The Radical Faces of
Godard and Bertolucci

CONTEMPORARY FILM AND TELEVISION SERIES

A complete listing of the books in this series can be found at the back of this volume.

The Radical Faces of Godard and Bertolucci

Yosefa Loshitzky

 Wayne State University Press   Detroit

Library of Congress Cataloging-in-Publication Data

Loshitzky, Yosefa.
    The radical faces of Godard and Bertolucci / Yosefa Loshitzky.
        p.   cm. — (Contemporary film and television series)
    Filmography
    Includes bibliographical references and index.
    ISBN 0-8143-2446-0 (alk. paper). — ISBN 0-8143-2447-9 (pbk.
alk. paper)
    1. Godard, Jean-Luc, 1930– —Criticism and interpretation.
2. Bertolucci, Bernardo—Criticism and interpretation.   I. Title.
II. Series.
PN1998.3.G63L67 1995
791.43'0233'0922—dc20   94-30602

Designer: Elizabeth Pilon

To the memory of my father Moshe Loshitzky
and for Doba Loshitzky

Contents

Acknowledgments

As an Israeli scholar situated at the periphery of the academic and film world, obtaining access to primary and secondary sources for my book was difficult and costly. My search for research materials and films achieved at times almost global proportions and therefore I have many people and institutions to thank.

First, I would like to thank Bernardo Bertolucci for inviting me to his home in London and for an unforgettable interview, which added insight into my reading of his films as well as of his complex relationship with Jean-Luc Godard. Bertolucci was kind in other ways as well, providing me with the opportunity to view *Agonia* as well as other interesting materials. I also wish to thank Julie Oudot of The Recorded Pictures Company (Jeremy Thomas's production company, which produced *The Last Emperor, The Sheltering Sky,* and *Little Buddha*), who was not only extremely efficient and helpful in arranging meetings and providing a variety of materials on Bertolucci's films, but was also kind and warm. Bruce Sklarew gave me access to rare materials, such as videotapes of a press conference with Bertolucci at the Mill Valley Film Festival. His friendship and support for my project were indispensable.

In the summer and fall of 1989 I was a visiting scholar at the Department of Cinema Studies at New York University. Due to William Simon's help and generosity, I was able to view films and conduct research at the department's Film Study Center as well as at the university's Bobst Library. Simon was kind enough to review my initial proposal for the book and made some helpful comments. Robert Stam from the Department of Cinema Studies at New York University was also kind enough to review my project at that initial stage and also provided useful suggestions. Summer and fall 1989 in "The Big Apple" was an opportunity to use New York's excellent resources. Charles Silver from the Study Center of the Department of

Film at the Museum of Modern Art in New York was the most considerate and helpful archivist I have ever met. In particular I wish to thank him for sympathizing with my frustration at not being able to attend the MOMA retrospective on Godard in 1992. He tried to compensate by updating me about the retrospective and sending me relevant materials. I am also most grateful to the Donnell Media Center of The New York Public Library and Electronic Arts Intermix in New York City for the opportunity to view films and videotapes. I also wish to thank the Motion Picture Broadcasting and Recorded Sound Division of the Library of Congress in Washington where I also viewed films.

In the summer of 1990 I received a grant (through the Israel Research Authority and Israel Ministry of Science and Technology) from the French Centre National de la Recherche Scientifique (CNRS) and the Italian Centro Nazionale di Ricerca (CNR) to conduct research in France and Italy. I would like to thank, in particular, Daniel Dayan who played the part of my "Parisian Virgil." I am also indebted to Sylvie Pliskin of the Cinematheque Universitaire et Service Informatique at the Department d'Etudes et de Recherches Cinematographiques et Audiovisuelles at the Université de Paris III—Sorbonne Nouvelle, Centre Censier; and to Deborah Glassman and Annette Wilson of The Critical Studies Program of the University of Paris III, Censier. In Italy I would like to thank especially Stefania Zittelli. A special thanks to Serge Toubiana, the editor of *Cahiers du Cinéma*, who sent me an original videotape of Godard's *Nouvelle Vague* and gave me some insights (upon his visit to Israel) on Godard's most recent creative phase. In London I would like to thank the British Film Institute and especially Colin MacCabe.

In Israel I would like to thank both the Smart Communications Institute and the Authority for Research and Development at the Hebrew University of Jerusalem, and the Department of Communication and Journalism. I would like especially to acknowledge the help of Elihu Katz for the many ways in which he has been my advocate over the years. I would also like to thank a wonderful librarian, Irit November, at the library at the Mount Scopus campus. I would like also to thank the Instituto Italiano di Cultura and the Institut Français at Tel-Aviv for their help, and Irma and Uri Kline for lending me videotapes. A special thanks to George Prochnik, whose stylistic suggestions, intellectual rigor, and devotion have been more than I could ask.

Again across the Atlantic, a very special thanks to Arthur Evans, the director of the Wayne State University Press, who has been more cordial and supportive than I could expect. I also am indebted to my teachers at Indiana University: Harry Geduld, James Naremore, Matei Calinescu, and Breon Mitchell for their support over the years, and to Robert Burgoyne and Patricia Erens whose helpful and insightful comments and their faith in the appeal of my book brought this project into its final and blissful state. Finally I am grateful to the Annenberg School for Communication, University of Pennsylvania, for generously providing my year as a visiting scholar. I would like to thank Lisa Henderson for her excellent stylistic suggestions regarding the photo illustrations of this book and to Larry Gross and Roberta Pearson for their stylistic suggestions regarding the catalogue and cover description of my book. A special thanks to my friend Barbie Zelizer for her always good professional advices.

Some of the material used in this book has already appeared in print in a somewhat changed form. A slightly different version of the section in chapter 2 dealing with *Partner* and *The Conformist* appeared in *History and Memory*, Vol. 3, No. 2 (Fall 1991): 87–114, under the title " 'Memory of My Own Memory': Processes of Private and Collective Remembering in Bertolucci's *The Spider Stratagem* and *The Conformist*." The analysis of *The Last Emperor* in chapter 4, which was co-authored with Raya Meyuhas, appeared under the title " 'Ecstasy of Difference': Bertolucci's *The Last Emperor*" in *Cinema Journal*, Vol. 31, No. 2 (Winter 1992): 26–44. The other part of chapter 4 discussing *The Sheltering Sky* appeared in a slightly different version in *East-West Film Journal* Vol. 7, No. 2 (July 1993): 110–137, under the title "The Tourist/Traveler Gaze: Bertolucci and Bowles' *The Sheltering Sky*."

The help of my personal dear friends will be acknowledged in the private space of our friendships.

Introduction:
Anxiety of Influence/
Celebration of Influence

This book aspires both to fill gaps left by other scholarly books on Bertolucci and Godard and to relocate the discussion of the two filmmakers within new theoretical frameworks such as feminism, postmodernism, and multiculturalism that dominate contemporary critical discourse. With the "new world order" of the 1990s providing some measure of historical distance, this appears to be a particularly productive time to review the politics of both directors. Such endeavor is all the more urgent in view of the much discussed historical debate over the ultimate, correct definition of political cinema or of *film progressist* (progressive film), a notion derived from the heritage of the May 1968 events. This book (in particular chapters 1 and 2) suggests substituting the notion of Oedipal struggle between Bertolucci and Godard during the radical 1960s and 1970s with that of "founding fathers" of two competing paradigms of radical cinema which emerged in the aftermath of the May 1968 upheavals.

Godard has been championed by critics, filmmakers, and scholars as the most important film artist since Sergei Eisenstein. Of Bernardo Bertolucci, Robert Kolker has said that he "is one of the strongest personalities to emerge in cinema since Jean-Luc Godard."[1] Kolker's observation could be expected to provoke considerable debate. Critical and scholarly praise is generally reserved for the young Bertolucci, the author of *Before the Revolution*,[2] *The Spider's Stratagem*, and *The Conformist*. *Last Tango in Paris* is often cited as the high point of his serious directorial career.

For me, however, the question of auteurist ranking is negligible, if not obsolete, compared with the question of influence. The concept of influence I am invoking in this book is more comprehensive than the one implied by the classic Oedipus complex, and should not be seen merely as a derivative of that complex. Instead, the Oedipal struggle of Bertolucci against Godard should be understood as a cultural and historical phenomenon transcending the Italian director's personal conflict. Indeed, Kolker was the first critic who argued that Bertolucci's work should be considered as an ongoing aesthetic and political struggle with Godard, the rebellion of the son against the father (see particularly Kolker's first chapter, entitled "Versus Godard"). Godard, as he rightly observes, is both mentor and tormentor to Bertolucci, "l'enfant terrible" (or "l'enfant prodige") of the militant Marxist cinema of the 1970s. Yet, within the framework of the heated debates of the May 1968 generation and its derivatives in contemporary discourse on and of radical cinema, Bertolucci's Oedipal struggle against Godard can be viewed as a paradigmatic case study on the politics of cinematic "anxiety of influence."

Although the notion of anxiety of influence has become an household term in literary studies it has never entered the arena of film studies—except perhaps in a disguised form under the rubrics of "intertextuality" or "self-reflexivity". Consequently this book, which is a comparatist study in two parallel and cross-influencing careers, provides the first attempt to study this issue on both the thematic and formal levels. Applying Harold Bloom's theory of poetic influence to the realm of cinema, one may say that cinematic history is indistinguishable from cinematic influence. This history is essentially a process of strong filmmakers misreading one another, so as to clear imaginative space for themselves.[3] Bloom clarifies that his concern is only with what he calls "strong poets," namely, "major figures with the persistence to wrestle with their strong precursors, even to death." [4] But poetic influence, as Bloom also observes, "need not make poets less original."[5]

Regarding Bertolucci's anxiety of influence, the paradox is, of course, that he deliberately abandoned poetry because of that very fear—even though his 1962 collection of poetry *In Cerca del Mistero* (*In Search of Mystery*) received the "Premio Viareggio Opera Prima" for that year. Bertolucci chose cinema as his medium of expression in order to escape his father's (the poet Attilio Bertolucci) influence. However, his cinematic career has been marked by an anxiety of influence from its inception.[6] In his first feature film, *La commare secca* (*The Grim Reaper*), he imitated Pier Paolo Pasolini (his first mentor), and in his following film *Before the Revolution*, which he called "my first own movie," he celebrated Godard's influence.

At the beginning of his career, Godard's films, *Breathless* in particular, were a sort of genuine revelation and a model for homagistic emulation. Since then, the dramatic and structural organization of Bertolucci's *oeuvre* has reproduced the Freudian theme of rebellion against paternal authority (the *padre/padrone* theme). Of all Bertolucci's films *Partner* is the film most obsessed with the Godardian discourse. It was also, as Bertolucci confessed many times, the film that made him suffer the most. It is not an accident that for *Partner* Bertolucci chose Pierre Clementi for the role of Giacobbe, an anarchist revolutionary. Clementi was a favorite actor of both Pasolini and Godard, Bertolucci's first "fathers."

In *Before the Revolution* and *Partner*, the assimilation of Godard's style and spirit is not charged with any of the ambivalence that characterizes Bertolucci's later films. On the contrary, these two films are invested with deep admiration and an open acknowledgment of Godard's role as the director's enlightened cinematic father/tutor (*padre*). Bertolucci's ambivalence towards Godard's cinema as a prime model of radical cinema began to be expressed only in *The Conformist* (see chapter 2). The film is, as Bertolucci himself confessed, a story about Godard and himself transferred into the Oedipal relationship between Quadri, the anti-Fascist professor, and Marcello, his former student who eventually assassinates him. *The Conformist* signifies a change in the symbolic role of Godard's place in Bertolucci's cinema, with Bertolucci "killing" his spiritual father. The killing occurs on the level of the fictional narrative as well as on the level of style through Bertolucci's departure from his former experimental cinema *à la* Godard to a more conventional narrative. This symbolic patricide is, however, charged with guilt feelings. Part of the film's criticism of Godard is an attack on impotent militant intellectuals not unlike Godard himself (see chapter 2).

Tango offers, perhaps, the most curious evidence of Bertolucci's anxiety of influence. In *Tango*, Bertolucci satirizes Godard quite viciously through the figure of the ridiculous Tom. Perhaps, Bertolucci says, Godard is not the pure revolutionary he would like to be. *Tango* is a subjective act of liberation not only because "Bernardo was getting free of his sex problems" by making Brando and Schneider transfer "them to the film,"[7] but also because, more than *The Conformist*, *Tango* is a liberation from Godard.

Bertolucci's next film, *1900*, brings the Oedipal conflict almost full circle. This epic film concerns the decline and fall of the *patron*, the tyrannical boss and demonic father figure (*padrone*). By now Godard has definitely lost the aura of the enlightened and enlightening father (*padre*) and has become, rather, the tyrannical *padrone* whose presence Bertolucci attempts to exorcise. *The Tragedy of a Ridiculous Man* reveals, however, that the Italian director's

Last Tango in Paris satirizes Godard quite viciously through the ridiculous figure of Tom (Jean-Pierre Leaud). Tom and Jeanne (Maria Schneider) fight in the Paris Metro against the backdrop of a typical Godardian composition. Courtesy of The Museum of Modern Art, Film Stills Archive.

attempts at exorcism have failed. *The Tragedy of a Ridiculous Man* exemplifies the Oedipal struggle through its thematics (the resurrection of the son) but also, and principally, through its formal organization which alludes to and quotes from the visual style of Godard's Marxist films, and *Tout va bien* in particular (see chapter 3). Nevertheless, Bertolucci's most recent films, *The Last Emperor* (1987) and *The Sheltering Sky* (1990), which are marked by the quest for non-Western otherness (see chapter 4), are completely free of Godard's influence. Bertolucci's choice of the life of the Buddha as the topic of his most recent film (*Little Buddha*) indicates that he intends to continue his quest for the Other.

Although Bertolucci, the son, is the one to suffer from anxiety of influence, Godard, the father, is not therefore immune from Bertolucci's influence. For example, *Prénom Carmen* (First Name Carmen) (1984), pays tribute to *Tango* (see chapters 3 and 5). In fact, quite unusually it is Godard, not Bertolucci, who initiates a dialogue. *Carmen* pays tribute to *Tango* through its investigation of the metaphor of anality which is at the center of *Tango*'s political analysis, wherein an anal rape turns out to be a reification of social relations under capitalism. Yet, Godard's tribute in the early 1980s came after a decade of bitter criticism aimed at Bertolucci, his former disciple, who, in Godard's estimation, had become a conformist. Godard's and Bertolucci's close personal and intellectual ties were seriously damaged as a result of Bertolucci resorting to conformism and his resentful attitude towards Godard's purist and dogmatic revolutionism. For example, in *Vent d'est* (Wind from the East) (1969), Godard says that "to be a militant moviemaker means to explore the history of revolutionary cinema and not to show the decadent life style of the bourgeoisie" thus alluding to *The Conformist*'s critique of bourgeois decadence.[8]

Related to the question of influence is the Franco-Italian connection which is a recurrent motif in both cultures. The Franco-Italian dialectic is most evident in Bertolucci's first auteuristic movie *Before the Revolution*. At that time, as he later confessed, he considered himself more of a French director than an Italian director. Godard himself romanticized Italy as the land of freedom and escape from urban life in *Breathless* and *Pierrot le fou*. In both films the protagonist, played by Jean-Paul Belmondo, indulges in utopian dreams about escaping to sunny Italy.[9]

Although the book discusses some of Godard and Bertolucci's films within the context of influence, I am trying to avoid thinking about them in terms of oppositions that may suggest a relationship of master and slave, important and non-important. I prefer to discuss the two filmmakers' work in terms of difference or even disjunction.[10] The centrality of the disjunction in any discussion of Godard and Bertolucci's work is supported by the evident disproportion between the overall production of each director. Whereas Bertolucci has made only twelve feature films to date, Godard has made more than thirty (this does not include his video work and the short films). Godard is, as Jacques Aumont claims,[11] an iconoclast and this, perhaps, explains his amazing productivity and the speed that characterizes his work.[12] Obviously Godard's insistence on making low-budget movies, and his customary resistance to spectacle and the fetishization of production values have also contributed to his productivity.[13] Part of Bertolucci's liberation from Godard's oppressive influence was to accept his role as *autore di film spettacolo* (director of spectacle)[14] and to invest his films with Hollywood-type production values. This attitude, necessarily, requires more time and money and it explains Bertolucci's relatively low productivity. There are of course other reasons that explain Bertolucci's slow speed such as the personal difficulties he encountered after the trauma of *1900*.

Godard has always enjoyed popularity among critics and academics despite and perhaps because of his apparent lack of appeal to larger audiences (with the noticeable exceptions of *Breathless* and the *succès de scandale* of *Weekend* and *Hail Mary*), and there are quite a few books on him. However, the most comprehensive book in English on his work *Godard: Images, Sounds, Politics* by Colin MacCabe was published more than a decade ago. During the 1980s Godard seemed to fall out of grace even with his academic admirers, and since that time, only a few sporadic analyses of several of his films have been published. No attempt, however, was made during the 1980s to reconceptualize Godard's work, and, especially to probe his shift towards a new religiosity (see chapters 3 and 5). A recent retrospective of Godard, tracing the relationship between his film and video work from 1974 to 1991, opened at the Museum of Modern Art in New York City on October 30, 1992. It was joined by the publication of an anthology entitled *Jean-Luc Godard: Son+Image* (edited by Raymond Bellour), and constitutes an attempt to fill this lacuna in the critical reception of Godard's more recent work. An exhibition, "Postcards from Alphaville: Jean-Luc Godard in Contemporary Art," at New York's P.S. 1 gallery complemented the Museum of Modern Art's retrospective.

The scarcity of material on the late Godard is rather surprising given his privileged position within the theoretical discourse on film. Yet recent developments in film studies and the gradual disintegration of the discipline into cultural and critical studies might at least help explain the dwindling interest in studies of auteurs.

Compared with the critical neglect of the late Godard, Bertolucci has in recent years enjoyed more critical attention. At present there are two in-depth English books on Bertolucci: *Bernardo Bertolucci* by Robert Phillip Kolker and *Bertolucci's Dream Loom: A Psychoanalytic Study of Cinema* by T. Jefferson Kline.[15] In addition there is a book of interviews with Bertolucci (*Bertolucci by Bertolucci*). Another more recent valuable contribution to the scholarly literature on Bertolucci's work is Robert Burgoyne's *Bertolucci's 1900*.[16] The entire book is devoted to a narrative and historical analysis of one of Bertolucci's more notorious films. Angela Dalle Vacche's *The Body in the Mirror* provides yet another important discussion of Bertolucci's by now classic films *The Spider's Stratagem* and *The Conformist*.[17]

Despite the differences in their critical approaches—Kolker is concerned more with form and ideology, Kline with psychoanalysis and myth or literature—both books are primarily close textual studies of individual films. Although Kolker argues that Bertolucci's cinema should be considered an ongoing Oedipal struggle with Godard's cinema, he does not examine the idea from the other side, i.e., from *père* Godard's point of view. Furthermore, neither books analyzes (due to their publication dates) Bertolucci's most recent films, *The Last Emperor* and *The Sheltering Sky*. These films (as I demonstrate in chapter 4), as well as the available material on Bertolucci's *Little Buddha*, reflect the Italian director's present interest in non-Western cultures. Bertolucci's interest coincides with the recent interest, expressed within different academic disciplines, in multiculturalism and colonial and postcolonial discourse, thus making his later work all the more intriguing for the cultural studies scholar.

The first chapter of my book examines in depth the intellectual, political, and philosophical roots of Godard's radical period from 1968 to 1978. The chapter reviews Godard's involvement with the French *Gauche*, from his initiation (through Anne Wiazemsky) into the radical Maoist circles of Paris during the late 1960s, to his political activity during the May 1968 events, the formation of the Dziga Vertov Group and its dissolution, and his collaboration with Anne-Marie Miéville on experimental video work during their "voluntary exile" in Switzerland. The analysis of the individual films in this chapter focuses on Godard's radical critique of the image culture we live in. Special attention is devoted to the film *Tout va bien*. The chapter's study of *Tout va bien* shows that, in line with Louis Althusser's theoretical premises regarding the role of art in the process of knowledge production and Maoist principles of self-criticism, this film is constantly engaged with exposing the process of its own production and deconstruction of the codes of the classic narrative.

Chapter 2 examines Bertolucci's radical period from 1968 to 1976. It reviews his involvement with the Italian Communist Party up to his resignation in the late 1970s. The chapter also compares Godard's radical *Gauchisme* with Bertolucci's "revisionist" Communism, particularly in their attitudes toward the May 1968 upheavals and how they influenced politics and film culture. The chapter argues that, for Godard, the lesson of the May 1968 events was a personal rejection of his prepoliticized cinema of the esthete. For Bertolucci, however, the lesson was quite different, involving the discovery of a plane on which political revolution is functioning as highly individual and subjective phenomenon. Bertolucci's search for the individual level in political revolution motivates the synthesis of Freud and Marx that characterizes all his films. It recalls the Freudian/Marxian synthesis at the core of Herbert Marcuse's *Eros and Civilization* and, further, derives from a correspondant belief in the possibility and necessity for a Marxist styled individual liberation.

The chapter excavates the politicization of memory in *The Spider's Stratagem* (1970) and *The Conformist* (1970), which deal directly with questions of national identity and processes of collective remembering through an exploration of Italy's Fascist period. Both in *The Spider's Stratagem* and *The Conformist*, Bertolucci chose to mediate the national by appealing to processes of remembering which involve the tension between individual and public memory. The complexity of these films is due to their appeal to the notion of memory as articulated in other discursive practices such as literature (Alberto Moravia's *The Conformist* and Marcel Proust's *Remembrance of Things Past*), philosophy (Henri Bergson), and psychoanalysis. *The Spider's Stratagem* and *The Conformist* are based on literary works that problematize the relationship between memory and history.

The chapter also concentrates on the film *Last Tango in Paris*. The film, so I suggest, is closely linked to the historical momentum of the May 1968 events. But unlike in *Tout va bien* (Godard's film released in the same year, which uses the student-worker uprising of May 1968 as a concrete historical referent) in *Tango* the historical referent is absent from the overt level of the narrative. Yet its absence is an active absence, guiding the underlying theoretical premises on which the film is based. The chapter's close study of *Tango* reveals ideational affinity between Marcuse's thought, in particular his reading of Freud in *Eros and Civilization* as a utopian thinker, and Bertolucci's attempt in *Tango* to analyze the language of sexuality in revolutionary terms but within the boundaries of the classic realist text.

Chapter 3 explores the 1980s conceived as a new stage in both Godard's and Bertolucci's works. The chapter examines in detail Bertolucci's *Tragedy of Ridiculous Man* (a film which generated very little critical attention) in light of Jean Baudrillard's postmodernist notion of spiralling negativity. It also reads the film as Bertolucci's most curious tribute to Godard, in particular on the level of visuals that constantly fight against the modernist style typical of Godard's radical period. *Tragedy*, Bertolucci's last film to be shot in Europe, anticipates through its Baudrillardian flavor Bertolucci's flight to the East in pursuit of new utopias no longer tenable in the postmodern West.

The chapter examines also Godard's transition through *Sauve qui peut (la vie)* (Every Man for Himself) to his cosmic period exemplified by the "triology of the sublime" (*Passion, Carmen,* and *Hail Mary*) which expresses a semi-religious quest for spiritual rejuvenation. Whereas Bertolucci's dialogue with the cosmos departs from Emilia Romagna, the "paradise lost" landscape of his childhood, and takes place in the utopian landscapes of the East and Africa, Godard's dialogue takes him back to the landscapes of his childhood, the Swiss lakes. The chapter also analyzes some of Godard's video works such as *Soft and Hard*, as well as his more recent film *Nouvelle Vague*.

Chapter 4 focuses on Bertolucci's quest for the Other in *The Last Emperor* and *The Sheltering Sky*. The chapter investigates how both films foreground discussions taking place on several disciplinary fronts concerning the problem of the Other. The chapter considers discussions among anthropologists, sociologists, and literary and film scholars and applies them to the cultural problematics associated with Bertolucci's Orientalism.

The chapter examines *The Last Emperor's* representation of processes of political reeducation and psychoanalytic therapy in Maoist China which is ultimately portrayed as a projection of the West's utopian Other. As for *The Sheltering Sky*, the chapter (drawing heavily on recent literature on tourism and its colonial/postcolonial implications) investigates the film's oscillation between the tourist and the traveler discourses as well as its use of the myth of American expatriates, the road film genre, the motif of the journey, and the Existentialist heritage. This investigation is aimed at deconstructing the film's ambiguity in relation to the colonial discourse.

Chapter 5 provides an overall feminist reinterpretation of Godard's work beginning with the early libertine misogynism of the New Wave period. It continues through the political/public feminism of the radical period, the domestic/private feminism (the discourse of metapornography) of the video work with Miéville to the meta-heresy of the sacralizing images of feminine flesh in his quasi-religious, cosmic period in which sexuality is no longer linked (as in his previous films) to the world of prostitution, consumption, and pornography, but to the world of nature, the universe, and cosmic contemplation. The chapter also investigates

Godard's representation of female sexuality through the recurrent motifs in his films of woman as consumer, woman as commodity, woman as prostitute, anality as a metaphor of the capitalist system of opression/repression, and incest and pedophilia.

Chapter 6 investigates Bertolucci's sexual politics. It explores what I call Bertolucci's "poetics of sexual indeterminacy," i.e., his fascination with sexual ambiguity, gender ambivalence, and sexual confusion. The chapter provides a feminist critique of Bertolucci's work which betrays the promise of sexual emanicipation inherent in images of sexual contamination. A feminist critique of *Tango* deconstructs the Marcusian (and perhaps too celebratory) reading of *Tango* suggested in chapter 2.

The chapter criticizes Bertolucci not only for the absence of women (except in *La Luna*) as protagonists in his films, but also and mainly for his portrayal of women as the representatives of the hated bourgeoisie. His mostly mediocre heroines are dwarfed by the existential *angst* of their male counterparts. Bertolucci also makes use of cultural misogynist traditions such as the myth of the spider woman and the femme fatal of the *film noir*. His use of metaphors of sexual repression and political oppression are not favorable to women either. His use of the themes of dance, incest, the Oedipal complex, the primary scene, and anality betray their emanicapatory potential and fail to transgress patriarchal binarism.

CHAPTER 1

The Radical Period of Godard: 1968–1978

For Godard the May 1968 events were a genuine turning point in his cinematic career. Godard's involvement with the extreme French *Gauche*—which denounced the policy of the PCF (Partie Communiste Française, the French Communist Party)—began only with his initiation (through Anne Wiazemsky, his second wife) into the radical Maoist circles of Paris during the late 1960s. Godard's transition from cinéphilism to political radicalism was accompanied by a complete rejection of the films he made between 1959 and 1968 as bourgeois. His transition into radical politics is most evident in *La Chinoise* (1967), an almost prophetic film in its anticipation of the May 1968 events and their political aftermath (in particular the growth of urban terrorism). However, in retrospect, one might argue that the seeds of much of his later political work are already contained in his earlier films.

Pierrot le fou (1965), for example, despite its *l'amour fou* escapism, contains latent criticism of the Vietnam War, as well as nature utopianism.[1] *Deux ou trois choses que je sais d'elle* (Two or Three Things I know about Her) (1966) is even more overtly critical of consumer society in general and of de Gaulle's urban planning of Paris in particular. Some critics argue that *Les Carabiniers* (1962–1963), an even earlier film, contains a radical political critique. Despite the film's "universalism" (the fact that its anti-war message does not refer to any specific war but to the phenomenon of war in general), Dana Polan, for example, views it as a critique of the ideology of spectacle and Bruce Kawin regards it as the foundation of Godard's political cinema.[2] Colin MacCabe, on the other hand, sees

Masculin/Féminin (1966) as the beginning of Godard's series of explicitly political films which ended with his withdrawal from the traditional cinema in the early 1970s.[3] Godard himself said that the exact point in time when his break from bourgeois to revolutionary filmmaking occurred was during the May–June events in France in 1968. He also said that the only earlier films that have any positive merit for him were *Pierrot le fou*, *Weekend*, and "some things" in *Two or Three Things*.

The Influence of May 1968

The dramatic events of 1968, one of the most tumultuous years in the second half of the twentieth century, included the eruption of riots in cities around the world and in particular student and worker protests in Germany, Italy, and Paris (which witnessed some of the worst violence); political assassinations (Martin Luther King, Jr., and Robert F. Kennedy), racial riots, and student demonstrations in America; the Tet offensive in Vietnam; and the Soviet invasion of Czechoslovakia, which resulted in the crushing of the Prague Spring. All of these had far-reaching ideological ramifications as well as enormous effects in immediate political and social terms.

The May 1968 events in Paris were a reaction to the authoritarian Fifth Republic of General de Gaulle, and they became the focus for major political reassessments. The left—both in its radical and established manifestations—suffered further internal divisions over the issue of whether to promote reform or revolution.[4]

The film world in France had already been engaged with political struggle earlier in 1968 through what came to be known as "l'Affaire Langlois," the public scandal surrounding the dissmissal of Henri Langlois the legendary head of the Cinématheque Française. The efforts of the French film people to fight against then Minister of Culture Andre Malraux's decision to replace Langlois with a Gaulist bureaucrat (Pierre Barbin) were successful. This success made the French cineastes realize the importance of political struggle in the realm of culture as well as against the threat of the authoritarian Gaulist regime. It created, perhaps, the ideological foundation for the formation of the *Etats Generaux du Cinéma* (Estates General of the French Cinéma), an organization founded by several thousand filmmakers, critics, and technicians.

The intention of the Estates General was to revolutionize French cinema in terms of production, distribution, and film content. Not all the decisions accepted by the organization were carried out, but it succeeded in getting some documentary projects under way. The greatest impact of the revolutionary spirit of the organization was registered in the arena of film theory. Jean-Louis Comolli and Jean Narboni, the editors of the famous periodical *Cahiers du Cinéma*, adopted a radical political stance, and a new militant film journal, *Cinéthique*, was founded. Another characteristic of the radical spirit of May 1968 in the arena of filmmaking was the creation of revolutionary film collectives. The most notable were the Dziga Vertov Group which included Godard, and SLON (later Groupe Medvedkine) which grew out of the collective work Chris Marker organized for *Loin du Vietnam* (Far from Vietnam) (1966) and in which Godard participated.

Godard and Bertolucci reveal in their films and in many interviews diametrically opposed views regarding the influence of the May 1968 events on their lives and work. The polarization of their views on this issue likewise affected their personal and professional relationships. For Godard the lesson of the May 1968 events was a personal rejection of his pre-politicized cinema of the "esthete."[5]

Godard shows during his radical phase an affinity to Louis Althusser, the French Marxist theoretician whose philosophy—in terms of both philosophy and applied politics—is influenced by the teachings of Mao Tse-tung. Indeed, *Lotte in Italia* (*Struggle in Italy*) (1969), one of the films made by the Dziga Vertov Group, is based on Althusser's concept of ideology, as articulated in his essay "Ideology and Ideological State Apparatus," published in France in 1971.[6] It is important to understand the impact of Althusser's ideas—as well as the French philosopher's position within the PCF (the French Communist Party)—on the radical Godard, because it also explains the difference between Godard's and Bertolucci's cinema during the 1970s. Moreover, it explains Bertolucci's "betrayal" of "pere Godard" and his resort, after the 1968 events, to conformist cinema.

Louis Althusser and Roger Garaudy represent, according to Michael Kelly, the major polarization of the 1960s within the PCF.[7] A full discussion of the political and conceptual difference between the two Communist theoreticians is obviously beyond the scope of this study; however, it is important to mention that during the 1960s, the two represented symmetrical oppositions between, as Kelly observes, "opportunism and sectarianism, and between speculative humanism and theoretical anti-humanism." [8] Whereas Garaudy's policy advocated broad alliance with non-Communist parties as an alternative to the Gaullist regime, Althusser advocated a policy of radical extra-parliamentary independent action. In terms of the international Communist movement, Garaudy's orientation was towards the Italian Communist Party while Althusser sympathized with the Chinese. Bertolucci, a registered member of the Italian Communist party since 1969 (in fact he joined the Communist party in reaction to the growth of militant Maoism in the European left), was revisionist in the eyes of Godard whose politics were close to sectarian Althusserianism and to the ultra-left groups that flourished in Europe (and especially in France, Italy, and Germany) in the years immediately following 1968.

The enormous influence of the intellectuals on politics, as dramatically demonstrated in the eruption of the May 1968 events, was also significant in the radical cinema created during these years. The former division between workers and intellectuals was abolished. The seeds for the political role of the intellectuals as a social group had already been planted in Antonio Gramsci's theoretical writings which distinguished between organic and arbitrary intellectuals.[9] During the 1960s, Althusser elaborated on Gramsci's conception of the intellectuals and introduced an integration between the working class and the intellectuals. The growing role of the intellectuals in the revolutionary process both reflected the emphasis on an integration of praxis and theory, a central concern in the May 1968 discourse, and expressed an integration of theorist and political positions which, in the realm of film, placed great importance on practical experimentation motivated by theoretical presuppositions. This type of integration is best exemplified by Godard's *Le Gai Savoir* (1968). During the 1960s even Bertolucci, who later became an opponent of the excessively theoretical orientation typical of French filmmaking (and especially that of Godard), confessed that: "I used to think—in '68, I thought that the camera was like a gun and then I discovered that it was an illusion."[10] This confession clearly alludes to Godard's famous dictum pronounced during what came to be known as the utopian years: "I think an idea is a theoretical weapon and a film is a theoretical rifle."

Throughout his radical period (from 1968 to 1978) Godard made eighteen films. They include the six films made by the Dziga Vertov Group; two films made in collaboration with Jean-Pierre Gorin, *Tout va bien* (1972) and the short film that accompanies it, *Letter to Jane* (1972); as well as the films and television work he did with Anne-Marie Miéville.[11] Nevertheless, unlike Bertolucci's commercially successful films (with the exception of *Partner* which emulates the Godardian style) all of Godard's films of the period (with the significant exception of *Tout va bien*) were produced and distributed outside of the traditional commercial circuit and were aimed at militant audiences. Despite his surprising productivity during these years,

Godard was silent in reference to the world of commercial cinema. None of his militant films (except for the American-backed *Tout va bien*) have appeared on the circuits of commercial cinema. Godard's break with the past was complete during these years.

From *Le Gai Savoir* to the Films of the Dziga Vertov Group

More than any other film made during his radical phase, *Le Gai Savoir* (1968) (which is also the French title of Nietzsche's book) is the purest product of this period because of its attempt at a radical break with the past and a return to zero degree. It is the first film of the "utopian years" ceremonially announcing the birth of the new Godard as well as the birth of a new phase in his career. In fact the film was commissioned initially by the French television, O.R.T.F, before the May events, but was edited and released after them. The finished film was rejected by the O.R.T.F. It is not surprising, therefore, that the film ends with a utopian appeal to start film language from zero degree. Through what became his stylistic signature during his radical phase, the cardboard characterization, Godard announces that this is not the film that should be made. Rather, it is a film that only suggests the future path for cinema. At this point he also names the promising revolutionary directors including Bertolucci who will respond to his appeal to create new cinema. The voice-over narration says that "in Freudian Marxist terms Bertolucci will shoot them in Rome," Straub in Germany, and Rocha in Brazil.

Le Gai Savoir is shaped like a television free adaptation of Jean Jacques Rousseau's eighteenth century *Bildungsroman Émile*, a treatise on education. The film comprises a series of seven conversations in a television studio between two characters, Patricia Lumumba[12] (played by Juliet Berto) and Emil Rousseau (Jean-Pierre Léaud). The characters' dialogues focus on the nature of language, especially on words as the primary building blocks of language, and the need to dissolve words' traditional associations in order to purify language of its ideological burden and to create a new and liberated language of knowledge. These dialogues are punctuated by a series of images, handwritten signs, and words that interrogate the meaning and ideology assigned to them. The rigorous exploration and scrutiny of these systems of signs is conducted both visually (through the breaking down of the words and written signs on the screen) and visually/verbally through fictive interviews with real people (an old *clochard*, a young boy, and a young girl). The interviewees (through a technique recalling the surrealists' automatic writing) are asked to verbalize their associations in response to words delivered by the whispering interviewer. Thus, they are forced to rethink the customary meaning of images and words.

Through this original process of learning Godard is trying to empty and naturalize images and words, hence anticipating his famous aphorism (which appeared as a slogan written on a blackboard in *Vent d'Est*), "Ce n'est pas une image juste, c'est juste une image" (It is not a just image, it is just an image). The attempt to empty the ideological connotations of dominant images in our culture is theoretically formulated by the motto of the film drawn from Herbert Marcuse's *Eros and Civilization*: "The history of man is the history of his repression." The ideology-laden meaning assigned to images in our culture is perceived by Godard as part of this repression, and the role of a truly liberating education is to teach us how to emancipate ourselves from it. Therefore, it is rather logical that Godard, despite his avoidance of psychoanalysis in his own films, will assign the task of using it as a liberating political force to Bertolucci, the cinematic expert on the subject.

. *Le Gai Savoir*, which announced Godard's initiation into revolutionary zero degree cinema, was followed by the production of *Cinétracts*, a kind of film poster with a still photograph and a revolutionary message, usually written out in Godard's handwriting, or a simple animated design like a red flag with a growing bloody stain. These two- or three-minute films were made by Godard at home with a 16mm camera and were distributed through revolutionary groups. In August 1968, Godard made *Un film comme les autres* (*A Film Like Any Other*) which was composed of images taken during the *Evenements* and a soundtrack of conversations between students and workers. His next film, *One Plus One* with the Rolling Stones, was made in England and appeared in the producer's version as *Sympathy for the Devil*.[13]

Godard's subsequent *One American Movie* (*One A.M.*) was originally planned as a joint film by Godard and the American *cinéma vérité* film-makers Richard Leacock and D.A. Pennebacker; however, because of disagreements concerning the treatment of the documentary material and Godard's insistence that "art is not natural" (a sentence which dominates his documentary-style discussion with the Black Panther Eldridge Cleaver), he abandoned the project. Pennebacker edited the material shot by Godard and added some material of his own to make *One P.M.* (*Onex Parallel Movie*).

One American Movie was designed to blur the distinctions between documentary and fiction, echoing Godard's famous dictum about "the reality of fiction and the fiction of reality." Godard wanted it to consist of ten sequences: five "real" (two interviews with radicals, Tom Hayden and Eldridge Cleaver, and one with a Wall Street woman; shots of a girl from Ocean Hill-Brownsville carrying a phonograph playing soul music through the streets of Harlem; a performance by the Jefferson Airplane on a hotel roof), and five "fictional" (professional actors doing the same sequences). Pennebacker's version maintains some of the original structure; however, he added self-reflexive sequences showing Godard himself shooting scenes or engaged in discussions with the film's participants on the relationship of cinema to reality. To a certain extent one might speculate that despite Godard's abandonment of *One American Movie* the film expressed his wish to collaborate with other filmmakers who shared his radical political views. In this respect the failure of this specific collaboration anticipated the foundation of the Dziga Vertov Group with its emphasis on collective work. Another abandoned project of "television libre" in Canada, provisionally entitled *Communications*, made the time ripe for collective filmmaking.

In the summer of 1968, Godard and Jean-Pierre Gorin (with Gerard Martin, Armand Marco, Nathalie Billard, and Jean-Henri Roger) founded *le groupe Dziga Vertov*, a film collective whose proclaimed goal was to make "political films politically" in an attempt to revolutionize the language of cinema. The notions of class struggle and dialectical materialism determined the films' mode of production, form, and content; above all, they demanded a new relationship be created between the film and the spectator, the image and the sound, and the content and the form of the films themselves. Despite the proleterian aspirations of the films, which were motivated by an attempt to revive a *Proletkult* (proletarian culture), their circulation was limited to militant circles. In fact, even today they are not even available in large and well-known film archives. This phase in Godard's career was conceived by some as creative suicide. Some critics even talked about the "vampirization of Godard by the Maoists."[14] The name of the collective was taken from the Soviet filmmaker Dziga Vertov and his original group called the *kinoki*. Godard's choice of Vertov over Sergei Eisenstein was significant as well. Contrary to the common view of Eisenstein as the paradigmatic revolutionary filmmaker, for Godard, Vertov and not Eisenstein was the real Marxist moviemaker.

Vertov's *The Man with a Movie Camera*, as Annette Michelson suggests, was a natural choice to "become the key film-text for the generation of filmmakers who called into question the grounds and claims of cinematic representation through the political uprisings of 1968."[15] *The Man with a Movie Camera* is the culmination of Vertov's theoretical and practical work and it deals with all the theoretical issues that became central to post-May 1968 film criticism. The film not only epitomizes the success of intellection elicited by the dialectical organization of montage; it also generates a critique of cinematic representation which is united in the film with cinematic production. Furthermore, the whole process as depicted by and analyzed by *The Man with a Movie Camera* takes place within the constraints of a socialist economy, which for post-May 1968 film criticism signified the only arena free of bourgeois influence.

The Dziga Vertov Group was committed to producing and exhibiting films differently—both economically and aesthetically—from the way they had been exhibited previously. The films were exhibited primarily in non-theatrical situations, and seen solely by students and militant activists. They were filmed in 16mm on very low budgets. Their film theory, according to Godard, rested on a perceived cultural and ideological exchange value in cinema. Each film was a continuation of the one before and the avant-garde of the one to come.

British Sounds (*See You at Mao*) (1969), the first film of the Dziga Vertov Group, demonstrates more than any other film made by the collective the importance attributed by Godard to the relationship of sound and image. As the title of the film suggests, the main concern of the film is to reconsider the role of sound in cinema by confronting rather than intensifying the impression rendered through the film image. The film was commissioned by London Weekend and produced by Kestrel Films but it was never shown in its entirety on television. The film consistently attacks the authority accorded in Western epistemology to the image to define, if not—as Jean Baudrillard argues—to replace the real.[16] The moving image, which has become the most privileged site of visual representation and the prime reflector of reality, is questioned through the stuggle between the image of Britain provided by the Union Jack and the "correct" sound of the Maoist analysis, as well as the "live" sound recorded in the factory. This struggle, on the level of the film's means of representation, is echoed and reproduced by one of the more famous aphorisms coined by Godard, which appears as a handwritten slogan in the film: "photography is not the reflection of reality but the reality of that reflection." The use of sound in this film verges on the sadistic. The sound tests the extent to which the spectator is able to endure the horrible noise produced and recorded in the factory. Implicitly Godard suggests to his audience, "if the workers can take it, you can take it as well and if you can't take it then you should do something about the class struggle." The implicit message rendered through the use of sound is explicitly suggested by the closing written message of the final shot which says "no end to the class struggle."

Pravda (1969), another film essay made by the collective, questions Godard's ability as a foreign filmmaker to document another country. The two narrators, carrying the names Lenin and Rosa after the first names of Vladimir Ilyich Lenin and Rosa Luxemburg, anticipate the last film made by the collective, *Vladimir et Rosa* (Vladimir and Rosa) (1971). In line with the Maoist spirit of its makers, *Pravda* aims at providing "a concrete analysis of a concrete situation." Overall it stresses the importance of the class struggle and attacks the revisionists. The first part of the movie is composed of images recalling the iconography and the visual rhetoric of tourist films. These touristic images are accompanied by American popular music and a voice-over narration, which ironically recalls the crushing of the Prague Spring: "Il y a des tanks, tu entends, oui, des tanks qui surveillent les paysans" (There are tanks, you understand, tanks that watch over the countrymen). The struggle between sound and image and the attempt to create a "just image" dominate the film's dogmatic tone; it ends with quotations from Maoist texts regarding the need to reeducate the intellectuals and to fight the revisionists. The group's main practical and theoretical project to analyze images is epitomized and dogmatized by the film's repeated use of the image of a red rose which comes to signify the purity of the anti-revisionist camp.

Vento dell'est (Vent d'est; Wind from the East) (1969), the third film of the Dziga Vertov Group, is a revolutionary "spaghetti western," "western de gauche" (leftist Western) as envisaged by Daniel Cohn-Bendit, the famous leader of the May 1968 students' revolt in France, who wrote the script with Godard and Sergio Bazzini. Unlike the group's other films made during the period, it was financed, as Colin MacCabe reveals, by a rich left-wing supporter and starred the Italian revolutionary actor Gian Maria Volonte. The film attacks the ideology of spectacle, facing it off with the Marxist notion of struggle. The idea of spectacle as epitomized in Hollywood movies is analyzed in terms of "the repression of representation" conveying Godard and Gorin's original intention "lutter contre le concept bourgeois de représentation" (to struggle against the bourgeois concept of representation). The voice-over narration and written text contend that Hollywood films use images of domination in an attempt to lead their viewers to believe that an image of a horse is a real horse. The role of revolutionary cinema, therefore, is to fight spectacle and cultivate struggle and to explore its own history. Since there is no cinema beyond the class struggle, cinema as a mode of praxis is a second duty only. The first duty is the class struggle. The film argues that the exploration of the history of what is known as revolutionary cinema, demonstrates that some of the revolutionary directors (such as Sergei Eisenstein and Gillo Pontecorvo) only "pose as Marxists," whereas in reality they enable imperialism to invade their films (Godard and his collaborators go so far as to label Eisenstein's *Potemkin* a Nazi film).

Against Hollywood's ideology of spectacle, the film advocates struggle and criticism—self-criticism in particular. Following a written title: "critique," the film shows a flutist advocating "auto-critique" and playing the "Bandiera Rossa." Toward the end of the film Godard discusses contradiction, both primary (between labor and capital) and secondary (between sex and labor), concluding in a direct appeal to the viewer: "You've made a film, you've criticized it, you've learned something about sound and image." This conclusion, indeed, continues the struggle to correctly define sound in relation to the image while emphasizing the political and ideological dimensions of the sound/image clash.

Vent d'est was followed by *Lotte in Italia (Struggle in Italy)* (1969) and *Vladimir et Rosa* (1970). The last film attempted by the group was *Jusqu'à la victoire (Until Victory)* (1970), on the PLO in Jordan. The events of "The Black September," however, and the dissolution of the ultra-leftist groups in France, resulted in the disintegration of the Dziga Vertov Group and the abandonment of *Jusqu' a la victoire*. Footage from the film, however, was used in a later Godard movie *Ici et ailleurs (Here and Elsewhere)* (1974).

The Intermediate Stage: *Tout va bien*

Tout va bien and History: The Cultural Mediator Meditates about His Role in the Revolution

Godard's and Gorin's *Tout va bien* (1972) signaled the collapse of the Dziga Vertov Group. It was made with American money in an attempt to break into the conventional commercial circuit and bring the revolutionary message to a larger audience. The film simulates a fictional situation, a seizure of a factory by its workers. Although the film's narrative is deliberately fictional, it bears resemblance to similar events that occurred during the May 1968 upheavals. The film depicts and analyzes the reaction of some fictional representatives of the CGT (*Confédération générale du travail*, the largest French workers' union controlled by the PCF, the French Communist Party) and two media people (Susan [Jane Fonda] and Jacques [Yves Montand]) to the revolutionary acts of the workers. Their interactions provide a dialectical cinematic meditation on the problem of reform versus revolution and a critique of power relationships. The film focuses on the personal involvement of Susan and Jacques ("cultural workers with bourgeois backgrounds") in the factory occupation and the effect it has on their private lives and political consciousness. The fragility of the film's cultural workers—a French filmmaker (Jacques) and an American radio broadcaster (Susan)—is not ignored. Nevertheless, there is a sense of strength in this very weakness which derives from their privileged positions of intellectual power (i.e., the ability to analyze the historical situation and to engage in analysis and struggle at the level of ideology). The optimistic ending of *Tout va bien* emphasizes strength and hope from a *gauchiste* (leftwing) perspective. In the end, a voice-over states that the characters have begun to live historically.

The immediate political context of *Tout va bien* is one in which the legitimacy of Communist organizations after May 1968 was being questioned. The fact that the French Communist Party had condemned the *gauchistes'* involvement in the May 1968 events sharpened the already existing tension between the far left groups (Trotskyists, Maoists, etc.) and the French Communist party. The *gauchistes* tried to put pressure on the PCF from outside and oblige it to return to a revolutionary line. Thus in *Tout va bien* the *gauchistes* of the Salumi factory reject the political line of the CGT. The *gauchistes'* bitterness against the CGT was rooted in CGT support of De Gaulle's call for general elections in response to political unrest caused by political uprisings of students and workers. The CGT acceptance of the government proposal signified a willingness to act within the boundaries of a parliamentary system. Furthermore, the moderate political line adopted by the CGT reasserted the central debate of the May 1968 events: the question of reform or revolution.

It should be pointed out here that the complexity of the political/intellectual background that stimulated the making of *Tout va bien* goes beyond the factual account of historical events. The revival of the extremist left in France as a result of the May 1968 events had reverberations in film culture as well. French film criticism joined the militant *gauchistes* and committed itself zealously to the left's cause. For his part, Godard, a filmmaker who writes essays with his camera and incorporates criticism into all his films, began his private revolution on the screen. *Tout va bien* reflects Godard's decisive shift toward the far radical left, and consequently questions the role of intellectuals, like himself, in the political arena. From this vantage point, the fictional schematization of the factory seizure in *Tout va bien* not only mediates historical events symbolically; it also conveys a self-reflexive meditation on the political role of the cultural mediator himself.

Godard's job since his politicization has been—as Jacques, his alter ego in the film, says— "to find new forms for new content." Yet *Tout va bien*, though radical in form by the standards of mainstream cinema and Hollywood cinema in particular, is not a truly radical breakthrough. *Tout va bien* is in fact a product of either a political/commercial compromise or a new conscious political strategy, adopted by Godard and Gorin. This strategy was adopted in order to win a large audience. The failure of the Dziga Vertov Group to complete *Jusqu' à la Victoire* (1970) and the increasing disintegration of Maoist groups in France forced Godard and Gorin to return to commercial cinema. *Tout va bien* is the product of these changes, and its prologue reflects on the ingredients necessary for a commercially successful film (money, stars, narrative, romance and conflict, etc.). Since Paramount provided the money (due to the casting of Fonda and Montand) and the target audience was larger and more eclectic than the usual militant audience for the Dziga Vertov Group's films, *Tout va bien* retains some traces of the traditional narrative. The fact that the film contains its own criticism (in the prologue and epilogue as well as in Montand's monologue) and confesses its ideological sins (the use of stars, the focus on love story, etc.) does not redeem it. *Tout va bien* does not finally come up with any convincing revolutionary form to replace bourgeois cinema.

Tout va bien and Hollywood Cinema

Godard's cinema is usually tagged as counter-cinema. Critics refer frequently to the "Godardian code" as opposed to the "Hollywood code."[17] Many critics equate the relationship between the classical Hollywood film and Godard's cinema to that between opera and Brechtian epic theater. This equation suggests that Godard, like Bertolt Brecht, does not invent new forms but rather renovates ex-

isting forms (Hollywood film). Kristin Thompson, to cite one example, suggests that the "radical separation of the elements" in opposition to the fusion of elements, is the major characteristic of
Brecht's Epic theater, as well as what "makes *Tout va bien* a Brechtian film."[18] Her thesis thus proposes that *Tout va bien* is Brechtian
because it violates the Hollywood code. The "separation of elements" as such is Godard's counter-strategy, his method of violation. The result is that "*Tout va bien* remains within the realm of
the standard narrative film but with innovations."[19] In fact, "*Tout
va bien* provides two major alternatives to Hollywood cinema: (1) an
argumentative, rhetorical structure instead of a linear chain of
causality; and (2) "a movement towards social solutions rather than
purely personal ones."[20] Although essays and rhetorical/reflective
structures also typify Godard's pre-politicized cinema, these elements are more evident and elaborate in his politicized work. Naturally, the Marxist/Maoist theoretical framework is responsible for
the two central innovations that he introduces to Hollywood narrative in *Tout va bien*. The argumentative, rhetorical structure liter-
alizes the "scientific authenticity" of the Marxist discourse and
leads to an inevitable conclusion: the protagonists have begun to
think themselves in historical terms.

The Ubuesque elements in *Tout va bien* are yet another anti-
Hollywood narrative device. The factory manager is portrayed as a
contemporary version of Ubu, the hero of Alfred Jarry's trilogy. He is
a clownish buffoon, a comic caricature of middle management.
When Susan and Jacques come to interview him they say, "We are
visiting for Toto." Toto (1898–1967) was a great Italian comedian
and, sure enough, the factory manager is an Italian actor (Vittorio
Caprioli).[21]

The Ubuesque, grotesque elements are further developed in the
metaphoric reduction of the class struggle to the primal problem of
urination. The suffering and misfortunes of the workers are neither
sentimentalized nor seen as the suffering of real people, but, instead,
are viewed in a spirit of carnival and ritual. In an hilarious comic
scene the manager is prevented from using the toilet to urinate;
while he waits impatiently near the occupied toilet, two workers
play a spontaneous, absurdist game with a child's ball. A sense of
childish indulgence in nonsense and the infantile pleasure of utter-
ing dirty words mark this scene.

The scene also recalls the famous "parler Ubu" fascination
with variations and neologisms of *merde*. As in Mikail Bakhtin's carnivalesque approach to the grotesque, the body principle domi-

nates[22] the presentation of class struggle in *Tout va bien*. The deprivation of the workers' elementary right to urinate becomes in turn their act of revenge against *le patron* (the boss).[23] Godard here embodies the principle of grotesque realism according to Bakhtin: "The essential principle of grotesque realism is degradation, that is, the lowering of all that is high, spiritual, ideal, abstract; it is a transfer to the material level, the sphere of earth and body in their indissoluble unity."[24] The high ideals of class struggle are stripped down to their bare bones. The workers, unlike the CGT representatives who deal with figures and numbers, fight for elementary rights that come down to basic bodily needs. The class struggle is not a struggle for abstract ideas; it is a struggle for the right to urinate when one needs to. The urination scene thus follows Brecht's paradigm of *gestus* (social gesture).

The carnivalesque spirit manifests itself also in the supermarket scene. Again the comedic, anarchic spirit provides a statement against the consumer society, celebrated in the manager's speech. In a dadaistic and surrealistic manner these two scenes echo these movements' advocacy of the artistic value of shock (*épater le bourgeois*). Here the film asserts its aggressiveness. It is an aggression designed to encourage the audience to question social reality and its representation in the film image.

The prologue of *Tout va bien* not only exposes the economic forces behind the film industry, it also lays bare the clichés of Hollywood narrative: romance, an inevitable conflict, precision of situations, clarity of motivations, and so on. The progression of the narrative in *Tout va bien* itself makes use of these very same worn-out ingredients; however, it twists their habitual representation and consequently their ideology. The love story is politicized and the personal affair is displaced into a social context.

Godard's use of quotations in *Tout va bien* as the major device through which characters express their positions is another counter-Hollywood device. In some cases this procedure is in part ironic. For example, the factory manager's statements are an extract from Jean Saint-Geour's *Vive la societe de consommation*. His caricature-like delivery of these quotations further ridicules the glib generalities of the text. The speech of the union delegate is cited from the Communist Party's CGT union magazine, *La vie ouvriere*. Paradoxically, it is highly abstract because it is full of facts, figures, and numbers. Jacques refers to Brecht's "Preface of Mahagonny" but in a more spontaneous manner than that of the manager and the CGT representative. On the other hand, the workers rarely quote. They refer to their own experiences in a more hesitant and inarticulate manner. The speech delivered by Georgette is the most simple and concrete. While it, too, is a cited text from *La Cause du Peuple*, a Maoist journal, it is less formally articulated than the other texts. This "mobilization of quotations" likewise follows Brecht, who regarded it "as basic to dialectical argument, being listed as one of the objectives of his proposed 'Society of Dialecticians.' "[25]

Although *Le Gai Savoir* is much more advanced in terms of research and instruction aimed at creating a "society of dialecticians," *Tout va bien* is still entitled to be called an instructive/dialectic film because it encourages the audience to criticize the ontology and ideology of film images through deconstruction. Moreover, in *Tout va bien* Godard debunks certain film conventions, such as Hollywood's use of representation to achieve verisimilitude, in order to combat their powers of persuasion.

The Criticizer is Criticized: Auto-Critique in *Tout va bien*

Auto-critique is another eminent strategy in *Tout va bien*, although not something new in Godard's cinema. Even his pre-politicized films contain critical dimensions subsumed within the narrative. Structurally, auto-critique manifests itself openly in the prologue and in Yves Montand's monologue. Godard and Gorin explicitly express their discomfort and guilt feelings about using the same system they despise. Thus they put a finger on the paradoxical position they occupy in a capitalist society, as artists who presume to call themselves revolutionaries. In addition to being, in this sense, a critique of itself, the epilogue is also a critique of Godard's previous work. The dialogue in which Susan tells Jacques that she loves him and lists all the parts of his body that she loves has been taken from *Le Mépris* (*Contempt*) (1963). *Contempt* is a film about the process of making a film which contains a critique of filmmaking. Yet *Tout va bien* by quoting the love dialogue from *Contempt* emphasizes first that *Contempt*'s "idealist view of love is no longer tenable,"[26] and second that *Contempt*'s "passionate critique of filmmaking is no longer enough, because it confines itself to aesthetic and cultural analyses while scanting economic and explicitly political ones."[27]

Breathless (1959) is another film which *Tout va bien* bitterly criticizes. Godard's "repeated statement that it is one of his films that he likes least and that he finds it fascist"[28] is understood in the context of his politicization. *Tout va bien*'s analysis of economic forces as the molder and shaper of both filmmaking and film narrative explains his renouncement of *Breathless*. Its Fascism, according to Godard:

> resides in its refusal of the reality of social relations and the propagation of the myth of an existence outside those relations. If *A bout de souffle* represents the criminal as someone who has abolished any restraint on desire, Godard's later films reveal this image as too simple, as indeed an image of money which disregards the money in the image.[29]

Tout va bien echoes *Breathless* in many respects. For instance, Gorin said, "Fonda and Montand's roles here are in one sense a reprise of Seberg and Belmondo's in *A bout de souffle*."[30] The two protagonists are again a French male and an American female. Yet the American woman in *Tout va bien* is the "correction" of Patricia, the traitress of *Breathless*. Both American women are journalists, yet whereas Patricia betrays Michel for the sake of her career, Susan, the correct heroine of *Tout va bien* does not prostitute herself professionally to advance her career. On the contrary, she finds out that what the network wants her to write is crap. She also finds out that the broadcasting organization imposes a uniform "objective" style that distorts the reality behind the representation. Susan's discovery of her dependence on the means of representation, and furthermore on the owners of the means of producing representation (the fictive ABS American Broadcasting System), culminates in her resignation.

Tout va bien also implicitly criticizes the idolization of American cinema in *Breathless*. The nostalgic romanticizing of Hollywood cinema in *Breathless* is replaced by a cynical disclosure of Hollywood's economic motivation and its impact on codes of narrative. The romantic existentialist love story of *Breathless* is dislocated. Love is reduced to its barest elements: "cinéma, bouffe, et baise" (film, food, and fucking). These bodily/materialist activities are analyzed with a scientific precision leading to the conclusion that personal problems exist only as part of a larger economic/socio/ political system. Yet, Godard not only criticizes his previous film, he criticizes himself and the role he played as a cinéphile *Nouvelle Vague* director. *Tout va bien* is, in this respect, very autobiographical. The auteur (although rejecting the notion of authorship and personal cinematic vision) strips himself and becomes his own historian. Moreover the protagonists, Susan and Jacques, parallel Godard and Gorin and especially Godard. Yves Montand in his monologue introduces himself as an ex-*Nouvelle Vague* director who now makes television commercials. Not only has Godard done television commercials, but *Tout va bien* was itself produced and distributed commercially. Furthermore, like Godard, Jacques realizes after May 1968 that mere support of the leftist cause means nothing. Finally, and perhaps, most importantly, like Godard, he defines his "vocation" as "finding new forms for new content." Jacques's romance with Susan, as he reveals in his monologue, flourished during the May 1968 events, and this recalls Godard's own romance with Anne Wiazemsky, who actually introduced Godard to the Maoist groups in Paris. Susan herself also functions as a semi-alter ego of Godard. Like Jacques she also concludes "that everything is a matter of style." Hence, her professional/political/personal crisis opens new avenues for her to find and explore "new forms."

"The Cinema Plays with Itself": Exemplary Brechtian Self-Reflexive Strategies in *Tout va bien*

Self-reflexivity has always played a major role in Godard's cinema. The "Godardian touch" has been primarily characterized by the extensive use of self-reflexive methods. However, in his pre-political films, reflexivity was mostly playful, non-programmatic, and lacking in didactic missionary aspirations. Nevertheless, it was always critical and reflective. *Contempt* (1963) criticized moral corruption in the film industry, *Masculin/Feminin* (1966) criticized the consumer society and its addiction to images manufactured by advertisement, and *Les Carabiniers* (1963) criticized the futility of war (although in a very vague and uncommitted manner).

Godard's fascination with language and other means of communication was also evident in his pre-political phase. Implicitly his obsession with questions of verbal and sign language[31] conveyed a critique of representation both in life and cinema. Godard often shows characters imitating representations, i.e., conforming to social molds via what they see and read. In *Breathless* (1959), Patricia compares her profile to a profile of a woman in a reproduction of a Renoir painting *Portrait de modèle ou Margot*. In *Une Femme mariée* (A Married Woman) (1964), Charlotte examines herself in the mirror after looking at a sequence of bra advertisements in *Elle*, the French women's weekly magazine. In *Bande à part* (Band of Outsiders) (1964), a woman in the restroom paints her eyes to become more attractive in terms dictated by a magazine. When her boyfriend tries to talk to her, she brushes him off, claiming that he interferes with her efforts to become attractive. Godard has always been fascinated by this interaction of life and art, life and representation, self-identity and social identity.

In *Tout va bien*, as in his other politicized films, this fascination is reformulated in political (especially Marxist) terms. The major self-reflexive techniques in *Tout va bien* are: the use of the "star system" and documenatry conventions, the politicization of the love story, and the employment of various strategies to organize the narrative and to unveil the means of representation peculiar to cinema.

The "Star System" Exploits Itself

The conscious exploitation of the star system in *Tout va bien* is another major example of Godard's struggle against the Hollywood system. The main reason for employing Fonda and Montand was their star value. The use of big-name stars (Godard and Gorin reasoned) was the only way to obtain financial backing for such a film. They believed it would also help them appeal to a larger audience. Yet the two were also selected because of their association with left-wing politics and their support for progressive political causes. Fonda was an anti-Vietnam war activist (for a more detailed analysis of her representation in the film see chapter 5), and Montand has always been a prominent supporter of the *Gauche*. Furthermore, Montand's portrayal of the famous Lambrakis in Constantin Costa-Gavras' *Z* (1969) anchored his image as a left-wing hero in the public mind. Costa-Gavras's *The Confession* (1970), which followed *Z*, strengthened this image. Although in *The Confession* (which deals with the Prague trials) the evil forces are associated with the Stalinist regime, Montand, who portrays Slansky, is still the good, righteous leftist hero. Stalinism in this film is presented as a distortion and corruption of socialism. Montand is not an anti-socialist, but rather a victim of Stalinism. In *Tout va bien*, Godard implicitly mocks Montand's leftist heroic aura, by his deliberate humiliation of him (Montand) as a star. Godard, who meditates in *Tout va bien* on the fragility of left-wing intellectuals, considers Montand himself to be one of them. Therefore, Godard finds any attempt à la Costa-Gavras to cast Montand as a traditional melodramatic hero (whose only deviation from Hollywood standards is his political commitment to the left cause) unacceptable. Furthermore, Montand's casting in *Tout va bien* accentuates Godard and Gorin's quest for the form most appropriate to political film. In other words, Godard is trying, in *Tout va bien* to answer the question "how to make political films politically."

This question is deliberately built into *Tout va bien* so as to recall the *Cahiers'* theoretical debate about the notion of the political film. In this debate, Costa-Gavras's political melodramas, and *Z* in particular, played a key role. Costa-Gavras could be considered the most important commercial political filmmaker of the period. *Z*, as George Lellis suggests, "might even be considered the film which gave commercial potency to the treatment of leftist themes in the French cinema."[32] This is the reason why the Greek-born director's work became the *Cahiers'* prime negative model.

The attack on Costa-Gavras's treatment of political issues intensified with the appearance of *The Confession. Cahiers* critic Jean-Louis Comolli, as Lellis suggests, "takes the opportunity to treat general issues of film and politics as they apply to the Costa-Gavras film."[33] Comolli structures his review of the work in the form of fifteen propositions about politics and film. His point of departure is that: "Like many films, *The Confession* is in the forefront of the dominant ideology but puts up a smokescreen to hide its ideological operations; in no way does it try to subvert socio-cultural standards."[34] Comolli claims that "identification with the central character in *The Confession* [played by Yves Montand] is achieved by illusionist techniques, the artificial techniques creating the effect of reality."[35]

Against the politically incorrect films of Costa-Gavras, *Cahiers*, in a subsequent issue, presented *Tout va bien* as the "correct" political film and the prime example of Brechtian cinema. *Tout va bien*, according to *Cahiers*, fulfills all the conditions that Comolli and Narboni indicate as necessary for a progressive film. Moreover, it epitomizes Comolli's ideal type of film, *le direct*: it promotes alternatives to conventional cinematic representation since it is concerned not with reproducing events for the camera but with producing events that could not exist without the camera.

We could claim that Montand's casting in *Tout va bien* is a cinematic reaffirmation of *Cahiers*'s position by Godard and Gorin. Montand, the merchandized working class hero is displaced into a correct political film that exploits Montand's on- and off-screen image in order to make a political statement. The melodramatic Montand of *Z* and *The Confession* is transformed into the self-critical Montand of *Tout va bien*. Like Godard, who criticizes his politically incorrect cinematic past in *Tout va bien*, Montand implicitly criticizes his continual casting as a sentimentalized left-wing hero in the politically incorrect films of Costa-Gavras. In his confessional monologue, he even mentions the Soviet invasion of Czechoslovakia, thus invoking his role in *The Confession*. The scene in which Montand is shown, or imagined, as a worker in the Salumi meat factory is a visual culmination of Godard's criticism of Montand's melodramatic roles in Costa-Gavras's films. The scene mocks the exploitation of the star system by conventional left-wing filmmakers. Even though we actually see Montand working in the factory, we do not believe, even for one moment, that he is a real worker. We cannot even indulge in a suspension of belief. Rather, we are completely conscious that we are watching a star playing or imitating a worker. (The same is true of Jane Fonda's performance in this scene.) There is even a hint of deliberate intention to humiliate the star. From a glamorous leftist hero who fights for abstract moral ideals in Costa-Gavras's films, Montand in *Tout va bien* is reduced to a participant in a monotonous and alienating process of sausage production. The gap between real worker and star is fully exploited. The same approach guided Godard's selection of actors to play the roles of the workers.[36]

Yves Montand's star quality is interlinked with his other functions in the narrative. His status as a fictional character is enormously complex. In fact, he is a curious mixture of fictional and authentic personalities which locate his performance within the Brechtian tradition of acting. The actor always remains present as an actor, both demonstrating and commenting on that character's actions. The fictional Jacques is thus composed of the following personas:

1. the authentic "real" Yves Montand; the "persona" projected in his off-screen activities
2. the image of Montand; the "persona" built and projected by his continual casting as a left-wing hero
3. the fictive Jacques, whose character exists only in relation to his specific fictional situation in *Tout va bien*
4. the surrogate and semi-alter ego of Godard himself
5. a caricature portrayal of François Traffaut
6. a caricature portrayal of Roger Vadim
7. the star Montand in the film *Tout va bien*.

Montand's off-screen image is exploited through his well-known and outspoken affiliation with the French *Gauche*. His on-screen image is utilized, as was mentioned before, by way of his melodramatic roles as a left-wing hero in Costa-Gavras's films. However, he still possesses special traits that distinguish him as the fictional Jacques. At the same time he is also a fictional version of Godard. He defines himself as a former New Wave director, who, in May, became disgusted with his "films d'esthète." Furthermore, Yves Montand comments within the film on his role in the film. In his monologue he confesses that in the factory with the workers

"C'était comme si je n'avais plus de texte, je ne savais plus quel rôle suivre" (It was as though I had no more text, I didn't know what role to play any more). This is actually what happened to Montand and Fonda on the set in the factory scene. Visually they were pushed away from the center of the frame. Godard deliberately deprived them of any opportunity to demonstrate their star qualities. Instead the workers/extras occupied the center of the frame and the focus of the narrative in this sequence. Montand and Fonda were in a position of undefined and confused observers.[37]

"The Reality of Fiction and the Fiction of Reality": Documentary and Fiction in Tout va bien

The cinematic institution's categories of documentary and fiction have continuously been thrown into crisis in Godard's work. Godard's unconventional blending of these modes expresses his complex attitude toward the relationship between art and life, life and cinema. Godard believes that the moment one departs from fiction in film one inevitably departs from truth; yet he always combines documentary or quasi-documentary elements in his films because, as he has been known to say, "Cinema is not the reflection of reality, but the reality of that reflection." Unlike the Eric Rohmer-André Bazin phenomenological approach, Godard distrusts verisimilitude as the means to render reality. By contrast, his cinema epitomizes Comolli's ideal film, le direct, which extends the original conception of cinéma vérité. It is not a crude transformation of reality into cinematography, but rather a presentation of representation. It is a documentation of the process of producing events in front of the camera. Since Godard believes that the film image is fundamentally and profoundly ideological, he insists that film does not exist as a neutral medium to convey reality.

In Tout va bien Godard integrates into the romance (the fiction) "various devices traditionally coded as belonging to documentary modes."[38] The film uses one of the central conventions of the documentary, the interview. In so doing, it challenges the main philosophical assumptions of this cinematic mode, namely, the assumption that the interview provides the most direct access to truth, and that it gives a fair chance to the interviewee to express his opinions and ideas. Godard mocks these naive assumptions by inverting traditional interview conventions. When the CGT shop steward and the manager of the factory respond to unheard questions in long takes filmed in frontal medium shots, it is unclear by whom these questions are being asked. The same disorientation occurs when Jacques and Susan talk about their backgrounds. Jacques seems to answer an unheard questioner. Susan's whole speech is a mock interview. She sits by a microphone and a voice-over translator speaks along with her. Yet the next shot makes clear that this is actually her taping session.

The same logic, rooted in Godard's mistrust of documentary's claim to be truer than fiction, guided the selection of unemployed actors to play the workers. Godard's choice of the fictional mode was highly praised by *Cahiers*. *Tout va bien* was compared to Marin Karmitz's *Coup pour coup* (Blow for Blow), which was released in Paris at almost exactly the same time and which also deals with workers' strikes and the sequestration of employers from a Maoist point of view. Yet "the Karmitz film was shot with a group of workers themselves; shooting was done simultaneously with camera and videotape, so that workers could critique the material as it was shot."[39] In their analysis of the two films, the *Cahiers* article attacked what it perceived as the naive empiricist philosophical assumptions that underline the documentary mode à la Karmitz. "The *Cahiers* critics assert that what is needed in a film is an understanding of social, political and economic *processes* and that those processes cannot be seen merely through the observation of reality."[40] The *Cahiers* review concluded that: "By presenting the film as a closed discourse and not discussing how the making of the film itself enters into the political process, Karmitz avoids any genuine political comment on the film's own place in the struggle."[41] The *Cahiers* related this conclusion to the question that had been asked throughout the 1970s, a question, likewise asked by Godard and built into *Tout va bien* itself, namely: "Can one make a revolutionary film without criticizing bourgeois representation?"[42]

The Politicization of the Love Story

The politicization of the love story in *Tout va bien* is in line with the film's conscious violation of the Hollywood code. As such it is part of the overall self-reflexive strategy employed by the movie. Furthermore, Godard and Gorin's decision to write a love story with a political twist posits two interrelated issues. On the one hand, the film investigates the possibility of conveying radical politics through a traditional topos (romance). On the other it challenges the traditional conception of the political film by blurring the customary and artificial division between personal and public. The romance is presented in the prologue as an economic compromise imposed on film-makers who work in a capitalist system. Yet interweaving the ro-mance into the overall political situation (the occupation of the factory and the aftermath of May 1968) does not contradict Marxist thinking. On the contrary, in Marxist thought the sharp opposition between work and leisure has always been considered (by Brecht in particular) an artificial division peculiar to the alienating capitalist system. Godard and Gorin show how Jacques's and Susan's relation-ships to their work affect their marital and sex life. In their con-frontation, Susan claims that she has only an image of them together sexually because they have tried to alienate their jobs from their ex-perience of living together. She demands an image of both of them working in order to abolish this alienation.

Since *Tout va bien* challenges the bourgeois conception of the political film, Godard and Gorin's definition of politics here is broad-ened to include sexual politics. While central to Jacques and Susan's relationship, these politics also play an important role in the lives of the women workers. They complain at length about physical deteri-oration, sexual harassment by male workers, multiple pregnancies due to ignorance of birth control measures, chauvinistic husbands, and so on. The Marxist framework of the film specifies historical ma-terialism as the meeting point of the personal and the public. Thus, in order to understand their dissatisfaction, Susan and Jacques, as Thomas Kavanagh observes, "must see themselves and each other not as self-enclosed psychological units, but as part of a concrete eco-nomic and political situation."[43]

Another issue that is raised by the politicization of the love story is the relationship between popular forms and revolutionary politics. Critics like Judith Mayne and Kristin Thompson suggest that Godard and Gorin's adoption of mass culture forms is "not un-like Brecht's work with standard, banalized forms of opera."[44] Mayne asserts that both the love story and opera "are genres performing a certain social function, that of mystification or, as Brecht referred to it 'dishing up pleasure.' Rather than dismissing these genres as empty and useless, however, Brecht proposed working on them as a point of departure, thus attacking the society that *needs* such for-malized conventions."[45] Mayne adds, "The possibilities of an 'epic cinema' take as their formal point of departure the recognition of techniques, the most obvious being those associated with the love story, as extremely codified practices, codified by the social produc-tion of reality."[46] We might also see this adoption of popular form as another facet of Godard's modernist subversion of the cliché. Along these lines, *Tout va bien*'s love story also eliminates psychological dimensions. The conflicts, not only those between the workers and the manager, but also between Jacques and Susan, are defined politically. The psychological causality of Hollywood cinema is replaced by Marxist economic and political analysis.

Interruptions in the Narrative and Authorial/Directorial Presence

In terms of narrative structure, the film's self-reflexivity is manifested by systematic interruptions of the narrative, by the displacement of Hollywood causality into dialectical rhetorical argumentative structures, and by conscious authorial/directorial intrusions. For Godard *Tout va bien* signified his return to narrative, and in returning to narrative he also returned to his familiar methods of interrupting narrative. *Tout va bien*, like all Godard's films, subsumes criticism within its narrative pattern; therefore, structurally, the film is composed of the representation of life (the dramatic scenes) and its theoretical/critical analysis. Each dramatic unit comments about itself and develops an argument. This structure is systematically interrupted by a confrontation of characters who explain their arguments by the use of printed material, and the like.

The auteurist intrusion is yet another type of interruption. It exists through intratextual references, but mainly via the prologue and the epilogue. In the prologue the codes of narrative (including Godard's pre-political narratives) are exposed via the externalized process of self-reflection that operates through the voices of the two directors. In the epilogue they intrude again in the voice-over narration. They reiterate the notion that love stories are ultimately nothing more than "rules of the game," generic conventions that construct the narrative. They illustrate their reflective intrusion by exposing two ways of ending the story, each of which satisfies the codified form of the love story. The phenomenon of the directors entering the text directly not only interrupts the flow of the narrative but also defines blatantly their own relationships to their film.

Sound/Image

On the level of style/technique, the most apparent reflexive strategy in *Tout va bien* is the separation of sound and image.[47] In *British Sounds/See You at Mao* (1969) Godard says: "There are times when class struggle is the struggle of an image against an image and of a sound against a sound. In a film, it is the struggle of an image against a sound and a sound against an image." This quotation speaks for itself. It emphasizes that Godard understands the notion of a correct relation between sound and image in exclusively political terms:

> We said: Jean-Pierre Gorin told Martin Walsh "We don't know if film is image or not, and we're going to start by saying film is just as much image as it is sound and to do that and to make it perceptible we are going to start from the soundtrack, we are going to overcrowd the soundtrack and we're going to skip the image."[48]

Examples of conflict between sound and image in *Tout va bien* are numerous. The two central characters represent the split between sound and image in their jobs. She is a radio broadcaster, and he is a filmmaker. "This is emphasized by the placement of a camera to the left of the frame during his 'interview,' while there is a microphone in a comparable position in hers."[49] Another instance of conflict between sound and image occurs in the sequence in which Susan tells us about her job. We hear not only fragments of her actual interview, but also her own voice translating her English into French. Sometimes her French is ahead of her English, sometimes her English is ahead of her French and neither is a precise translation of the other. Thus, at this point, fracturing is occurring at a basic level: "Susan's instantaneous translation of her own comments renders her interview difficult to follow at points: her own discursivity negates itself, as well as the fundamental union between sound and image."[50]

Another example of this occurs when Georgette tells her story to Susan. A man's voice (whose source in the image is invisible and unknown) announces a "chanson gauchiste" (a leftist song) and Georgette's face fills the frame. We see her lips moving, and she delivers her bare recital of facts in a monotone voice. However, she does not *sing*. A woman humming is heard in the background but the source of the sound is not visible in the frame. In fact, the spectator has no way of determining whether the sound is on-screen diegetic or off-screen diegetic. This conflict between sound and image is pushed to limits beyond even the operatic alienating song of the Brechtian theatre. Brecht in the *Three Penny Opera* wrote: "Nothing is more revolting than when the actor pretends not to notice that he has left the level of plain speech and started to sing. The three levels—plain speech, heightened speech and singing—must always remain distinct."[51] Godard and Gorin not only made each level distinct, they separated the levels to the extent that they negated even the notion of "chanson."

Godard's use of non-image enhancing sound takes on a synecdochical life of its own as it breaks down into "sounds." The last tracking shot of the film (there are a total of only three) summarizes the relationship between these sounds and the image, as Gorin himself told Martin Walsh:

> The last tracking shot sums up the whole film—the slum landscape with that incredible song. You pass along the wall, and on the soundtrack you have the three principal sounds of the film—the leftist sound, the Communist Party sound, the boss sound. They're like sound vignettes stamped on that bare wall. And then you get back into landscape again. That's the summary of the film. It's a film done on a number of sounds and the way they interact with each other.[52]

The first lateral tracking shot in the film clearly shows the Salumi factory to be a stage set, built in a studio. In an epic Brechtian manner it breaks the illusionism of the fourth wall in Aristotelian theater.[53] The second tracking shot, which occurs in the supermarket scene, creates a rigidly formalized shot parallel to the first one. The third and the last long tracking shot across the slums and over the surface of a brick wall at the end of the film seems also to suggest the two-dimensionality of the cinema screen. The three formally parallel tracking shots call the spectator's attention to the means of representation that the film itself employs.

Tout va bien, with its almost obsessive exploration of screen surfaces and inquiry into its modes of representation, stresses that artworks are constructions, objects produced by people, and as such obey ideologically determined codes. Hence Godard's main problem in constructing *Tout va bien* became a formal one; i.e., "how to make political films politically." Vertov's[54] and Brecht's notions of new form for revolutionary content helped him to confront this problem, and *Tout va bien* (through its acknowledged contradictions) epitomizes Godard's solution.

Letter to Jane (1972), which followed *Tout va bien* (for a lengthier discussion of the film see chapter 5), is a 52-minute, 16mm film that provides a combination of semiological and ideological analysis of a newspaper photo of Jane Fonda visiting Hanoi during the American bombardment of the city. It is the last film made by the couple Godard and Gorin.

A New Turn: The Collaboration with Miéville

Tout va bien was Godard's only attempt to come back to the commercial circuits of production and distribution during his radical period. After the failure of the movie and the termination of his collaboration with Gorin, Godard began to work with the person who was to become his long-time partner: Anne-Marie Miéville. In 1972 Godard left Paris and moved to Grenoble intending to equip a video studio and to build alternative strategies of production and distribution (disseminating video cassettes through networks of friends). The collaboration between the two between 1974 and 1975 resulted in three movies: *Içi et ailleurs* (1974), *Numero deux* (1975), and *Comment ça va* (1976).

Ici et ailleurs combines footage shot for *Jusqu'à la victoire* by the Dziga Vertov Group about what it called "the Palestinian revolution" (actually it was about the Fatah, the largest faction in the Palestinian Liberation Organization) and images of domestic scenes from the life of a French family in France. The juxtaposition of domestic images borrowed from the private domain (the family) and political images borrowed from the sphere of the public space (politics) is evidence of Miéville's growing influence on Godard and her feminist leaning towards the politicization of the intimate and familial. The footage selected from *Jusqu'à la victoire* emphasizes the role of women (and even little girls) in the Palestinian armed struggle as well as in the process of educating the Palestinian people. The film also contains a scene of feminist criticism aimed at Godard himself. In this scene a young Palestinian woman is talking about the willingness of Palestinian women and even pregnant women to sacrifice their children for the Palestinian cause. The voice-over narration criticizes the scene asking why Godard chose a beautiful young woman and not a pregnant one in order to convey this political message.

The merging of the "here and there" raises the question of the relationship between what Godard perceived as the Palestinian revolution and the French revolution that he envisaged in the 1960s. The naive idealization of the PLO by Godard and Miéville is accompanied by an anti-Israeli position equating the Israeli retaliations against Jordan (and in particular the Karame operation) with Nazi atrocities. The climax of this anti-Israeli stance (which verges on anti-Semitism) is conveyed through the image of the wedding of Golda Meir, Israel's prime minister at the time, with the voice-over of a Nazi speech delivered by Adolph Hitler. The film, like many of

Godard's other political movies, is extremely naive and dogmatic, if not infantile in its approach towards the East/West conflict. This conflict is presented and explained through a montage technique whereby images of advertising and consumption are associated with the West, while images of violence are linked with the East. This manipulation reaches its climax in the ideational and audio-visual link Godard creates between the events of 1917, 1936, and 1968. Through this simplistic and horrifying equation Godard claims that the sum of 1917 and 1936 is the image of "Black September," which occurred a few months after the shooting of *Jusqu'à la victoire*. This simplistic and monstrous equation is carried further in an association aligning the capitalist system (visualized by images of mass production lines) with images of the Nazis' mass murder of Jews.

In 1975 Godard and Miéville made two films, *Numero deux* (see chapter 5) and *Comment ça va*. *Comment ça va* (defined by Godard and Miéville as "un film entre l'actif et le passif" [a film between the active and the passive]) explores the problems of the mass media and the transmission of information in photojournalism through the analysis of one photo in particular which shows a violent clash between a journalist and a soldier in Portugal. Unlike *Letter to Jane*, in which the analysis of a photo of Jane Fonda in Hanoi (see chapter 5) is strictly verbal and essayistic, in *Comment ça va* the analysis employs fictive narrative techniques as well. *Comment ça va* is about a member of the CGT who participates in a video report on the modernization of print journalism. He works with Odette (played by Miéville whose face is never seen in the film) a gauchiste secretary who teaches him how to look critically at images of information (with a special reference to the image from Portugal). The principal opposition of the film is not between the text and the image (as is the case of *Letter to Jane*) but between the hands (writing) and the gaze (reading). The gaze which is controlling everything is superior to the hands and therefore "ce qui ne vas pas aujourd'hui avec le travail manuel, c'est qu'il est d'abord un travail intellectuel" (the trouble with manual work today is that it is primarily intellectual work). Much like Bertolucci's *The Conformist* (see chapter 2) the refusal to see (closing one's eyes) is perceived as enabling the rise of Fascism. The strong criticism leveled at the press and journalists in this film anticipates, to a certain extent, Godard and Miéville's video work aimed at creating an "alternative television" that would provide information in a new communicative form (in *Comment ça va* Godard and Miéville claim that information is a matter of form since the word "form" is contained in the word in "form"ation). The film's interest in problems of dissemination of information takes epistolary form in a letter that a father (the CGT member) writes to his daughter. Godard attempts to analogize genetics—the language of information—with biological birth symbolism; the genetic theme of the reproduction process will be reflected in a communicative act of writing.

Between 1976 and 1978 Godard and Miéville moved to Rolle, a small Swiss town between Geneva and Lausanne, and shifted to video/television work. During most of his radical period, Godard rejected his personal pre-politicized cinema. Godard's comeback to subjectivity occurred only in the mid to late 1970s through his video work with Miéville. He thus moved back from his Maoist collaboration with Gorin to explorations of individuality and subjectivity—but always within the context of a larger system of social and political institutions. Miéville, as MacCabe explains, "insisted on the quotidian realities of life in France, including television's dominance as both producer and distributer of images."[55] In fact the video work started with the 1974 foundation of Godard's company, Sonimage, which functioned as an experimental laboratory concerned with the image. How does the image come into existence? What meaning does it convey? What social and ideological conventions decide on the relationship between the image's signified and signifier?

The change of power in France and Valéry Giscard d'Estaing's election in 1974, which brought about the dissolution of O.R.T.F. into separate units, advanced Godard's efforts in this direction. One of the units, Institut National Audiovisuelle (INA), comissioned a televison program from Godard: "Six fois deux (Sur et sous la communication)" (1976), a series of six two-part programs which were broadcast on French television in 1976 (unlike, for example, *Le Gai Savoir* which was commissioned by O.R.T.F. but never broadcast). As the title implies, the programs are concerned with processes of communication in contemporary society—in particular how the production and consumption of images affects the division of labor and leisure time. These issues are explored through various interviews and visual essays on aspects of contemporary European life. The presence of Godard himself in text and image in these explorations exposes his subjectivity as much as that of the human and ideational subjects he studies. The programs' concern is not only to explore subjects and subjectivity but also, and mainly, to question traditional television structure, aesthetics, and politics and to offer a radical alternative.

Godard and Miéville divided the programs into daytime and nighttime episodes. The daytime interviews are more complex and composed of interviews with different people on social and communication issues. The nighttime programs are more documentary in nature and maintain real time as opposed to the screen time used in the daytime programs. The titles of the programs use ideational/descriptive titles (day) paired with names of people (night).

The first program, "Ya Personne (Nobody's There)" presents Godard as a prospective employer who interviews a number of jobseekers; in its companion piece, "Louison," a dairy farmer discusses French peasantry. The second program is a theoretical essay on the production and social reception of cultural images ("Leçons de Choses") accompanied by an interview with Godard by two journalists from *Liberation* ("Jean-Luc"). The third program, entitled "Photos et cie," deals with photography and includes a critique of photojournalism and television news, and is paired with "Marcel," an interview with an amateur filmmaker and nature photographer. The fourth program is about women ("Pas d'histoire No History/No Story"). It relates their problems to the problems of storytelling while its counterpart consists of the autobiographical accounts of four women ("Nanas"). Program five, "Nous trois" presents a romantic melodrama, followed by "René(e)s" an interview with the French mathematician Rene Thom, the inventor of the catastrophe theory. "Avant et après" concludes the series with an attempt to "do television differently." "Jacqueline et Ludovic"—the final nighttime program—presents a couple whose personal communication is "different."

Six fois deux's call for counter-television (echoing Godard's appeal in *Le Gai Savoir* for an alternative cinema) is continued in the couple's second television project from this period entitled "France tour/détour deux enfants" (1977–1978). It is a series of twelve half-hour episodes structured in a very rigid repetitive format. It is loosely based on G. Bruno's nineteenth-century popular novel *Le Tour de la France par Deux Enfants*, which tells of the extraordinary adventures of two children exploring France. Godard's children (Camille Virolleaud and Arnaud Martin), however, are not engaged in any out-of-the ordinary adventures. On the contrary, they are seen engaged in quotidian activities in school and within the family. Their activities are interspersed with serious questions from Godard. The questions are not the usual questions adults ask children. They concern metaphysical issues (death, silence) or social, cultural, and ideological topics (what is an image? what is the significance of communication?). The two children are not treated as kids, but rather as individuals whose observations may carry more weight than the wisdom of adults. The school system is presented both visually and ideationally as a prison or a military institution that represses and oppresses the child. The family is represented as a similarly oppressive institution, crushing the child's subjectivity and imagination. Perhaps the most memorable scene occurs in the eleventh program. In a take of more than ten minutes the camera remains fixed on the face of the little girl at the family dinner table. We can hear the family's conversation taking place, but we are deprived of our voyeuristic and auditoristic impulse to peep at the faces of the other family members.

One may speculate that this pessimistic view of France, and in particular of its educational system as the locus of civilized repression, is influenced by both Althusser's critique of the ISA (Ideological State Apparatuses) and Michel Foucault's histories of the structures of repression in prisons and mental hospitals. However, where Althusser differentiates between the symbolic repression of the family, education system, and media (the ISA) and the overt repression of such institutions as the army, the prison system, and the police (the RSA, Repressive State Apparatuses), Godard and Miéville do not. For them the two systems work together. The children's observations accompanied by the analyses of the two adult narrators reveal the extent to which the children are programmed, repressed, and silenced by the governing institutions of family, school, and television.[56]

France tour/détour was the last video production of Godard and Mieville during the Swiss period. *Sauve qui peut (la vie)* (1979) was produced and distributed by M.K. 2, Marin Karmitz's production company, and signaled Godard's return from the seclusion of Switzerland to the circuits of commercial cinema. Much like *Tout va bien*, the first commercial film made by the radical couple Godard/Gorin after the dissolution of the Dziga Vertov group, *Sauve qui peut (la vie)* is the initial commercial enterprise of the feminist couple Godard/Miéville after the Grenoble and the Swiss experience. It signals the close of Godard's so-called radical period.

CHAPTER 2

The Radical Period of Bertolucci: 1968–1976

Godard's transition from cinephilism to radicalism was conceived by many of his fans as surprising. Bertolucci's fans have experienced no such surprise. Bertolucci was a registered member of the Communist party from 1969, and his sympathy for the Communists was nothing out of the ordinary for an Italian director of his generation. As an assistant director to Pier Paolo Pasolini, himself a Gramscian Marxist, Bertolucci's cinematic career, right from its beginning, has been marked by radicalism. Indeed it is possible to see the whole of Bertolucci's *oeuvre* as a cycle of cinematic meditation on the fate and prospects of revolution in our time. His is a Marcusian revolution which is both subjective and collective and therefore relates to both Marx, the visionary of social revolution, and Freud, the founder of depth psychology.

Bertolucci's films from *Before the Revolution* (1964) through *Tango* (1972) can be seen as a submission to pessimism. Nonetheless, a melancholic aura was not enough to prevent *Tango* from attaining tremendous commercial success. The film's popularity contributed significantly to Bertolucci's self-confidence—and (perhaps ironically) to his faith in revolution as well. *Novecento (1900)* (1976) made after *Tango*, reflects the euphoria of this new phase in Bertolucci's development. American money and international stars were mobilized to project a utopian image of a primitive rural commune inspired by revolutionary ideas. Yet, for all its revolutionary romanticism the film was also conceived as a pragmatic platform: its release occurred in an election year when the prospects of major wins by the Italian Communist Party appeared extremely favorable.[1]

The logic of Bertolucci's revolutionary/utopian impulse, however, is immersed with a paradoxical sense of nostalgia for the present best exemplified by the motto of *Before the Revolution*: "He who did not live in the years before the revolution cannot understand what the sweetness of life is." This motto echos, to a certain extent, Tancredi's words to Don Fabrizio (the Leopard) in Luchino Visconti's *Il Gattopardo* (The Leopard): "Things have to change in order to remain the same."[2] Indeed of all the Italian directors, Visconti is the closest to Bertolucci.[3] Both directors convey in their films, as well as in their public pronouncements, a belief in the dialectical relationship between progress, change, and the future on the one hand, and decadence, destruction, pessimism, and nostalgia for the past, on the other.[4]

This sense of contradiction, so typical of Bertolucci, may explain his relative indifference to the May 1968 events. For Bertolucci the lesson of the events was quite different from what it was for Godard and Marco Bellochio: "I think the most important discovery I made after the events of May 1968 was that I wanted the revolution not to help the poor but for myself. I wanted the world to change for me. I discovered the individual level in political revolution."[5] This individual level is applied to the fundamentally political dialectic of sexual repression and liberation in his films.

Bertolucci's search for the individual's revolution within the political one motivates the synthesis of Freud and Marx that characterizes all his films. It recalls the Freudian/Marxian synthesis at the core of Herbert Marcuse's *Eros and Civilization* and it derives from the same awareness of what Douglas Kellner calls "the absence in Marxism of emphasis on individual liberation and the psychological dimension."[6] Indeed, in an interview on *The Last Emperor* Bertolucci confessed that: "back in '68 I was fascinated by the theatrical element of the Cultural Revolution . . . by that idea of Utopia. I was never involved with the pro-Chinese movements in Europe, although all my friends were, starting with Godard and Bellochio. In fact, I think I joined the Italian Communist Party specifically to be against the pro-China people."[7] Bertolucci's hostile attitude towards the European Maoist groups was shared and perhaps influenced by his other cinematic mentor and tutor, Pasolini. Despite being a Gramscian Marxist, Pasolini, as Bondanella explains, nevertheless attacked radical students during the 1968 events "as anticultural, antihistorical, and ignorant sons of the middle class, while he defended the embattled policemen, usually sons of peasants who had been drafted by the Italian government to defend a system that provided them with little benefit."[8]

The Politicization of Memory: From *Partner* to *The Conformist*

From 1968 to 1978 Bertolucci made only five feature films: *Partner* (1968), *The Spider's Stratagem* (1970), *The Conformist* (1970), *Last Tango in Paris* (1972), and *Novecento (1900)* (1976). He also made a short documentary under the auspices of the Italian Communist Party (PCI), *La salute e malata o I poveri muoiono prima* (*Health is Sick, or The Poor Die First*) (1971).

Partner fits the radical spirit of the late 1960s both stylistically and politically. However, as a film obsessed with the Godardian spirit it swallows Bertolucci's personality and erases, almost completely, his unique auteuristic signature. The film contains not only a Godardian critique of consumerism, but also many announcements such as "Free the passions" and "Prohibit the prohibitors" which echo Antonin Artaud's appeal for a revolution of the senses as well as Marcuse's advocation of a liberated society emancipated from "surplus repression." These slogans recall ones such as "Be realistic, ask the impossible" and "Imagination is realism," which dominated the May 1968 events. *Partner*, although marked by Godardian discourse, nevertheless introduces the theme of the interchangeability of sexual repression and political oppression which comes to prevail in Bertolucci's subsequent films.

La strategia del ragno (*The Spider's Stratagem*) (1970) is a free adaptation of Jorge Borges's short story "Theme of the Traitor and the Hero." Athos Magnani (Giulio Brogi) returns to his hometown thirty years after the assassination of his father, an anti-Fascist hero, and tries to discover through his father's former mistress Dreyfa (Alida Valli) and friends the truth behind the events leading to his father's death.

The film further refines the controlling theme and metaphor of *Partner*, that of doubling and repetition, once again invested with political and historical significance. Joel Magny suggests that in *The Spider's Stratagem* Bertolucci casts his political problematics in the form of an oscillation between the cinema and its myths on the one hand and history on the other.[9] Athos Magnani's attempts to discover if his father was a traitor or a hero, a Fascist or an anti-Fascist, are doomed to fail because, in the Bertoluccian universe, objective truth along with objective history does not exist. Historical time in *Stratagem* is replaced by mythical time in which things, events, and historical figures repeat themselves. Just as the son is the double of his father, so the father's assassination is a repetition of Caesar's murder.[10] Thus, history is conceived as a theater stage, a repetitive form of political spectacle in which events not only copy past events but, following Borges's idea, go so far as to "copy literature."[11] The cult of the hero/father is disassociated from any valid historical truth, and the fundamental issues of political cinema such as "the revelation of the truth" and "the representation of true history" remain locked within the duality of being/appearance. Therefore, the son is prevented from knowing for sure if his father was a hero or a traitor, if the little child is a boy or a girl, if the rabbit is female or male, and consequently, if the past as a myth of resistance belongs to the right or to the left.

The prime manifestation of this unresolved duality, however, is rendered through the protagonist's, as well as the spectator's, difficulty in distinguishing between treason and heroism. This invokes the problematics associated with the notion of the social practice of commemoration, one of the emergent themes in the contemporary discourse on collective remembering.[12] Commemoration as a social practice reconciles contested pasts by suppressing the mutable potential of the past—yesterday's heroes are today's or tomorrow's traitors and vice versa.

This view of history as a past inaccessible to truth, or to the process of demythification ("circular labyrinths" in Borges's words), is visually represented through repeating shots in which the camera circles around a statue of the father whose eyes are painted so as to create an impression of blindness.[13] This visual metaphor, loaded as it is with heavy Oedipal connotations, suggests the blindness of myth to history. Moreover, the camera movement as well as the blank unchiseled eyes of the statue allude to the statue in Godard's *Contempt*, a film that deals with ancient classical myths (the *Odyssey*) and their projection on what seem to be the more modern myths of the cinema and its heroes (Fritz Lang in *Contempt*). The camera movements—which imitate the circular labyrinths of the highly self-reflexive movement of Borges's story—create a kind of eternal repetition of the past and a sense of historical *cul du sac*. The son cannot escape from his father, nor from his past. The final scene in which he is seen waiting for a train that never comes (anticipating the train in *1900*) demonstrates the power of the past as a kind of eternal presence in human life.

Borges's "Theme of the Traitor and the Hero" is set in Ireland in 1824; Bertolucci changed the time of his film to 1970 (to include the Fascist past within its scope) and the place to Sabbionetta, Italy (or Tara as Bertolucci calls it in the film, after the plantation in *Gone With the Wind*). This preserved Renaissance town in the Po valley— the scene of Bertolucci's earliest memories and the location of most of his Italian films—links history and the characters' psychology to the geographic and mental landscape of Bertolucci's childhood. The displacement in time and space accentuates the political dimension of the film and its engagement with issues of historical conscious- ness and the development of collective myths. It is also in line with Borges's labyrinthic conception of history according to which time can move forward or backward in a linear fashion and yet always rep- resent the reenactment of previous myths. The plot takes place si- multaneously on several temporal levels. In terms of historical temporality, it is set in contemporary—as well as Fascist and Re- naissance—Italy. In terms of ahistorical mythical and literary time it is set on a Shakespearean stage that simulates the murder of Caesar. Hence, Bertolucci creates, to use Jean Baudrillard's thesis, a world of a simulacra, in which images refer to other images but never to real referents. History, to use Anton Kaes's observation regarding the relationship between film and history, "dissolves into a self- referential sign system cut loose from experience and memory."[14]

The film carries over the idea of spectacle from *Partner* where Giacobbe, following Antonin Artaud's advocation of total spectacle, suggests that the spectacle should become the mise en scène of the entire world with revolution as its text. Similarly, in *Stratagem* the father suggests "a popular spectacle so that the people will continue to hate fascism." This, of course, reverses the more common prac- tice in which fascism alone is represented as spectacle. It can there- fore be interpreted as Bertolucci's attempt to redeem spectacle from the charges made against it by Godard in the May 1968 discourse.

The Conformist continues to develop the topic of fascism, and much like *Stratagem*, it emphasizes the question of memory, public as well as private. Its treatment of the past is complex because of the intertextual relationships that exist between Bertolucci's film and other works. Bertolucci's *The Conformist* is based on Alberto Moravia's novel *Il Conformista* (The Conformist) which is, in itself, loaded with allusions and references to other literary texts, Marcel Proust's *À la recherche du temps perdu* (Remembrance of Things Past) in particular. The relationship between Moravia's novel and Proust's prose poem is based primarily on an attempt by Moravia to articulate his protagonist's "data of consciousness" through a narra- tive technique reminiscent of that employed by Proust. How- ever, more than imitating Proust's style, Moravia pays homage to the decadent French writer through the characters' names. Not only does the protagonist's first name, Marcello, recall the Proustian Marcel, but his family name, Clerici, recalls Albertine du Clarici,

Marcel's greatest love object. The character of Albertine is a com-
posite drawn from Proust's homosexual experiences with Reynaldo
Hahn, Lucien Daudet, and, in particular, Alfred Agostinelli, his
chauffeur-secretary. As such, Albertine is an effeminate, masked
version of a male figure. The complexity of the fictional liberty taken
by Proust, and its appeal to bisexuality, (the "inverted")[15] finds expression in Moravia's novel through a symmetrical configuration of
characters whereby each character has his double/other in the same
or opposite sex. Thus, for example, Lino's female double is Lina
(Anna in the film),[16] and Marcello's mother's chauffeur, Alberi (a
name likewise suggestive of Proust's Albertine/Agostinelli) is doubled twice in Lino and in Manganiello who also serve as father figures for Marcello.

However, the importance of Proust's influence on both the
novel and the film goes beyond the referential act of naming characters. The appropriation of the notion of memory in Bertolucci's film
is indebted to the Proustian notion of involuntary memory derived
from the philosophy of Henri Bergson (1859–1941) and the early
twentieth century French tradition of philosophical spiritual realism. Bergson's work, as Richard Chessick points out, "enjoys a
spectacular revitalization in Proust's *Remembrance of Things Past*
(or *In Search of Lost Time*)" and "the two works continuously complement, refresh, and restore each other to higher and higher levels
of intuitive validity."[17] According to Chessick, Bergson's collection
of essays called *Mind-Energy* (1910) "could serve as the crucial thesis of Proust" although in *Matter and Memory* (1896), Proust's
theories are already anticipated. "Both men described how a tiny
link of similarity between present and past can provide a sudden
spreading of recollection with all its continuous elements. This
spontaneous explosion of memories produces a mystical ecstasy in
Proust's Narrator."[18]

The notion of involuntary memory in its Proustian sense refers
to the occasion of rare privileged moments when a chance sensation,
such as the dipping of a madeleine cake into a cup of lime tea, or the
observation of an irregularity in the Paris paving-stones, hauls to the
surface its twin sensation of long ago, and abolishes time for a fleet-
ing second by merging our past—the whole living past to which it
belongs—into our present.[19] Similarly, most of the action of the film
occurs in flashbacks prompted through a seemingly random association of ideas as Clerici travels to the ambush of the professor. As
Joan Mellen observes, Bertolucci's structuring of time and space, unlike that in classical Hollywood films and in Moravia's novel, is

Proustian, based as it were on the notion of involuntary memory.[20] This in turn resembles the Freudian concept of free association (*freier Einfall*) in which ideas occur to one spontaneously, without straining.[21] Temporal and spatial dimensions as such are subordinated in Bertolucci's *The Conformist* to the Protagonist's data of consciousness (or to his stream of consciousness to use terminology developed in relation to James Joyce's work)[22] rather than to the cause and effect structure so typical of Hollywood classical narrative. Bertolucci employs a narrative technique indebted to the surrealists' films, Luis Buñuel's in particular, in which the unfolding of events is closer to the mechanism of dreaming with its disrespect for the coherence of time and space.[23] For example, when Marcello confesses to a priest before his marriage to Giulia he returns to the seduction scene with Lino. The confession scene itself is recalled while he and Manganiello pursue the anti-Fascist professor. Time is organized in a mise-en-abime fashion whereby flashbacks are contained within each other, some referring to the near past and some to the distant past of infancy. Thus, for example, the car chase in the opening credits returns Marcello to the first flashback at the radio station where Italo Montanari, the blind Fascist and one of Marcello's father figures (tutor/padre), is delivering a Fascist speech. This flashback leads to another one involving a visit to the Fascist ministry and then returns to the car chase—which then circles back to another return scene at Giulia's home.

The movement back and forth in time as well as in space (the car chase, the energetic but stiff movement of Marcello in the Fascist space of monumental architecture and large empty space) also emphasizes the film's allegorical treatment of fascism and recalls Bertolucci's repeated insistence that *The Conformist* is about the present. The free movement in time and space follows a key Bergsonian theme: "True memory is beyond the reach of intellect and we labor to find it in vain. Rather, it is called up in a spontaneous way by such unexpected impressions as the taste of the madeleine."[24] The film, much like Proust's book, is filled with examples of how sudden, unexpected sensations trigger the explosion of pure memory.

The Conformist poses, through the means of representation peculiar to film (editing, the long take and camera mobility), the Proustian question of how to capture the past and to register it on the screen of memory.[25] But whereas Proust's engagement with the question of memory is more philosophically oriented, Bertolucci's quest for the past is imbued with political ramifications. How should Italy's Fascist past be treated? What is the relevance of this past to the country's present, and perhaps most importantly, in the case of

The Conformist and Bertolucci's other films dealing with the legacy of fascism, how can we prevent ourselves from revisiting the past? In fact the reawakened interest of Bertolucci as well as of other European filmmakers during the early 1970s in fascism is, according to Mellen, an interest in the analysis of the process of the decline and dissolution of capitalism resulting in Fascist revivalism.[26] The liberation from the Stalin era and the rise of the protest movements of the 1960s created in young intellectuals like Bertolucci a need to reassess the recent political history of their own countries. This explains why Bertolucci claimed that *The Conformist* is a film about the present intended to promote disgust towards and the rejection of fascism.

The Conformist's complex intertextual relationship with the Proustian text implicates it as being what the militant directors of the radical era, especially Godard, denounced as revisionist. As Bertolucci himself noted, one of the precepts of 1968 was "that time was only a poetic construction and was inadequate in so far as it had nothing to do with politics. So much so that Proust, in those years, almost became a dirty word. It was an injustice comparable to that perpetrated by anti-semitism but Proust lovers have been vaccinated against fads and fashions and felt instinctive repugnance for those views."[27] Bertolucci's words twenty years after the May 1968 events add an element of political protest to what, at first, seems just an innovative technique to manipulate cinematic space and time. Against the conformity of the militant directors, Godard in particular, in their rejection of decadence (Proust was reproached by the realist and naturalist critics for his lack of a political creed, his neglect of the masses, his indifference to economic issues, etc.), Bertolucci explores the poetic aspects of time only to expose its political relevance.

In his article on Proust, Walter Benjamin defines the writer's individual remembering ("the weaving of his memory" in his words) as "the Penelope work of recollection" or better still "a Penelope work of forgetting." And he adds: "Is not the involuntary recollection, Proust's *memoire involontaire*, much closer to forgetting than what is usually called memory?"[28] Benjamin's words cannot but recall Freud's theory of memory which is in reality a theory of forgetting. In *The Conformist*, Bertolucci expands and politicizes the boundaries of individual memories and oblivion by acknowledging that the memories of individuals do not act passively but transform past experiences according to present circumstances, producing either "collective memory" or "socially constructed oblivion."[29]

Despite Bertolucci's claims concerning the film's anti-Fascist message, one cannot ignore some of the criticism leveled at Berto-

lucci's visually indulgent reconstruction of the 1930s. In fact
Bertolucci defined *The Conformist* as a "memory of my own memory."[30] By that he meant that unlike *The Spider's Stratagem*, which
was influenced by "life and by memories of childhood," *The Conformist* was influenced by "cinema . . . by the memories of American and French films of the 30s."[31] Indeed, Bertolucci describes here
the tension between private and public memory. Whereas *Stratagem*
integrates into its construction of the Fascist era traces of personal
memories through the depiction of the landscape, *The Conformist* is
completely artificial and stylized. The memory recaptured and re-
lived through the film is not an authentic, re-experienced memory
but rather a cinema memory produced and recycled by the movie industry. It is, to use Kaes's words, part of a "succession of endlessly
recycled déjà-vu images,"[32] a world of hypersigns and simulacra. The
conscious reliance of *The Conformist* on the constitution of film as
a collective memory thus weakens the link between public memory
and personal experience, a link that still exists in *Stratagem*.
Whereas, as Walter Benjamin reminds us, the remembering author
of Proust's novel "did not describe a life as it actually was, but a life
as it was remembered by the one who had lived it,"[33] the cinematic
author of *The Conformist* uses remembered images drawn from the
public memory produced by cinema in order to narrate a life of an
imaginary Fascist conformist. And yet Benjamin shows an unre-
served preference for the remembered event over the experienced
event, making the point that while "an experienced event is finite—
at any rate, confined to one sphere of experience; a remembered
event is infinite, because it is only a key to everything that happened
before it and after it."[34] The distinction here, one might argue, is between closed text (the experienced event) and open text (the remembered event). Although Bertolucci's text is a collective rather
than personal type of remembered event it is still open in its infinite
potential for interpretation.

    The question of memory is enmeshed in further questions of
looking and action, the spectator and the film, the individual and
politics. The question of the gaze assumes political meaning through
the contrast of mobility (action and being *engagé* in the Existentialist sense, i.e., politically and morally committed.) with immobility
and passivity. Marcello, as Joel Magny describes him, "est le specta-
teur de sa propre vie, de ses propres actes" (is the spectator of his own
life, of his own acts).[35] This is most evident in the assassination
scene, throughout which Marcello is seen sitting, as if frozen in a
kind of an anxiety dream, watching through the car windshield the

brutal murder of Quadri. His immobility, like that of the cinematic spectator, the dreamer, and the enchained people in the Plato allegory, is not disrupted even when Anna rushes to the car and presses her face to the glass in an appeal for help. Marcello's passivity, and immobility as such, is not only a variation on Plato's cave—the controlling metaphor of the movie—but also an allegory of the dangers inherent in the role of the film spectator, and by implication, the role of the observer of fascism in action. Within the framework of the psychoanalytic theory of film, Plato's cave, as Jean-Louis Baudry suggests, is the first theoretical model of the spectators' experience. On the other hand, cinema, more than any other visual art, is a movement-based medium and therefore is more vulnerable, as Bertolucci's film implicitly suggests, to "fascinating fascism" and its seductive movement.[36] Action, ranging from sheer physical action to the more general phenomenon of war, has always enjoyed prestige in Fascist thinking. Filippo Thomaso Marinetti and the Italian futurists' apotheosis of the dynamism and energetic movement of war is a prime example. The metacinematic question of identification/passivity/spectatorship epitomized in this scene thus assumes the role of moral drama, warning the spectators, in a Platonic manner, against the seductions of both fascism and its passive reception.

The film, as many critics have noted, is not only a moral and political allegory but also a self-reflexive critique of cinema itself as the embodiment of the Platonic cave. It is centered on the epistemological question of seeing and believing and the authority of the moving image to define or even displace the real. Walter Benjamin reminds us that: "To be sure, most memories that we search for come to us as visual images. Even the free-floating forms of the *mémoire involontaire* are still in large part isolated, though enigmatically present, visual images."[37] The crisis of representation in the age of mechanical and electronic reproduction and dissemination is rendered through the film's motif of blindness (with its Oedipal overtones). The engagement with the binary oppositions of blindness and seeing operates on the level of thematics and style alike.

Moravia's novels, *The Conformist* in particular, are centered around the problem of self-knowledge: light and darkness, mirrors, masks, and puppets are principal elements. The degree of each character's consciousness of the self determines the amount of suffering each endures. The quality of light is an integral part of the setting and is noted with each change of scene by the author and his characters. The same Moravian dialectic of light and shadow is adapted in the film's brilliant allusions to the chiaroscuro lighting so typical

of the Hollywood studio film—particularly as realized in the work of
Josef von Sternberg, Orson Welles, and Max Ophuls. Many scenes
in the film—echoing Plato's critique in the cave allegory of the epistemological authority attributed to seeing—mock and challenge the
status of the image. For example when Italo, the blind Fascist and a
father figure for Marcello, praises normalcy and claims never to be
mistaken in detecting it, the camera moves down to his shoes showing us that he is wearing shoes of different colors. Other famous
scenes are the scenes of Clerici's recitation of the cave allegory to the
professor,[38] and the quasi-love scene between Marcello and Giulia at
her apartment when the backdrop of Venetian screens and Giulia's
zebra-patterned dress both imply light, shadow, and entrapment.
The confession scene and the love scene between Giulia and Marcello on the train to Paris [39] also, of course, create a chiaroscuro in-
terplay of light and shadow so as to visually reproduce the dominant
motifs of blindness and entrapment and to echo Plato's allegory.

Of special interest in this regard is the scene in which Marcello
is being driven to his fatal meeting. He tells his chauffeur of a strange
dream he has had: "I was operated in Switzerland by Professor
Quadri. I could see again and the Prof's wife fell in love with me."
Not all physical blindness in the film is associated with not seeing
the truth. While this is obviously Italo's case (Italo standing for Italy),
it is not the case of the blind girl from Parma (Bertolucci's birthplace)
who sells violets in a Parisian street and sings the "International."
This ambiguity of blindness and seeing, truth and lies, knowledge
and ignorance of truth, only reinforces the crisis of spectatorship and
further challenges the authority of perception itself.

It is no wonder then that the name of the major father figure in
the movie, Marcello's spiritual father whom he betrays, is Luca
Quadri, recalling the word light (luce in Italian).[40] The Fascist assas-
sins smash Professor Quadri's glasses before they murder him in a
symbolic gesture destroying the light of truth. Because of the Oedipal dimensions of this murder, the glasses also hint at Oedipus'
blindness and the dialectic of blindness and knowledge that dominates the Sophoclean text. The final sight of the film articulates the
ambivalent nature of blindness and seeing and relates it, as in the
Moravian text, to issues of self-knowledge and identity. In this
scene, the Roman boy whom Lino tried to seduce starts to strip down
for the night. Marcello stands watching him, his glance fixed on the
boy's naked body, and he blinks. The focus of the film at this privileged moment on Marcello's active seeing suggests, if not a redemp-

tion, then at least a moment of self-awareness as the protagonist comes to terms with his "weakness" (homosexuality), accepting thus his own non-conformity.

The questions of memory, and the motifs of blindness and knowledge are intimately connected to the Oedipal complex, a major thematic and narrative axis in all of Bertolucci's films.[41] The Oedipal complex is also related to the theme of the double, another recurrent motif in Bertolucci's work. Indeed Marcello has no less than four double father figures. Most of them, in one way or another, are physically or mentally deformed. Italo (a figure who does not exist in Moravia's novel) is blind, Marcello's biological father is insane, and Quadri is a short-sighted hunchback. Manganiello is the only physically "undeformed" father figure.[42] There is also a secondary succession of father figures such as Lino who is both father and double to Marcello, and Marcello's mother's young chauffeur and lover (usurping the place of Marcello's biological father) who doubles Lino and Manganiello and Marcello himself in that he materializes his incestuous desire. The male figures are further doubled by female figures so as to accentuate the ambiguity of the characters' sexual identities. In fact the film is more subtle in its occupation with the double theme than the novel. Moravia has continually maintained that a literary work should exhaust its subject; and indeed there is very little left unexplained in his fiction. Therefore, the structure of the novel is repetitive, and the parallelism of situations and characters is fashioned symmetrically. Thus, for example, Lino is the double of Lina (Anna in the film) and the relationship between Lina and Giulia—Lina trying to impose herself on Giulia—parallels that of Lino and Marcello. Marcello and Giulia are also quasi-doubles—both were sexually abused as children. Moreover, in the novel, Marcello and his family, like Quadri and his wife, are killed on the road. In the film, however, the symmetrical configuration is less obvious and the parallelism of characters and situations is suggested but not explicit. Marcello's entire existence revolves around the desire to both please (identify with) these surrogate fathers, and/or to rebel against them. In fact the origins of Clerici's repressed homosexuality and subsequently of his fascism are located by Bertolucci in the Oedipal scenario. The search for a strong father figure leads him to perceive the Fascist state as the ultimate patriarch.

The education theme, called by Robert Kolker the padre/padrone theme, epitomizes the dialectics of the Oedipal complex. The father figure in all of Bertolucci's films is perceived as either a good tutor/educator (padre) or a tyrannical boss (padrone), and the quest for the father involves a process of growth in which the protagonist defines himself through identification with but also differentiation from the father.[43] According to some critics the character of Professor Quadri is modeled to a certain extent after the figure of Antonio Gramsci.[44] Despite the undenied influence of Gramsci on many left-oriented Italian directors—including Bertolucci, especially in *1900*—there are some problems with this thesis. Quadri in the novel, if less so than in the film, is depicted as an impotent and even decadent intellectual.[45] It is rather evident that he derives a voyeuristic pleasure from watching his lesbian wife, and his presumed sexual impotence is projected onto the political sphere as well. In many interviews Bertolucci emphasized the decadence and negativity of the couple: "The professor and his wife were the other side of the medallion of bourgeois Fascism, linked to it by a chain which is decadence. They are sympathetic, they are on the right side of the barricades, but they are still bourgeois and they are not saved."[46] This kind of accusation definitely does not fit Gramsci, who in June 1928 was imprisoned by the Fascists and eventually died under guard in a clinic. It seems more applicable to Palmiro Togliatti, the Italian Communist Party's leader throughout the Fascist, Resistance, and postwar reconstruction periods, who flew to Paris on the same day that Gramsci was arrested.[47]

According to Mellen, *The Conformist*, like other European and American films made during the early 1970s, reveals a social interest in the psychological roots of the "mass man" who is most susceptible to fascism. Mellen claims that the film's depiction of the development of the Fascist personality is influenced by Wilhelm Reich's theory about the connection between repressed and distorted homosexuality and vulnerability to fascism. The theorists of the Frankfurt School (notably in their classic study, *The Authoritarian Personality* [Adorno et al. 1950]) also developed a theory that could serve as a theoretical framework to Bertolucci's treatment of the subject. Their studies endeavored to establish connections between potentially Fascist character traits and political opinions. Using psychoanalytic concepts, the school examined the way in which society constitutes the individual, thus producing character types. They found that in the socialization process, the importance of parents is diminishing. Families provide ever less protection against the overpowering pressures of the outside world, which in turn, undermines the legitimacy of the father's authority. The male child does not aspire to become like his father, but more and more like images projected by the culture industry in general (or by fascism). The father's power appears arbitrary and the child retains an abstract idea of force and strength. He searches for a more powerful father adequate to this image. In this situation, time is ripe for the acceptance of Fascist demagogues or even of the Fascist state as a surrogate father.[48]

The Conformist, being directly or indirectly influenced by these mass society theories, is more interested in the construction and development of Fascist subjectivity and its configuration of latent homosexual and sadomasochistic tendencies, than in an analysis of the process and the political and social circumstances that enable the rise of fascism. According to Mellen, Bertolucci in both *The Spider's Stratagem* and *The Conformist* criticizes the intellectuals' impotence to resist the emergence and growth of fascism. Only with fascism's defeat does Clerici accept his own "abnormality," his homosexual state.

In the film, the desire to find a father figure in the "healthy," "normal" Fascist state is also a reaction against the cultural decadence epitomized by Clerici's old decaying family mansion and by his opium-addicted mother. Decadence is evoked also through allusions to Proust. The visual evocation of the past provides a psychological explanation for Marcello's quest for normalcy in the form of the Fascist state. It is an attempt to fill the vacuum created by the absent patriarch in a decadent society with a culture that represses sexuality.

The use of spectacle in *The Conformist* cannot but raise questions concerning the anti-Fascist message of the film. Frederic Jameson rejects this film, as well as others, on the basis of their historicism, which he interprets as the displacement of the historical referent into the sphere of beautiful visuals designed to invoke nostalgia. Perhaps this is what Susan Sontag meant when she coined the catchy phrase "fascinating fascism." Marilyn Goldin's interview with Bertolucci indirectly touched upon this problematic issue. "There is still some nostalgia in Italy for the Fascist period, isn't there?" she asked Bertolucci who answered: "Yes! That's why I say *The Conformist* is a film on the present."[49]

In *The Conformist* the narrative in a self-reflexive manner— through nostalgic quotations—surpasses the boundaries of realism and history and becomes a moral drama on fascism. This kind of moral drama[50] explains why Bertolucci told Joan Mellen that "*The Conformist* is also in the present, but it's the present dressed as the past."[51] The spectatorial experience of *The Conformist* as such is not confined to the diegesis alone but is both alluding to and constructed through the imaginary collective memory of the movies. The self-reflexive dimension subsumed within the nostalgia film critiques both the past and the present, thus acknowledging that history is as much a constructed narrative as fiction is. Consequently what Jameson refers to as the flat historicism of the postmodern nostalgia film is indeed an analysis of the deep structure of film and history as different modes of narrative.

The Politicization of the Love Story: *Eros and Civilization* Revisited in *Last Tango in Paris*

In her review of *Last Tango in Paris* (1972) in the *New York Times*, Pauline Kael wrote that the film festival opening of *Tango* is a date "that should become a landmark in movie history comparable to May 29, 1913—the night *Le Sacre du Printemps* (The Rites of Spring) was first performed—in music history. . . . This must be the most powerfully erotic movie ever made and it may turn out to be the most liberating movie ever made. . . . Bertolucci and Brando have altered the face of an art form. Who was prepared for that?"[52]

Kael's enthusiastic reception of *Tango*, one of the most controversial films of the 1970s, captures the radical spirit of that era by fusing the notions of liberation, eroticism, and art. Yet despite the movie's significant commercial and critical success, it was dismissed by militant directors on the grounds that *Tango* reflects Bertolucci's withdrawal from the political domain (manifest in his films prior to *Tango*) into the depths of introspection, subjectivity and, even worse, indulgence in privatization.[53] What the militant criticism failed to notice is that, despite *Tango*'s flight into inwardness, the utopian demand for political and social transformation remains a central ingredient in the film's vision. In this respect the sexual in Bertolucci's *Tango* is fundamentally political.

A close reading of *Tango* suggests an ideational affinity between Herbert Marcuse's thought, and in particular his reading of Freud in *Eros and Civilization* as a utopian thinker, and Bertolucci's attempt in *Tango* to analyze the language of sexuality in revolutionary terms.[54] The film is marked by its emphasis on the subjective level in revolutionary praxis.

Tango is closely linked to the historical *momentum* of the May 1968 events, but unlike Godard's *Tout va bien* (also released in 1972), which uses the student-worker uprising of May 1968 as a concrete historical referent, *Tango* does not include a historical referent in the overt level of the narrative. Nevertheless, its absence is an active absence, guiding the underlying theoretical premises on which the film is based. As Marcuse was one of the inspiring figures in the May 1968 upheavals, one may well expect to find traces of his thought in Bertolucci, who like Marcuse, emphasizes the subjective level in revolutionary praxis.[55] *Tango* explores the emotional extremes of the love story only to politicize it by displacing the assault on bourgeois ideology to the exploitation and destruction of the love object.

Trying to situate Bertolucci's films within the framework of the debate over the nature of political cinema, critics and scholars alike agree that *Tango* signifies a turning point in his *oeuvre*. It is a departure from an experimental, uncompromising cinema that, following Jean-Louis Comolli and Jean Narboni's classification in "Cinema/Ideology/Criticism," attacks the dominant capitalist ideology on the levels of both form and content, to a commercial mainstream cinema that pleases the masses but fails to adhere to the rigid, purist demands of militant avant-garde cinema. To my mind, however, the shift signaled by *Tango* should not be perceived as a withdrawal from the political sphere, but rather as an attempt to redefine the political.

For Bertolucci, in *Tango*, it is eminently logical, indeed essential, to combine a Marcusian analysis of the ideology of advanced industrial society with Artaud's ideal of theater, as well as with elements borrowed from Hollywood melodrama, because these eclectic sources of influence emphasize the necessity of expressing rather than suppressing the subjective level in artistic discourse. Bertolucci himself proposes that the clash between Jeanne and Paul transcends the uniqueness of an individual love story. Instead it becomes "a centrally symptomatic affair for our time."[56] Furthermore, he argued that the encounter between Jeanne and Paul "ends up being an encounter of forces pulling in different directions; the kind of encounter of forces which exists at the base of all political clashes."[57]

According to Bertolucci, Paul's search for authenticity and his challenge to Jeanne's bourgeois lifestyle is the political/didactic dimension of *Tango*. It is not didactic in the Godardian sense in which knowledge is acquired through a theoretical/argumentative process. Rather, knowledge is acquired through experience, through Paul's search for "the roots of human behavior,"[58] his desperate belief "that he must seek absolute authenticity in relationships."[59] This search for authenticity is common to both the fictional and the metafictional levels of *Tango*, as well as to its production history. Paul's quest was joined by Brando/Bertolucci for authenticity, an experience that turned Brando into a co-author of *Tango* but exhausted him emotionally.[60]

As a devoted Communist, Bertolucci was concerned that the film was apolitical; while making it he must have been saying to himself, "Watch out! You'll end up making another love story!"[61] But eventually he realized that one does not have to use a direct political statement in order to make a political film: "I quickly realized, shooting, that when you show the depths, when you drown yourself, as it were, in that feeling of solitude and death that attaches to a relationship in our Western, bourgeois society, and when you begin to identify the reasons for this feeling of death, you inevitably make a political statement."[62]

A Marcusian reading of *Tango* (which, in fact, is close in spirit to Bertolucci's own reading) makes it possible to see the sexual in *Tango* as essentially political and therefore potentially subversive. Paul's search for authenticity in relationships expresses the quest of a Marcusian one-dimensional man for liberation from a surplus repression. Indeed, the film opens with a powerful image of pain that contains the basic Marcusian elements. The first post-credits shot is a crane down to the agonized figure of Paul. He is standing under an elevated stretch of the Paris Metro, a train roaring over his head. As the camera bears down on him, Paul raises his head, hands over his ears; his face expresses an intense despair reminiscent of the paintings of Francis Bacon, and he screams back at the noise: "Fucking god!"[63] in a fashion that recalls yet another work of art—expressionist Edvard Munch's *The Scream*. The Metro's oppressive noise becomes a metaphor for advanced technological capitalism and Brando/Paul's blasphemy delineates and anticipates his later behavior, his desperate attempt to rebel against "a capitalist era incapable of human relations."[64]

In *Eros and Civilization* Marcuse asks, "Can we speak of a juncture between the erotic and political dimensions?" His answer is decisive. "Today," he asserts, "the fight for life, the fight for Eros, is the *political* fight."[65] For Marcuse, the liberation of instinctual needs is a precondition to liberation from repressive affluence. Marcuse challenges Freud's identification of civilization and progress with a necessary libidinal and instinctual repression. To replace Freud's thesis (or rather to extrapolate the hypothesis of a non-repressive civilization from Freud's theory of the instincts), Marcuse proposes that erotic sublimation grounded in emancipating the libido and re-eroticizing man's relations to man and nature might give rise to an entirely new, non-repressive civilization based upon the pleasure principle. "A changed society," Marcuse suggests, "no

longer based on the repressive and antiquated 'performance principle' would end historically rooted 'surplus repression,' thus freeing
the individual from his tension-producing alienated labor."[66]

Several major elements of Marcuse's bold attempt to read Freud
as a revolutionary utopian are found in *Tango*'s politicization of the
sexual. Indeed, Paul/Brando/Bertolucci's attempts to substitute sexuality as a new type of language[67] deny the equation of reason with
repression on which the ideology of culture is built. Paul's struggle
is an attempt to reject Freud's thesis that the conflict between sexual gratification and civilization is unavoidable and that the history
of man, therefore, is the history of his repression. If Paul, through his
relationship with Jeanne, stimulates the "return of the repressed"
which "makes up the tabooed and subterranean history of civilization,"[68] then the exploration of his history reveals not only the secret of Paul as an individual but also that of civilization. In this
respect, *Tango* becomes a cinematic thesis on sexual repression as it
is transmitted through a system of oppressive political institutions:
the bourgeois family, the church, the military, etc. The Freudian on-
togenic level (the growth of the repressed individual from infancy to
societal existence) manifested in Paul and Jeanne's individual histories is interrelated with the phylogenetic level (the growth of repressive civilization from the primal horde to the political state). Hence
Paul's revolt is against surplus repression, a synthetic term coined
by Marcuse, drawn from Marx's economic theory and Freud's theory
of the instincts, denoting "the restrictions necessitated by social
domination"[69] which " introduce *additional* controls over and above
those indispensable for civilized human association."[70]

More specifically, *Tango* makes reference to the Marcusian
analysis of advanced technological societies (which combines Marx
with Freud) through its exploration of the reification of the body,
phantasies, polymorphous perversity, the family institution, and the
patriarchal order.

Reification of the Body and Alienated versus Libidinal Work

Paul's new order stresses the corporeal element in true happiness, echoing Marcuse's "seeing in the most extreme reification of
the body an 'anticipatory memory' of genuine joy."[71] In *Eros and
Civilization* Marcuse claims that only a breakdown of the sexual
tyranny of the genitals and a return to the "polymorphous perversity" of the child promises true liberation and happiness. "Only if
the entire body were reeroticized," he argued, "could alienated labor,

which was grounded in the reification of the nongenital areas of the body, be overcome." Marcuse suggests that "the entire body [become] libidinally cathected as it was before the localizing of the sexual instincts (polymorphous perversity) so that it would no longer be an object of labor and the subject of political manipulation."[72] Through this libidinal cathexis, Marcuse hoped to transform Freud's instinct theory into the foundation of utopia. Hence Marcuse shows "that Freud's correlation 'instinctual repression-socially useful labor-civilization' can be meaningfully transformed into the correlation 'instinctual liberation-socially useful work-civilization.' "[73]

The Edenism of the Marcusian utopia is conveyed in *Tango* through the character's retreat from capitalist (the Marcusian performance principle) civilization to the seclusion of the apartment in rue Jules Verne and the savage pleasure it provides (Eros). Indeed, Jeanne describes love in the following way: "The workers go to a secret apartment . . . they take off their overalls, turn back into men and women and make love."[74] Here Jeanne is, in fact, describing her relationship with Paul. Her seeing Paul and herself as workers in blue overalls invests the metaphor with Marcusian visionary connotations. The irreconcilable conflict in this metaphor follows Marcuse's interpretation of Freud's theory of the instincts. The conflict "is not between work (reality principle) and Eros (pleasure principle), but between alienated labor (performance principle) and Eros."[75] Jeanne's metaphor confirms this thesis and invites the notion of non-alienated, libidinal work. Her metaphor describes the transition from the existing order (alienated labor) to a utopian order (libidinal order, re-eroticized man and nature). The content of Jeanne's conversation with Tom—which invokes such subjects as advertisement as marriage as pop-commodity—also reinforces a reading of Jeanne's metaphorical definition within a Marcusian framework. Despite the parodic tone of this conversation (with its reference to Godard's obsession with advertisement and consumerism), it provides a critique of the capitalist/consumer society in which, according to Marcuse, "scientific management of instinctual needs has long since become a vital factor in the reproduction of the system: merchandise which has to be bought and used is made into objects of the libido."[76]

Phantasy

The Paris apartment in *Tango* is a place where phantasies come true. In a Marcusian fashion, however, these phantasies are invested with a political dimension: an urge to destroy the existing order (bourgeois reality: the performance principle) and move to a new utopian order based on the pleasure principle.

Phantasy plays an important role in Marcuse's theory of liberation. According to Freud, phantasy is the only mental activity that remains free of the rule of the reality principle and stays committed to the pleasure principle. Marcuse elaborates on Freud's thesis and suggests that phantasy and utopia are the major mental forces that, by virtue of their freedom from the reality principle even in the realm of the developed consciousness, demonstrate "the possibility of a non-repressive development of the libido under the conditions of mature civilization."[77]

Phantasy is not confined to the mental apparatus of the individual; it links the deepest layers of the unconscious with the highest product of consciousness: art. Thus, Marcuse claims, "art retains the tabooed images of freedom."[78] Phantasy is also imagination, which preserves the collective archaic past of the genus through the *id*, to which it is committed. Art is, as Marcuse suggests, the most visible "return of the repressed" on both the individual and the generic-historical level. Thus, the artistic imagination shapes the unconscious memory of liberation that was betrayed and denied by the reality principle.

In *Tango*, the roots of phantasy's commitment to Eros are investigated on the fictional level through Paul and Jeanne and on the metafictional level through the metaphoric status of the apartment as a reflex of Bertolucci's own cinema. The apartment, which functions as a stage for the spectacle of Paul and Jeanne's phantasies, projects the critical function of imagination that Bertolucci attaches to his cinema and that challenges the commitment of Godard's cinema to the reality principle. Through the doubling process, Paul/Bertolucci recognizes the revolutionary implications of Freud's discoveries concerning phantasy and imagination and projects them onto Paul's fiction. Paul and Jeanne's phantasy play also contradicts the values of productiveness and performance so crucial to the capitalist system. It cancels the repressive and exploitative traits of labor and leisure, thus providing a political commentary on the established order. On the reflexive level, their playing insists on the revolutionary potential existing in phantasy and in imagination as vehicles of artistic expression.

Perversions

Bertolucci's films are crowded with perversions such as incest, masturbation, sodomy, bestiality, and so on. Within the very self-conscious framework of his work, the extensive use of preversions provokes an awareness of the perverse nature of cinema itself and the spectatorial pleasure it offers.

The theme of anality [79] (the sodomy scene; the verbalizing of anal phantasies by Paul; the repetitive, almost compulsive preoccupation with "shit" stories—Paul/Brando's story about the cow shit; the obsessive use of anal metaphors in Paul/Brando's discourse: "You won't be able to be free of that feeling of being alone . . . until you go right up into the ass of death . . . till you find the womb of fear") seems to be crucial to *Tango*'s dealing with perversions. The metaphor of anality is certainly at the center of *Tango*'s political analysis, whereby an anal rape turns out to be a reification of social relations under capitalism. This is most evident in the sodomy scene in which Paul/Brando (wearing a red sweater) compares his rape to the symbolic rape enacted by the whole social system, represented in his "red" sermonizing rhetoric by the bourgeois family and the church. The dialectic of anal-sadistic/anal-erotic in *Tango* investigates anal perversion as a phantasy of regression that ultimately assumes a progressive role. The anal regression/perversion is deployed within the narrative so as to maintain the traditional patriarchal Freudian binarism, assigning sadism to the male protagonist and masochism to the female.[80]

Marcuse attributes progressive value to perversions because they express rebellion against upholding sexuality as an end in itself under a repressive social system that channels libidinal energies into monogamic reproduction within the structure of the family. Perversions, like phantasy, Marcuse suggests, "seem to give a *promesse de bonheur* greater than that of 'normal' sexuality."[81] Through their rejection of procreative sex they express rebellion against the institutions (family, religion, etc.) that guarantee the order of procreation. They also manifest a revolt against paternal domination and an attempt to disrupt the perpetual reappearance of the father. As against the employment of sexuality to the ends of productiveness and usefulness, "the perversions uphold sexuality as an end in itself; they thus place themselves outside the dominion of the performance principle and challenge its very foundation."[82] The practice of perversions, to Marcuse, seems to be an integral part of the utopian process of re-eroticization of man and nature, leading to the establishment of libidinal relationships to replace the process by which civilization turned the body and the organism into an instrument of toil and exploitation.

Father/patriarchy

The father/son struggle comprises the major dramatic and symbolic conflict of *Tango*, and on the metacinematic level it addresses the relationship between Godard and Bertolucci. In *Tango*, as in the Freudian system, the rebellion against the primal father eventually develops into institutionalized social and political forms of domination. Paul's revolt against paternal authority deteriorates into a form of sadistic tyranny which symbolically, in the final scene, is represented by the military, that most oppressive of the state's institutions (the state itself being the ultimate organizational transference of the father's despotism). Paul's mockery of the primal father, the archetype of domination, initiates a chain of enslavement, rebellion, and the perpetuation of self-imposed domination that, according to Freud, marks the history of civilization. The reenactment of the Oedipal complex, the primal crime in *Tango*, emulates the Freudian model. First there is the conflict between old and new generations, reflected in Paul and Jeanne's relationship; then a rebellion against established authority through Paul's mockery of the two "ghost" fathers (his and Jeanne's); and finally repentance, culminating in the restoration and glorification of authority. This last is expressed through Paul's proposal of marriage, which signifies both accep-tance of the reality principle and preservation of the satisfaction of his needs. Thus, *Tango*'s dramatic and structural organization is focused on the Freudian recurrent cycle of "domination-rebellion-domination."

Paul and Jeanne's retreat to the seclusion of their apartment/ paradise illustrates Marcuse's explanation of why Freud's reconstruction of the prehistory of mankind, from the primal horde through patricide to civilization, was so violently rejected. According to him, the Freudian hypothesis "does not lead back to the image of a paradise which man has forfeited by his sin against God but to the domination of man by man."[83] Marcuse's hypothesis could be a description of the dynamics in the Edenic apartment of *Tango*. The relationship between Jeanne/Eve and Paul/Adam (in the original script they are explicitly compared to the biblical pair) deteriorates because gradually sexuality loses its purity and begins to be used as a tool of oppression, exploitation, and domination.

Family

Paul/Brando/Bertolucci's ultimate attack on the family institution as the locus of oppression/repression is expressed in the sodomy scene. Paul's repression of Jeanne (the forced sodomy) is echoed in the dialogue ("Holy family . . . Where the will is broken by repression . . . Where freedom is assassinated . . . You fucking fucking family! . . . You fucking family! Oh God, Jesus!").[84] Paradoxically, Paul's actions contradict his preaching against oppression/repression and he himself becomes the demonic parody of the oppressive father he despises. Furthermore, he is consumed by the narrative, which uses him as an agent to deconstruct/construct the ideology of romance; and despite his rebellious rhetoric, he becomes the ultimate symbol of phallic authority.

The assault on the family as "the moral foundation of the social system of domination"[85] is at the core of Marxist theory. "The reality of the bourgeois family," Marcuse elaborates on Marx, "like all forms of life under capitalism" is determined "by the character of the commodity economy; as a 'property' with its specific costs and expenses, profits and surplus value, it is entered into the general account. Economic interests govern not only the choice of partners (mostly prescribed by the father) but also the production and upbringing of the children."[86] The interrelation between marriage and the commodity economy is explored in *Tango*, which interprets Jeanne's final choice of Tom as her husband as conforming to bourgeois ideology.

The critique of the bourgeois family in *Tango* leads directly to a critique of religion, another institution of domination according to Marx. Brando's "holy family" invokes the Christian one as well as Marx's book, *The Holy Family*. Bertolucci's allusions in the sodomy scene, and the names Jesus and God that accompany Paul's orgasm, are perfectly explicit. The critique of religion is also central to Freud's theory, which explains the phenomenon of religion as the institutionalized expression of guilt concerning the primal crime of overthrowing the king-father and the necessity of restoring him in order for civilization to progress.

Indeed, *Tango* is the first significant departure from the more experimental cinema that characterized Bertolucci's work prior to *The Conformist* (1970). *Tango* was also Bertolucci's first international success—*The Conformist*'s considerable international recognition was still marginal compared to that of *Tango*—and it elevated its author to the status of celebrity. Yet the film, like most of Bertolucci's films, is infested with conflicts between the fascination of the bourgeoisie and the radical commitment to destroy it.

Prima della rivoluzione (Before the Revolution) (1964) explicitly articulates this painful, inner conflict.[87] The conflict is expressed in the epigraph from Talleyrand that opens the film: "He who did not live in the years before the revolution cannot understand what the sweetness of living is." Here Bertolucci uses Talleyrand's nostalgia for France's bourgeois pre-revolutionary past to reflect upon his own "nostalgia for the present," the acute neurotic syndrome of Fabrizio, the film's protagonist and Bertolucci's semi-surrogate. The present of Bertolucci is the bourgeois present, the sweetness of living that he both loves and hates and that expresses the anomaly of his situation. His nostalgia expresses a yearning for the cinema before the French revolution begun by Godard, which Bertolucci at the beginning of his career hoped to carry on in Italy, thus echoing the "Italian/French connection" of Stendhal's *La Chartreuse de Parme*, the text that inspired *Before the Revolution*. But whereas Talleyrand's words express healthy, normal nostalgia born of the present (the French Revolution), and directed toward the past (the pre-revolutionary stage in French history), Bertolucci's nostalgic sentiment, projected upon his protagonist Fabrizio, is sickly because it springs from the present and is aimed at the present.

Through the acknowledgement of the contradictions he lives with and transforms into art, Bertolucci not only reveals his subjectivity, but also addresses one of the central issues in the tension between theory and praxis in Marxist thought, that of the role of intellectuals in the revolution. By expressing and asserting his bourgeois sensibilities and uncertainties, Bertolucci emphasizes his status as a traditional non-organic intellectual who, despite all his efforts, remains an outsider to the revolutionary process.

Tango's regression into past cinematic forms—in its use of the conventions of bourgeois melodrama for example—and the regression of the characters within the narrative reflect the contradictions inherent in the "nostalgia for the present." This regression makes *Tango* a far more self-exposing work than Godard's political films. The latter suppress the tension between bourgeois withdrawal and political activism so as to display scorn for bourgeois "inwardness," a scorn that the politicized Godard (not unlike Brecht) interpreted as a sign of revolutionary consciousness. For Bertolucci, the crucial, formal political question becomes not how to replace narrative, but how to work within and against it. *Tango*'s regression is manifested on both the fictional and the metafictional levels, and eventually assumes a progressive function. On the fictional level, Paul and Jeanne regress to childhood to rediscover their past. The apartment where they meet in secret embodies visually the idea of regression by assuming the role of the intra-uterine condition. (Bertolucci intentionally lit this scene so as to underscore what he termed the "uterine" or "prenatal" state.) It symbolically focuses on the enactment of a regressive childhood play space. Furthermore, Bertolucci moves Paul/Brando through a process of *percorso* (advance by going backwards). To quote Bertolucci himself on this point:

> At the beginning of the film he is supervirile, desperate but determined in his despair. But slowly he almost loses his virility. At a certain point he makes the girl sodomize him: going backwards he has arrived at the anal stage. Let's say, the sadico-anal stage. Then he goes back even further and arrives in the womb of Paris, dying with mother Paris all around him, her rooftops, TV-aerials, her grey, grabbing anonymity.[88]

The notion of *percorso* describes the progressive value attached to the characters' regression/retreat into phantasy. The psychoanalytic liberation of Jeanne and Paul's memories explodes and negates the rationality of their repression as individuals. Their *recherche du temps perdu* reveals the potential emancipatory power of the psychology of depth, the regressive nature of which, according to Marcuse, assumes a progressive role:

> As cognition gives way to re-cognition, the forbidden images and impulses of childhood begin to tell the truth that reason denies. Regression assumes a progressive function. The rediscovered past yields critical standards which are tabooed by the present. Moreover, the restoration of memory is accompanied by the restoration of the cognitive content of phantasy.[89]

The regression of Paul and Jeanne also assumes a political dimension since, as Marcuse suggests, "The manifold forms of regression are unconscious protests against the insufficiency of civilization: against the prevalence of toil over pleasure, performance over gratification."[90] The non-repressive, instinctual order Marcuse advocates (and Paul in *Tango* fails to establish) is based on regression, on advancing by going backward:

> The emergence of a non-repressive reality principle involving instinctual liberation would *regress* behind the attained level of civilized rationality. This regression would be physical as well as social: it would reactivate early stages of the libido which were surpassed in the development of the reality ego and it would dissolve the institutions of society in which the reality ego exists.[91]

In addition, the regressive movement of the narrative and characters in *Tango* is progressive because it emulates the inner direction
of Freud's critical theory. As Marcuse points out, Freud's instinct
theory (in contrast to his therapeutic program) moved from consciousness to the unconscious, from personality to childhood, from
the individual to the generic source. This movement was crucial for
Freud's critique of civilization because

> only by means of the 'regression' behind the mystifying forms
> of the mature individual and his private and public existence
> did he discover their basic negativity in the foundations on
> which they rest. Moreover, only by pushing his critical regres-
> sion back to the deepest biological layer could Freud elucidate
> the explosive content of the mystifying forms and, at the same
> time, the full scope of civilized repression.[92]

The same demystifying, critical logic orients the process of regression in *Tango*. The film uses regression on all levels to protest
the discontents of civilization and to expose its repressive mechanisms. Regression is also manifested through the film's generic
choices. *Tango* is a pastiche of the classic American cinema, which
is intimately connected to Bertolucci's childhood memories. On the
metafictional level, Paul/Brando is the icon of this historic text and
the agent of the melodramatic discourse which, nevertheless, becomes a stage of conflict between modernism and romanticism. This
conflict is suggested by the title of the film and reaches its climax in
the dance hall scene to which it refers. The tango,[93] the classic signifier of the mythology of romance, is mocked and ridiculed by
Paul/Brando whose fictional character in *Tango*, as well as his con-
noted *icon persona*, embody the contradictions of modernism (progress) and postmodernism/romanticism (regression and nostalgia).
Whereas the fictional Paul, as the bearer of melodrama, exploits the
emotionalism of the genre, Brando the icon forces the spectator to
examine the structure of those emotions and to reflect on their cultural significance.

Through the doubling process (Paul/Brando/Bertolucci being
the *Doppelgänger* of Tom/Leaud/Godard) the Paris apartment becomes a metonymy for the political spectacle of Bertolucci. Echoing
the double theme in *Partner*, where Giacobbe (inspired by the theatrical theories of Artaud and Julian Beck's Living Theater) suggests
that the stage should become the entire world with revolution as its
text, *Tango* suggests that the apartment/womb (the intra-uterine
state) is Bertolucci's revolutionary *spettacolo* with sexuality as its

progressive text. And here again, the regression into the apartment/ womb assumes a critical function. It defines the nature of Berto- lucci's cinema as regressive/progressive through its attachment to phantasy, to the Freudian pleasure principle, and to the Lacanian "imaginary." Hence Bertolucci asserts his independence from Godard whose cinema is closely connected to the reality principle, the Lacanian symbolic order. (It is no accident that Paul, in his effort to revive the imaginary order, attempts first to destroy language, the signifier of the Father and Law in the Lacanian symbolic order.)

From this perspective, Brando's *avance en reculant* (what Bertolucci called the *percorso* of Brando's character in the film) is also the regression of Bertolucci himself (the double of Brando/Paul) from radical cinematic experimentation to the roots of cinema. This retreat is an attempt to question the structures of cinema through a continual inquiry in filmic terms as well as a quest for cinema history in terms of narrative. Paradoxically enough, in this advance by going backward, Bertolucci provides his answer to Go- dard's call in *Le Gai Savoir* (1968) for a return to a degree zero cin- ema. Godard's plea in *Le Gai Savoir* was advanced by Jean-Pierre Léaud who plays Tom in *Tango*. Tom is Paul's Other and Godard's double; but their Otherness is reversible. Thus, *Tango* has its own internal justification as a postmodernist progressive film: the seem- ing nostalgic regression into conventional narrative is in fact *per- corso*. Insofar as Godard's films are regarded as progressive texts because of their rupture with old forms, so too is Bertolucci's *Tango*, which embraces these forms only to inform us that they are no longer tenable.[94]

Politicization of Politics: *1900*

1900, the film which follows *Tango*, is, perhaps, Bertolucci's most ambitious attempt to make a revolutionary film. Bertolucci's newly acquired status as a celebrity and the unprecedented box-office suc- cess of *Tango*, coincidental with the political situation in Italy, en- couraged him to make the ultimate revolutionary spectacle. This spectacle is inspired by what he called the dialectics of the green dol- lars (the American financial backing of the film as well as its assim- ilation of Hollywood production values) and the red flags (the visual signifiers of the envisaged revolution that dominate the film's lean- ing towards the iconography of socialist realism). The film's internal and external contradictions[95] render in a dialectical fashion not only the problematic situation of Bertolucci himself, an Italian revolutionary director working within the capitalist system, but also a sense of the end of an epoch. Although the film that follows, *La Luna* (1979), is Bertolucci's last movie made during the 1970s, symbolically, *1900* indicates the end of this radical decade.

CHAPTER 3

Dialogue with the Cosmos: The Films after the Revolution

The 1980s seemed to signal a new phase in both Godard's and Bertolucci's work. In 1979 Godard made his second comeback (the first one was in 1972 with *Tout va bien*) to the circuits of commercial cinema with *Sauve qui peut (la vie)* (*Every Man for Himself*), also known as *Slow Motion*). Bertolucci, after the grand failure of *1900*, made a more intimate film, *La Luna*, in 1979, introducing for the first time in his career a woman as a protagonist. Godard's return to commercial cinema and to the international film scene with *Sauve qui peut (la vie)*, which was presented at the thirty-third annual Cannes International Film Festival,[1] was accompanied by a publicly acknowledged desire to reach the audience he had lost during his radical period. However, contrary to expectations, Godard refused to acknowledge that *Sauve qui peut (la vie)*, which was distributed under the banner of Francis Ford Coppola's Zoetrope, marked a return from his self-imposed exile in Switzerland to the world of commercial feature filmmaking. Instead Godard insisted that he had never been away.[2] The truth, of course, is that except for *Tout va bien* (a box-office disaster), Godard's association with theatrical commercial film had been minimal if not nonexistent since *Weekend* (1967). In many public appearances and interviews Godard defined *Sauve qui peut (la vie)* as his "second first film" and stressed over and again his feeling of being born again as a filmmaker.

For Bertolucci, however, 1979 was neither a year of euphoria nor a year of rebirth, but rather a year of recuperating from the trauma of *1900*. The vehicle for this recuperation was *La Luna*, a film he compared to Godard's *Breathless*. "*La Luna*," Bertolucci said, "is not only the consequence of a disappointment. *1900* had enabled me to explore thoroughly, personally, the mechanisms and contradictions of production. . . . Without that experience, I never would have dared make *La Luna*."[3]

It is of great significance that in 1979, the year that ended the European and American radical decade, and anticipated the neoconservativism of the 1980s, both directors made more personal and quasi-biographical films. These films were also, to use the language of their critical reception, more "accessible" to the public at large. For both directors, the desire to communicate with the public became more urgent during the 1980s. For Bertolucci, who in an attempt to free himself from the oppressive influence of Godard had long before defined himself as a director of film *spettacolo*, the wish to please the audience was only natural. For the reborn Godard, however, this desire was novel. His reawakened interest in popularity led him to try to reintegrate into the international filmmaking scene. In 1980 he was planning to make a gangster film based on the figure of the legendary Bugsy Siegel. Reflecting on this rather sharp transition from voluntary seclusion to the big capitalist market he said: "My Grenoble experience has been fascinating. But I realize now that it was too abstract, lacking in contact and means. I cut myself off from certain subjects and from a certain public. Whereas we must base our aims on the public's desires and prolong them. So this winter, I'm going to shoot 'Bugsy' with Vittorio Gassman and Charlotte Rampling in the U.S., Italy and France."[4] Yet, the project of *The Story*, subtitled *Bugsy*, never came to fruition despite Coppola's assistance.

It is quite interesting to see in retrospect how in the early 1980s, Godard reconciled his still existing radical impulse with his newly rekindled interest in commmercial cinema. Godard's compromise was expressed by his somehow schizophrenic collaboration on two different (if not incompatible) projects at once. One project was in Mozambique. His Switzerland-based Sonimage company was employed as a consultant by the government of Mozambique, which was starting a film and television industry. His other project was in California where he had a contract with Coppola "to study a script but to study it not only with a pencil but with a camera."[5] Reflecting on this seeming paradox of working simultaneously on a Third World project and on a project based in the postmodern center of late capitalism, Godard said:

It's very logical. In California, you have so many images, and in Mozambique, there are none. Eighty percent of the population has never seen an image—only nature. It's like a child opening his eyes and there's no code, no sense: he's just looking. In Mozambique, the image is the raw material. But in Hollywood, the images are so sophisticated you can't even read them anymore.[6]

Reflecting on Godard's logic one cannot but recall Bertolucci's own reconciliatory announcements regarding the dialectics of the green dollars and the images of the red flags in *1900*, a film that reproduced (on the level of its history of production as well as on the level of its thematics and style) the historical compromise of the Italian Communist party. Moreover, the dialectics of lack of images versus dense implosion of images continued Godard's prior interest in the study of the image through deconstructive methods of ideological analysis. However, Godard's former militant and semiotic interest in the image's process of signification was replaced, in the 1980s by a reflection on the society of the simulacra where the image is the real thing. For Godard, then, Mozambique was a sort of laboratory, a virginal public space as yet uncontaminated by the commodified images of multinational capitalism. Only in a place like Mozambique could Godard's plea in *Le Gai Savoir* to create a film from zero degree be fulfilled. Only a society innocent of the knowledge of an endless reproduction of recycled images could both produce fresh and authentic images, and also revitalize the lost and forgotten link between the image and its original referent, thus reconciling culture with nature. In the same period, Bertolucci made *Tragedy of a Ridiculous Man* which not only took Godard's *Tout va bien* as its point of reference, but used the idea of the simulacra society in order to criticize the tragic and ridiculous political situation of Italy in the 1980s.

The "Spiralling Negativity" of the Terrorist Game: Bertolucci's *Tragedy of a Ridiculous Man*

Tragedy of a Ridiculous Man is based on a true event in southern Italy that Bertolucci read about in a newspaper. "It was Mafia country," Bertolucci said. "A man's son had been kidnapped. Everybody knew the boy was dead. Yet the father raised the money for the ransom, and then diverted it to his own use."[7] It is worth quoting in full how Bertolucci himself summarized the plot of the film.

He [the father, the owner of the cheese factory] sees the boy kidnapped before his very eyes. When the ransom fails to arrive, he
realizes he must sell all that he's worked for—his cheese factory with its "Fort Knox" of golden *parmigiano*, his villa on top
of the hill, the pompous luxuries of his life, like his yacht—and
all to buy back the life of a son he discovers he hardly knows
and comes to suspect of fixing the whole affair.[8]

The title of the film encompasses its contradictions and ambiguities. Can a ridiculous man be tragic? Furthermore, are not tragic
characters *passé* in twentieth century art? One cannot but recall
Arthur Miller's largely debated definition of *Death of A Salesman* as
a "modern tragedy" as well as Samuel Beckett's labeling of his *Waiting For Godot* as a "tragic comedy." Miller named his hero Willy Lo-
mann (low man) to consciously subvert the traditional highness (of
class as well as character) of the tragic hero. Bertolucci, in a similar
fashion, named his protagonist ridiculous in order to question the essential distinction between the high and the low. Bertolucci's playful contradiction, the blurring of the sublime and the ridiculous, is in
line with the postmodern spirit of the film. As a cultural dominant,
postmodernism is bereft of seriousness and grandeur, the essential ingredients of the tragic, and the very act of quoting this dead genre reaf-
firms the postmodern petition for a dissolution of the hierarchy of
discourses. The film leaves black holes and loose ends in the narrative and never provides any closure. Many events in the narrative are
understood neither by the protagonists, nor by the spectators. The
main question "What happened?" remains unresolved, and the protagonists and the spectators alike are left without answers to basic
questions: Was the son really kidnapped? Who kidnapped him? Were
the kidnappers terrorists? Did the son himself stage the kidnapping?
Indeed part of the film's confusion and ambiguity derives from what
Bertolucci himself described as "a complex, sinister and tragically
ridiculous reality which is Italy today, a confused reality."[9] This type
of confused reality, deprived of master narratives and real referents,
is responsible for trapping the characters and the spectators in a web
of speculative interpretations regarding what really happened. It recalls Jean Baudrillard's thesis regarding the disappearance of the real
in the postmodern simulacrum society in which the political, the
moral, and the financial are only floating signifiers of real politics,
real morality, and real capital. The terrorist game in the film can be
read as a cinematic variation on Baudrillard's notion of the "spiralling
negativity," the model of which is the Moebius strip.

According to Baudrillard, all hypotheses concerning the political discourse (scandals, crises, and the like) are possible: "All the hypotheses of manipulation are reversible in an endless whirligig. For manipulation is a floating causality where positivity and negativity engender and overlap with one another; where there is no longer any active or passive."[10] Only by "putting an *arbitrary* stop to this revolving causality," Baudrillard claims, can a principle of political reality be saved. The predominance of the spiralling negativity in postmodern political life blurs the traditional distinctions between right and left and further diminishes the moral meaning of political struggle. In this respect, as Baudrillard observes, "the work of the Right is done very well, and spontaneously, by the Left on its own" whereas "the Right itself also spontaneously does the work of the Left."[11] It is not surprising, therefore, that the first example given by Baudrillard to explain his idea is the terrorism in Italy (perhaps it is not accidental either that the original publication date of "Simulacra and Simulation" is 1981, the year in which *Tragedy of a Ridiculous Man* was released). Interestingly enough, his words seem to apply perfectly to the dynamics of the narrative in *Tragedy* in which it is never made explicit who committed the kidnapping (the terrorist act) and for what reason. Furthermore, it is never clear whether the characters themselves and even the two representatives of the leftist group, Laura and Adelfo, know exactly what is happening. There is a surprisingly perfect fit between the logic of Bertolucci's narrative and Baudrillard's thesis about the logic of simulation which he explains by resorting to the Italian case:

> Is any given bombing in Italy the work of leftist extremists; or of extreme right-wing provocation; or staged by centrists to bring every terrorist extreme into disrepute and to shore up its own failing power; or again, is it a police-inspired scenario in order to appeal to calls for public security? All this is equally true, and the search for proof—indeed the objectivity of the fact— does not check this vertigo of interpretation. We are in a logic of simulation which has nothing to do with a logic of facts and an order of reasons.[12]

Tragedy of a Ridiculous Man is perhaps Bertolucci's most curious tribute to Godard. It is also the final exorcism of Godard from the Bertoluccian discourse.[13] The Italian/French connection is manifested through the rather unlikely couple Primo Spaggiari (Ugo Tognazzi) and his wife Barbara (Anouk Aimée). But it is also promoted, because as Kolker observes, "*Tout va bien* stands behind

Tragedy of a Ridiculous Man as a mark of difference."[14] The inter-textual relationships between the two films operate on the level of the narrative, but more so on the level of visual style. On the level of narrative, the allusions to *Tout va bien* include the factory itself (there are allusions to Salume, the sausage factory in *Tout va bien*; however, in *Tragedy* the role of the cheese factory is more strongly emphasized). Even the interior walls of Primo's factory are painted blue as in *Tout va bien* and hung with pictures of the factory itself (for the analysis of this scene in *Tout va bien* see chapter 1). Furthermore, the Italian comedian Vittorio Caprioli who plays the patron in *Tout va bien* plays the *maresciallo* (the police marshall) in *Tragedy*.[15]

The *Tragedy of a Ridiculous Man* exemplifies the Oedipal struggle not only through its thematics (the resurrection of the son), but also and principally through its formal organization which alludes to and quotes from the visual style of Godard's Marxist films, *Tout va Bien* in particular. Most critics agree that the film deviates from the classic Bertoluccian style. Ric Gentry, to cite one example, claims that: "Stylistically, *Tragedy of A Ridiculous Man* contains none of the operatic grandeur of *1900* or *Luna* . . . nor the fluid, baroque camera moves that are typical of his visual signature."[16] The reason all the critics give for this switch is the change in cinematographers. Vittorio Storaro was at work on Coppola's *One from the Heart*, and Bertolucci hired Carlo di Palma.

It is, however, rather interesting that the most bitter Oedipal struggle with the Godardian style occurs in a film that most critics agree is not typical of Bertolucci. Yet to my mind, although Storaro was not involved with this production, his style is pastiched by di Palma and contrasted with Godard's modernist style. The most peculiar thing about the Oedipal struggle in *Tragedy* is that the color scheme of each individual shot in the film becomes a stage of conflict between the contrasting visual styles of the two directors. Thus, although most of the shots retain the lush and almost excessive style typical of Bertolucci (brown golden colors; outdoors shots of pastoral nature, romantic imagery, and so on), each of them also contains a visual element that alludes to Godard's visual texts. These artificially inserted elements such as cars, pieces of furniture, clothes, and other articles bearing the primary colors and the rectangular forms used in *Tout va bien* do not assimilate into the dominant visual tones of the shots but, to the contrary, subvert and contradict them. While on the one hand they function as homage quotations to Godard, on the other hand they display the incongruity of his style with that of Bertolucci (which is obviously a question of more than mere style).

The curious collision in *Tragedy* on the level of the individual shot recalls the early stages of Sergei Eisenstein's montage theory (Eisenstein himself is invoked in this film through the scene involving the slaughter of the pigs, which alludes to *Strike*); however, this strain of intercinematography disappears toward the end of the film, which submits itself to the allure of the true Bertolucci style. The shots become more and more Bertoluccian in form and mood. The brown and gold colors take over, while the primary colors associated with *Tout va bien* vanish. The intensification of Bertolucci's style is accompanied by the replacement of intertextuality with intratextuality. Bertolucci no longer quotes from Godard's visual style, but rather cites from his own films. The beautiful shots of autumnal landscape invoke the ending scene of *The Conformist*, and the lyrical soft cinematography of the Po river reminds us of *Before the Revolution, The Spider's Stratagem,* and *1900.*[17] In addition, the constructivist elements and the industrial setting cited from the Godard text (which in turn pays tribute to Vertov and not to Eisenstein) are replaced by the rural landscape of the country of Parma, Bertolucci's birthplace and his primal source of visual imagery. Thus, in *Tragedy,* we have the opportunity to witness how the exorcisism of Godard's trademarks from the visual discourse enables Bertolucci to consciously cope with his anxiety of influence, and to assert his own directorial signature.

The film's Baudrillardian flavor is in harmony with the postmodernist confusion of the 1980s and the developing skepticism regarding the master narratives of the West. It is not surprising, therefore, that the film that opens the 1980s is also Bertolucci's last film to be shot in Europe. His next three films, *The Last Emperor, The Sheltering Sky,* and *Little Buddha,* turn to the East as a source of inspiration and rejuvenation. *Tragedy* thus signifies Bertolucci's fatigue with the West, and anticipates his pursuit of the East as a new source for "ecstasy of difference."

The Transition to the Cosmic Period: Godard's "Trilogy of the Sublime"

If the 1970s were Godard and Bertolucci's radical years, then the 1980s were their cosmic years.[18] After *Sauve qui peut (la vie),* Godard created what Marc Cerisuelo calls "the trilogy of the sublime:" *Passion* (1982), *Carmen* (1982), and *Hail Mary* (1983).[19] In contrast to the political militancy of the Dziga Vertov Group and the radical social critique typical of the video work with Anne-Marie Miéville, the work of the early 1980s reveals a new Godard. This is a Godard who shows a keen interest in the exploration of the idea of beauty. His "triology of the sublime" is preoccupied with reflections on the beautiful, the mystique of feminine flesh, and the transcendence of nature. The connoisseurs of Godard's materialist films were caught by surprise by this shift towards what seems to be a spiritual cinema on the verge of metaphysics, if not mysticism. For many, it appeared that Godard had traded Marxism for mysticism. A tangible spiritual fervor seems to motivate Godard's films of the 1980s. Indeed Godard's and Bertolucci's utopian years turn into the cosmic years. Bertolucci made *The Last Emperor* (1987) in the Forbidden City of Bejing; in 1990 he made *The Sheltering Sky* in Africa; and in 1994 he released a film on the life of the Buddha. Whereas Godard's cinephile as well as radical periods were confined to an urban or industrial milieu (usually associated with Paris) his triology of the sublime shows a renewed interest in nature and the elements (water, sky, and earth). In fact this interest manifested itself already in *Sauve qui peut (la vie)*. Whereas Bertoluuci turned to the East as a new reservoir for utopias, Godard returned to the landscape of his childhood, the Swiss lakes. Bertolucci began his film work through evocation of his own childhood landscapes. Most of his stories were set in his birthplace, Parma, which represented the keynote symbol for his antagonistic coupling of nostalgia with an acute belief in progressive historical change. With *The Last Emperor*, however, Bertolucci departed from the regions of his childhood and traveled farther and farther East to discover new exotic and pure spaces. His themes became more and more non-Italian, universal, and even metaphysical in nature. Italy disappeared from the new Bertoluccian discourse and the East became, in opposition to the West, a utopia. *The Sheltering Sky*, Bertolucci's second non-Italian film, seemed to follow the track begun with *The Last Emperor*. Godard, on the other hand, in the 1980s went back to the nature scenes of his childhood with films such as *Sauve qui peut (la vie)*, *Hail Mary*, and *Nouvelle Vague*.

The Triology of the Sublime

Passion opens Godard's triology of the sublime. The plot involves a group of characters linked to each other by work and love relationships: Isabelle (Isabelle Huppert), a factory worker; Hanna (Hanna Schygulla), an hotel owner; Piccoli (Michel Piccoli); a factory owner, and Jerzy (Jerzy Radziwilowicz), a Polish expatriate filmmaker. Part of the plot takes place on the set of Jerzy's film called *Passion*, which reconstructs and resurrects several famous paintings of past masters. *Passion*, according to Cerisuelo, fits the canonic definition of the sublime: the sublime is the presentation of the unpresentable. Or to use Jean François Lyotard's definition, following Kant, "la présentation qu'il y a de l'imprésentable" (the presentation of the impresentable).[20] More specifically, it is that which tries to represent the fact of unrepresentability, the gap between the conceivable and its presentation. Although traces of the old, politically conscious Godard are in the film, the interrogation of the relations between love and work, and the attempt to articulate working class consciousness through the stuttering of Isabelle (who plays an exploited factory worker)[21] display a new aspect of Godard's cinematic self. The fact that *Passion* deals with two realms (the realm of the political and its passion for social justice, and the realm of the aesthetic with its passion for art) posed for Godard a dilemma. The director, as Peter Wollen observes, must make a choice between the two counterposed realms, which are the modern versions of the sacred and the secular.[22] Godard said that the "grandeur of the ordinary" was the purpose of the film *Passion*.[23] This grandeur is achieved through the juxtaposition of scenes of ordinary life and the banal situation of the triangle with reconstructions through *tableau vivantes* of the paintings of the masters.[24] According to Cerisuelo, Pascal Bonitzer claims that the tableau vivantes invoked by Godard act like an oxymoron, a sublime figure *par excellence*.[25]

A major metaphor in the triology of the sublime is the sky, which perhaps more than anything else, reveals the new quality of the nouveau Godard: the preoccupation with the question of the sublime and the impossibility of representing it. In the films of the triology of the sublime, as Cerisuelo suggests, Godard created a new relationship with the spectator, a relationship based on homology.[26] The spectators face the film as Godard is facing the world. Godard first named the film *Passion: The World and Its Metaphor*.[27] The film suggests that if indeed film is a metaphor for the world than the screen is a metaphor for the sky.[28] The sky in these films mark the limits, the borders of the presented world. In both *Sauve qui peut (la vie)* and *Passion* it marks a double limit, that of the film and the world. But since the concept of the sky suggests the infinite, the total absence of limits and boundaries, it becomes a metaphor for the mystery of art.

Scénario du film Passion was commissioned in 1982 by Channel 4, Great Britain's independent television network. Made as a complement to his theatrical feature *Passion*, Godard's short feature video presents the director in a video editing room in front of a blank white screen ruminating on the creative process and on the labor that informs the conceptual and image-making process. This work, like his other televison work produced between 1976 and 1985, explores the production and consumption of images through television and cinema. In *Scénario du film Passion* Godard says "I think that first you see the world," thus he proclaims the precedence of seeing over writing/reading. According to his somewhat paradoxical aphorism, the word (the script) makes the world probable while the image (the camera) makes the world possible. The homology developed in *Passion* between Godard facing the world and the spectator facing the film is most evident in *Scenario du film Passion* in which Godard is seen sitting in front of a white screen musing: "Our subject: how to fill the white screen, or the famous blank page of Mallarmé" (l'invisible, l'énorme surface blanche la fameuse page blanche, de Mallarmé). While *Passion* can be seen "as Cinema regained after a detour through television, the decision to shoot it in the television ratio 1:1.33, and the production of *Scenario de Passion* on tape alongside the feature film, indicate . . . that it is an integral part of contemporary audio-visual practice."[29]

Godard, more so in *Scenario* than in *Passion*, elaborates on his oscillation between the aesthetic and the political by using contradictory metaphors to describe the homology between the world and its metaphor (film). According to one metaphor suggested by the text, a film is like a factory (a factory that produces images). Implicit in this metaphor is the idea that the director is a worker/producer of images. This conception is, obviously, not far from the materialist approach of the highly political, militant Godard. According to the other metaphor used by Godard, "the body of the film is like Christ's body." Implicit in this religious metaphor is the idea that the director is not a manufacturer of images but rather a lover/*creator* of images. This religious metaphor invokes the romantic notion of the artist who like God creates the world by word (the logos). Godard projects in *Scenario du film Passion* an ideal type of artist who like Mallarmé is facing the white sheet in an attempt to create a new poetic world. "Was the Law first read or seen?" Godard asks in the beginning of *Scenario*, and he answers: "I think that first you see the world." The primacy of seeing over writing is thus hypothesized. The antinomy of word/image is compared to that of labor/love and is transposed in Godard's thinking in this film to a utopian vision in which words are linked to images as labor is to love. The act of God's creation (grace) thus is like the act of labor (labor also in the sense of childbirth). Both acts result in the creation of something new.

The dialectic of love/labor is visually materialized through a shot in which Godard is seen as a sillhouette from behind caressing the white blank screen as images of Isabelle and Jerzy from the film *Passion* appear on it, invoking the scene in *Les Carabiniers* in which Michel Ange is caressing the image of a bathing woman that appears on the screen. As much as God created human beings through an act of grace, and as much as a woman gives life to her child through labor, so the director creates characters and images through love. The film ends on a note of the pure sublime, when love and labor merge through music, the music of the angels.

In *Scenario du Film Passion* Godard asks "How did the masters represent moments of life?" thus suggesting an homology between the masters and himself. The artist (the master) is like God, the Creator, and Godard, in *Scenario*, is shown in the process of creating images and explaining them through words. *Scenario du film Passion* is "*process as product* not product in progress."[30] Both films thus constitute a reflection on the creative process—a notion much despised by the former militant Godard. Creation is passion, a combination of love and labor.[31] The function of the word as such is to reconcile and mediate the contradictions of love/labor, fiction/documentary, and black/white that the film exposes. It must tell the truth that has been obscured by the lies of images. In *Scenario du film Passion* the filmmaker is no longer presented as a worker, but rather as "a tormented artist projecting his confused creativity."[32]

Godard denied that *Passion* is a film about filmmaking. Yet one cannot ignore the intratextual relationship that *Passion* establishes with *Contempt*. In *Contempt*, Michel Piccoli is a director who is being tyrannized by a ruthless and greedy American producer (Jack Palance). In *Passion* Piccoli himself is transformed into the capitalist, greedy producer, while the figure of the Italian producer is reminiscent of Vittorio Caprioli in *Tout va bien*. Yet, in *Passion*, unlike in *Contempt*, the nexus of cash and aesthetics surpasses the boundaries of moral idealistic criticism of the film industry, and becomes a philosophical treatise on the creative process.

Prénom Carmen (First Name: Carmen) is the second film in the trilogy of the sublime, and it won the Gold Palm Award at the Venice Film Festival in 1983.[33] In fact, the beginning of the 1980s witnessed a rash of *Carmen* films: Carlos Saura, *Carmen* (1983); Peter Brook, *La Tragedie de Carmen* (1983); Jean-Luc Godard, *Prénom Carmen* (1983); and Francesco Rosi, *Carmen* (1984). Of all these, Godard's *Carmen* is the furthest from Bizet, Spain, and the Mediterranean.

The plot is about a bank robber named Carmen with whom a cop named Joseph falls in love. The bank robber goes to her rich and sick uncle Jeannot (played by Godard) to ask for money to make a film about a very elaborate kidnap plot. In an interview with Ranvaud, Godard said: "At first I thought of doing the film around terrorism but then felt that too many things would be brought to it from the outside by critics and audience. *Carmen* is just a picture."[34] *Carmen* with its band of *deseperados*[35] pays tribute to Bertolucci's *Tragedy of a Ridiculous Man* through the equation it draws between experimental Godard-type filmmaking and the deliquency or terrorism represented by Carmen's elaborate kidnap plot. But it also, through a complex network of references, alludes to *Tango*. As in *Tango*, the spectacle of *l'amour fou* and contempt (mépris), between Joseph and Carmen takes place in an interior space (a suite in the Intercontinental Hotel) which, like the empty apartment in *Tango*, is bathed in yellow light. There are even more explicit allusions to *Tango*'s use of the anal metaphor in one of the dialogues between Joseph and Carmen (see chapter 5).

Most of the film takes place indoors inside the hotel but there are a few intercuts of shots of the sea and the sky. The intercuts of the sea recall the imagery of the French symbolist poet Mallarmé which is, to a large extent, dominated by the sea (for example *Un Coup de Des*). Mallarmé's white sheet of paper was invoked in *Scenario du film Passion*. The motif of water is a recurrent poetic motif, and it was an important theme for philosophers and artists of the *fin de siècle* such as Arthur Schopenhauer, Friedrich Nietzsche, Richard Wagner, and Thomas Mann. Despite these sublime aspects of the film, it marks a continuation of Godard's interest in the relationship between sound and image—an interest that was almost an obsession for him during his radical years. However, in *Carmen*, the exploration of this relationship is motivated by the new Godardian spiritualism, and therefore, as David Wills points out, "the introduction of the soundtrack into or onto the image track, as both an attempt to redress the primacy given the image, and . . . disturb the coherence of the image track by lodging the other of cinema within what it assumes to be its fullness" is done by "exploiting the furthest supplement, the most dependent or repressed element of the film process, music."[36] The music (from certain Beethoven quartets for strings and not from Bizet's Carmen), as Delvaux says, penetrates the image. The film is also full of homage references to the early burlesque cinema which was the first victim of the sound film.

Godard's *Hail Mary* caused a stir. Undoubedtly this is Godard's most scandalous film and its *succès de scandale* is comparable only to Bertolucci's *Tango*.[37] The film caused protests from the Pope John Paul II, who denounced the film as blasphemous, and from demonstrators around the globe. Even today the film retains the power to stir and provoke, and its screenings are invariably followed by demonstrations organized by Christian groups. Yet Godard denied that he had any intention to provoke. "To provoke," he said "is no work for a moviemaker."[38] And indeed, for those familiar with Godard's work this statement does not sound naive or hypocritical. Godard's new spiritualism anticipated in *Sauve qui peut (la vie)* is evident even in this somewhat bizzare interpretation of the immaculate conception "with Mary as a sullen basketball-playing teen pumping gas in her father's station, Joseph as a sexually frustrated cabdriver, and the archangel Gabriel as an unshaven tough with a cherubic little girl spouting lines like 'Be pure, be rough, follow thy way'."[39] Godard's new mildness, his new policy of compromises and no provocations, manifested itself also in his willingness not to release the film in Rome, the Papal city. When Katherine Dieckmann asked him why he told his Italian distributor to pull the film from Rome, he answered: "It's the house of the church, and if the Pope didn't want a bad boy running around in his house, the least I could do is respect his wishes. This Pope has a special relationship to Mary; he considers her a daughter almost. There were other cities for the film. We didn't need Rome."[40]

Indeed the movie, as Robert Seidenberg observes, "doesn't mock those who have faith or ridicule Catholicism à la Luis Bunuel."[41] Rather like Pasolini in *The Gospel According to Matthew*, *Teorema* and *Accattone* it provides an heretical interpretation of Christian myths by invoking the sublime. Contrary to public expectations of "the most controversial film of our time" the film's "obscenity," as Dieckmann notes is limited to some nudity "and a brief, graphic quasi-masturbation scene over-laid with a juicily blasphemous Artaud quotation."[42]

Although Godard was raised as a Protestant he said in his interview with Dieckmann:

> But I'm very interested in Catholicism. I think there's something so strong in the way the Bible was written, how it speaks of events that are happening today, how it contains statements about things which have happened in the past. I think, well—it's a great book! And somehow I think we need faith, or I need faith, or I'm lacking in faith. Therefore maybe I needed a story which is bigger than myself.[43]

Hail Mary continues the interest expressed in *Passion* in the relationship of word and image. But here the relationhip is located within the framework of what Baudrillard calls "the quarrel of the Iconoclasts."[44] As Godard said: "The Vatican newspaper said, 'Pictures shall not deal with sacred things,' which is the Church opinion. I think it shouldn't be said so fast, but there is probably something important in that opinion. Sacred things are sacred. But as a moviemaker I ask why they are sacred for the image but not for words, why you can say the word 'sacred' and why you can't just shut up and show 'sacred'."[45]

The sublime effects of the film and its rendering of the sense of the presence of the inexplicable in our world derive both from its use of sound, which juxtaposes bird sounds and music of Bach,[46] and from its nature photography. In *Hail Mary* Godard abandoned his modernist aesthetics. The Godardian modernist iconography, which borrowed bits of traffic signs, neon, advertisements, and cartoons from the urban and industrial milieu, was replaced in *Hail Mary* by natural signs: a moon, a sun, water, and apples. As Dieckmann pointed out in her interview with Godard, "Some of the images are even a little corny, like *National Geographic* photography." To which Godard answered:

> What we wanted to show in *Hail Mary* was signs in the beginning. Immaculate signs in a way. And not just to give a feeling of nature, in order to be poetic, but to show the physical process of making nature possible. A philosophy of nature, just as we tried to show the spirit and flesh of Mary. Also to bring science close to the natural, not to show them as oppositions. Because there's a scene where the professor is talking about creation— the text comes from the work of a British physicist—and it sounds very Biblical or religious. We are an extraterrestrial people, as it says in the film. We come from the sky. And it's not by chance, but by design.[47]

Miéville contributed what Godard called "a long short story" to his "short long story" with her *Book of Mary*, which prefaces *Hail Mary*. Her movie looks at how a parental separation affects a girl named Mary who expresses her anger through recitation of Baudelaire and freestyle dance. Although Godard claims that both films were conceived, written, and shot separately, they seem constantly to refer to each other.

The story of the Virgin Mary appears at first to be an odd choice for a filmmaker who never overtly concerned himself with religion.

Godard himself said: "I prefer to say it that way. Maybe all my movies have dealt with couples—men and women—and I tried probably to go back to the archetypal couple. I'm always interested in the first time . . . So let's do the first love story ever told."[48] This apologetic kind of answer recalls Bertolucci's interest in the archetypal couple in *Tango*. The couple in Bertolucci's original script was modeled on the biblical Adam and Eve.[49] Godard's new-found religiosity is perhaps not so surprising given André Bazin's influence and status as a spiritual father for the young Turks of the New Wave. The emergence of Bazin's brand of humanistic Catholicism, with its reverential attitude toward reality as the manifestation of divine presence, emerges in the new Godardian discourse in the form of the "return of the repressed." "I think that politics today is the voice of horror," Adam tells Eve in Godard's *Hail Mary*. And Mary in another scene says: "Earth and sex are inside us. Outside are only the stars."

On the one hand *Carmen*, *Passion*, and *Hail Mary* constitute Godard's triology of the sublime. Yet, when taken together, *Passion*, *Hail Mary*, and *Nouvelle Vague* (New Wave) can be seen as a separate trilogy of Protestant theology. The three films deal with "les grands objets theologiques" (the big theological issues): the crucifixion, the annunciation, and the resurrection.[50] For Godard, the iconoclast, the Bible is a good scenario. Its universally known stories simplify the filmmaker's quest for subjects and plots. In this, Godard follows Bertolt Brecht who believed in the popularity of the Bible and its potential as a reservoir of "moral stories" (Brecht's *Good Person of Szechwan* is of course a prime example). Godard was raised in a Protestant family, and his return to the landscape of his Swiss childhood (Lake Leman situated between Lausanne and Geneva) is a return to a lost paradise. Furthermore, it also signifies a return to the Protestant faith of his childhood.

With *Nouvelle Vague* (1990), Godard returned to some of the issues that permeate the whole of his oeuvre. Yet, the film can be seen not only as a return but also an intensification of Godard's new interest in religion and nature as the manifestation of divine creation. The plot (if one can apply this term to the highly fragmented and frequently confusing narrative of this film) is set on a lush Swiss estate from which a beautiful woman (Domiziana Giordano) controls an industrial empire. One day, while traveling in her luxurious sportscar through the countryside, she picks up an injured hitchhiker (Alain Delon). The rest of the plot portrays the developing relationship between the wounded, mysterious stranger in town and the woman, presented as a sort of "queen of Capitalism" surrounded by a group of rich and greedy industrialists of "the Age of the Conglomerate."[51]

Other social groups besides the industrialists are represented in this semi-religious parable on the spiritual bankruptcy of modern materialism through the figures of the servant girl (who reads and quotes Schiller) and the gardener (Roland Amstutz) who ruminates on how nature makes its own suggestions for creation. Godard's former political interest in the class struggle is transformed in *Nouvelle Vague* into a Christian framework that articulates the tensions between rich and poor in religious terms.[52]

As in his trilogy of the sublime, nature is celebrated through adoring shots of the Swiss forests, lakes, and meadows which serve as contrapuntal points of reference to the decadent world of the power-lustful industrialists.[53] The film, as Roland Amstutz suggests, "tells the story of our epoch . . . the story of the world of money and the world of nature."[54] In *Nouvelle Vague*, Godard continues to develop the nature/factory dichotomy, yet he takes it one step further so as to generate an opposition between spiritualism and materialism. Whereas the beauty of the Swiss landscape is a natural beauty, that of the factory is a fabricated beauty. It is a modernist Mondrian-like beauty dominated by the red color so popular with the radical Godard.

Godard's negation of the world of big corporations and multi-national capitalism portrayed through the shadowy world of the greedy industrialists (we never see their faces and they are always photographed from behind in dark shadow) is the only trace of his former radical politics. Yet, despite the film's critique of the crimes of international finance (emblematized by Swiss banking and corporate takeovers), the tensions between rich and poor are no longer grounded in the Marxist notion of class struggle, but in the ideas of primitive, early Christianity and its utopian promise of egalitarian society. The waitress, as Robert Stam suggests, "forever being reprimanded and slapped, stands in for all the oppressed once foregrounded in Godard's films."[55] As the film puts it: "Soon certain social conventions, customs, principles, and internal attitudes will vanish. We can take defunct society as we know it. Future ages will recall it only as a charming moment in history. Back then, they will say, there were rich and poor." One may argue that Godard's former subscription to the Marxist utopia of a classless society has been replaced by a belief in the Christian utopia of the "Kingdom of Heaven" promised by Jesus to his poor followers. According to

Godard's new semi-religious vision, the world of money is the world of materialism and the world of nature is the world of spiritualism. *Nouvelle Vague*, as Stam suggests, "has some of the visual exhilaration of discovering the world before names."[56] The image in the form of seeing precedes the logos and, as in *Passion, Scenario du film Passion*, and *Hail Mary*, the shots of the sky and its cloud formations imply a celestial backdrop. Furthermore, they seem to suggest the second coming of the Messiah, whose figure is hinted at by the character of Delon, the stranger with the cross. (When the rich woman finds him lying injured on the road she pulls out a chain with a cross which is hanging on his neck.) The theme of resurrection (suggested by the poem motto of the film)[57] and by the reappearance of the Delon character (who appears first as Roger Lennox and after as Richard Lennox) invokes a Messianic hope for the second coming of Christ.

Perhaps the most important figure in this film, which reflects Godard's new quest for spiritualism, is the gardener, who plays a sort of poet/philosopher. The biblical, edenic associations of the garden emphasize the religious utopian dimension of nature, envisioned by Godard as the last resort from late capitalism. Hence, one cannot but recall Voltaire's concluding wisdom in *Candide*: "We must cultivate our garden." In fact the whole plot of the film is accompanied by Godard's voice-over aphorisms and fragmented lyrical meditations on the nature of God and humankind and the destiny of civilization. *Nouvelle Vague* is, as Stam observes, an "aleatory collage of sententious phrases culled from Nietzsche, Faulkner, Raymond Chandler, Rimbaud, Dante, and Lucretius."[58] A series of Latin intertitles such as "Incipit Lamentation," "Te Deum," and "Ecce Homo" betray a rich spectrum of cultural allusions to poetic, literary, and philosophical origins.

The plot of the film recalls to a certain extent Pasolini's *Teorema* and its heretic invocation of Christian themes. Pasolini's *Teorema* can be interpreted as a Marxist parable (and even more specifically as a Stalinist parable), as a religious allegory, as a Freudian lesson, and as a modern myth. Each reading of the film can exclude the other, as well as incorporate the other, or can be read in conjunction with the other. In *Teorema*, according to Peter Bondanella, Pasolini asks, "What if . . . a god or some form of divine being appeared before a middle-class family, formed relationships with each of its members, and then departed? His unequivocal answer is that the bourgeois family members would achieve a sense of self-consciousness and would self-destruct."[59] The enigmatic stranger coming to town in *Nouvelle Vague* recalls the mysterious stranger (Terence Stamp) in *Teorema* whose encounter with the upper bourgeois family of the factory owner ends with the total physical and mental disintegration of all the members of the family. In *Nouvelle Vague*, however, the encounter of the stranger (who like Terence Stamp has blue eyes associated in Italian/Catholic iconography with the figure of Christ) with the rich industrialist woman ends not in destruction but in Christian (non-corporeal) love. Whereas the message of Pasolini's heretic parable was that of a complete destruction of the bourgeoisie, the message of the late non-Marxist Godard is that of love. The man's and woman's hands become, in the film, Godard's visual symbol of Christian, spiritual love and the film ends with an intertitle reading "love conquers everything." Yet, despite the Christian aspects of the film and its reference to the archetypal story of Christ, *Nouvelle Vague*, unlike *Hail Mary* which is deliberately designed as a modern version of the annunciation, is a modern, yet latent and disguised version of the resurrection.

Andre Dumas suggests that Godard does not need to go to Rome, to Jerusalem, or to the Sahara in order to find his paradise.[60] His is an internal journey that is not directed towards the "exoticism" of the Other. Bertolucci, on the other hand, turns in the mid 1980s towards the Other situated on the periphery of the globe, in Bejing and in the Sahara, in a quest for his own paradise lost.

CHAPTER 4

The Quest for the Other: Bertolucci's *The Last Emperor* and *The Sheltering Sky*

Bertolucci's *The Last Emperor* and *The Sheltering Sky* are his first films shot in the Third World rather than in Europe. Perhaps as a consequence, both films address concerns and sentiments regarding the problem of the Other that recur in debates about the inscription and representation of another culture. The right to inscribe or represent another culture is a power that, as Johannes Fabian and Bernard McGrane claim, traditionally has been granted to the anthropologist/ethnographer.[1] Nevertheless, the links between ethnography and film are by now well known and in dominant cinema, as Ella Shohat points out, "the spectator is subliminally invited on an archeological and ethnographic tour of celluloid-preserved cultures."[2] Moreover, the fact that these films are Western productions made in the Orient raises the question whether Bertolucci's object is a restoration of "authenticity" to this region or an attempt to construct it, in Jane Desmond's suggestive phrase, "as the imaginary geography of ('the West's') desire."[3]

The Last Emperor

"China. Geographical region, nation, political regime, culture, tradition, rice, wall, cultural revolution, Mao, ideograms, danger, hope. China is an abstraction, a chain of abstractions."[4] This is how in 1969 Tommaso Chiaretti opens his short introduction to the published script of Marco Bellochio's *La Cina e vicina* (*China is Near*) (1967). Bellochio, like other militant Maoist filmmakers of the 1960s, Godard in particular (see *La Chinoise* which may be seen as a preview of May 1968), turned the abstraction "into the pivot of a metaphor"[5] by saying that China is near. In contrast, Bertolucci, despite his fascination with the theatrical dimensions of the Cultural Revolution, which he perceived as a spectacular mise en scène of living street theater,[6] saw the growing militancy on the part of left-oriented filmmakers as a disastrous historical error. Like his first mentor, Pier Paolo Pasolini, he denounced what he regarded as the political immaturity of the extremist left and in a gesture of protest he joined the Italian Communist party, "the revisionists" as they were called in the May 1968 discourse.

Only twenty years later, when the revolutionary spirit vanished from the European scene, did Bertolucci return to China, the favorite yet abstract metaphor of the May 1968 revolutionary generation. Although like Godard, Bellochio, and others, Bertolucci used China in his *Last Emperor* as a utopian metaphor for the West, he attempted at the same time to flesh out the metaphor by actually shooting in the geographical region called China. Furthermore, his Chinese metaphor is imbued with historical depth due to the time perspective provided by the almost twenty years that separate the last historical event (the Cultural Revolution) represented by the film and the present of its shooting.

The film is an interpretation of the life of Pu Yi (1906–1967) the last Chinese emperor. It is loosely based on the memoirs of Sir Reginald Johnston, the emperor's Scottish tutor between 1919 and 1922 and on Pu Yi's own autobiography, *From Emperor to Citizen*, written with the encouragement and approval of the Maoist government after his "reeducation" in a reform camp. The film spans all the major events of modern Chinese history including its transition from empire to republic and then to a Communist state.

Pu Yi was placed on the throne at the age of three in 1908 by his dying great aunt Tsu-Hsi, the Empress Dowager. He was taken from his family and raised by the court eunuchs in the Forbidden City in the center of Beijing. Shortly after his coronation he was deposed by republican nationalists and became a prisoner in the Forbidden City. In 1924 he was evicted by a warlord and stayed in Tianjin where he lived the lifestyle of a Western playboy. Eventually, he agreed to collaborate with the Japanese by serving as a king of the puppet state of Manchuria (the birthplace of his ancestors). He was captured by Soviet troops in 1945 and was transferred in 1949 to the Communist regime founded in China by Mao. The Maoist authorities sent him to a rehabilitation center where he underwent Maoist reeducation. After ten years in the government prison, he was released as an ordinary citizen and began working as a gardener in Beijing's botanical gardens. In 1967, in the midst of the Cultural Revolution and after publishing his autobiography, he died.

Bertolucci got permission to shoot in the Forbidden City in the spring of 1984 after only a month of negotiation. This was due to the fact that he was a registered member of the Italian Communist party until 1978. The Chinese even assisted the film crew by providing thousands of Chinese soldiers as extras. This big production (it was the first collaboration between Bertolucci and the British producer Jeremy Thomas) won nine Oscar awards.

The Sino-Italian connection has a long history, beginning with Marco Polo, the Venetian who first revealed China to the West. As Zhang Longxi points out, China has furnished the West since that time with "a better reservoir for its dreams, fantasies, and utopias."[7] Michelangelo Antonioni's documentary film on China, *Chung Kuo*, is but one expression of Italy's continued fascination with China. In his discussion of Antonioni's film, Umberto Eco emphasizes "the search for China as a potential utopia by the frantic, neurotic West."[8] Similarly, Bertolucci, the first Western director permitted to shoot in the Forbidden City, the traditional capital of the Chinese emperors, has said that "China had become the front projection of our confused utopias."[9] Bertolucci's *The Last Emperor*, thus, invokes the problematic image of China as myth and symbol of difference and as the ultimate Other/double of the West.

The Last Emperor, like Bertolucci's other films, is about revolution and utopia. The focus of Bertolucci's meditation on the fate and prospects of revolution in our time has evolved from an imaginary revolution (as envisaged in *1900*) to a real one which, however, in Longxi's words, "is obviously not concerned with China per se but with learning about the self in the West."[10]

Yet *The Last Emperor*'s utopian vision implies the expulsion of the feminine from the new and improved society. Toward the end of the movie, no women remain in it. Women (except perhaps in *1900*) are excluded from the Communist utopia envisaged in most of Bertolucci's films, but the *Last Emperor* goes one step further and banishes them from the text. The symbolic annihilation of women in this film is enacted through the film's dialectics of interior/exterior and darkness/light, which ultimately assume the orthodox Freudian binarism of feminine/masculine and the Lacanian division of the imaginary versus the symbolic.[11]

In *Emperor* both the protagonist's desire and the text itself follow an Oedipal configuration generated by the search for the father-tutor and by repudiation of the mother. This configuration entails the acceptance of the Lacanian symbolic and rejection of the imaginary, the latter being articulated through the infant's dyadic relationship with the mother. Whereas *The Last Tango* (1972) demonstrates attachment to the Lacanian imaginary through the regressive movement of its narrative towards the interior or womb (as visually embodied by the apartment representing the "nostalgia for a lost paradise"),[12] *The Last Emperor*'s counter-movement is, on the one hand, an escape from the womb (as represented by The Forbidden City signifying the M/Other)[13] and, on the other hand, a striving towards the exterior of the symbolic order governed by the law of the father. Hence, the film's dialectics of light and color becomes a dialectic of enlightenment that would also be seen as a dialectic between the metaphors of sexual difference:

Feminine/M/Other	*Masculine*/tutor/educator
The Forbidden City	the outside world
dark	light
internal	external
closed (prison)	open .
unknowledge	knowledge
unconscious	conscious
immanent	transcendental

Moreover, this dialectic is transformed into political terms, and suggests an analogy between psychoanalytic therapy and the Maoist didactic process of reeducation, the goal of both being the rebirth of a new enlightened and liberated man. To achieve this ideal, the emperor must be educated by *male* tutors (the Scottish teacher and the head of the prison) who eventually, through transference, assume the role of the *padre*. The acceptance of these father figures as *padre* (good educator) and not *padrone* (tyrannical boss) enables the emperor to accomplish his education successfully and to acquire true enlightenment.

The gradual removal of women from a film that Bertolucci defines as "the only positive film that I've made"[14] is quite disturbing and therefore calls for a feminist critique. Moreover, this film has special appeal for feminist analysis because, as an epic film exploring both individual and national psychohistory, *Emperor* invokes the problematics associated with the representation of women in our culture. In particular, *Emperor* raises questions about the absenting and marginalization of women both from the patriarchal ordering of narrative and from the history emplotted[15] by men.

The stylistic structure of *Emperor*, as well as the organization of the narrative, inevitably lead to the symbolic annihilation of women. The first part of my discussion of *The Last Emperor* deals with the representation of the feminine in the film, specifically the representation of the Forbidden City as the M/Other, and the role of the eunuchs in the film's process of structuring sexual differences. The second part of the discussion analyzes the two major processes that take place in the film, the psychoanalytic and the political. The analysis there seeks to demonstrate that the film's design can be seen as a reconstruction of psychoanalytic therapy. The flow of flashbacks generated by the protagonist's free associations emulates the process and structure of psychoanalytic therapy as conducted by a male therapist (the prison governor played by the former Chinese minister of culture, Ying Ruocheng). It can also be shown that the psychoanalytic process is tightly linked to the political one, and the ideal of the Maoist reeducation process (changing the individual and integrating him or her into the collective) intersects with the psychonalytic goal (freeing the individual from traumas of the past and paving the road towards social integration). Both processes are conducted by the same male tutor and are aimed at the resolution of an Oedipal complex through positive identification with the ultimate father, the Maoist educator. Thus, these processes lead to the absenting of women from the domains of personal and political education as well as to their exit from the stage of history,[16] which then becomes the exclusive sphere of male presence and dominance.

The major metaphor of femininity in the film, the Forbidden City, appears in the opening credits, in the flashbacks, and at the end when Pu Yi returns to see the Forbidden City in 1967. Pu Yi's last visit represents a different image of the city, which under Mao's regime has become the "Unforbidden City." The transition from the forbidden (the "taboo" in Freudian terms) to the unforbidden is at the core of Pu Yi's personal, as well as political, education. This transition assumes the character of a progressive regression in which Pu Yi emplots his life story to the investigator (the prison's governor, the symbolic "good father" figure and analyst). Through this emplotment, Pu Yi reconstructs, in a metonymic fashion, the most important phase of Chinese history: the transition from the Imperial past to the Communist present.

The opening credits scene introducing the Forbidden City is used as an advancing symbol for all the subsequent flashbacks representing the city. The city's visual perfection and *will-to-spectacle*[17] requires the spectator to conceptualize the city's image.

This psychoanalytic process derives from the connotations assigned by the Western mind to the name "The Forbidden City" and is further conditioned by the cinematographic representation achieved through the camera movement and framing in this scene and in other scenes, which echo and mirror our initial encounter with the Forbidden City.

The camera movements in the first scene create a dialectic interaction of perceptions. The slow penetrating movements of the camera bring the spectator closer to the center of the city, thus threatening to invade the city's interior and to expose its riddles. Simultaneously, these camera movements blur the spatial distinctions between foreground and background: the farther the camera penetrates the city, the more distant and inaccessible the city becomes. This *trompe-l'oeil* effect, whereby what seems to be interior eventually becomes an exterior, imitates the architecture of the city itself, which was designed as a Chinese box, each part containing—and at the same time being contained—within another part. The city's mise-en-abime materializes the metaphor of the city as the body of the mother and projects the infantile fantasy of total fusion with this body.[18]

The camera movement toward the structures in front of it (such as pavilions and temples) is repeatedly blocked, and penetration into the city becomes impossible. Decorated glass doors block access to the Forbidden City and turn the camera's gaze, as well as the spectator's gaze, into an act of peeping into the unknown behind the walls. The repetition of close-up shots of glass doors and gates emphasizes that the view taken in by both the camera and the spectator is never whole at any given moment during the act of spectatorship. Thus, again and again, the spectator is required to use his or her imagination in order to fill visual gaps in his or her own movement and in the camera's movement through the text. The activity of filling gaps in the film's visual presentation neatly parallels the filling of gaps in the film's narrative, which links the flashbacks to the story frame. The cinematography and the gaps in the narrative render a feeling of "lack" and create the impression that we are engaged in a conscious voyeuristic activity of peeping into the forbidden, which is never to be fully seen or touched.[19]

On the level of psychoanalytic conceptualization, the camera movement visually emulates the metaphor used by Freud to describe his inquiry into the nature of femininity. In the introduction to his lecture on femininity, Freud—aware of the weakness of his endeavor to explore the enigma of femininity—tries to excuse himself by appealing to the sympathy of his male audience, emphasizing that "throughout history people [i.e., men] have knocked their heads against the riddle of the nature of femininity."[20] In contrast to Freud's visually vivid metaphor, the film demands abstract conceptualization or mythification of its concrete visual imagery of the Forbidden City.[21]

Freud's visualization of his male construct of female mystery as a prison-like essence is a controlling metaphor in *Emperor*. The metaphor is epitomized by the representation of the Forbidden City as a womb-like prison inhabited only by women and castrated men. In a few scenes, each presenting an attempt on Pu Yi's part to escape from the Forbidden City, the camera's tracking shots emphasize the claustrophobic feeling generated by the thick walls of the city and conceptually turn the attempted escapes into visual signifiers of emergence from this womb-like enclosure.

The attempts to escape from the body of the mother manifest a process of differentiation in which Pu Yi tries to achieve his distinct male identity. In order to attain his maleness, he denies identification or oneness with his mother. This strategy is what Jessica Benjamin, following Nancy Chodorow,[22] describes as "the intense repudiation of the mother and maternal nurturance" that "seems also to stamp the formation of male gender identity."[23] In Lacanian terms, the attempted escapes from the city/M/Other prepare Pu Yi for the transition from the imaginary to the symbolic order, the domain of phallic authority.

Freud's reading of femininity as an enigma, the culmination of the "Other," is not far from the image of China as perceived by the Western mind. As Longxi points out, China has traditionally been perceived by the West "as the paradigm and locale of the Other."[24] China's cultural Otherness mirrors our first encounter with the Other, which, as Jessica Benjamin reminds us, is "our mother." China's—and, in particular, the Forbidden City's—Otherness in this film is especially rich in its appeal to gender divisions and to structures of sexual differences. Bertolucci has used the phrase "ecstasy of difference" to describe a special sensation he felt while walking at dawn in the streets of Shanghai surrounded "by the sea of Chinese faces and bodies buzzing in all directions simultaneously."[25] As a Westerner, he was struck "by the almost feminine, very soft nature of Chinese men," which forced him "to play a silly game of wild generalizations" by saying that "Japan is macho and China is feminine."[26] Within the framework of feminist critique, which tends to theorize the place woman occupies in the patriarchal order as man's

Other, Bertolucci's wild generalization does not sound so silly. Just as the conceptualization of the Other is crucial as a point of contrast to Western self-conception, so too is the conceptualization of woman as man's Other. The problematics involved in the representation of exoticism and otherness is, as Roland Barthes long ago observed, intimately linked with questions of the Other's becoming a pure object, a spectacle. Indeed, in no other domain, as Barthes himself emphasizes, is the indispensable symbol of the exotic other so salient as in the representation of the body of the woman.[27]

The uniqueness of the Forbidden City's architecture lends a certain complexity to the point of view in the opening sequence. On one hand, the gaze of the Western spectator identifies with the camera: both regard the city as a metonymy of China's enigma, as the Other. But the City is also represented through its inhabitants' eyes. The Empress Dowager Cixi on her deathbed announces to the three-year-old Pu Yi (and to the Western spectator) that, after sunset, the entrance to the City is forbidden to all men but the emperor. The spectator thus sees the city as it is seen by Pu Yi, from the inside, but at the same time sees it (like any Chinese man during the Empire and, in particular, toward the end of the Qing dynasty) as the *forbidden* Other.

For Pu Yi, the world beyond the city is an absent presence. Both Pu Yi and the camera define the physical limits of the young emperor's world. The child's point of view is bound by the roofs and towers of the City that surround him. Stationed on the rooftops and simultaneously performing a spectacular 360-degree tracking shot around the boundaries of the Forbidden City the camera manipulates the framing and similarly defines these boundaries. The framing is repeated in several scenes, intensifying the spectator's identification with Pu Yi's limited angle of vision. Since the city does not enable a real differentiation, the self is threatened with the grim prospect of being swallowed by the Other, which merges femininity and the city-as-spectacle. According to Dana Polan, the *will-to-spectacle* banishes everything beyond the image frame.

In the final scene of the film, the Forbidden City of the Maoist regime becomes the Unforbidden City. From an Imperial city forbidden to all citizens, it becomes a Communist city open to all citizens. The city's enigma, which in the film is conjured up through visions of Oriental mystique and splendor, is demystified in the final scene. The city is no longer reified or masked by exotic Orientalism. On the contrary, the once Forbidden City now appears as a gray dreary mini-metropolis that functions as a national museum, in marked contrast with the lush gold colors and the seductive Imperial past. In the final scene, the city is represented as it was first seen by Bertolucci himself when he received permission from the Chinese authorities to shoot it. This is the actual city that Bertolucci saw when he first came to China, before he turned it into "the set that Hollywood never dared to build."[28]

What we the spectators see in the final scene is the contemporaneous city dispossessed of its Imperial mystique, a mystique that was constructed by Bertolucci's mise en scène in an attempt to consciously rewrite the past. For the first time in the film, Pu Yi and the spectator (both of whom receive Bertolucci's virginal impression of the city) see the city naked, unfetishized, almost an anti-spectacle. Yet, to use Barthes's words on striptease, so relevant to the representation of the Forbidden City in the final scene, the enveloping memory of a luxurious shell is still there. According to Barthes, exoticism is the first barrier of a "whole series of coverings placed upon the body of the woman in proportion as she pretends to strip it bare . . . for it is always of a petrified kind which transports the body into the world of legend or romance."[29] Through the final striptease of the city, the spectators thus become aware of the fact that they are engaged as they watch the first Western movie to venture behind the walls of China's Forbidden City. In addition, the spectators become conscious of their participation in a collective Western voyeuristic desire both to mystify and demystify the Other.[30]

As much as the Forbidden City exemplifies Bertolucci's own ambivalence about sexual identity and gender, so do the eunuchs, the largest group inhabiting the city. There are some interesting analogies between Sophocles's Thebes and the Forbidden City.[31] The prohibition against men entering the Forbidden City after sunset recalls the prohibition against entering Thebes. The riddle of the Sphinx is mirrored by the riddle of Pu Yi's sexual identity, and the Sphinx of the Forbidden City is the collective group of eunuchs who govern the city in accordance with the instructions of "the great tradition," i.e., Confucianism.[32] Similarly, the architecture of the city is both metaphor and metonymy of the riddle.

The representation in *Emperor* of what Taisuke Mitamura calls the "artificial third sex"[33] raises some interesting questions. The film's concretization and materialization of the unconscious castration threat challenges the basic premise of major feminist theoretical models of cinematic spectatorship, Laura Mulvey's in particular, which claim that narrative cinema induces mechanisms of voyeurism and fetishism in order to disavow the threat of castration aroused by the image of woman.[34]

The theoretical problems raised here are admittedly rare, because the representation of castrated men in cinema is not common. Moreover, eunuchs are perceived by the modern Western audience as grotesque rarities of the past who are associated with the Otherness of exotic cultures, such as those of ancient Egypt, Rome, and the Ottoman Empire. In *Emperor*, however, the spectator is confronted with the fact that eunuchs existed in the twentieth century, as well as with the materiality of the mise en scène that makes their presence real. Bertolucci exploits the voyeuristic potential of cinema to confront the spectator with real eunuchs. However, unlike the eunuchs in Balzac's *Sarrasine*, those in *Emperor* are not literary figures but rather a visual spectacle, something to look at.

Emperor's eunuchs are the representatives of the Dowager Empress, who possesses phallic power due to her acting in the service of patriarchal interests, as is evident in the opening scene and in her introductory conversation with Pu Yi.[35] The eunuchs are introduced to the audience in the separation scene when they take Pu Yi from his mother and bring him to the Forbidden City. In this nighttime scene, the eunuchs appear as silhouettes, dark shadows acting behind screens. Eventually, the eunuchs become Pu Yi's shadows or, rather, his doubles, and they follow him everywhere.[36] Within the framework of power relationships in the Forbidden City, the concept of shadow signifies absence of distinction between the monarch and his subjects, yet, from a psychoanalytic perspective the concept also symbolizes the lack of differentiation in the relationship between subject and object, or between self and Other. The eunuchs become Pu Yi's surrogate ego and the substitute for his parents. The process of differentiation reaches its climax when one of them is punished instead of Pu Yi.

The total control of the eunuchs over the child-emperor is associated with voyeuristic patterns of behavior. The camera reveals the eunuchs hiding behind walls, or in interior rooms, always monitoring Pu Yi. Their hide-and-seek strategy of control is made possible by the city's architecture, which exploits the tension between interiors and exteriors and the difficulties of orientation. Originally measures of the eunuchs' limitations, voyeurism and auditeurism become means of power and control, depriving Pu Yi of any intimacy or privacy and subordinating the needs of the "I" to those of the imperial order. Like the Platonic cave allegory in *The Conformist*, the shadow metaphor with which the eunuchs are associated and their scopophilia become a kind of built-in, self-reflexive commentary on spectatorial voyeurism and the relationship between sadism (the control of the Other) and voyeurism, which, according to Mulvey, are always intertwined.[37]

The inescapable presence of the eunuchs serves as a sort of metaphorical collective unconscious, a monstrous materialization of society's collective nightmares, the Freudian "return of the repressed." To use Robin Wood's phrasing, "The *Doppelgänger* motif reveals the Monster as normality's shadow."[38] Thus the mass expulsion of the eunuchs from the city expresses an attempt to repress a collective nightmare and to disavow the threat of what Freud called the uncanny.

The expulsion scene, a flashback told to the prison's governor (the analyst) from Pu Yi's point of view, is linked through editing to the scene in which Pu Yi has sex with both wives. In the expulsion scene, Pu Yi is seen standing on a wall, a wife at either side of him, and looking down at the 800 eunuchs holding small jars containing their severed organs while pleading for the emperor's mercy. The composition and framing of the expulsion scene not only confronts the ruler with his subjects/shadows but also confronts the "I" with its double/other and the whole person with the deficient man. The shadow, thus, is the reflection of the "I"'s castration anxiety.

The expulsion scene is a visualization of the repression not only of the castration fear, but also of latent homosexuality. As in all of Bertolucci's films, homosexual inclinations are hinted at but never fully realized.[39] Pu Yi is associated both with homosexuality and, through his loss of power, with the eunuchs. In his progressive loss of eyesight,[40] Pu Yi is also symbolically castrated.[41] The composition of the shot and the low camera angle in the expulsion scene symbolically turn Pu Yi into one of the eunuchs, one of the *kao sheng*.[42] The eunuchs raise the *pao*, the containers with their severed sexual organs, towards the one who is not—physically at least—an eunuch. The dance of the eunuchs around the little Pu Yi's bath, which reflects the Chinese myth concerning the four eunuch stars,[43] is thus displaced into repression of the internal and external threat of the castrated men in an attempt to create an illusory sense of manhood and omnipotence.

In order to deal with his psychological/sexual anxieties regarding his masculinity and potency, Pu Yi uses political authoritarian means. In contrast, the eunuchs, his shadows, use their loss of masculinity to advance their political careers. With masculinity represented by images of power, or by the pursuit of power, the worship

of the phallus becomes inseparable from the worship of political authority, as is especially evident in the expulsion scene, when the eunuchs bow to Pu Yi, who is wearing glasses for the first time. The
glasses acquire almost a fetish status, symbolically representing the
penis. According to Freud, who in "The Uncanny" establishes the relationship between castration anxiety, the fear of losing one's sight,
and the fear of one's father's death, and who sees the eye (in his discussion of the Oedipus myth) as a substitute organ for the penis, the
glasses (the "artificial eyes") become the signifier of illusory sexual
and political omnipotence. The expulsion scene in *Emperor*, enact-
ing a symbolic representation of the worship of the phallus as the
prime signifier of power and authority, recalls Paul/Brando's warning to Jeanne/Schneider in *Last Tango in Paris* regarding the dubious
benefits of bourgeois marriage in which the man feels "comfortable
and secure enough so that he can worship in front of the altar of his
own prick."

The eunuchs holding the *pao* in their hands and bowing to the
emperor render a powerful image of the desire to own the phallus and
to have what they are not permitted to have, namely power. The
scene symbolically articulates the typical Bertoluccian dialectic of
political oppression and sexual repression. The expulsion is dialectical in the sense that it is, on one hand, an attempt to suppress the internal fear of homosexuality, and on the other hand, an attempt to
externally project an image of authority, leadership, and potency. In
the patriarchal Fascist order, this image is intimately linked with the
notions of manhood, masculinity, and heterosexuality. The entire
scene is embedded with Fascist iconography. The figure of Pu Yi and
the choreography of the masses (the eunuchs) echo famous images
drawn from the collective memory of the Fascist (but also Communist) personality cult. Just as Marcello's appeal to fascism in *The
Conformist* is presented by Bertolucci as an attempt to repress homosexuality, so too is Pu Yi's emerging fascism. Hence, the spectacle of expulsion directed by Pu Yi becomes a synthetic metonymy
for the spectacle of history as interpreted by both Marx and Freud, a
metonymic spectacle of civilization marked by both sexual repression and political oppression.[44]

The temptation to compare the eunuchs with women seems almost inevitable. Both groups represent the lack and absence of the
phallus. Yet, it is obvious that the process of structuring absences in
the two cases is different. The question regarding the essence of eunuchism is a question of sexual identity (are eunuchs indeed the
"Third Sex"?). Moreover, eunuchism induces ambivalence: in one

sense, eunuchism is perceived as a barbaric, archaic, and uncivilized phenomenon and therefore as an anachronism; in another, despite its archaism, eunuchism is also a real concretization of the fear of castration.

As opposed to woman, the eunuch is unequivocal evidence that masculinity/manhood can be lost. The eunuch's husky, hoarse voice is an acoustic mirror of the visual imagery of castration. Moreover, unlike the fetishized image of the women in the film, the eunuchs' image is neither seductive nor pleasurable. The eunuchs are represented as anti-objects of desire. They are ugly, aging, and deformed and their presence is never alluring or tempting. These two images, one might speculate, increase the level of male unconscious anxiety regarding castration and consequently intensify the male spectator's identification with Pu Yi who himself is haunted by the eunuch, his shadow. The eunuchs who subvert binary definitions of sexuality seem to bring to full bloom, if not to crisis, Pu Yi's sexual identity.

Robert Kolker views Bertolucci's representation of women as problematic, observing that Bertolucci not only neglects to analyze their situation but "often places them in inferior or, worse, destructive roles."[45] Despite his apparent critique of society's reproduction of oppression/repression through the relationship of fathers and sons, Bertolucci himself seems imprisoned by the patriarchal order. This imprisonment is most evident in one of the first scenes of the film. When the little Pu Yi enters the Forbidden City for the first time, the camera moves from him crying inside the canopy of his carriage to the gates of the city, where three crying women tied to each other on a pillory reach their hands out to the rushing carriage.[46]

The image of the three women is a proleptic symbol in the film's overall formal and thematic economy, and most of the female characters in the film echo this economy by being punished through acts that are, first and foremost, social, public, and collective. Pu Yi's mother is destroyed through opium addiction and suicide, while his first wife suffers punishment through opium addiction, involvement in a lesbian relationship, infanticide, and the destruction of her health, beauty, and youth. Although the second wife, who demands a divorce from Pu Yi, seems to be free and independent, she quite quickly disappears from the narrative. Eastern Jewel, the pilot, is punished through the total collapse of her plans and conspiracies and the suicide of her Japanese collaborator. In the third and final part of the film no women remain, and their exit from the stage of history and from the spectacle of the epic film genre is complete, as is the history rewritten and emplotted by Bertolucci.

The concubines, perhaps, epitomize the film's representation of what it perceives as the female collective "I." When the twelve-year-old Pu Yi sucks Ar Mo's breast, the concubines watch the"perverted" scene with binoculars and are thus inscribed into the text as a collective built-in voyeur. Constituting an Imperial collective "I," the concubines do not fulfill a feminine function for Pu Yi. They are neither his mothers nor the objects of his desire, nor even sexual playmates as the eunuchs are. Instead, the concubines control Pu Yi by withholding sensual pleasure. Their collective identity as such is traditional and Imperial, although it also represents the constant tension between woman and mother. Whenever they appear, they are depicted as an enigmatic group whose main occupation is spying on Pu Yi and observing him from afar. When the optometrist discusses with Johnston Pu Yi's need for glasses, the concubines hide behind columns and listen to the conversation.[47]

Bertolucci does not individuate the characters in the group of concubines. In some scenes, such as the disrobing of the emperor and his new bride, the concubines perform their duties even though their faces do not appear in the frame. In contrast to the lack of power and influence displayed by Pu Yi's mother, the concubines maintain political power and do make decisions, such as expelling Ar Mo from the City. In this respect, their power, like that of the Empress Dowager Cixi, is phallic.

The processes and psychological/structural patterns related to the female characters, namely, the traumatic patterns of desertion, echo and mirror each other. Ar Mo's expulsion parallels the forced desertion of Pu Yi's mother, while the first wife's desertion, her opium addiction, her affair with Pu Yi's driver, and her lesbian relationship with Eastern Jewel echo the decadence of Pu Yi's mother (her opium addiction). The second wife's departure is a repetition of the same motif. To a certain extent, even the eunuchs' expulsion and Johnston's departure are variations on the same theme. Concerning La Luna, the only Bertolucci's film that has a woman as protagonist, Kolker observes: "[in] the Freudian-Lacanian model, he [Joe] must be 'saved' from this [the Oedipal crime] by that other owner of the phallus, the father. But in the body of the film there are no men present to 'save' Caterina or Joe . . . there are only homosexuals."[48] In the case of Emperor's symbolic incest, enacted through the adolescent Pu Yi's suckling of Ar Mo's breast, these men are the male tutors who save Pu Yi.

Presented in the opening scene of the film as a mother substitute and a nurturing environment, Ar Mo in the suckling scene is the epitomy of the two feminine functions of mother and wife. Despite the Oriental context of the scene the seductive imagery alludes to Christian mythology—specifically to the Virgin Mother—by invoking a portrayal of the maternal that, to use Julia Kristeva's words, "reduces social anguish and gratifies a male being."[49] The fetishization of Ar Mo in the suckling scene and her position as an incestuous object of desire is paralleled in the scene between Eastern Jewel and Pu Yi's first wife. The fetishization is carried even further in the latter scene, culminating in the punishment of the deviant wife and her expulsion from her husband's home and finally from the narrative itself.

Not only do the emperor's two wives have no impact on Chinese history in the transition from empire to republic, but the role of women in the Maoist and Cultural Revolution is totally suppressed by Bertolucci. In a film spanning sixty years of Chinese history, women are represented as subjugated to the symbolic order, ineffective, and associated with desertion, opium addiction, suicide, mental breakdown, and the destruction of their own sex through sexual seduction. This unimpressive repertoire of feminine attributes results in the narrative's treatment of women as objects of desire and signifiers of castration threat rather than as sovereign subjects participating in history. Man is in the center of the narrative. It is he who undergoes reeducation and psychological/political change, and the film does not touch upon the sexual and familial revolution in Communist China. Furthermore, as noted, the female characters in the film become nonexistent, almost ethereal. The disappearance of females from the narrative has varied manifestations. For example, Ar Mo is taken away by carriage from the palace, the second consort disappears in the rain in a mock homage to *Singin' in the Rain*, and Eastern Jewel fixes a desperate look at a vacant room after the suicide of her collaborator.

Eastern Jewel, the female pilot and spy, is another of Bertolucci's variations on the theme of bisexuality so typical of his work. Her occupation, appearance, and behavior challenge binary thinking related to sexual identity. Although the signifiers of her identity belong to the phallic domain, her representation as a destructive *femme fatale* and as a "spider woman"—borrowing from the misogynist tradition of *film noir*—foregrounds her femininity as a cultural construct that draws on the resources of genre tradition in cinema. Her punishment can be seen in the dispossession of her phallic power, with the suggestion that such power wielded by a woman is only temporary and illusory.[50] The sexual ambiguity of the

A fetishized image of lesbian decadence in *The Last Emperor.* Empress Wan Jung (Joan Chen, r.) is turned into an opium addict by the Japanese spy Eastern Jewel (Maggie Han), a destructive *femme fatale* and spider woman. Courtesy of The Museum of Modern Art, Film Stills Archive.

film's characters, what we may call Bertolucci's "poetics of indeterminacy," does not stop the film from symbolically annihilating its women. Significantly, Pu Yi is the film's pivotal character and his voice is the privileged one.

Bertolucci's "poetics of indeterminacy," which results in the annihilation of all women in the text, is supported by the structure of the narrative and by the director's choice of the epic film genre. Victor Turner uses the term "social drama" to describe the universal form of political processes and social/cultural changes.[51] According to Turner some genres, and, in particular, the epic genre, can be used as paradigms for the actions typical of important political leaders. Social drama provides them with style and emplots their lives accordingly. *Emperor* combines the psychohistorical approach (the view that personal history is no less important than public history)[52] with the epic genre while inverting one of the conventions of the genre through the portrayal of an anti-epic hero. As a psychohistorical film, *Emperor* presents its anti-hero, Pu Yi, as if he were a patient in analysis and renders China's political and historical events through his neuroses, or, rather, psychopathology. Yet Bertolucci himself, in an attempt to revise the Western view of brainwashing, has described the analysis that Pu Yi goes through as *psicanalisi forzata* (forced analysis).[53]

Linked to the issue of analysis is the issue of the symbolic order which, after all, is the ghost behind the forced analysis. A unique aspect of *Emperor* is its depiction of two symbolic orders, the Confucian and the Maoist. According to Kolker, *1900* "creates two symbolic orders, the capitalist and the socialist—each with their own modes of discourse—with a third, the fascist, beginning as an extension of the first and overwhelming both."[54] In contrast, *Emperor* creates two competing (but also completing) orders, and the spectator follows the development of the individual from one order to the other. The existence of two orders emphasizes the dominance and continuity of fathers and the patriarchal structure.

Despite the political impotence of Pu Yi's biological father and his neglect in the narrative, his absent presence (recalling the absent presence of, to use Kolker's words, the "ghost fathers" in *Last Tango*) embodies Confucian ideology which, symbolically, castrates Pu Yi. The Maoist order replacing the Confucian seems to castrate Pu Yi as well. Politically, it turns him into the last emperor and, sexually, it announces the appearance of a new father, a new emperor. The personality cult of Mao during the Cultural Revolution is evident in the scene of the Red Guards' procession in Beijing's streets, for this scene reproduces the Freudian theme of rebellion against paternal authority (the *padre/padrone* theme), culminating in the recurrent cycle of domination-rebellion-domination. According to Freud, this cycle marks the history of both the individual and civilization.

At this late stage in Pu Yi's life the sexual dimension seems marginal to the process of creating a new man, and the question of whether communism castrates desire is left open. The emphasis shifts from desire to collective action. The Communist uniformity (the grayness, dreariness, and colorlessness of the rehabilitation center, the near-facelessness of the masses on the streets, and so on) is contrasted with the luxury, splendor, and colors of the Imperial style—with the comparison working to the benefit of Communist uniformity. Chinese communism is presented as "le temps retrouve" (time regained), a worthy substitute to the loss of parents and childhood and as a successful solution to the Oedipus complex. In this respect, politics wins over sexuality, and Bertolucci's dialectic of political oppression/sexual repression is resolved in non-dialectical fashion.

When emplotting Pu Yi's life, Bertolucci chose not to present the last emperor's homosexuality or his sadism in its more perverted aspects (beating to death young boys and girls, for example). Bertolucci also chose not to mention that Pu Yi was married to five women or that, when he was released from prison, the authorities forced him to marry a nurse who was a member of the Communist party. Bertolucci's conscious liberties with and omissions from the historical text are obviously meaningful. In interviews he has repeatedly stated "I didn't try to make the film a historical documentary. What I'm interested in is history refracted by imagination."[55]

Although Bertolucci's omissions emphasize the film's moral drama, that is, the human potential to change and transform, their didactic dimension is dubious from a feminist point of view because they marginalize, perhaps even abolish, the role of women in the political/educational process. Identification with an anti-hero like Pu Yi is possible and moral only if he can become a hero through a process of self-correction (the film's notion of reeducation). Yet, this psychoanalytic/political process is exclusively conducted by male tutors and assigned to and enjoyed by the male protagonist alone.

Bertolucci, like Borges (one of his favorite authors), is, as Longxi says, "particularly sensitive to the problematic of the Other, and the theme of double identities runs throughout his works. In these works, the Other often turns out to be no other than the Self."[56] Within the context of Emperor, the theme of the double operates on many levels, the autobiographical as well as the didactic/ideological. In addition to being a Bildungsroman unfolding the history of the self, the film is a political didactic discourse suggesting that the Chinese Other is also a potential correcting and corrected mirror of the Western capitalist world. Furthermore, the political didacticism of the film is a latent statement on the power of cinema to reinvent the past and to reconstruct history, a process that parallels the reconstruction and correction of the self through analysis. The transition of China from the illusions of the Imperial past to the reality of the present is similar to the ability of the film spectator, on the film's reflexive level, to resist the seduction of the "imaginary" (the feminine) and to recognize, in Althusserian terms, "the effective presence of a new reality: ideology."[57]

The word revolution in Chinese is heh ming meaning "to change the mandate" (the emperor's "mandate of Heaven"). Bertolucci's Emperor brings the Italian director's cycle of utopian revolutionism to its final stop: the realm of the real in which women's difference is liquidated and woman becomes man's double.

It is most significant that women appear in the movie only in association with China's past. Whenever the film deals with the Maoist order, the domain of the real, women are absent. This statement is not contradicted by the fact that women do appear in the scene of the Red Guards' procession in Beijing's streets, a scene depicting what Bertolucci called the "mise en scène" of the Chinese Cultural Revolution. In this Chinese living theater, masses of men and women perform gymnastics, while rhythmically and energetically waving red flags and Mao's red book. The women are dressed like the men and all the demarcation lines of sexual difference are blurred and dissolved for the sake of uniformity. The victory of the collective thus is represented as the victory of the male discourse over the female's with the result that women are rendered effectively absent.

The structure of *Emperor*, and especially its oscillation between reflective distancing and spectacular pleasure, require a multifaceted analysis that goes "beyond the pleasure principle." The text of Bertolucci's film maneuvers the reader and the critic alike through an endless dialectic of desire. But the victory of the real over the imaginary, the symbolic annihilation of women, and the absence of signs of difference from the utopian vision of Maoist China as the West's Other suggest, in the last instance, the death of desire.

The Sheltering Sky

The brochure-like book published by Scribners as part of the publicity campaign surrounding the release of Bernardo Bertolucci's film *The Sheltering Sky*—based on the novel by Paul Bowles—starts its portrait of the film as follows: "1947. An ocean liner from New York sets Kit and Port Moresby down in Tangier. They are seasoned adventurers with no plans to return. Their friend Tunner wants to return with snapshots and stories of sexual conquests. He is a tourist. They are travellers."[58] This description, and the distinction made by both the novelist and the scriptwriters of *The Sheltering Sky* between tourists and travelers, recalls an emerging interest in tourism research: points of convergence and divergence between pilgrimage and tourism.[59]

Any analysis of *The Sheltering Sky* should consider some of these current discussions among anthropologists, sociologists, and literary and film scholars to provide, to use Clifford Geertz's words, a "thick description" of the film.[60] If, indeed, *The Sheltering Sky* is yet another manifestation of colonial discourse, then it may well be read as a tourist film, exploiting the exoticism of the Other. Yet the film is open to negotiated readings, and, in many respects, it may be seen as subverting rather than enforcing the colonial discourse. The fact that it partially draws on the road film genre as well as on the Existentialist tradition (whose influence can be easily detected in Bowles's novel) obviously goes beyond its concern with the anthropological Other.

Although Camus's brand of Existentialism is intimately—if not physically, mentally, and geographically—connected to the North African/Mediterranean landscape while the issue of the Other occupies Sartre's Existentialist analyses, their presence in Bertolucci/Bowles's *The Sheltering Sky* provides both film and book with the dignity of a soul-searching and existential/metaphysical journey/quest that goes beyond anthropology. From this vantage point the film can be read as a travel film, expressing a movement toward the religious/cosmic Other and not the anthropological one.

The nature of the relationship between *The Sheltering Sky* and colonial discourse assumes special interest given the fact that the plot of the film, as well as that of the novel, occurs in the immediate aftermath of the Second World War—that is to say at the moment when the long chapter of decolonization was just beginning. In that period "Africa alone held out the hopes of a new continent" and "the Sahara could still serve as a backdrop to the kind of radical self-interrogation to which Port and Kit Moresby subject themselves."[61] Bowles himself who moved permanently to Tangier, Morocco, in 1950 was fleeing "imperialist land, the America of John Wayne. Similarly his protagonists flee those continents where the war has left too many traces; they abandon a world in which they no longer recognise themselves. The idea of remaining in this self-styled civilization has become intolerable to them as it would imply their complicity in what is happening to it."[62]

John Urry distinguishes between the mass character of the gaze of tourists and the individual character of the gaze of the traveler. His definition of a tourist as someone who has "a clear intention to return 'home' within a relatively short period of time"[63] fits perfectly the definitions of both Bowles and Bertolucci regarding the distinction between tourists and travelers.[64] The nostalgic, elitist view expressed by Bowles is not surprising given the historical context of his novel (the end of World War II and the rapid development of mass transportation which engendered the rise of mass tourism) and his status as an American expatriate and literary pilgrim. The nostalgic view expressed by Bertolucci, however, is rooted in different ground. Bertolucci's disaffection with the West manifested itself in the 1980s through a romantic search for new utopias in the East. *The Last Emperor* is the first example of this quest, and its last scene, in which a group of tourists gaze at what is left of the Imperial glamour of The Forbidden City, epitomizes the victorious gaze of mass tourism. This scene can be read as "the archetypical tourist's (or ethnographer's) frustration at witnessing the paradox of his activity: tourism (like colonialism) destroys the very authenticity it desires."[65]

The romantic conception of the traveler in Bowles's and Bertolucci's works invokes the current sociological/anthropological analysis of tourism as sacred quest, displacing "the profound spiritual quest of the past, epitomized in the ancient traveller or pilgrim."[66] Erik Cohen, following Mircea Eliade, distinguishes between pilgrims and travelers. According to Cohen, while the Center is the goal of the pilgrim, the Other is the goal of the traveler.[67] Socially and religiously the traveler's attraction to the primordial chaotic Other is conceived, in traditional cultures and societies, as dangerous and heretical. Yet, the traveler's role became socially more acceptable with the coming of modernity and the replacement of a mythic/religious world view with rationality. The perceived shrinking of the world engenders a situation in which only the wild regions beyond the boundaries of civilization preserve some qualities of Otherness. In the process of the growth of modern travel, "landscapes are transformed into 'attractions', not because they symbolize one's own culture, but precisely because they are different—allegedly harboring an 'authenticity' which modernity has lost."[68] Hence, tourism becomes "an invasion outwards from the highly developed and metropolitan centers into the uncivilized peripheries."[69] The "traveler-tourist" version "grew in importance as modern man became increasingly alienated from his world, and departed, or escaped, in search of recuperation and relief, into its periphery. . . . For those most alienated from modernity, indeed, the search is crowned by the discovery of a new, personal or 'elective' Center not shared by the co-members of their society of origin."[70]

Porter, the male protagonist of *The Sheltering Sky* and Bowles's alter-ego, is a combination of two of the four modes (the diversionary, the experiential, the experimental, and the existential) of the touristic experience of alienated individuals described by Cohen. He is both the experimental and the existential.[71] Bowles's description of the difference between a tourist and a traveler expresses his rejection of the American center. For Bowles, an American expatriate alienated from his own civilization, the new "elective center" is Arab civilization encountered in the periphery of the modern world.

What Bowles calls "Arab fatalism" becomes for him an authentic alternative to the"huge monstrous 'non-culture', a 'non-civilization' " and"apocalypse" that is America today.[72]

Bertolucci inherited his romantic nostalgia for a pure civilization—i.e., one onterior to Western contamination—from his first cinematic mentor, Pasolini, whose heretical ideas concerning the reverence of primal pre-industrial reality were strongly criticized at the time he expressed them.[73] His polemics against the cultural logic of late capitalism, as Giuliana Bruno suggests, "were generally taken as nostalgia for an archaic world."[74] Pasolini's hatred of the worldwide spread of what he termed "cultura homogenieta" (homogenious culture)—characterized by consumerism, and the destruction of "authentic" cultures—moved him in 1973 to create *The Arabian Nights*, the last movie in his "trilogy of life."[75] The film was shot on various exotic locations in Nepal, Yemen, Iran, and Ethiopia in the hope of discovering in these uncontaminated regions a free sexuality devoid of the repression and exploitation typical of industrialized Western societies.

The intertextual links between *The Sheltering Sky* and *Arabian Nights*, such as the evocation of Oriental landscapes and the film's homosexual motifs,[76] further accentuate Pasolini's influence on Bertolucci. The fact that Pasolini synthesized several remote geographical regions of the Third World to construct a concept of the Orient, in particular a concept of liberated Oriental sexuality, emphasizes the function of the East as the desired imaginary of the West. The hypersexualization of the East, with its promise of, to use Edward Said's words, "excessive 'freedom of intercourse' "[77] and "freedom of licentious sex,"[78] is a European invention whose cinematic expression in the 1970s and 1980s can be found in works of directors such as Pasolini and Rainer Werner Fassbinder.[79] Pasolini's celebration of imaginary Oriental sexuality, as well as of violent sexual encounters—in his cinema and life alike—was intimately related to his proclaimed beliefs in the purity of the Third World and the world-historical victory of "the agricultural subproletariat of the Third World (and the Italian South) over Europe's weakening and thoroughly compromised bourgeois civilization."[80] A similar view is expressed by both Bowles and Bertolucci whose depiction of Kit's (the "sophisticated daughter of Scott and Zelda Fitzgerald," as Bertolucci called her) erotic obsession with the Tuareg Belqassim, can be read as analogous to the West's confrontation with the violent and vital sexual vigor of the Third World. Yet, instead of being rejuvenated by the more virile Other, Kit is physically and mentally destroyed. Her loss of mind signifies the victory of the dark-skinned races over white decadence.

Pasolini, as Roy MacBean rightly observes, "unbashedly became a tourist of the *'exotic'* as *erotic liberation,* and tried to pass this off as the 'real' revolution."[81] Paul Bowles's *The Sheltering Sky,* like Pasolini's *Arabian Nights,* embodies all the old colonialist projections concerning the imaginary Arab sexuality. The second part of the novel, beginning with Port's death, takes the form of a rape narrative rife with white male fantasies on the sexual energies of dark-skinned peoples. At the begining of the novel, as Millicent Dillon observes, "Kit Moresby is the observer, while her husband Port is the protagonist. . . . But by the end of the novel, Kit is no longer the spectator outside the action. After Port's death, she goes deeper and deeper into the Sahara and descends into darkness and madness."[82] The penetration into the Sahara and Africa with its inevitable fall into madness assumes the form of colonial travel literature exemplified by Joseph Conrad's *Heart of Darkness.*

Kit's rape in the novel by the imaginary Tuareg Belqassim follows the tradition of colonial Orientalist discourse in its representation of the Other's sexual prowess.

> There was an animal-like quality in the firmness with which he held her, affectionate, sensuous, wholly irrational—gentle but of a determination that only death could gainsay. . . . In his behavior there was a perfect balance between gentleness and violence that gave her particular delight . . . but she knew beforehand that it was hopeless, that even if they had a language in common, he never could understand her.[83]

Bertolucci, it should be pointed out, resisted this sexually overcharged Orientalist fantasy of rape. "Discussing with the Tuaregs," he said, "I learnt that they deny that rape, or any form of carnal violence, exists in their culture. Theirs is a matriarchal society. So it occurred to me perhaps the end of the book was a kind of fantasy on Bowles' part. It was not to be taken too seriously. . . . This is why there is no explicit violence in the film. In this sense the film is different from the book."[84]

Although Bowles's fantasy of gentle/violent rape was expelled from Bertolucci's text, the film *The Sheltering Sky* is immersed with fantasies and fetishizations of Oriental/African/Arab Otherness, most of them concerned with the hypersexualization and hypersensualisation of the Other. Such are, for example, the nudity and dance imagery which exhibit the body of the Other as a site of sensuality and exotica. Even Bertolucci's by now famous poetics of sexual indeterminacy, potentially promising a truly liberated sexuality (see chapter 6), is burdened with the weight of this colonial discourse. His famous preoccupation with themes of bisexuality and the double are echoed in a series of bisexual figures. One such example is a young girl/boy in the wagon of nomad Arabs who wears a Panama hat, and resembles a similar character (also wearing a colonial hat) in *The Spider's Stratagem*. Kit herself, with her short hair, is modeled after Jane Bowles and communicates a bisexual energy.[85] In the beginning of the movie she is wearing the heavy makeup of a Manhattan sophisticate. Gradually her look becomes more natural, she becomes suntanned and seems more adapted to her surroundings. In the second part of both the novel and the film Kit is disguised as an Arab boy in an attempt to fool Belqassim's wives. She eats, sleeps, and thirsts for her Tuareg's secret visits. These trysts become the obsessive center of her existence.

Themes of bisexuality and sexual disguise are common in colonial discourse. Josef Von Sternberg's *Morocco*, for example, tells the love story of a vaudeville singer and a foreign legionnaire. The ship's captain who brings the vaudeville actresses to Marakesh calls them "suicide passengers," explaining that they buy one-way tickets because they never return home. As in *The Sheltering Sky* and other colonial narratives (for example Conrad's *Heart of Darkness*, and E. M. Forster's *Passage to India*), the text suggests that the alluring fascination of the Other and the desire it invokes culminate in madness. In *Morocco* Amy Jolly (Marlene Dietrich) follows her lover Tom Brown (Gary Cooper), the legionnaire, into the heart of the Sahara Desert. The last shot shows her kicking off her high-heeled gold sandals as she vanishes in the sand dunes of the desert. Amy Jolly, like Kit in *The Sheltering Sky*, immerses herself (literally) in the sands of the desert. Hence, the power of the desert/Orient, the film suggests, causes women to transgress social conventions, to surrender to archaic forces (the id). The image of the Sahara Desert becomes an image of madness, uncontrollable passion, and irrationality that leads to the destruction of the white race.[86]

Marlene Dietrich, herself a legendary bisexual cult figure, first appears in *Morocco* with a veil to accentuate her status as an object of desire and to suggest unveiling. In the film *The Sheltering Sky*, Debra Winger appears, while with Belqassim, with a blue Indigo veil that masks her face, but brings out the color of her blue (non-Oriental) eyes. Her veiling, although justified by the logic of the narrative, is problematic given the fact that in Tuareg culture only men cover their faces with an Indigo turban.[87] However, in accordance with Bertolucci's poetics of sexual indeterminacy, and within the tradition of colonial discourse, the real object of desire is Belqassim, the Other, whose face is always veiled during their journey in the desert and is only briefly unveiled in the harem during an erotic scene with Kit. Like Fassbinder's Moroccan man—played by one of Fassbinder's own homosexual lovers, El Hedi Ben Salem—in both *Ali: Fear Eats the Soul* and *Fox and His Friends*, and Pasolini's southern "ragazzi" and "sacred barbarians," Belqassim personifies stereotypes of racial virility and vitality. Bertolucci said on the casting of Eric Vu-An (a leading dancer with the Paris Opera) as Belqassim that "perhaps the explanation is that Belqassim is a figure who, both in the book and in the film, stands outside all known psychological convention."[88] The Western association of Belqassim with transgression of conventional morality and Western inhibitions follows in the tradition of colonial discourse with its depiction of the Orient as a place which "seems to have offended sexual propriety"[89] and suggests "untiring sensuality, unlimited desire, deep generative energies"[90] and "escapism of sexual fantasy."[91] Hence, as Said suggests, the Orient becomes "a place where one could look for sexual experience unobtainable in Europe."[92] "Hiding beneath that turban," Bertolucci said, "is desire, the desirer, and the desired—all at once. He is the man without a face and without a country. The true nomad."[93]

Interlinked with the representation of the Oriental Other in *The Sheltering Sky* is the view of women as Other. Women in *The Sheltering Sky*, as in other colonial narratives, are seen as being especially susceptible to madness and hysteria. The desert seems more dangerous to women than to men because of the traditional equation between nature and woman. In the novel, and the movie, David Thomson suggests, Kit is the true traveler "who will go deeper into the unknown than Port."[94] This explains the notion of the feminization of the Orient suggested both by *The Sheltering Sky* and other colonial narratives. As Urry points out, until the nineteenth century access to travel was largely the preserve of men. But this changed with the development of Victorian lady travelers, some of whom visited countries considered at the time to be uncivilized and uncharted.[95] Although Kit is portrayed as a sophisticated twentieth century woman, her being swept way into an irrational sexual adventure with Belqassim recalls the sexual fantasies of the heroine in *Passage to India* whose encounter with the sensuality of India engages her (actually her male narrator-creator) in fantasies of rape. The

An "escapism of sexual fantasy" in *The Sheltering Sky.*
The unveiled Kit (Debra Winger) and the veiled Belqassim
(Eric Vu-An) penetrate the heart of the Sahara Desert. "Hiding beneath that turban," Bertolucci said "is desire, the desirer, and the desired—all at once. He is the man without a
face and without a country. The true nomad." From the author's private collection.

intensity of the involvement of the fictional heroine in both the
novel and the film with the natives was projected into real life as
well and incorporated into the narrative of the film production.

So involved did she become in the character of Kit that at the
end of filming Winger could not face an immediate return to the
western world. To "come down" from her weeks in north Africa
she took off for a week to explore the deserts of Tenere and Air
in Niger, guided by the Tuaregs who appear in the film. She describes the film as "the story of the journey of a relationship. As
it is an inner journey so it is also a journey in a landscape."[96]

The scenes of nudity in *The Sheltering Sky* are marked by anatomical mapping of exposure for white and dark women. While only the bottom parts of the white woman (Debra Winger) are exposed, only the full breasts of Mahrnia, the Arab girl who seduces Port, are shown. Mahrnia is played by the young Moroccan singer from Carthage in Tunisia, Amina Annabi. The use of Annabi, who is currently enjoying immense success on the wave of Arab pop music now being taken up by the West (she appeared in the 1991 Eurovision with an ethnic song and won second prize), goes hand-in-hand with the use of ethnic music from the Jajouka band, for centuries court musicians in Morocco.

The images of Paul/Port and Jane/Kit as the lonely individual travelers penetrating the mysterious periphery of the cosmic world of the Other (emblematized by the penetration into the Sahara and its Arab/African culture) is interlinked with issues of exile and displacement regarding both the life and work of expatriates and, in particular, expatriate artists. Indeed within the theoretical framework of the sociology of tourism some emigrants, Graham Dann and Erik Cohen claim, can be classified as expatriates or even as "permanent tourists." As they observe, an element of fantasy exists in both emigration and tourism.[97] The articulation of relations between "home" (the Center in anthropological discourse which stresses the travel dimension of tourism) and "voluntary exile" (elective Center) was central to the life and work of the American expatriates living in Paris in the 1920s and 1930s.[98] The tradition of American expatriates in Paris was established by writers like Ernest Hemingway, and continued to flourish with e. e. cummings, Henry Miller, Norman Mailer, Gertrude Stein, and others. In fact Paul Bowles himself left for Paris in 1929 where he wrote compositions and poetry. Gertrude Stein discouraged him from writing poetry and dispatched him and his master Aaron Copland to Tangier. Bowles visited Tangier for the first time in 1931 with Copland and returned to live there permanently in the 1950s with his wife Jane, whom he married in 1937. Also a writer, Jane published the novel *Two Serious Ladies* in 1942. She died in 1973.

There is a certain irony in the fact that Bowles, who left the metropolitan Center in search for a new elective Center in the peripheric East, became himself a sort of elective Center and a site of pilgrimage for the Beat Generation. Tangier, city of sinister repute, became home to the Beat Generation of William Burroughs, Allen Ginsberg, and Gregory Corso. For many of the 1960s hippies, Bowles became a guru, and his home at Tangier attracted many pilgrims who were in the process of finding themselves.[99]

Bertolucci imagined Port and Kit as two sophisticated intellectuals from Manhattan. They are, he said, "like the children of Zelda and Scott Fitzgerald who in 1947 find out that what used to be the cultural oxygen of their milieu was the glamour of the Fitzgerald genre. They leave and go looking for something else. They leave because they feel their story is broken into a thousand pieces and they come to North Africa to try to reconstruct the broken thing."[100]

Paul Bowles's choice of the Orient as an elective Center followed, to rely on Said, a long and established tradition of nineteenth-century French pilgrims who

> did not seek a scientific so much as an exotic yet especially attractive reality. This is obviously true of the literary pilgrims, beginning with Chateaubriand, who found in the Orient a locale sympathetic to their private myths, obsessions and requirements. Here we notice how all the pilgrims, but especially the French ones, exploit the Orient in their work so as in some urgent way to justify their existential vocation.[101]

Bowles, the existential traveler-tourist, according to Robert Briatte, the author of the only authorized biography on Paul Bowles, had on a May night in 1947 a dream of Tangier, the "white city." "In the labyrinth of the unconscious the images of his dreams delineated a landscape of quite startling precision: narrow little alleys designed to make one lose one's way, terraces looking out over the ocean, staircases ascending nowhere."[102] As a result of this vocational dream, Briatte observes, Bowles decided to spend the summer in Morocco and to write. He left his wife Jane in the United States and that August in Fez he began writing *The Sheltering Sky*. Bowles's delirious moment of unconscious epiphany, and his hallucinatory vision of Tangier as a chaotic, mysterious, and labyrinthine city, invokes the archeological and geographical metaphors prevalent in colonial discourse on the Orient. Bertolucci, also, used a similar vocabulary to describe Port and Kit's journey into the Sahara.

> They go back into the past of North Africa. To reach the truth they have to go deeper into the Sahara, they have to pass through the ruins of the Kasbah and the abandoned ksour that takes them into the labyrinth of tunnels . . . somewhere very

obscure and somewhere very big. There isn't anything in the world that gives you a sense of timelessness like the desert. Port and Kit's trip to the desert is parallel to their trip into the past.[103]

The Oriental desert in both Bowles's and Bertolucci's discourses becomes the id of Western civilization. Here colonial, anthropological, archeological, and psychoanalytic discourses are clearly interwoven. The trip to the desert is the quest for the past, that of the individuals Kit and Port, as well as of Western civilization in search of its Eastern roots.

Bowles's abandonment of the metropolitan centers of colonialism is reenacted by his protagonists in *The Sheltering Sky*. In a way, both deny complicity in the conditions of these centers, as well as of the colonies. Yet what Said claims with respect to the presence of a European in the Orient can be applied to the presence of an American in the East, particularly a very European American like Bowles: "To be a European in the Orient *always* involves being a consciousness set apart from, and unequal with, its surroundings."[104] Even the innocent presence of a literary pilgrim, a traveler-tourist in search of elective Center poses questions regarding cooption in the colonial discourse.

The complexity regarding the relationship of literary pilgrims or expatriates like Bowles to the colonial discourse must be considered first on the level of their physical presence in the colony or ex-colony which, as Said observes, sets up a consciousness alien to its surrounding. Second, it can be studied on the textual level. When examining the textuality and ideology of the novel *The Sheltering Sky*, the dominance of the colonial discourse vis-à-vis the hypersexualization of the Other is especially apparent. Yet, despite the prominence of Orientalist presuppositions in the representation of the Arab/African Other, there remains a certain ambiguity. The fascination with the Sahara and the desire to penetrate to the interior of Africa can be read, as was suggested before, as the desire to conquer and demystify the Other, as well as to unveil the past of the West.[105] Yet this very attraction, within the conceptual framework of the novel in its historical context, is presented as subversive in relation to the metropolitan center. This is best illustrated by the interior monologue of Miss Ferry, the woman from the American consulate in Algiers who takes care of Kit after she manages to escape. Presumably giving voice to the official and dominant American ideology of the late 1940s, Miss Ferry meditates: "There is something repulsive about an American without money in his pocket. . . . She asked herself what possible attraction the parched interior of Africa could have for any civilized person."[106] Here Kit's (and indirectly Port's and Bowles's) fascination with the unconscious of their own American civilization (the interior of Africa) is presented as a threat to the American way of life. It also suggests why the rights to produce the film have never been supplied by Hollywood. As William Aldrich, the son of Robert Aldrich who owned the rights for the novel, notes, "Some readers in Hollywood were frightened by the implied criticism of capitalism—what else, after all, could so tarnish two beautiful, talented people? Remember, this was mid-McCarthy time."[107]

The questions regarding the implications of Bertolucci's film in colonial discourse touch, of course, on issues of representation and textuality and their celebration of primitivism. But, in addition, they relate to issues of production. Here, in fact, we deal with a problematic associated with a much larger phenomenon regarding film productions in the Third World. Classical questions regarding colonialism, recalling those relating to tourism in the Third World, cannot but be raised in this context: Does the production destroy the very authenticity it strives to represent? Are the natives (those who become the object of the cinematic gaze, and those who help the film crews or provide services for the production) being exploited?

The brochures accompanying the release of Bertolucci's *The Sheltering Sky* emphasize the producers' persistent search for uncontaminated regions of authenticity: "The filmmakers traveled thousands of miles across mountains and deserts surviving illness, storms and flood to end up in Niger where no feature film crew had ever been before."[108] Yet the same brochures emphasize the destruction of authenticity in other locations by earlier film productions. This is how the brochures describe one of the shooting locations (Ouarzazate in Morocco): "Ouarzazate was once a small village with no paved roads and only a mud-built Kasbah, but now is a sprawling town with three modern hotels perched on the hillside facing the Kasbah, courtesy of the film business. Films such as *Lawrence of Arabia* and *The Man Who Would Be King* came in search of sunshine and sand and created a whole new industry."[109] In order to avoid any impression that the natives or the Tuaregs were exploited, the brochures also emphasize the benefits brought to them by the film crews.

Cinema's craze for the authentic and exotic spectacle (what Ella Shohat calls "the National Geographic mania") is fully exploited in those films shot at the periphery of the globe, in Third World countries. *The Sheltering Sky* is no exception. In fact in the second part of the film, the narrative becomes secondary and the desert landscape, and later the idealized Otherness of the Tuareg culture, become the real protagonists. The vastness and beauty of the desert, as in the classical Westerns, dwarf the human subjects and overwhelm the heroine and the spectator alike. Whereas *The Last Emperor* is characterized by excessive signifiers of the Orient (lush foliage, peacock feathers, brocades, and silk) *The Sheltering Sky* emphasizes the simplicity and purity of the desert and its sand dunes. The blue and yellow color schemes prevail in the scenes in which Kit and the Tuaregs journey deeper into the Sahara. Bertolucci's customary ornamental tendency is restrained in these scenes but it blooms again in his portrayal of the tribal people whose bodies, clothes, and jewelry are paraded and fetishized recalling Pasolini's parades of "sacred barbarians" in films such as *Medea, Arabian Nights,* and *Oedipus Rex.*[110]

The desert is a geographic metaphor for the private id of the heroine as well as for the collective id of Western civilization. But the geographical desert is also a metaphor for an inner desert. The journey takes place on two planes simultaneously: in the actual desert, and in the inner desert of the spirit. As the menacing id of Western civilization, the desert causes the physic and psychic disintegration of Port and Kit. As they journey deeper into some of Africa's most inhospitable terrain, so they move further apart from each other and surrender to the alien surroundings.

The brochures of the film, posing as tourist brochures promoting "authenticity" and "idealized typicalities of the other,"[111] emphasize that the movie was filmed entirely on location in Tangier, the Kasbahs and lush oasis towns of Erfoud and Ouarzazate in Morocco, remote villages in Algeria and Niger, and the extraordinary sandscapes of the Sahara. Indeed all the signifiers of the desert and Arab/African culture are condensed in the film: camels, sand dunes, turbans, authentic jewelry, and so on. The visual rhetoric of the African Orient resembles the staged and contrived authenticity typical of postcards, perhaps the most commodified product of tourism culture. The first shots of the film representing New York City are in brown colors, invoking the nostalgic look of old 1950s postcards. The nostalgic postcard-like look of the film emphasizes that the film is both a visualization of an inner journey and a journey into external landscapes.

Marc Peploe who wrote the script for *The Sheltering Sky* (with Bertolucci) notes:

I read *The Sheltering Sky* in 1964 and felt an extraordinary sense of recognition about the world it describes. Five years later, when I gave up documentary film-making and decided to write a screenplay, this was the novel I wanted to adapt. But Robert Aldrich owned the rights and wouldn't part with them. So I wrote another story called *The Passenger* which begins with a man who dies in the desert and another man who takes his identity and inherits his journey. Life as a road movie.[112]

Cinema, travel, and identity, as Peploe suggests, are inextricably linked.[113]

Paul and Jane's and Kit and Port's searches for something different to replace the American dream directs them to another continent, to North Africa. At the very same moment in precisely the same place, Existentialism was being born. The novel *The Sheltering Sky* actually starts with Kit, Port, and Tunner disembarking in the Algerian harbor of Oran. However, a different choice was made in the film. Tangier was substituted for the legendary free port of Oran, where West meets East and North meets South, thus imaging a colorful gateway to Africa. The replacement of Oran with Tangier may be seen as a preference for the tourist discourse over the Existentialist. Oran is the city that falls prey to the plague in Albert Camus's Existentialist novel *The Plague*. Camus's antiromantic style and vision, tending toward what Barthes later called the "zero degree of writing" emphasizes, especially in *The Stranger*, the centrality of the "geographic presence" in metaphysics. There, the Mediterranean experience (the glittering sun, the sea, and the dazzling heat) are in part responsible for the otherwise inexplicable and absurd murder committed by Meursault, the protagonist to whose field of vision the narrative is restricted.

The title of the novel *The Sheltering Sky* is taken from a song popular before the First World War, "Down Among the Sheltering Palms." Paul Bowles said that from the age of four he was fascinated, not by the tune, but by the word *sheltering*. "What did the palm trees shelter people from, and how sure could they be of protection?" he asked. "We think of the sky as light and bright but in fact it is black if you get beyond the earth. With the book I was saying 'don't believe in the sky except that it protects us from the dark, beyond it is just blackness.' When Port says it protects us from what lies behind, what lies behind is nothing."[114] This metaphysical Existentialist quality (with its flavor of Camus's Mediterranean brand of Existentialism signified by the palm tree) was adapted to the film through the materiality of the mise en scène with its emphasis on the geographic presence of the landscape. But the Existentialist quality is conveyed even in the indoor scenes and in particular in the room where Port dies, which recalls Sartre's *Huis Clos (Closed Door)*, a play depicting the hell that for each of us is the Other.[115]

The nexus of discourses invoked by and interwoven between the novel and the film *The Sheltering Sky* defies any monolithic reading. Hence, colonial discourse must be seen to represent only one strand of the text's signification. The ambivalence built into both texts also parallels and mirrors contemporary debates in tourism research: Is it a modern version of a sacred quest for the Other? Is it a frivolous leisure time activity typical of consumer society? Or is it a postmodern game of staged authenticity? Whichever reading we prefer, the question of the Other is still there. Whether the Other is the unstructured cosmic order, the fetishized and exoticized object of desire, or the touristic, staged "sacred barbarian," the question of what makes a description of the Other legitimate is still there. Some contemporary anthropologists no longer believe in the notion of correct representation of the Other; they posit the idea that the anthropological concept of the Other is invented much as science fiction is.[116] In fiction film the demarcation between positivistic factual correctness and invention is obviously less problematic than in anthropology.

The Other of both Bowles and Bertolucci can be read simultaneously as utopian or destructive in relation to the West, America in particular. The only American survivor in both texts is Tunner, the rich capitalist tourist from Long Island. Port and Kit, the travelers, are physically and mentally destroyed by the Other. Hence both texts render an apocalyptic vision of the West symbolically annihilated by the East. Ultimately, the desert is shown to have the upper hand in the long standing struggle between wilderness and civilization. This reading is in fact suggested by Bertolucci himself who described the film as a sort of Existentialist/ecological allegory.

We could also speak of the renewed search for alternative values developing as a reaction to the overdose of consumerism, and it isn't surprising that existentialism should once again take

White *angst* in the Sahara Desert in *The Sheltering Sky*. John Malkovich as Port, the existential traveler, is dying in a room that recalls Sartre's *Huis Clos* (No Exit), as well as the apartment in *Last Tango in Paris*. "Isn't the empty flat of *Last Tango* a kind of desert and isn't the desert an empty flat?" Bertolucci asked. From the author's private collection.

hold of the popular imagination. Due to the media bombardment, the encroaching desert, so pervasive in the book, also pervades our thoughts now. A desert world about to become
tomorrow's reality. A symptom of the greenhouse effect.[117]

The sophisticated children of Scott and Zelda, the children of
Coca Cola, are devoured by the Arab/African desert. The binarism of
culture and nature, super-ego and id, New York City and the Sahara
Desert, decadence and primitivism, East and West, is thus resolved.
New York, the city jungle, the capital of capitalism, is conquered by
the Sahara Desert, "the only place in the world where even memory
disappears."[118]

CHAPTER 5

From Metapornography to Meta-heresy: Godard's Images of Sexuality

Surprisingly, little work has been done on Godard's sexual politics. The most important works are MacCabe and Mulvey's seminal essay published as a chapter in MacCabe's book *Godard: Images, Sounds, Politics* (1980) entitled "Images of Woman, Images of Sexuality,"[1] and a special issue of *Camera Obscura* on Jean-Luc Godard which was published in 1982. Laura Mulvey's more recent discussion of *Carmen, Passion,* and *Hail Mary* in her essay "The Hole and the Zero: Carmen and Marie: The Janus Face of the Feminine in Godard" which was written for the catalogue of the Fall 1992 retrospective on Godard's cinema in the Museum of Modern Art in New York is an attempt to fill the gap in a feminist reassessment of Godard's work during the 1980s.[2] Although Godard's work cries out for a feminist reinterpretation, the scarcity of material on this issue is rather surprising given Godard's privileged position within the theoretical discourse on film, as well as his own interest (albeit inconsistent and contradictory) in feminism and the representation of images of woman and sexuality in cinema.

Paradoxical as it may seem, Godard's prestige among academics and his progressive politics are responsible for the difficulty one confronts when analyzing his approach to imaging woman. The contradictions in Godard's films as well as in his career and public pronouncements[3] can also be found in his treatment of woman's image. There is, however, one difference. An overview of Godard's sexual politics reveals a rather clear pattern of growth and development. Perhaps more than any other director's career Godard's can be neatly divided into stages or periods. From a feminist point of view, however, the intriguing aspect of the periodization of Godard's work is that each of the stages of his career is associated with another woman/actress/collaborator. The cinéphile/New Wave stage is associated with Godard's first wife, Anna Karina; the beginning of the Maoist period with Anne Wiazemsky, his second wife; and the video period with Anne-Marie Miéville. The only exception is the Dziga Vertov period, which was marked by a collaboration with a man, Jean-Pierre Gorin. This exception is not deviant if one relies on Gorin's confession in 1974: "With Jean-Luc and me, it was a love story; we really were deeply in love with each other, with no shame, no guilt; it was a very deep involved sexual thing; we played on our fears and neuroses, it was something which went far beyond movies, and that's why it was effective."[4]

In 1969 someone on the set of one of Godard's movies (his identity is not revealed) is quoted by Walter S. Ross as saying: "He [Godard] can't work unless his wife is in the film."[5] Ross added to this observation that "His permanent wife is Anne Wiazemsky. . . . And when his wife is not in the film, he makes the lead imitate her. Bardot had to change her walk and her delivery to be more like Anna Karina (his first wife) in *Le Mépris*."[6] What Ross did not mention is that Godard even made Brigitte Bardot, in some scenes, wear a wig that resembled Karina's hair style especially in *Vivre sa vie*. The collaboration of Godard and Karina constitutes, as William Simon suggests, "one of the most complex and fascinating cases of a director and actress working closely together in the history of film."[7] Karina, according to him, "apparently brought out the more romantic aspects of Godard's temperament, especially to the degree that this romantic attitude was essentially worshipful. "In the earliest Karina films, Simon observes" there is a high degree of this worshipful attitude, expressed through the male character's reverence for the Karina character. The male characters are, to an extent, surrogates within the narrative for Godard himself."[8]

But Godard's periods are also associated with different types of male leads. In the New Wave period Jean-Paul Belmondo is the actor favored by Godard. Cast as a small criminal (*Breathless*), or a runaway journalist in search of adventure and escape from the city (*Pierrot le Fou*), Belmondo projects an image of a macho, a tough but vulnerable guy, emulating the male heroes of *film noir* (Humphrey Bogart in particular) one of the New Wave's favorite genres. In the 1960s, however, the image of Godard's male leads changed. Instead of the tough detective, Godard increasingly focused on the student/intellectual/revolutionary associated with the then popular actor Jean-Pierre Léaud—an actor with the image of a child-man.[9]

Despite the celebratory reception of Godard's representation of women by many critics, one cannot ignore the misogynist tendency of his films, and in particular of the early ones. This tendency is already displayed in Godard's first short films and in *Tous les garçons s'appellent Patrick (Charlotte et Véronique)* (1957) (*All Boys Are Called Patrick*). Romanticism and idealization, as Janet Bergstrom observes, "has characterized the position of the desired woman within the logic of the enunciation in most of Godard's films."[10] In his first feature film, *Breathless*, Godard introduced a new type of woman to the cinema: a young woman with very short hair whose appearance opposed the Hollywood feminine ideal. In his New Wave films with Anna Karina, Godard developed a Louis Brooks's type of woman noted for her famous Care style hair.[11] Godard's image of woman, especially during the New Wave period, is that of a child-woman. Jacques Rivette said: "Have you ever noticed that he [Godard] never uses women over twenty-five? Godard was asked to direct *Eva* (before Joseph Losey), but he refused because of Jeanne Moreau. An adult woman frightened him."[12] In *Le Petit Soldat*, Michel Subor (Bruno Forestier) claims that no woman should ever pass twenty-five.

Godard's women, especially in his New Wave period, are youthful and concerned with attractiveness in a narcissistic fashion. Their representation recalls the findings of the sociologist Erving Goffmann (popularized in his book *Gender Advertisments* [1979]), in which he discovered that ads are conceived of as ritualized versions of the parent-child relationship, with women represented largely as children. Godard represents his women and especially Anna Karina as very playful, and many of the scenes in his early movies display fascination with their movements. They dance and jump but never too energetically or dynamically—always gracefully in a girl-like manner. Related to the child-woman type is the fact that women in Godard's films are always dressed simply, in regular, everyday clothes. They never wear fancy evening dresses, provocative costumes, or revealing, sexy ensembles. This, it should be stressed, holds true for all the stages of his career. Women, are never glamorized and their clothes are never used to fetishize or elevate their bodies. This attitude toward feminine masquerade is in line with Godard's habitual anti-star attitude. During his New Wave period, it also matched the spirit of the time and the generational flavor of other New Wave productions. Godard's attraction for non-French actresses is also one of his trademarks. Several of his most prominent heroines are foreigners. Jean Seberg was an American, Anna Karina is Danish, and Marina Vladi is of Russian origin.

"The Last Romantic Couple": Images of Women in Godard's New Wave Period

To a certain extent, one may argue that Godard's early misogynism, and his tendency to portray cinematic versions of the romantic idea of woman as a treacherous enigma, are consistent with existentialism and its view of woman as the Other. *Contempt* (1963) is one of the more interesting examples of Godard's work during this period. The film is an adaptation of Alberto Moravia's *Il disprezzo* (translated into English as *A Ghost at Noon*).[13] Coming three years after *The Conformist*, the novel, as Walter Korte observes, "presents his [Moravia's] full-length treatment of a theme that was to dominate his work increasingly thereafter: the relation of art to sexuality."[14] The protagonist Piccardo Molteni (Paul in Godard's film, played by Michel Piccoli) "begins to write filmscripts, a kind of artistic prostitution in his eyes, and a betrayal of his masculinity from Emilia's [Camille in the movie, played by Bardot] point of view."[15] The film's juxtaposition of Fritz Lang, the mythic director, and Bardot, the sex goddess, is the juxtaposition of "Le dinosaure et le bebe" (the dinosaur and the baby) as Godard called it.[16] This juxtaposition, however, is quite problematic from a feminist perspective. *Contempt* tends, like many of Godard's other movies, to demythify the star system, and Bardot is used (and sometimes even abused) as the target and vehicle of this process.

This is most evident in the scene in which Lang quotes the famous lines from Bertolt Brecht's ballad in which the German playwright describes his work as a scriptwriter in Hollywood as prostitution: "Every morning to earn my bread I go to the market, where they buy lies. Full of hope I get in line with the peddlers." Brigitte Bardot asks Lang where this quote comes from and he answers: "That's Hollywood . . . as described in a ballad by our late BB." In response Michel Piccoli asks knowingly: "Bertolt Brecht?" and Lang answers: "Yes." The joke is of course that Brigitte Bardot's nickname was BB (composed of the initials of her private and family names and pronounced like *bebe*—baby—in French). The confusion between Brecht (Godard's idol and a man of intellect) and Bardot (a dumb blond, a sex bombshell, and child-woman) could not but elicit laughter from the knowing audience. Paul/Piccoli, Godard's surro-

"Le dinosaure et le bebe." Fritz Lang, the mythic director, and Camille (Brigitte Bardot), the sex goddess, in *Contempt*. Bardot is wearing a wig that recalls Anna Karina's hair style, especially in *Vivre sa vie*. Courtesy of The Museum of Modern Art, Film Stills Archive.

gate, is used in this practical joke as a mediator between the knowing spectator and the smart director.

The joke at Bardot's expense is visually illustrated in the movie through the position and the framing of the shots of the naked Bardot. In these shots Bardot is positioned in the way babies used to be photographed for family albums with their backsides up. Bardot's nude positions in the film also anticipate Godard's later preoccupation with the anal theme. Bardot's sexy childishness and cute mindlessness is intensified in the scene following Lang's citation of Brecht. In this scene the director and Lang discuss the philosophy behind *Ulysses*. Having finished the discussion the producer asks Bardot: "Why don't you say something?" and she responds: "Because I have nothing to say." Yet in another scene of a fight between Camille and Paul, Piccoli asks Bardot: "Why do you look so thoughtful?" to which she answers: "Believe it or not I'm thinking." The allusion here is to the Cartesian notion that equates thinking with existence. Hence Bardot's statement can be read either as a claim for subjecthood, or as another attempt by Godard to question her intellectual capacity and to reaffirm her image as the dumb blond.

Despite the film's deliberate humilation of Bardot (as an image of sexuality and also as a female subject), its use of her body is neither pornographic nor explicitly exploitative (as it is with Roger Vadim). Producers Carlo Ponti and Joseph Levin complained that Bardot's sexiness did not come out in the film (indeed it was the least popular of her films). As Jacques Aumont explains, the celebrated shots of the naked Bardot were imposed by the producers.[17] In an attempt to indirectly resist the producer's demand to use Bardot's body Godard inserted in one of the scenes a subversive comment on the exploitation of the image of woman's body in the cinema. The scene takes place on a yacht in the sea. Piccoli is seen sitting with Bardot on the deck while young women extras rush from one side of the yacht to another. Piccoli asks: "They're going to get undressed?" and Bardot answers: "Naturally." Piccoli, then, in a mock-soliloquy responds: "There's nothing like the movies. Usually when you see women they are dressed but put them in a movie and you see their backsides."

In *Contempt,* cinema (the producers who represent the business and the money aspect of the industry) is implicitly criticized for its abuse of the image of woman's body. Despite this criticism, Bardot is represented as narcisisstic and consumed with her looks and the desire to be desired, or to put it in Lacanian terminology "the desire to be the object of desire of the Other." Even the first scene, showing the naked Bardot, and presumably, as many critics claim, providing an anti-fetishistic image of a woman's body[18] is consumed with "feminine desire" to be desired. When Piccoli answers positively to Bardot's question if different parts of her body are pretty in his eyes, she does assert: "Then you love me totally." In many scenes Bardot (like Godard's other New Wave heroines) is seen scrutinizing her image in the mirror.

Violence against women occurs in *Contempt* when Piccoli slaps Bardot's face. The slap anticipates the harsher violence in *Numero deux* and *Sauve qui peut (la vie).* The boundaries of verbal violence are tested as well. During one of the couple's domestic fights Paul tells Camille: "This vulgar language does not become you," to which she responds with a long litany of names by which women were called in the Middle Ages ("sorcière, hameçon du diable, tison d'enfer" [sorceress, devil's hook, hell's brand]), a list that is later recited by Isabelle in *Sauve qui peut (la vie)*. Through these formalized verbal abuses, Godard questions and challenges the power of verbal obscenity and pornography. However, the scene in which Paul is shown browsing through an album of Classic art depicting different positions of lovemaking, examines the pornographic/erotic power of the image. Implicitly it suggests a comparison between the pornographic appeal of high/classic art and that of popular art (cinema and its use of "unspeakable bodies").[19]

The seeds of the anal theme that became one of the major metaphors in Godard's radical period are already planted in *Contempt*. It is most evident in the scene in which the producer writes a check on his secretary's "ass." As much as it is a total degradation of the image of woman, it is also a moment of reification that exposes the material/economic basis of cinema. It is used as a vivid visual image to symbolize the exchange value of women's sexuality within the economic system of the cinema industry. The anal theme as a critical metaphor is interlinked with the theme of prostitution, which is central to the work of Godard from its inception. The scene of the signing of the check occurs after the producer says (in a paraphrase of Joseph Goebbels's famous dictum "when I hear the word culture I get my revolver"): "When I hear the word culture I get out my checkbook." The producer here is compared to Goebbels and the established dichotomy of producer/director, American/Nazi Anti-Nazi (Lang)/European, businessman/artist, and money/culture reinforces Godard's portrayal of the new filmmaker (as opposed to the mythical auteur represented by Lang) as a prostitute.

Godard, attesting to the influence Bergman had on him as a young filmmaker, claimed in connection with *A Married Woman* (1964), that he "wanted to show someone who had influenced my way of making a woman into a character, into a hero, as in Hollywood."[20] Godard also referred to this film (approximately twenty years later) as pornographic. And indeed, the first love scene in the film showing the lovers Charlotte (played by Macha Méril) and Robert (Bernard Noël) sitting while facing each other is later quoted by Bertolucci in *Tango*. The theme of anality, which reaches its climax in *Numero deux*, is already established in *A Married Woman*, if not through the image (as in *Numero deux* and *Tango*) then through the following dialogue. Charlotte asks: "And from behind is it love?, and Robert responds: "No it is vice but it does not matter."

The film is dotted with misogynist aphorisms such as Robert's assertion that "Women live for men but do nothing for them." Charlotte, the protagonist, is portrayed not only as a bored and unfaithful upper-middle class woman but also as ignorant (she does not know, for example, what Auschwitz is). Yet this misogynism (masquerading as social critique) is moderated through dialogues such as the one between the husband's guest and the wife. To the guest's bombastic declaration that "In French all the great ideas are in the feminine," the wife responds that "Funny men never want women to do what men do." Godard's misogynism is also moderated through the contextualization of women's narcissism within the framework of consumerism and its cultivation of ideal images for imperfect bodies. Thus for example in one of the most memorable sequences, when Charlotte flicks through the pages of the woman's magazine *Elle* examining bras and men's underwear, her obsession with her looks and body is given a sociocultural/economic explanation. *A Married Woman*, thus, is the first film in which Godard made the relation between the image and sexuality his fundamental theme.

In *Pierrot le fou* (1965), Godard pretended to tell "the story of the last romantic couple." As many critics have noted, the film analyzes his separation from his first wife, Karina. Ferdinand (Jean-Paul Belmondo), Godard's surrogate, and Marianne (Anna Karina) run away to an idllyic island. They pass their time within a traditional division of labor: the man reads and writes while the woman shops, cooks, and complains. Soon she gets bored with their paradise and becomes involved with criminal activities and ultimately betrays Belmondo who blows himself up and dies. The film, as Simon observes, "in its negative representation of the 'female principle' (action over intellect), displays Godard's misogynist tendency more explicitly than his other films."[21] The misogynist tendency is also very apparent in the traditional cultural division of likes and dislikes of the man and the woman. Whereas Marianne likes concrete things such as flowers, Ferdinand likes abstract ideas. Ferdinand says to Marianne that: "It is impossible to have a conversation with you— there are only emotions." Whereas his world is populated by ideas, hers is occupied only by emotions. The woman is represented as being incapable of transcendence, forever locked in the prison of her interiority.

Godard's worshipful attitude towards Karina recalls, or perhaps even quotes, from the adulation scenes in *Le petit soldat*. Again, her "grey Velasquez eyes" are verbally contemplated in the voice-over narration and her portrait is compared to that of Renoir's *Portrait de modèle ou Margot* which appears also in *Breathless* (there it is Seberg who is being compared to the painting). Signs of Godard's obsession with consumerism and its relationship to images of sexuality, which were evident in *A Married Woman*, continue here also through his representation of ads for women's underwear.

Masculin Féminin (1966) is, as Joel Haycock points out, under the sociological mark. The film signals Godard's gradual shift from cinéphile concerns (the romanticization of the couple and heterosexual love) to social ones. This tendency started in *Masculin Féminin* and came full circle in *Two or Three Things I Know About Her*, which is above all a document of social critique announcing the initation of Godard into politics. The more clinical categories, masculine, feminine, Haycock observes, "point up a transformation in tone from that of most love stories, and already give the film a psychological or sociological inflection."[22] Some aspects of the film subvert Godard's earlier misogynism and hint of a new attitude towards women. Thus, for example, Madeleine (played by the popular French singer Chantal Goya) has two women roommates, and the film implies that she carries on some kind of lesbian relationship with one of them (Elizabeth). According to Haycock "In *Masculin Féminin*, the young women, particularly Madeleine and Elizabeth, have the upper hand on Paul, ordering him about (forcefully telling him to clear the table in one sequence) or willfully ignoring him."[23] Godard, the cinéphile, is still shy and the sado/masochist tendency revealed in *Masculin Féminin* comes full circle only in *Sauve qui peut (la vie)*. The masochist tendency, at this stage, is related to the image of Léaud as a child-man.

Godard's interest in the social inflection of pornography begins in this film. Madeleine and Paul are seen watching a porno movie (a mock-Swedish porno film used as a kind of parody on Bergman's films, *Silence* in particular). This film within a film shows a man brutally dominating a woman and forcing her to perform a sex act with him. The projected fantasies of violent sex, which in *Masculin Féminin* are mediated through the mise-en-abime device, are materialized in *Numero deux* and *Sauve qui peut (la vie)* which deliberately investigate the pornography culture. According to Haycock:

The eroticism of *The Silence* parody is disgusting, and the sequence implies that this brutality derives as much from the absence of language as it does from the man's rape of the woman, or rather that the two go together. Madeleine's remark about the film being in the original language takes on an added resonance here. The original language is no language, man before language, a beast: "Language is the house man lives in," says Julliette in *2 ou 3 choses*. The reduction of dialogue to grunts and whimpers is in complete contrast to Godard's own films, with their talky characters and their constant concern with written and spoken language.[24]

It is interesting to compare here Godard's conception of bestial sexuality to that of Bertolucci, especially in *Tango*.

Whereas in *Tango* language is presented as a corrupting force, a tool used by repressive civilization to prevent pure, and authentic sexual expressions, in *Masculin Féminin*, language is presented as a means of purifying sexuality from brutality and violence. The grunts and whimpers of the porno movie are ridiculed in the context of Godard's film, whereas in *Tango* they are elevated. In fact *Tango's* utopian vision reveals a mistrust of language. Language is perceived as a force that corrupts authentic sexuality. In *Tango* the relationship between Paul and Jeanne follows the rule of "no language." The meaning of true liberation in *Tango* resides not in language, but instead in an escape from language. In fact unlike Godard's meta-pornographic narratives, which analayze pornography through language, Bertolucci's *Tango* follows the favorite plot of mainstream porn in which, according to Tania Modleski, "the more the woman is subjugated and reduced to a slavering devotee of the phallus, the more she is seen to be discovering and liberating her *essential self.*"[25]

The Beginning of the Radical Period

Two or Three Things I Know about Her, which was made during the same year as *Masculin Féminin*, points clearly towards Godard's move to radicalism. The themes of prostitution, capitalism, and consumerism are crystallized into a mock-ethnographic-biological observation of French society under a microscope (Godard quotes frequently from Raymond Aron's book, *Eighteen Lessons on the Industrialist Society*). Godard's voice-over whispering in the film promises to "examine the city and its inhabitants like a biologist studying social pathology." Godard said that although *Two or Three Things* was sparked off by a newspaper anecdote, "what excited me most was that this anecdote linked up with one of my pet theories, that in order to live in society in Paris today, on no matter what social level, one is forced to prostitute oneself in one way or another— or to put it another way, to live under conditions resembling those of prostitution. . . . In modern industrial society, prostitution is the norm."[26]

A unique aspect of *Two or Three Things* is its deromanticization of prostitution (as opposed to *Vivre sa vie*, for example). Prostitution is dislocated from its natural environment (the street or the brothel) to the domestic sphere, the reign of the family and domestic sex. Thus, the tension between ordinary (familial) sex and "other" sex (extra-familial, forbidden) is blurred. Juliette, the domestic/suburban prostitute, the new protagonist of consumer society, is fully aware of her submissive function in this society. Yet she does not have the courage (as does Godard's later feminist heroine, Jane Fonda in *Tout va bien*) either to criticize or to rebel against a whole system that encourages prostitution and consumerism. "Being sexually independent of man is tempting. But actually it horrifies me," Juliette confesses to the camera in a frontal monologue facing the spectator and acknowledging his existence in a Brechtian manner. In *Two or Three Things* Godard developed his interest in anality to a level of "critical social theory." Western, capitalist society, he claims, is the society of the asshole. In *Two or Three Things* Godard establishes his use of anality (in particular anal rape) as a metaphor for the capitalist/consumer society.

In *Weekend* (1967), which intensified Godard's move toward radical social critique, the attack on the bourgeoisie, not unlike in Bertolucci, is associated with the critique of upper-middle class women as epitomizing the horror of the bourgeoisie. Corinne (Mireille Darc) is portrayed in the final scene of the film as a cannibal eating the flesh of her own husband. The final scene, with its semi-apocalyptic tones and its vision of the destruction of bourgeois civilization, is loaded with images of humiliated women designed presumably as "parodic" quotations borrowed from pornographic iconography. Such for example is the scene in which the cook of the wild band of hippies inserts live fish into Corinne's vagina (the title of the scene is "Totem et Taboo"). Corinne is portrayed as the culmination of the terror invoked by bourgeois civilization and its discontents. It is a civilization that moves from "advanced technology to primitive technology, from mass culture to barbarism from the present to the future—which is no more than a memory of the prehistoric past."[27] Godard says in this film "To overcome the horror of the bourgeoisie you need more horror." Godard is using the road film genre as an apocalyptic metaphor that appeals for the destruction of the bourgeoisie. A classic highway traffic jam turns into a metaphor for civilization's decline.

The point of disturbance here is that the critique of the pornography culture in *Weekend* not only betrays its critical intentions, but also adds new, original images to the museum of the degradation of women. In *Contempt, Weekend, and Tout va bien* Godard deliberately desexualizes and humiliates the women stars, who are also the sex goddesses of their times, as a gesture of socio/political criticism. Yet the delicate line in these films, between criticism and humilation, representation and enunciation, is unclear.

In *Weekend*, like in Contempt, Godard examines the boundaries of pornography and its dependence on the visual image. The film begins with Mireille Darc (dressed in panties and bra only) telling the spectators about a strange orgy in which she participated. In this scene Godard is both acknowledging and frustrating our voyeurism, awakening but refusing to satisfy our desire to actually peep into images of this orgy. Denying the scopophilic drive, Godard provides us with the verbal dimension only of this mock-pornographic narrative (the story of the orgy is actually a parody on pornographic narratives). In this scene Godard is trying to represent sex without images by testing the power of the spoken word. The spoken words are supposed to invoke imaginary sexual visions. Despite the problems associated with this film from a feminist point of view, it has some redeeming values. Thus for example when one of the hippies asks Corinne what her name is she responds by giving her family name to which he responds: "No! This is your husband's name." When she gives him her maiden name he responds "No! this is your father's name. So you don't know yourself."

The Radical Period

Of all the films made by Godard, *Tout va bien* is considered to be quite possibly the most feminist film. Certainly it is the least problematic of all his films from a feminist point of view. The film raises many classic feminist issues, in particular issues concerned with the double oppression/exploitation of working women. The women workers in the movie are economically exploited both by their specific factory manager as well as by the capitalist system at large; in addition, they are sexually abused by both their male fellow workers and husbands. Godard's concern with the relationship of love and labor is given full expression in *Tout va bien*. Susan (Jane Fonda) wants herself and her husband Jacques (Yves Montand) to function through images of both work and love. "I need his image at work and he needs my image at work," she says. As in Godard's other movies, the subject of society's sensitivity to the exploitation of women's bodies by the advertisement industry is raised. Jacques, a director who makes commercials for living, is shown shooting a commercial for Remington razors. He gives instructions to the actor and the model on how to perform his script. The spectators, however, never see this performance. Montand tells the male actor to put his cheek on the naked buttocks of the female model, and orders her to say that it pricks her ass. The male actor is then supposed to shave with his Remington, and when he puts his cheek on her ass the second time she is supposed to exclaim ecstatically how soft and nice it is with a Remington.

But if *Tout va bien* is politically correct from a feminist point of view, then *Letter to Jane* (1972), a forty-five-minute film made specifically by Godard and Gorin to be shown at the New York Film Festival to an American audience, is a dubious detour, frequently described as "a rape of one woman by two men." Godard and Gorin were aware of the rape implications and this awareness is subsumed within Godard's voice-over narration/analysis.

Susan (Jane Fonda) gives a feminist lecture about love and work to Jacques (Yves Montand) in *Tout va bien*. "I need his image at work and he needs my image at work," she says. Courtesy of The Museum of Modern Art, Film Stills Archive.

There is another problem too and one that we can't avoid. We are both men who have made *Tout va bien* and you are a woman. In Vietnam the question is not put that way but here it is. And as a woman you undoubtedly will be hurt a little, or a lot, by the fact that we going to criticize a little or a lot, your way of acting in this photograph. Hurt? because once again, as usual, men are finding ways to attack women. If for no other reason we hope that you will be able to come and answer our letter by talking with us as we go reading it in two or three places in the U.S.

The whole film (using only stills, black leader, and tape) is an analysis of a news photo of Jane Fonda on a visit to North Vietnam. In the picture, which was published in August 1972 on the front page of the French news magazine *L'Express*, the actress is in the foreground facing someone whose face is hidden by the brim of a hat. A Vietnamese is standing in the background. Gorin and Godard take turns discussing the photo and its ideological implications. They say, for example, that Fonda's expression is a "Roosevelt New Deal expression" which all Western movie stars (including her father Henry Fonda in John Ford's *Grapes of Wrath*) have acquired since the talkies; the expression is also labeled Cartesian because it reflects the belief "I think therefore I am." The reason for Fonda's face being in focus while the Vietnamese face remains out of focus is discussed in depth. Actually, what Godard and Gorin have done with Fonda's photo is similar to what Roland Barthes has done in his semiological/ideological studies in *Mythologies*. At a Lincoln Center press conference Godard and Gorin emphasized that they were not attacking Jane Fonda personally. Yet the visciousness with which Fonda is criticized cannot be ignored.[28]

The "Miéville Period"

Godard's awareness of feminist issues grew as a result of his collaboration with Miéville. "Like Jean-Pierre Gorin before her, Miéville seems to function as Godard's guilty conscience ('You know, your program about women was a bit weak,' she tells him in one of the segments of *Six Times Two*. 'You set them up, you question them, you more or less tell them how to reply, and then you're surprised that you can't find anybody [there].')."[29]

The paradox is, of course, that the more sensitive Godard became to feminist issues (in particular to those concerned with pornographic images) the more problematic, from a feminist point of view, his films became. Yet the complexity inherent in the issue of pornography (on the legal and representational levels alike) has the potential of turning any attempt (however serious and sincere it may be) to challenge the issue into part of the pornography culture itself.

More than any of Godard's and Miéville's films, *Numero deux* (1975) and *Sauve qui peut (la vie)* exemplify the problems involved with any attempt to deal with "metapornography."[30] *Numero deux*, with its multiple TV monitors, displays in the first scene images drawn from traditional public politics (anti-war protests, workers' demonstrations), popular culture (Bruce Lee Kung-fu movies), semi-high culture (Bergman's *Scenes from a Marriage*), and pornography (the film *Les Devoreuses de sexe*). By juxtaposing these images taken from different spheres of life and asking in the voice-over narration: "Is this film about sex or politics?" Godard unites the private and the public domains, thus politicizing sexuality and sexualizing politics.

From a feminist point of view what is most surprising and refreshing in this film is its treatment of old people's sexuality. Actually the film presents three generations of the nuclear family (girl and boy, mother and father, grandmother and grandfather). The film, as Julia Lessage observes, "depicts symbolic situations rather than dramatic ones."[31] Godard's former disgust with older women is replaced in this film (presumably due to Miéville's influence) by a sympathetic look at the naked bodies of an old woman and an old man. The grandmother is seen peeling carrots, cleaning the house, and washing herself—all in the nude—at the sink. The grandfather is seen sitting nude with his family watching television, or else sitting at a table facing us (genitals visible), and talking to the camera about his past life as a radical. In *Numero deux* Godard subverts several taboos regarding the representation of sexuality in cinema. Not only does he depict images of "imperfect old bodies" but he also shows the genitals of an old man.[32]

The exploitation of women in our society, the film claims, is double. Not only are they sexually abused, their housework also constitutes a form of economic abuse. For women (as the feminist social analysis of Germaine Greer which accompanies shots of the grandmother and the young wife doing housework makes clear) the home is a factory. Therefore, the young man, pausing during a love making scene with his head between his wife's knees, says: "It's hard for me to do the housework, to see shit on her dirty underwear. For her, it's the factory; for me, it's home."

The film also deals with the child's sexuality, another taboo topic in cinema. The mother is shown washing her daughter in the bath and the camera takes a shot of the girl's genitals. The shot recalls the tight shots focusing on the genitals and pubic hair of the female protagonists in *Carmen* and *Hail Mary*; these, in turn, both invoke Godard's New Wave image of the child-woman and anticipate Paul's pedophilia (his incestuous desire for his daughter in *Sauve qui peut (la vie)*). The film ends with an image of the girl bathing and asking her father a question that betrays her incestuous desire: "When I'll be a mother will you still be my father?" The mother and the father explain sexual intercourse to their kids through an oral metaphor. The mouth of the father embraces the mouth of the mother. Coitus, they explain, is death putting a finger on the lips.

In *The Conformist* (see chapter 6) Giulia is described as "all bed and kitchen." The experience of the petit bourgeois woman is reduced to these territories. In *Numero deux* the experience of the working class woman is also limited to bed and kitchen. But Godard's reduction here is part of a critical discourse on the narrowing of the female universe. The young woman says that she does not know how to do anything except cook and make love. Images of the young woman fixing a bed, and the grandmother peeling carrots in the kitchen appear on two monitors in the same shot, accompanied by a feminist text of Germaine Greer analyzing the social oppression of women and the origins of men's hatred of them. Women, the voice-over narration says, are the object of fear, disgust, and hatred because of their "magic holes." The old woman peeling the carrots and represented in a traditional female activity (preparing food) occupies a traditional female space (the kitchen) and is reciting quotations from Greer's feminist social analysis: "la préservation masculine de la violence est le facteur fondamental de la dégradation des femmes" (the male preservation of violence is the fundamental factor in the degradation of women). To represent this degradation Godard, in a Brechtian fashion, juxtaposes images of women's subordination (women doing kitchen work) with a progressive feminist text. The sound of emanicipation accompanies the image of oppression. Women, the grandmother continues, are trash—entirely at the disposal of men in our consumer society. Ironically (or not) the old woman affirms the essential immanence of women saying: "Woman has no consciousness because her sex is interior." This text follows an image of a woman scratching the floor.

The feminist critique in *Numero deux* is aimed at women as well. Woman's narcissism is bitterly attacked. The world is at your service, the grandmother, quoting Greer's text, says. The sun is there to color you, the flowers are there to give you perfumes: "You're the masterpiece of this world." On the delivery of this line we watch a naked elderly woman doing her toilet in a basin (an indication of her lower class origins). A huge list of luxury products originating in nature (furs, pearls, crocodiles, ostriches) and used by women to adorn themselves is invoked to portray woman as the ultimate consumer and the prime exploiter of nature. Woman adorns and fetishizes her body so as to turn it into a perfect object/commodity to be desired. While the grandfather talks about his work, the grandmother talks about sexuality. Hence Godard's preoccupation with the themes of love/labor, sexuality/work is worked out both visually and orally.

Godard also hints at the homosexual fantasies induced in consequence of the various divisions in this film. The husband explains to his child that because his wife betrayed him with another man, when he makes love to her he feels as if he makes love to a man (which makes him feel like a woman does). In perhaps a deliberate allusion to *Tango*, the husband says that he wants to be penetrated and wants his wife to put a finger in his "arse." Male fears of being "swallowed" by woman are conveyed by the husband who, in response to his wife's question: "Do you like oral sex?" says: "I feel eaten by oral sex."

Sauve qui peut (la vie) (Every Man for Himself) (1979), made in collaboration with Miéville, is Godard's most discussed film (at least by the writers of *Camera Obscura*) in terms of its treatment of sexuality and pornography. The film is structured around three characters: Isabelle Riviere (Isabelle Huppert), a prostitute; Paul Godard (Jacques Dutroc), a TV producer; and Denise Rimbaud (Nathalie Baye), his mistress. Each character dominates one movement in the film (The Imaginary, Fear, Commerce) and the three characters converge in the final movement (Music).

In their introduction to the special issue of *Camera Obscura* on Godard, the editors make it clear that they take as their point of departure *Sauve qui peut (la vie)* which was, at the time of the issue's publication, the most recent of Godard's films to be released in the United States. The editors explain that they chose the film and certain issues it raises such as violence and enunciation, pornography and eroticism, and the work of Marguerite Duras "in order to give readers a sense not only of the importance that we accord to Godard's work, but also the complexity of our relation to that work as it bears on our own project, namely, the examination of women and representation in film and the other arts."[33]

Although the film includes many disturbing images and verbal texts on the subject of women, one senses that the writers of *Camera Obscura* make an almost desperate effort to read them positively as a manifestation of feminist critique rather than as a reinforcement of misogynist and anti-feminist sentiments. Elisabeth Lyon, for example, redeems the film from charges of misogynism by seeing it as a film that connects the possibility (or in this case the impossibility) of sexual relations to the "concept of *parole de femme*, metaphorically as well as in the form of direct citation and appropriation of a figure whose work is as controversial and influential for feminists as Godard's own: Marguerite Duras."[34]

Constance Penley begins her article by describing the film's most disturbing scene in which Paul Godard asks his eleven-year-old daughter's (Cécile) coach, who told him that he has a daughter the same age as Cecile, if he ever "feels like caressing her tits or fucking her up the ass?" This scene, Penley claims, "and others like it that mention or depict homosexual propositions, bestiality, prostitution, masturbation, sadism, masochism, sodomy and voyeurism, do indeed afford the spectator a wide-ranging iconography of the pornographic. But is the film pornographic?"[35] Her answer is that "for all of its pornographic 'images,' the film is, rather, about the refusal or failure of a controlling male gaze, that gaze designated here as a pornographic one."[36] Furthermore, for Penley, the film is "the antithesis of eroticism."[37] If a criticism is to be made of this film, Penley claims, "it cannot be along the lines of an alleged pornographic debasement of women. The point of disturbance, the site of possible objection, lies, rather in the film's specific *privileging* of women."[38] Janet Bergstrom, on the other hand, seems more sensitive to what she calls the film's "system of sexual ambivalence (aggression/ eroticism)" which she sees as "*this* film's motivating anxiety."[39]

On the popular front, however, the film generated a great deal of criticism. In a public discussion with Godard at the Walker Art Center in Minneapolis, one woman said: "I'm disturbed by all the scenes of abuse to women in this film, and I want to know why you included them." Godard responded to this question (after the angry audience cited disturbing scenes such as the suggestion of incest, the pimps hitting the prostitute, the scene in the parking lot where two men slap a woman, violently forcing her to choose between them, and the prostitution scenes) saying: "I didn't invent prostitution or violence, I just show it." And later, "I'm a man so I am showing that viewpoint, and maybe criticizing myself. . . . I say a film is like an X-ray, where you can see disease and health together."[40]

The whore played by Isabelle Huppert is very cold and practical. Isabelle Huppert's prostitute in *Sauve qui peut (la vie)* is a new variant on the characters played by Anna Karina in earlier Godard films like *Vivre sa vie*. Through her business-like attitude she disassociates herself from her body, retaining her soul and freedom. In this paradigm Godard returns to his former idealization of prostitution. Her business-minded prostitution is designed to enable her to live a free life.[41] Her control over her profession and life is evidenced through the fact that she works also as a pimp (for her sister Denise). Prostitution thus is presented as the only escape from oppressive society. On *Sauve qui peut (la vie)*'s whore-heroine Godard said: "The whore's trade brings more money to dried-up scriptwriters than it does to pimps. I myself am only a whore fighting the pimps of cinema."[42] Here Godard returns to the metaphor of *Contempt* and its portrayal of the director as a prostitute and the producer as a monstrous pimp. Godard said also: "So I can say I'm a whore, but I don't like pimps. The first enemy is the pimp, not the other whore."[43]

The theme of anality in *Sauve qui peut (la vie)* is mixed with bestiality. Isabelle lets the cows lick her buttocks. She says "sometimes they give you a hard lick." Anality is conveyed also in the scene when the client (M. Personne) tells Isabelle to show her ass to the street. The film also contains a homosexual motif: Paul Godard is chased by a man. "Mr. Godard," he cries desperately, "I love you." The pedophilia motif, on the other hand, appears not only in Paul's desire for his daughter but also in the scene in which the client asks Isabelle and another prostitute to play a lesbian game between mother and daughter. If in his New Wave period Godard invoked the child in the woman, in *Sauve qui peut (la vie)* he invokes the woman in the child.

The film's most memorable (and disturbingly funny) metapornographic image is that of the sex-chain machine, the *combinatoire* scene used "as a mild pastiche of de Sade's more elaborate combinations."[44] The image of the sex-machine epitomizes the ultimate reification and commodification of sexuality under advanced capitalism. It is a picture of assembly-line sex representing the ultimate image of metapornography: sex as a soulless, Pavlovian behaviorist machine. During the sex-chain orgy the prostitute is sucking the boss's penis while he [("le patron")], imitating the social gesture of a film director, says: "The image is o.k. let's do the sound." Le patron (echoing *Tout va bien*'s caricatural portrayal of a factory manager), who is the director of the orgy scene, gives acting instructions to the participants: "When I grab your tits you lick his ass, etc. etc.," exposing the ideological mechanism behind the mass-produced pornographic fantasies.

Godard said that the title of the film would be better translated as "Save Your Ass" and indeed Denise is trying to save hers by keeping a journal and moving to the country. Unlike his non-intellectual heroines in the New Wave period, Denise is an aspiring writer who wants to retire to the country in order to write and contemplate the meaning of life. Her family name, Rimbaud, indicates her literary inclinations, and within the film's economy of ambivalence it can be read either as making fun of her literary pretensions or as crediting her with the hope of becoming the French female Rimbaud (not unlike Duras herself). Yet even Denise, the woman with the intellectual aspirations, turns to prostitution. Again the image of woman here, as in all of Godard's movies, the early ones in particular, is that of the survivor, the one who "saves her ass" and throws her man to the dogs. Godard said that the movie is about movement and "that the two women move faster than the pessimistic life around them while Paul does not—they save their asses."[45]

Soft and Hard (subtitle: A Soft Conversation Between Two Friends on a Hard Subject) was released in 1986. It was commissioned by Great Britain's Channel 4 and was shot in the village of Rolle, Switzerland, where Godard and Miéville live. This video film comments on cinema as a type of domestic activity, a home movie, and Godard and Miéville, the two conversing friends, reflect and sum up fifteen years of work together. In the first part of the program they are seen simulating different types of domestic activities inside the house. Miéville is ironing clothes while Godard, mockingly, is practicing his tennis strokes. This simulation of quotidian activities performed in the private space provides a visual/symbolic critique of the traditional division of labor between the sexes (housework versus sport). The outdoor scene that follows takes place on the lake, in nature. The dialogue here is with the cosmic space and the elements: the sky, the water, and the earth. Godard recites passages from Hermann Broch's *The Death of Virgil* while Miéville walks through the Swiss countryside. But, very soon, the cosmic space is displaced back into the private sphere, the interior of the house where the conversation between Miéville and Godard began. Godard is shot from the back, his face is never fully shown. Miéville, on the other hand, is facing the camera, Godard, and the spectator.

This conversation, as well as the arrangement of the domestic mise en scène in this intimate space, is an act of acknowledgement on Godard's part of the existence of the other, the woman. Yet, the recognition of the "coupled space" is joined by the following sentence: "Parce que je fais des images au lieu de faire des enfants, est-ce que cela apeche que je sois un etre humain?" (So I'm doing pictures instead of children. Does it stop making me a human being?). The sentence is a paraphrase of a sentence in one of Vincent van Gogh's letters to his brother Theo in which he (van Gogh) says that the fact that he creates ideas and does not procreate children should not exclude him from humanity. It invokes Godard's reflection in *Scénario du film Passion* on the process of creation and creativity and the intimate link between the creation of life and art. Yet, as in *Scénario du film Passion*, Godard also returns in *Soft and Hard* to the image of cinema as a factory of images. Here creation/creativity is tainted with the processes of mass production and construction.

As in most of his films, in particular the early ones, Godard is the interviewer, and the woman (Miéville) is the interviewee. The woman is thus the researched object whose subjectivity is denied. Yet the subject/object relationship in this scene is more complex. The two discuss analysis, and Godard, playing a sort of analyst, reflects on the concept of projection which stands for both screening and the relationship of the analyzed to the analyst. You are the subject, Godard claims, but television subjects you and you become the subject of the king; "la télévision au contraire ne projette pas, elle nous projette et donc on ne se sait plus où est le sujet" (television, on the other hand, doesn't project, it projects us and therefore one no longer knows where the subject is). Godard's recurrent preoccupation with the theme of love/labor-private/public is revisited here through the links he establishes between the couple's intimate conversation about cinema, television, and their personal relationships, and the creation, production, and reception of images. Thus, the underlying sexual economy of image production and consumption emerges as a subtext to their domestic mise en scène.

Images of Women in the Cosmic Period

Godard's interest in feminism and his engagement with metapornography dwindled in the 1980s. Instead, he seemed to show a renewed interest in the "feminine enigma." Since then, this interest has been implicated in his concern for spiritual and religious issues. Already in *Passion* sexuality was engaged with religious images, and the film culminated with shots of the defloration of a virgin intercut with the camera's "penetration" of El Greco's *Assumption of the Virgin Mary*. Although Isabelle is shown dreaming of an egalitarian sexual relationship, images of women borrowed from the art of the masters (inspired by religious ideology) counter-balance her socialist utopian dreams. The irony is that in *Sauve qui peut (la vie)* Isabelle Huppert played a prostitute, while in *Passion* she played a virgin. This irony vanishes, of course, if one bears in mind the Christian dialectics of sin/redemption epitomized by Saint Mary Magdalene, the prostitute/saint. Godard's masculine investigation of women and their sexuality is linked in *Passion* with the problem of the sublime. In *Passion* Godard asks indirectly what makes the masters' pictures sublime and not pornographic. Despite the fact that the masters manipulated the eroticism generated by the tension between magnificent costumes and nudity, their art is not pornographic. *Passion*, as Marc Cerisuelo suggests, produces a new oxymoron, "le 'nu costume'," the nude costume.[46] And, indeed, a half-naked woman extra tries to escape from the tableau vivant of Eugène Delacroix's *Taking of Constantinople by the Crusaders on April 12, 1204* as well as from Godard's film set. Perhaps, Godard implies, her desire to escape questions the distinctions between pornography and sublimity. Later in the film we find out that Godard's escaping woman is also dumb. Her dumbness may be read as signifier of woman's symbolic silence in the patriarchal world of art.

In *Carmen*, Godard deals with the war of the sexes, which he prefers to call after the myth of Carmen "le dernier combat des femmes" (women's last battle). "Why do men exist?" and "Why do women exist?," the two protagonists teasingly ask each other. According to David Wills, Godard's film is very explicit in "its representation of Carmen as castrator, and her murder as an expression of male impotence, or the response to it."[47] Any adaptation of the *Carmen* text, he claims, cannot but be a modification on a classical sexual economy "even if it is also about a classical sexual economy in crisis."[48] In terms of a politics of representation, the focus is on the actress's lower parts. One of the scenes takes place in a bathroom and recalls a similar moment in *Tango* in which the camera shoots Schneider from below to the waist. *Carmen* pays tribute to *Tango*, also, through its investigation of the anal theme. One of its dialogues is a mild pastiche of the famous dialogue in *Tango* which also takes place in the bathroom: "If I put a finger in your ass. Is it clean?" Carmen asks Joseph. "No," he replies, adding: "The world is shit not us." Even *Carmen*'s hotel suite is bathed with yellow light like the apartment in *Tango*. *Carmen* as much as *Tango*, positions woman within the phallocentric economy. It is no longer a metapornographic film as was *Passion*, but represents, instead, a regression into the major cliché of the phallocentric order: "the eternal war of the sexes."

With *Hail Mary* Godard's socio/political detour into the image of woman in capitalist society comes to an end. "I think that politics today is the voice of horror," Adam says to Eve in *Hail Mary*. According to Berenice Reynaud, "Godard intended first to shoot *The Story of Dora*, about the difficult (transferential) relationship between Freud and his patient—then a story of incest between father and daughter—then drifted from there to tell a love story between a father, God, and his daughter, Mary."[49] The film returns the image of woman to its "natural" place: nature. Images of the circle and the moon signify Godard's new sexual economy. Woman, as in Bertolucci's *La Luna* and *The Sheltering Sky* (see chapter 6), is associated with the eternal sign of femininity: the moon.[50] In response to Katherine Dieckmann's comment: "And you have so many images of the circle, in nature and elsewhere, which gives the movie a strong feeling of unity," Godard answered:

> Yes, the circle. We used it metaphorically: the woman as circle, and the plane flying toward it. That's one signal: coming to a woman's center. But at a certain point there's no difference between metaphor and actuality. I had no idea we'd shot the moon so many times, but then suddenly we had all these shots of the moon, and I discovered then that the moon was like the basketball in Mary's games. So it was the same: Mary was playing basketball with the moon.[51]

Hail Mary is full of spiritualist aphorisms that link sexuality no longer to the world of consumption, prostitution, and pornography, but rather to the world of nature and contemplation. "Earth and sex are inside us, outside are only the stars," says Mary. Godard told Dieckmann that his purpose was "to try and shoot a woman naked and not make it aggressive, not in an x-rated picture way." There are "several shots which have more the purpose of an anatomical drawing." In *Hail Mary*, he said, "I was trying to make the audience see not a naked woman, but flesh, if that's at all possible."[52] Justifying himself for not showing Joseph's flesh he added: "And we had thought of having Joseph be naked also, as we had a nude male in *First Name: Carmen*, but decided the audience wouldn't understand, they would immediately think Mary and Joseph were going to have intercourse. So it was absolutely impossible. And I'm a man, still, I like to look at women naked!"[53]

The film is organized around binary oppositions, a structure that is typical of the phallocentric order. Dieckmann, commenting on this aspect of the film, told Godard: "You're dealing with this opposition between science and nature, or logic and illogic, in this movie. The men are associated with the logical, the women with the intuitive." Godard's response was: "Well, women are more casual. They accept more things. Whereas men always feel they have to master, to understand."[54] The point of disturbance in both the film and Godard's explanation is that it is an expression of a reformed director who underwent a feminist reeducation and was championed by critics and scholars for his interest in feminism.

Nonetheless to a certain extent one may argue that *Hail Mary* is the answer to Godard's *A Woman is a Woman*. Angela Recamier's (Anna Karina) desire to have a child is fulfilled here without her "having to enter the circuit of sexual relations, which, in biblical theology of the flesh, is characterized since the fall by male domination and mimetic violence and, in Godard/Anne-Marie Miéville's work *passim*, but especially in *Numero deux* (1975) and *Sauve qui peut (la Vie)* (1980) by fetishism, blockage, and mimetic violence."[55]

Detective, which Godard made to be able to finish *Hail Mary*, is seen by Fabrice Revault as an expression of *fatigue masculine*.[56] By masculine fatigue he means fatigue from the city, women, and a cinema made by technicians. "Je suis fatigue" (I am tired) is said repeatedly by Mr. Jim as an echo of Michel Poiccard in *Breathless*.[57] Cerisuelo notes that all the masculine characters in the film portray Godard as a tired artist.[58]

Armide (1986), which is a section in a collaborative film called *Aria*, foregrounds again Godard's former concern with images of sexuality in contemporary Western society. The whole film takes place in a gymnastic hall (salle de musculation in French). In this hall several very somber men are engaged in concentrated exercises, their hollow gaze is fixed on an empty space. The scene visually epitomizes male auto-eroticism. Two young women try desperately to seduce the men. They caress the developed muscles of the men and advance on them with clear sexual intentions, but nothing seems to work. The men remain indifferent, completely detached—fully absorbed in their male-narcissism. The unsuccessful seduction scene is impinged upon by images drawn from stereotypical soft pornography, such as naked women costumed in the furs of wild beasts and so on. The scene can be read as another manifestation of Godard's masculine fatigue. Whereas his movies of the 1980s deal, to a large extent, with the war of the sexes, *Armide* is already beyond war. The film represents a universe devoid of male passion. Men are so absorbed in cultivating their masculinity (their muscles) that they cannot even see the Other, let alone desire it. Desire in this kind of world belongs to women alone, and because of the dependence of female desire on the affirmation and response in the male gaze, here this desire is in vain.

Woman as Consumer Woman as Commodity

Godard likes the notion of commerce as a metaphor for various other forms of sexual/cultural interactions. Commerce, Godard said, "is a form of dialogue. It comes from the same Latin root as 'communicate.' Every time two people engage in a business transaction it's a kind of love affair. I think that's why most people are so fond of commerce. Women like shopping, because that's a way they can communicate."[59] This positive view of consumerism is not far from the positions currently held by researchers of popular culture such as John Fiske and John Urry. John Fiske has already pointed out the importance of shops as public spaces that are particularly attractive to women,[60] and John Urry notes that "indeed shopping is a sphere of social activity in that women are empowered. It links together the public and the domestic and involves activity in which women are permitted to demonstrate competence."[61]

Despite Godard's positive attitude towards the issue of woman and consumerism as expressed in the quoted interview, his films show woman as the main victim of consumer society. Shopping and consumption in Godard's films are represented as the secret vice of women. The issue of woman and consumerism is so important in Godard's cinema because it involves both the metaphorization of woman (especially the woman/prostitute) as the ultimate consumer of Western society, and the analysis of the process through which woman herself becomes a commodity in cinema. The paradox is, of course, that as a consumer woman consumes, more so than anything else, idealized representations of herself as a commodity.

The status of woman as commodity in feminist theory is, as Mary Ann Doane makes clear, "not merely the result of a striking metaphor or parallel. Its elaboration is a response to Levi-Strauss's description of the exchange of women as nothing less than the foundation of human society, of culture—the guarantee of an exogamy without which the family, and society along with it, would suffer an incestuous collapse."[62]

Godard's films are concerned mainly with the image of woman as a libidinal cathected commodity, and with the image of the woman/consumer obsessed with the imperfections of her real/ private body as opposed to the imaginary/public body of advertisement. The scenes from his early films showing women comparing their bodies and underwear to the figures and lingerie manufactured by the advertising business invoke Doane's suggestive phrase concerning the status of woman as commodity: "This objectlessness of the advertising discourse frequently prompts a return to the female body as the prototypical object of commodity fetishism."[63] Scenes such as that in *A Married Woman* in which Charlotte compares her breasts with the ideal ones of the Venus de Milo validate Godard's point—also evident from many empirical studies—that women view themselves and are viewed by others as sex objects.[64]

One disturbing aspect of Godard's critique of the culture of consumerism is that it strengthens the association, existing in advertising, between women and narcissism. In his early period, Godard's actresses/women are depicted, repeatedly, in narcissistic poses. They are either examining their bodies and faces in the mirror or comparing themselves to advertisments. They are also, in many instances, posed by Godard so as to be compared with portraits and representations of women in famous paintings. In *Breathless* Godard situates Jean Seberg so as to juxtapose her "portrait" with Renoir's painting *Portrait de modéle ou Margot*. Godard's posing of his women/subjects/objects and his invocation of woman's narcissism, are detours around the usual and pejorative sense of narcissism as "self-love."[65]

Woman as Prostitute

The motif of prostitution is a recurrent one in Godard's *ouevre*, and it manifests itself both literally and metaphorically. In *Vivre sa vie* and *Two or Three Things* (1966) the main protagonists are prostitutes. However, in *Two or Three Things*, prostitution is only a pretext: it is integrated into a much larger social picture. Juliette's prostitution is a metaphor for the capitalist reforming tendencies of the Gaulist regime, as well as for consumerism.

According to Brian Darling:

When he came to make *Deux ou trois choses que je sais d'elle*, Godard was saying that the notion of prostitution must be generalized throughout society since we are all betraying ourselves

Reflections of women. In his early period, Godard's women ac-
tors/characters are depicted in narcissistic poses. In *Breathless,*
Godard juxtaposes a portrait framing of Patricia (Jean Seberg) with
Auguste Renoir's painting *Portrait de modèle ou Margot.* Courtesy of The Museum of Modern Art, Film Stills Archive.

(our essential selves) for money. (See *Nouvelle Observateur,*
October 12, 1966). The idea of betrayal is, of course, ever present in Godard's work—though not always for money; many of
his characters betray for quiet life. And prostitution, of the
more limited, conventional kind, is the subject of the early
(1955) short *Une femme coquette.*[66]

Prostitution in its most specific and broadest sense (the selling
of one's personal morality for economic gain) is Godard's overriding
theme. In the early movies he deals directly with prostitution (as a
profession and as a hidden component of marriage). In his radical pe-

In *Masculin Féminin*, Elizabeth (Marlène Jobert) examines her face in the mirror while the spectator examines her body. Courtesy of The Museum of Modern Art, Film Stills Archive.

In *Weekend*, Corrine (Mireille Darc) is posed, half naked, against a portrait of a nude woman by Renoir. Courtesy of The Museum of Modern Art, Film Stills Archive.

riod he presents consumerism as a form of prostitution. The film industry as whoredom is another of Godard's variations on the theme of prostitution, and it runs over the whole of his career from the beginning to the present. In his New Wave period (and especially in *Contempt*), filmmaking is depicted as moral prostitution. In his radical period it is part of a concrete political critique of the capitalist system. In *Tout va bien* Montand's monologue alludes to François Truffaut, another New Wave director of Godard. Truffaut's *Tirez sur le Pianist (Shoot the Piano Player)* (1961) is evoked in this monologue, which implicitly suggests the commercialization/prostitution of Truffaut via his cultivation of what Godard considers to be self-indulgent narrative cinema.

Roger Vadim is another target for ridicule in Montand's monologue, and Jacques possesses some of Vadim's authentic characteristics. Like Truffaut and Godard, Vadim was also a New Wave director. However his direction has always been more commercial. Vadim discovered and married the French sex symbol Brigitte Bardot (who played in Godard's *Contempt*), and Jane Fonda was also briefly his wife. In *Barbarella* (1967) a filmic recreation of a popular and saucily erotic French comic strip, Vadim cast Fonda as the ultimate sex symbol. *Tout va bien* thus alludes to Vadim's prostitution (incorporated into the fictional Jacques) as well as to Fonda's own exploitability as a symbol of wicked sexuality. Thus Fonda, like Montand, is correcting herself politically in the role of Susan. In *Tout va bien* Jacques's stimulation of consumer demand through merchandized sex is also presented as prostitution. The motif of prostitution is reinforced also through the association of Fonda with the prostitute Danielle Brie in *Klute* (1971).

In the films of the late 1970s (*Numero deux* and *Sauve qui peut*[la vie]), the metaphor of prostitution is replaced with that of pornography. Pornography, as Constance Penley indicates, is one of Godard's

> most successful metaphors: the filmmaker as pornographer, sex and cinema (in our society) as pornographic. Like prostitution, pornography presents a configuration where sexuality cannot be seen apart from the selling of it. But pornography as a metaphor has an important advantage over prostitution insofar as it cannot be romanticized. 'Filmmaker as prostitute' has an air of proud martyrdom about it that 'filmmaker as pornographer' does not. Prostitutes as individuals can be romanticized, as Godard has done repeatedly in his films, but, in pornography,

as a business and as a fictional form, there are no martyrs or heroines.[67]

Almost all the women in Godard's films are "prostitutes." Even if professionally they are not prostitutes, metaphorically they are because like Patricia in *Breathless* they sell their bodies or their charms to advance themselves. However, in *Vivre sa vie* the prostitute is the one who sells her body but retains her soul. The introduction to Godard's *Anticipation* (1967) (a scene in the film *The Oldest Profession*) includes this statement: "And now the distinguished director J.L.G. will show us how the oldest profession will continue in the space age." Godard is also the only director in *Anticipation* who shows a half-naked woman. Of all the heroines in Godard's films, Jane Fonda in *Tout va bien* is the only one who is not a prostitute. Even more, she fights prostitution. She, unlike Patricia the traitor in *Breathless*, resigns from her job in the American Broadcasting System because of professional and political disagreements with the organization.

The complexity of Jane Fonda's fictional character is linked to the process of her de-prostitution, both as a real person/actress and as a fictional character. Fonda's off-screen image, which at that time depended on her reputation for political activity, is exploited in a Brechtian manner. Brecht suggested that actors in the epic theatre should have active roles in the class struggle in their real lives. Thus her personal traits as the fictional Susan presumably correspond to her real traits, or, rather to her media-defined style. At the same time, in her quarrel with Jacques, she is implicitly criticizing her former relationships with Vadim and her exploitation by him as a woman/star. As I suggested before, her performance also alludes to another American actress, Jean Seberg in *Breathless*. However, in *Tout va bien* Fonda is the politically correct American actress. The fictional Susan also alludes to Susan Sontag, another radical intellectual woman who was for a while, like Fonda herself, an American expatriate in Paris. On another level, Susan, like Jacques, is a surrogate for Godard. As a leftist intellectual involved with the media, she shares the Godardian sensibilities and frustrations concerning the role of intellectuals in the revolution, and like him she concludes that "it all comes down to a question of style." The fictional Susan here also echoes and duplicates Fonda of the 1970s. Susan/Fonda in *Tout va bien* is a radical activist, involved with the media and trying to define herself politically and professionally, not unlike Godard himself. In *Tout va bien* Fonda is shown in the process of creating a new image. Her sloppy, unstylish clothes deliberately demystify her former sexy image and her Marxist/feminist lecture to Jacques only reasserts her new image. In *Tout va bien* she not only abandons her old self but also criticizes it.[68]

Anality

Anality also plays a major role in Godard's cinema. However, it began to occupy Godard seriously only in his films of the 1970s, and in *Numero deux* in particular. As in Bertolucci's cinema, anality is a metaphor of the capitalist system of oppression/repression—or in Godard's language of the "society of the ass."[69] Godard's *First Name: Carmen* even pays tribute to *Tango* through its investigation of the anal theme. The anal theme is most evident in *Numero deux* in which a feminine voice-over says: "*Numero deux* n'est pas un film à gauche ou à droite, c'est un film devant ou derrière" (*Numero Deux* is not a film on the right or left, but the film before or after; before, are the kids; behind, the government, school teachers, and work). Anality as a metaphor for a rape enacted by the whole social system on the backside of the people is clearly conveyed in a scene in which Sandrine, the young wife (significantly she has a Southern France accent and we find out that she is from Marseille), comes in from shopping (an archetypal female activity in Godard's films) lies on her bed in exhaustion and proceeds to masturbate. When her husband tries to join her she brushes him off saying: "If you don't get along with a man, you can always leave him, but what do you do when it's the state and the whole social system that's a rape?"

The anal metaphor of the society of the ass is expressed both verbally and visually in the film. Godard claimed he was making a remake of *Breathless*, thus the title *Numero deux*. Yet the relationship of the title to the anal/shit motif is clear. "Is this film about sex or politics? Why always ask is it this or that? Perhaps it is both at the same time," says the voice-over narration. The film contains "a primal scene" in which the small girl Vanessa sees her parents having anal intercourse and hears her mother scream. In an allusion to the anal rape in *Tango* with its critique of the oppression inflicted by the family institution (see chapters 2 and 6) the raping husband says: "Family affairs, I guess." The husband explains that his obsession with his wife's anus (we actually see him looking at it) derives from the fact that she never sees it. His fetishistic scopophilia thus is an expression of the power of looking at what the M/Other cannot see.

In another scene, the young woman says: "Tout ce que je dis c'est de la merde. Tout ce qui devrait se passer dans le cul se passe ailleurs et dans le cul il ne se passe rien" (Everything I say is shit. Everything that should happen in the ass happens somewhere else and nothing happens in the ass). The relationship between the gaze, the control of the other, and anality are represented through shifts of sexual positions: whoever can see the other's anus has the power to control the other. The husband is looking at his wife's anus (she is sitting on him so that her buttocks are in front of his face) proclaiming (in response to her complaint that he is fixated on a single pose) that only in this pose can he see parts of her body that she cannot see. She goes on complaining that her gaze (regard) is denied the same privilege and they then trade positions.

The anal/sadistic metaphor controls the visuals and the thematics of the film. The woman complains of suffering from chronic constipation due to the anal intercourse that is imposed on her by her husband. She describes it as a torture, and when confronted with a woman militant on the street who distributes leaflets about women in Chile being raped and tortured because of their political activity she says that she is being tortured in precisely the same way. Thus, Godard suggests that political oppression is no different from domestic oppression—both the public and the private spheres constitute a political domain. The woman's manifestation of rebellion in the domestic sphere against her husband/tormentor is to resist sodomy. She claims ownership on her body saying that it is her ass and it is full of shit. "I can't accept any more shit" she says after having suffered from constipation for two weeks.

The anal metaphor is connected also to the Freudian belief about children's theories regarding birth (children according to Freud believe that babies are born from feces) and to the metaphor of woman as a factory. The experience of childbirth is compared by the young wife in *Numero deux* to defecation. Both are experiences of relief which she is being denied because of the repeated sodomies she is forced to endure. Because of the anal intercourse forced on her by her husband, the woman's buttocks can no longer fulfill their natural function. Sandrine thus moves from constipation to contamination: the shit is everywhere. Constipation here becomes a metaphor for the situation of the exploited woman and is contrasted to creativity. If childbirth, like defecation, expresses creativity (according to Freud the origins of creativity are anal), then constipation is the opposite of creativity. "Are there other women in France like me?" the woman asks. "Because I am not paid for my reproductive capabilities, because my husband is working instead of me," she complains "I suffer." She claims that not to work is a crime, " and "blames" the spectator for complicity in an "organized crime."

Godard chose in *Numero deux* to raise the issues of women's debasement and exploitation through the representation of working class women whose real life living conditions contradict the passionate theoretical feminist texts they frequently cite. Unlike the sophisticated feminist heroine of *Tout va bien*, the housewife heroine of *Numero deux* epitomizes women's humilation and degradation. She is neither liberated nor able to transcend internal and external imprisonment and so break the chains of her home/prison. Woman in *Numero deux* is the ultimate consumer of capitalist shit and trash whose productivity/creativity is denied, and whose subjectivity is transposed into oppressive immanence. As a metapornographic film, *Numero deux* is perhaps Godard's most pessimistic analysis of the place of women in late capitalism.

Incest and Pedophilia

Incest is a motif that appears only in the late Godard. Incest in *Sauve qui peut (la vie)*, for example, is evoked as a forbidden desire but is never explicitly materialized as it is in Bertolucci's cinema. The forbidden desire in Godard's *Sauve qui peut (la vie)* is directed toward the girl and originates in the father. In Bertolucci's cinema, however, the desire is Oedipal in the strict Freudian sense: it belongs to the male boy and is directed toward the body of the M/Other. Bertolucci focuses on the psychoanalytic aspect of the taboo whereas Godard's concern is with social phenomena in the larger sense. In *Numero deux* Vanessa, the daughter, sees her parents having sex (the primal scene). For Godard in this stage of his career, as for Bertolucci, the primal image (the confrontation with the sexual act) coincides with the origin of the cinema. When the couple in the film explains to their children the nature of the sexual act the little boy says: "C'est un film muet" (this is a silent film). This recalls the famous scene of the sexual chain in *Sauve qui peut (la vie)* in which first there is a production chain of images and only then of sounds. Communication between men and women, the film suggests, is linked to the evolution of the visible and the audible, the major modes of communication in cinema.

Interview

The use of the interview format, perhaps more so than any of Godard's other reflexive devices, expresses the power relationship between women and men. In the beginning of his career the interview format was used innocently. Godard was then unaware of its symbolic figuration of male/female power relationship. However, in his later career, Godard was perfectly conscious of the significance of the interview. In *Two or Three Things*, in the conversation that takes place in a cafe between Julliette's husband and a young woman (Juliet Breto), the woman says that "Men are always asking the questions. Women answer or not." An even more serious criticism of Godard's use of the interview, as was noted before, is rendered by Miéville in *Soft and Hard*. In *Soft and Hard*, as in most of Godard's films and in particular the early ones (the interview format was first used extensively in *A Married Woman*), Godard is the interviewer and Miéville is the interviewee. Woman, in most of Godard's films, is the researched object whose subjectivity is denied by man, the Socratic tutor. The Godardian man leads the conversation and directs it. Hence, many of Godard's films establish a Socratic relationship built around the dynamics between a male tutor and his female pupil.

Conclusion

Godard's representation of women metamorphosizes in direct relation to the different stages in his career. In Bertolucci's cinema, there is no sense of development in regard to the image of the woman. By way of contrast, in Godard's cinema the image of the woman is in constant flux. Whereas Godard's cinéphile New Wave period is associated with a romanticized image of woman and the dynamics of elevation/punishment of his heroines, his radical period is infused with political awareness of the status of woman as both consumer and commodity in the capitalist system. Godard's sensitivity to feminism in particular is evident during his video collaboration with Miéville. During this period, Godard's social critique focused on issues of sexual politics in the domestic sphere (*Numero deux*), and on the education system and the family (*France/tour/détour*). His so-called cosmic period with its new spiritualism, is accompanied by a rediscovery of the female body joined with a new, almost reverential, attitude towards feminine flesh. It follows logically that Godard's cosmic period, or as Frederic Strauss calls it, "period verte" (the green period)[70] is associated with a new interest in nature and its primary signifier in our culture: the female body. Here, it can be argued that Godard's apprehension of the image of woman comes full circle. The mystique surrounding his heroines in the New Wave period (represented through women's faces more than bodies) is recycled in his recent movies, which invest the feminine flesh with a new-found religiousity. If in *Vivre sa vie* Anna Karina's face is invested with spiritualism through her similarity to Carl Theodor Dreyer's *The Passion of Joan of Arc*, then in films such as *Passion* and *Hail Mary* women's bodies, rather than their faces are spiritually elevated and revered. It remains a question then, whether this new stage in Godard's career does or does not indicate a regressive reactionary position in relation to the image of woman.

From a feminist point of view, however, the most important aspect of Godard's cinema is his attempt, most evident in the 1970s, to challenge pornography.[71] Godard's examination of the boundaries of pornography are interlinked with his constant investigation into the power of the image. Does reciting dirty words (as Bardot does in

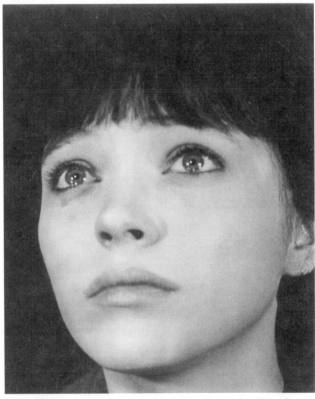

In *Vivre sa vie*, Nana's (Anna Karina's) face is spiritually endowed by a resemblance to Carl Theodor Dreyer's *The Passion of Joan of Arc*. Courtesy of The Museum of Modern Art, Film Stills Archive.

In *Hail Mary*, it is woman's flesh, rather than her face, that is spiritually elevated and revered. Courtesy of The Museum of Modern Art, Film Stills Archive.

Contempt), have the same status and effect as showing dirty things? The same questions that Godard asked about pornography (why a pornographic image is more pornographic than a pornographic word?) he later asked about the sacred. Why is it, he asks, that we can say sacred things but not show them? What differentiates an erotic image from a pornographic one? What distinguishes erotic art (as in the book of Roman/Greek art in *Contempt*) from sheer pornography? The investigation of pornography as that of the sacred thus is an investigation into the power of the image. Why do images have the power to become pornographic or blasphemous, whereas words do not?[72]

It can be argued that Godard's cinema traveled from romantic libertinage (the New Wave period) to metapornography (the radical period), coming finally in its current phase to embrace the Christian ideal of non-corporeal, spiritual love. In his cinéphile period, Godard's cult of "l'amour fou" is centered around the secret communication between man and woman. The ideal of love as potentially total, is obviously a romantic one.

Godard's transformations in regard to the question of woman are nowhere more evident than in his repeated use of one memorable dialogue in several movies. Yet despite the similarity of the oral text, the visual presentation in the different films as well as the different historical contexts reflect the changes in Godard's attitude towards the woman problem. Indeed, the fact that the same dialogue is deliberately used to convey different ideological attitudes toward women is even more interesting from a feminist perspective. The opening scene of *Contempt* in which Bardot lists all the parts of her body and asks Piccoli if he finds them pretty portrays, as I suggested before, an image of narcissistic woman whose essence is exhausted by the desire to be desired by the male gaze. Yet the verbal fragmentation of the female body in this dialogue and Bardot's asking of Piccoli if he loves each part in her body signifies the idea of total passionate love. The subtext of the scene can be read subversively as a critique on the exploitation of the female body in the cinema. In *Contempt*, whenever Piccoli lists one part of Bardot's body the camera shows us another part. Furthermore, we never see what we most want to see, the real thing (breasts and genitalia). This sexual teasing can be read as a protest against the producers's demand to use Bardot's sexiness, but it can also be read as a criticism addressed to the complicit spectator who comes to the cinema in order to satisfy his voyeuristic and fetishistic drives.

The scene from *Contempt* was later quoted and criticized in *Tout va bien* (see chapter 1). There, however, the criticism of cinema's sexual politics reached a climax. In *Contempt*, despite Godard's protest, Bardot was shown completely naked (from behind only). In *Tout va bien* both the man and the woman are completely dressed. Furthermore, Jane Fonda is dressed in the most unsexy clothes imaginable. In *Contempt*, the couple is shown in bed and the red lighting used to illuminate them evokes the aura of a bordello and wild sex. During this love scene there is a change from red filter lighting to natural lighting. These deliberate and unmotivated shifts of lighting draw attention to the highly constructed nature of the scene, potentially disrupting the spectators' voyeuristic pleasure. In *Tout va bien*, on the other hand, the whole monologue takes place outdoors in an autumnal landscape. There is still another significant difference between the two films. In *Tout va bien* Susan adds Jacques' balls to the list of the parts of his body that she loves. Here obscenity in the form of materiality replaces the former idealized notion of love. The same dialogue is echoed also in *Numero deux* where the former concept of love as total and passionate is replaced with a pessimistic notion of love as pornography. *Detective* with its masculine fatigue presents another version of the same verbal exchange: ("Vous n'osez pas le dire: la bouche, la queue, le cul, y'a que ca qui marche encore entre mon mari et moi) (You don't dare say it: mouth, prick, ass, that's all that works between my husband and me). In the film *Nouvelle Vague*, sexual love is transposed into deeply human communication. The hands become in this film an image of communication. As Strauss says[73] the origin of the couple in *Nouvelle Vague*, unlike that of *Numero deux*, is not sexual but creational (in the sense that it takes part in the universal process of creation and communication).

Sexuality, as a combinative presence of male and female bodies, disappears in *Nouvelle Vague*. Corporeal love is replaced by spiritual love modeled after the Christian ideal. If *Detective* expresses masculine fatigue, then *Nouvelle Vague* takes this fatigue one step further. Sexual desire as well as images of sexuality are absent from this film (with only one exception when the wife of one of the rich industrialists is shown dressed in a semi-pornographic attire). It is not an accident either that even the look of Domiziana Giordano, the Italian actress who plays the leading role, is so atypically Godardian, or even French. The former Godardian woman with the straight hair and the stereotypical French look is replaced by a Botticelli-like woman with long curly gold hair who resembles the Madonna found in Italian Renaissance paintings. Despite her characterization as a tough capitalist, in many shots Giordano is photographed in a manner that recalls Botticelli's "soft" female figures.[74]

Furthermore, in some of the shots Giordano is filmed in a style very different from Godard's customary approach toward his heroines. Not only does Giordano enjoy many close-ups, but in quite a few, the background is in soft focus, adding an ethereal, almost celestial aura to her face. If in *Hail Mary* feminine flesh is revered, then in *Nouvelle Vague*, as in traditional European religious paintings, the Madonna's face is worshipped as sacred.

The absence of sexual imagery is evident even in the fact that the man and the woman barely look at each other although the spectator is still invited to contemplate Giordano's face through the tight and revering close-ups. The erotic gaze as such has almost disappeared from the film's diegesis. The only signifier of the body of the two lovers in this film is their two hands "tentatively touching against a celestial backdrop so as to evoke both Michelangelo's Sistine Chapel and the initial 'lovemaking' sequence of his own *A Married Woman.*"[75] In one of the shots the woman kisses the man's hand in a reverential gesture recalling the way devoted Catholic women kiss the hands of a priest.

The film is loaded with typical Godardian aphorisms, some of them related to the relationships between women and men. Man, Godard says in one of them, poses the mystery, woman reveals the secret. Another disturbing aphorism states that "women are in love and men are lonely." In yet another dubious statement (accompanying the mock-baptism scene in the lake) it is declared that "women cannot harm men because the tragedy is that they can only disturb, irritate and kill them." Indeed, in *Nouvelle Vague*, Godard's attitude towards women seems closer to his New Wave films than to his radical/feminist ones. If, for example, in *Breathless* and *Pierrot le Fou* the male protagonists are portrayed as lonesome, individualist guys (dreaming about Italy as the land of freedom) then in *Nouvelle Vague* man's existential solitude is verbalized and forcefully stated. Furthermore, if in his triology of the sublime Godard invested woman's body with spirituality,[76] in *Nouvelle Vague*, he elevated and revered woman's face, as he did in his most celebrated New Wave films. Godard's career, in regard to the representation of women, can be described as a shift from the Nouvelle Vagueism of the 1960s, to the metapornography of the 1970s, and finally to the meta-heresy of sacrilized images of women of the 1980s and 1990s.

CHAPTER 6

The Spider's Sexual Stratagem: Bertolucci's Poetics and Politics of Sexual Indeterminacy

Bertolucci's fascination with bisexuality and androgyny is a recurrent motif in his work. On this matter he observes, "I would say that I like men who have something feminine about them and vice versa. Absolute virility is horrible. Absolute femininity, also."[1] Yet, as Will Aitken observes, "gay sexuality has never been the central concern of any of Bertolucci's films."[2] Bertolucci seems to be more interested in sexual ambivalence, than in pure and determinate sexual identity. Bertolucci uses one memorable image of sexual ambiguity again and again. In *The Spider's Stratagem* it is an image of a servant boy who provokes Athos's curiosity. The boy is always wearing a straw hat while smiling mysteriously. When eventually, Athos finds himself alone in the room with the boy, the boy smiles and then removes his hat and a shock wave of dark hair tumbles down revealing the image of a girl. In *The Conformist* this image is echoed in the seduction scene of the child Marcello by Lino, the chauffeur. Lino first shows Marcello his pistol and then takes off his uniform cap allowing his raven-black hair to tumble down to his shoulders. "Kill Madame Butterfly" Lino orders Marcello. The juxtaposition of the hard/phallic/Fascist symbol of the pistol with the soft/feminine/exotic Otherness of the luxurious kimono and the long silky hair, creates a disturbing poetic image of sexual ambiguity that anticipates the seductive Orientalism of Ar Mo in *The Last Emperor* ("She is not my wet-nurse! She is my butterfly!" Pu Yi cries after Ar Mo is expelled from the Forbidden City after the incestuous suckling scene). *The Conformist*'s poetics of sexual indeterminacy is expressed through the doubling process and the symmetrical configuration of the char-

174

Bertolucci's poetics of sexual indeterminacy. Giulio Brogi as Athos Magnani is fascinated by the "boy" who is always wearing a straw hat. Later the "boy" removes his hat and a shock of dark hair tumbles down, revealing the image of a girl. Courtesy of The Museum of Modern Art, Film Stills Archive.

acters, as well as through the bisexual inclinations of the protagonists of both sexes (see chapter 2).

In *Tango*, both Maria Schneider and Brando were selected, partially, due to what Bertolucci saw as their ambivalent sexual identity. One reason Bertolucci chose Schneider (although his first choice was Dominique Sanda, who could not accept because she was pregnant) was his perception of her androgynous quality (and perhaps her alleged bisexuality in real life). Bertolucci was impressed by her feminine upper part and her more masculine lower parts. This choice underscored his longstanding obsession with bisexuality and also matched the androgynous quality that some perceive as peculiar to Brando's grand machismo beauty. The sexy Jeanne exhibits masculine traits as well. She is wearing a mannish suit when she and Paul first meet in the real world on the Paris streets. When she kills Paul with the phallic pistol of her dead father, the colonel, she is wearing her masculine-fashion jacket. It is worth mentioning here that Ingmar Bergman said *Tango* would have been a much more truthful film had the Jeanne/Maria Schneider role been played by a boy.

The indeterminate image of boy/girl from *The Spider's Stratagem* is echoed in *The Conformist*, in the seduction scene of the child Marcello by Lino, the chauffeur (Pierre Clementi). Lino first shows his pistol to Marcello and then takes off his uniform cap allowing his raven-black hair to tumble to his shoulders. "Kill Madame Butterfly," Lino orders Marcello. Courtesy of The Museum of Modern Art, Film Stills Archive.

In *1900* the homosexual motif is manifested through the twinning/doubling motif of Olmo and Alfredo. There, however, it is immersed with Bertolucci's disturbing view of the working class as the embodiment of virility. This view is inspired by Pasolini and reveals an affinity with Fassbinder to whom Bertolucci feels very close.[3] In one of the scenes in *1900* Olmo (Gerard Depardieu), the sharecropper's son, and Alfredo (Robert De Niro), son of the landowner, compare the size of their penises, and Olmo jokingly notes that his is longer because he's a socialist. In *The Sheltering Sky*, supervirility is attributed to Belqassim, the Other from the Third World. This attribution assumes a visual representation in the set, which was erected as to show a Western fantasized image of Belqassim's harem. In the center of the set a towerlike construction looks like an erect penis, recalling Pasolini's mythic sets for the movies *Oedipus Rex* and *Medea* which were shot in North Africa and used Third World natives as extras.

In *Tragedy of a Ridiculous Man* there are several vivid images of sexual indeterminacy.[4] One of them occurs when the camera, through an extremely tight close-up of Laura's feminine lips, reveals a small moustache. The extreme close-up has no apparent motivation other than to reveal to the spectator the "blemish" in Laura's otherwise pretty face. There is also a scene in which two maids in Primo's household are dancing together to the sounds of rock music. One is a full, older woman and the other is a young and slim tomboy type. The spectator discovers that the young girl is a woman only after the camera approaches her bosom. The image of the two dancing women recalls the seductive tango performed by Anna and Guilia in *The Conformist*. But here, sexual liberation is the domain of the working class (associated with the low form of rock music), and not the dubious privilege of the decadent bourgeoisie (associated with the tango) as in *The Conformist*. In *The Last Emperor* although Pu Yi's homosexuality is never explicitly expressed in the movie, Bertolucci hints at it by presenting Lone's face in ways which emphasize its androgynous qualities. The eunuchs, representing the artificial third sex (see chapter 4) in *Emperor*, push sexual ambiguity into its grotesque limits. They are portrayed by Bertolucci as repulsive creatures and their sexual ambiguity is neither seductive nor sexually attractive.

In *The Sheltering Sky*, the image of bisexuality resonates in the image of a young, always laughing girl/boy in the Tuareg caravan to whom Kit gives her Panama (colonial) hat, and who resembles the boy/girl in *Stratagem*. Here sexual ambiguity is associated, as in *Stratagem* and *The Conformist*, with the symbol of the hat and its masking connotation. The hat veiling and unveiling the hair alludes to pubic hair, which veils the sexual marks of difference. Kit herself is veiled as a boy so that, paradoxically, both she and Belqassim can enjoy heterosexual relationship. There are also well disguised suggestions in the movie regarding Port's homosexual inclinations. The film, particularly in the beginning, creates an expectation that Port will have an affair with Tunner or with a local Arab boy. Port's soft voice and sometimes his body language seem to invite homosexual relationships. Some of the shots in which he is seen from behind, and others in which he is seen with the repulsive Erick—as well as shots showing him approaching Arabs—provoke homosexual associations. Another image of sexual ambiguity is associated with the veiled Belqassim. When we first see his eyes under the veil we, presumably like Kit, are not sure of his sexual identity. The scene that deconstructs all *The Sheltering Sky*'s sexual ambiguity occurs when the Arab whore pushes a breast into Port's open fly. This image fuses the sexual markers of the opposite sexes.

Sexual Indeterminacy and the Promise of Sexual Liberation

Bertolucci's openness to the bisexual aspect of human sexuality seems to suggest, if not feminist convictions, then at least sensitivity to the concept, suggested by bisexuality, of a truly liberated human sexuality. Yet, as Barbara Creed observes, the increasing emphasis on the androgynous figure in popular culture and the woman/man in the cinema is neither new nor necessarily progressive. On the contrary, "this postmodern fascination with the androgyne and the 'neuter' subject may indicate desire *not* to address problems associated with the specificities of the oppressive gender roles of patriarchal society, particularly those constructed for women."[5]

Bertolucci is perhaps a good reinforcement of Creed's suggestion. He has often been accused by feminists of conveying anti-women sentiments in his work.[6] This judgment is particularly evident in many feminist critiques of *Tango*. Bertolucci said in one of the interviews he gave after the phenomenal *succès de scandale* of *Tango*: "I like feminist women watching *Tango*. They have a primary reaction to this film—that because of the fact that Maria undergoes acts of violence it is therefore an anti-feminist film. That's much too primary a reaction for me." In the same interview he also said that: "It is not a male chauvinist film. That's too simplistic. It is a film about." And he added: "The movie is an accelerated course in Wilhelm Reich. . . . To make moral judgements is not interesting." Perhaps his most revealing remark in this interview is that "for men this movie is a more traumatic experience than for women" because "the men feel their virility challenged. Marlon takes great risks, and they identify with this."[7] Yet, despite Bertolucci's apologetic discourse, one cannot ignore the disturbing acts of sexual and verbal abuse committed against the character of Jeanne, as well as the representation of the Paul character as the sole bearer of suffering and social anger. The larger than life figure of the Paul character, and the tragic proportions of his agony, overshadow the petit-bourgeois concerns of the Jeanne character. The speech delivered by Paul sitting near the coffin of his dead wife, more than anything else fixes the notion of femininity as enigma, if not treachery, against the world of men. The authenticity attributed to Paul's search for pure sexuality denies Jeanne's subjectivity by embodying male fantasy, which ignores the humanity of the fantasized other.

Tango, Bertolucci's most controversial and disturbing film primarily because of its treatment of sexuality, violence, and death, is perhaps the director's most problematic film from a feminist point of view. In the second chapter I suggest that *Tango* be read as both a regressive and a progressive text that follows Marcuse's radical reading of Freud's analysis of perversions as the foundation of a better civilization based upon the pleasure principle. Aitken, to cite another example of a critic offering a favorable feminist reading of *Tango*, claims that the first intercourse between Paul and Jeanne inacts "the prototypical heterosexual male fantasy—pure lusty fucks, no encumbering attachments." But he adds that the fact that this relationship ultimately fails, "in fact proves fatal for Paul, seemed to indicate that Bertolucci was saying this sort of macho fantasy was over, impossible."[8]

Another disturbing aspect of *Tango* from a feminist point of view is the complete absence from view of Brando's penis, or even partial nakedness. Only in the last tango scene does he mockingly expose his buttocks to the shocked bourgeois audience in a gesture that ridicules the tango as a metaphor for heterosexual relationship and bourgeois respectability by suggesting anality and latent homosexuality. The historic absence of the penis in cinema is a well-known phenomenon and it has allowed, as Chris Straayer suggests, "the male body an independence from sexual anatomical verification."[9] When male sexuality is symbolized as the phallus, "power displaces sexuality rather than delivers it."[10] The displacement of the penis by phallic tyranny is most evident in *Tango* where Jeanne is asked to worship the phallus and the spectator is asked to admire Paul's transgression of social norms through his incestuous, Oedipal relations with Jeanne. In many interviews Bertolucci has admitted that he identified with Brando to such an extent that he could not show him naked in the final version. "It is also possible that I had so identified myself with Brando, that I cut it out of shame for myself. To show him naked would have been like showing myself naked."[11]

In *The Sheltering Sky*, however, we see Port's penis. Until his penis is revealed, it is difficult to determine if the visible lower parts belong to a man or a woman. The interesting thing about this shot is that the penis is not erect, a rare phenomenon in cinema. Whereas the absence of the penis in *Tango* only glorifies Paul's machismo, its presence in *The Sheltering Sky* exposes the problematic status of the phallus. It also alludes to the intratextual relationship between *Tango* and *The Sheltering Sky* discovered by Bertolucci, as he confessed to me, during an analysis only after he finished filming the latter.[12] In one of the shots of the dying Port in the room (which recalls the empty apartment of *Tango*) Port is seen wearing a T-shirt alluding to the famous Kowalski's T-shirt worn by Brando in *Tango*. Even some of the angles from which Port's face is shot during this agonizing scene (his face is seen from a high angle and from behind as if reversed) recall close-ups of Brando's face in *Tango*. The emphasis on male suffering locates the fictional situation of both films within an existentialist framework that assigns grandeur to male agony.

The representation of the Jeanne character in *Tango* is particularly difficult. The tragic greatness of Paul vis-à-vis Jeanne's petit-bourgeois worldview is, in a way, a reproduction of the imbalance in the two actors' star status levels. The utilization of Schneider, at that time an unknown actress (although the illegitimate daughter of a relatively famous French actor, Daniel Gelin), only emphasizes Brando's stardom. The collision of international star and anonymous actress created an intriguing yet problematic interaction. The curious thing about the characterization of Jeanne is that Bertolucci inverted Schneider's off-screen image as a young rebel. In *Tango* she plays the role of the French petite bourgeoise who submits herself to the American rebel. Bertolucci also selected Schneider, apparently, because he was impressed with her free attitude toward nakedness. Yet in *Tango* he preferred to invest her character with sexual submission and that of Brando with rebelliousness.

The investment of the Brando's character with the grandeur of the rebel is linked to his utilization as an icon of Hollywood cinema. "Why this fascination with the forties?" Tom asks Jeanne. She answers, "Because it's easier to love something that doesn't affect us too directly . . . something which keeps a certain distance . . . like you with your camera."[13] The cinematic allusions are clear. Jeanne's answer seems to express Bertolucci's own nostalgic fascination with the movies of the 1940s. Her explanation seems to be his. Jeanne appears at the beginning in a 1940s coat, flowered hat, and modern mini skirt. She appears as the combination of old and new. She is young and identified with pop art, but at the same time she has a special inclination for the old. Jeanne likes to collect antiques that once were revolutionary, because that makes her feel revolutionary. The allusion to Brando is obvious. Jeanne loves Paul/Brando although he is old (significantly, Paul is forty-five in the movie), because he once was a true revolutionary (Brando's movies from the 1950s are a re-

bellion against the 1940s) and because even in the present he remains
an anachronistic but romantic "revolutionary" type. Brando's romantic image is what attracts Jeanne as well as Bertolucci to him.
Tom, on the other hand, is the contemporary Godardian revolutionary who is disgusted by old things despite their revolutionary past:

> I don't have to think twice to choose between an antique house
> and a clean, clear room. You'll see . . . few pieces of furni-
> ture . . . glass and chrome . . . light even in the objects, every-
> thing new . . . new things. You are like a film with a technical
> error. The sound doesn't synchronize with the visuals. We lis-
> ten to you talking of old dusty things while we see your clean,
> healthy, modern appearance.[14]

As a representative of the New Wave and its radical conversion in
Godard's cinema, Tom expresses a childish zeal for everything that
is new, thus reminding us of Jacques's (Godard's alter-ego in *Tout va
bien*) quest for new forms for his revolutionary cinema.

Freudian psychoanalysis provides additional layers of signification for Jeanne's obsession with old things. Her Oedipal fixation on
her father, the colonel with the green eyes and the shining boots
(which still give her mother "strange shivers"),[15] motivates the narrative progression in *Tango*. Jeanne, who is defined by Paul as an old-
fashioned girl, kills him, finally, with an old-fashioned phallic pistol
that belonged to her father, while Paul mockingly wears the
colonel's hat. By killing Paul, Jeanne "has also killed the cinematic
fantasies which provide identity for all Bertolucci's generation."[16]
When Paul offers to marry her it means that the past becomes entirely real and that means "it can no longer provide a vital myth for
the present."[17] When the romantic rebel image of Paul/Brando is broken, he cannot be accepted any more. His existence is justified only
by his being the epitome of the Hollywood star as rebel hero.

In the beginning scene, Brando, like Schneider, is dressed in a
half modern, half old-fashioned manner. Under his elegant 1940s
coat, he wears the Kowalski's T-shirt, his on- and off-screen rebel
symbol. The semi-rape scene in *Tango* is an echo of the rape scene in
Streetcar Named Desire (1951), the movie adaptation of Tennessee
Williams's steamy play which established Brando as Stanley Kowalski as rebel anti-hero associated with class consciousness. We continue to see Kowalski's T-shirt in the following scenes. This shirt, we
should remember, was a powerful erotic image in the 1950s. Like the
blue jeans and the leather jacket (which Brando as Johnny, a leader of

the Blind Rebels Motorcycle Club, wears in *The Wild One*), to young audiences the T-shirt meant freedom, danger, defiance of authority, and refusal to conform to all established rules including the rigid sexual taboos of the time. Brando, whose roles in the 1950s established him as the rebel against the sexual repression intrinsic to the ideology of romance as elaborated by the movies of the 1940s, was therefore a natural choice for Bertolucci who, in *Tango*, launches an attack on the self-consuming discourse of romance.

Brando's Method acting during the 1950s also signified a rebellion—in this case against the dead expression typical of the acting style of the 1940s. Brando's relaxed postures, as opposed to the rigidity of the 1940s, represent his anti-Hollywood rebellion. In *Tango* the opposition of rigidity and free-spirited behavior is symbolically alluded to during the tango sequence. In this scene, Brando, dressed in the style of the great lovers of classical Hollywood cinema, is making fun of the very code he is supposed to obey. Not only does he disrupt and mock the ritualized movements of the dance, he also commits the ultimate gesture of assault on bourgeois/Hollywood respectability, baring his backside to the shocked dancers/spectators. Another facet of Brando's sexual rebelliousness during the 1950s was his tendency to play roles involving sado-masochism, a tendency fully realized by Bertolucci who moves him in *Tango* through a process of *percorso* (see chapter 2). Brando's play on the tension between sensitivity and brutality (a typical Hollywood strategy) is also exploited by Bertolucci's use of the American actor as the living rebel icon of the 1950s.

Significantly, in the last three scenes he is wearing an elegant suit. This is also "the first time they are together outside their island. It is their first contact with reality."[18] This is also the first time that Paul confesses his love and proposes marriage to Jeanne. Talking in bourgeois terms, he seems to break up his rebel image. But by the act of exposing his buttocks on the dance floor, Brando reminds us again that he is the eternal rebel, the last romantic cinema idol, "the essentially naive outsider, the romantic who is not a match for a French bourgeois girl."[19] Thus Brando's on-screen image as a rebel is preserved. He is metaphorically destroyed, but his screen image is revived. To reiterate this notion, he dies, curled in a fetal position.[20] The image is a quotation from Brando's death in *Viva Zapata*, where his role as the "essential revolutionary" established him as a hero for Bertolucci.

Whereas the main triangle in *Tango* retains Hollywood conventions of rivalry (weak male versus strong one), the secondary triangle is a sheer parody of the cinematic norm. We see Paul and Rosa's lover Marcel, sitting in identical red plaid bathrobes given them by Rosa, drinking the bourbon she gave her lover in emulation of her relationship with Paul. Trying to understand why Rosa has had relationships with Marcel, Paul says to himself, in English, after leaving Marcel's room, "I can't understand what she saw in you." The irony is that in her lover she saw Paul. She tried to make her lover a double of Paul.

This is a reversal of the Hollywood convention of rivalry according to which rivals are supposed to be opposites, and certainly not doubles. The parody is intensified by the atmosphere of the scene. Instead of an outburst of envy and hatred between the husband and the lover, we see a very friendly conversation between two ridiculous middle-aged men. Their discussion also centers around problems typical of middle-aged men, such as being overweight and losing hair. Perhaps it is the first scene in which Brando is shown not as a romantic idol, but as a real person, a human being who is even a little bit ridiculous. He is no more the legendary sexual animal, but an aging man concerned about losing his hair and getting fat, which reminds the spectator of the real problems of the aging Brando and re-emphasizes the question of where Paul ends, where Brando starts, and vice versa.

Paul becomes, despite his efforts to create a new symbolic order, the double of his own *padre*, a supermasculine figure who epitomizes the oppression of a phallic-centered culture. He also becomes symbolic of Jeanne's father, the ultimate symbol of Fascist oppression (he was a racist colonel who died in the Algerian war). Thus Paul becomes the double of two fathers who are themselves two ghost doubles united by the oppression/repression they inflict on their children (Jeanne and Paul). Despite Bertolucci's identification with the macho figure of Paul, his poetics of sexual indeterminacy complicates an explicit feminist critique of the movie. As much as Paul's character is a culmination of machoism it is also vivid evidence of the failure of macho fantasies.

Women and the Critique of the Bourgeoisie

Luna is the only Bertolucci film introducing a woman as a protagonist. It is about a widowed opera singer who goes to Rome for a summer engagement accompanied by her fifteen-year-old son. She discovers that her son is a drug addict and has a physical interest in her. Her response is animalistic, and she provokes her son to have intercourse with her. Bertolucci said that his inspiration for *Luna* was developed from the first memory he had of his mother. "I was 15 months or 2 years old. I was in the basket of a bicycle. I was looking up at my mother riding the bicycle, the moon behind her, and in my eyes confused the young face of my mother and the old face of the moon. I started from that memory and it became a story of a relationship between a mother and a son."[21]

The association of the mother and the feminine with the moon will be reinvoked in *The Sheltering Sky* when Kit's destiny after Port's death is controlled by the moon, the mythic symbol of the feminine. It is quite significant that in Bertolucci's only two films in which the protagonist is a woman (Kit is the sole protagonist of the second part of *The Sheltering Sky*, beginning with Port's death) women are explicitly associated with the moon. When Kit leaves the room after Port's death there is a spectacular shot of a moon in a dark blue sky (one might even find here a resonance to the corny images of the moon in Godard's *Hail Mary*) and from that moment on Kit is under the sign of the moon. This point was made clear by Storaro himself.

> *The Sheltering Sky* is a recounting of a journey in the lives of two characters, Port and Kit. The first part of the tale belongs to Port, the dominant one, the sun. The second part of the story belongs to Kit, the more submissive of the two, the moon. The fact that the story is set in Africa makes those two natural symbols of light, the sun and the moon, all the more important and the more difficult to ignore. At the beginning of the film it is day and Port is at the height of his powers. Kit is almost invisible, much the way the moon is when in the sky at the same time as the sun. But as Port sickens, the sun is going down. When he dies, it is nightfall. As Kit is left alone in an alien land, her moon begins to rise. It becomes her story. The journey of their lives parallels the journey of the sun and the moon. The sun, of course, represents the hot colours, the masculine colours, the reds and the oranges. The moon reflects the cooler colours, the indigos and the blues. Perhaps it is significant that as a couple, they only come to terms with their relationship as they sit and watch the sun go down, over a vast plain, at the time when the two lights pass each other. It is only then that they find their truth.[22]

Indeed the red/blue color scheme that dominates *The Last Emperor*'s dialectic of enlightenment is repeated in *The Sheltering Sky*, which bathes its interiors (the hotels' rooms and the room where

Port dies) in yellow/red colors and its exterior scenes in the desert when Kit is wandering with the Tuaregs caravan in blue. Kit is not only under the sign of the moon and the dark blue of the desert night, but the color of her blue eyes (unlike the dark brown color of Jane Bowles's eyes) is made even more salient by her blue clothes (the blue robe in the scene in the first hotel, the blue indigo turban, and finally the light blue dress and the blue sweater she is wearing after being saved and brought back to civilization). Thus, Kit's madness is portrayed as her inevitable destiny as a woman. The moon (itself the mythic symbol of the feminine element as well as the symbol of femininity in Bertolucci's private family mythology) is presented within the film's economy as being responsible for Kit's madness, i.e., for her dubious sexual liberation by the Other and her eventual hospitalization by the representatives of civilization. The moon, femininity, and madness, thus, are interwoven in accordance with an essentialist view regarding the true nature of woman.

The Sheltering Sky opens with an image of the strong and dynamic woman embodied through the famous energy of Debra Winger. In the beginning of the movie, when Kit, Port, and Tunner sit in the station, Kit reads aloud from a newspaper (with an ironic intonation) that the Italians gave the right of vote to women. Yet, in the second part of the film beginning with Port's death, Kit, being under the influence of the moon, becomes a submissive woman whose existence centers solely around her emancipatory sex with Belqassim. Her self breaks and dissolves after the sexual adventure is over and her story ends in madness. The dissolution of Kit's image of a strong woman begins in fact with the scene of Port's dying in the room. There, Kit is assigned the traditional maternal function of providing a nurturing environment for her man. She feeds Port with hot milk in a simulation of the idealized suckling mother of the oral stage.

It is rather interesting to note here that both *Tango* and *The Sheltering Sky* attempt to liberate their protagonists through sex and the rejection of language as a form of human communication. In *Tango* the negation of language (the "law of the father") fails and results in Paul's death. In *The Sheltering Sky*, the communication between Kit and Belqassim is purely carnal and devoid of any verbal or linguistic articulation. Eventually, as in *Tango*, this effort at achieving an articulate body language also fails.

In *Tango*, as in *The Conformist*, women are presented as mediocre, and their petit-bourgeois concerns are ridiculed relative to male existential *angst*. Marcello contemptuously describes Guilia to the priest during his confession as "petita borghesa" who is "all bed and kitchen." Yet as Mellen suggests, this view of women can be read differently.

> Perhaps taking cues from the actual history of fascism, with its suppression of the rights of women (a correlative to the latent or overt homosexuality of its men) Bertolucci, Visconti, and Petri reveal women under fascism to be either mainly promiscuous whores (Anna in *Conformista*, Agusta in *Investigation*, Draifa in *Spider's Stratagem*) or "all bed and kitchen," like Guilia, the mindless girl Clerici marries in his campaign not to be different. "To be normal is to turn to look at the ass of a pretty girl, see that others have done the same, and be pleased," says Clerici's best friend, the blind Italo—speaking Clerici's thoughts.[23]

Mellen's view suggests indeed a reading of what seems to be Bertolucci's view of women's inferiority as a critique of the Fascist view of women as sexual servants and procreation organisms. This recalls of course Bertolucci's insistence on reading *Tango* as about male chauvinism rather than as an expression of it. Yet one cannot ignore the impression that against the rebellious male protagonists in Bertolucci's films women are dwarfed by, if not indirectly blamed for, restricting their men's freedom. Women in Bertolucci's movies (with the exception of *1900*) do not have any intellectual interests, they live by animalistic instincts and for sensual pleasure. It is for the Bertoluccian male to suffer at length, and to prolong his suffering through conscious intellectualization of his problems.

The critique of the bourgeoisie in Bertolucci's cinema is immersed with anti-women sentiments correlating to the same strains in Fascist thought. Bertolucci's view of women as the locus of repressive bourgeois ideology is nowhere more evident than in the sodomizing scene in *Tango* in which the punished female body, as Lynda K. Bundtzen observes, becomes "a pathetic vessel of patriarchal and bourgeois values, a hiding place for 'family jewels'."[24] The difficulty in criticizing Bertolucci on this issue derives from the fact that this very strategy of sexual indeterminacy is projected to the sphere of sexual politics. Is Bertolucci's depiction of women part of his critique of the Fascist and patriarchal orders? As such is it reflective of dominant patterns of thought in these orders? Or is it an unproblematized mediation of women as seen by him?

Spider Women

There are two types of women in Bertolucci's movies: the domestic type, the petit-bourgeois, such as Guilia, or Celia in *Before the Revolution*, and Jeanne in *Last Tango*; and the destructive, neurotic, decadent type such as Marcello's mother, Anna in *The Conformist*,[25] the incestuous aunt Gina, in *Before the Revolution*, and Caterina, the seductive incestuous mother in *Luna*. Bertolucci's preoccupation with the surrealist theme of *amour fou* is joined with the myth of the spider woman, who resembles a destructive *femme fatale* borrowed from the misogynist tradition of *film noir*.

Kolker says on Draifa that she "may be the black widow of *The Spider's Stratagem*."[26] Tara, in *Strategy*, as Kline observes, is composed of "the first two syllables of the most dreaded of spiders."[27] When Athos junior insults Draifa's sexual prowess, she winds him "into a medical sarape, spinning him around and around, in a gesture that recalls both the action of a reel of film being *embobine* and a spider mumifying and embalming its prey."[28] In *The Conformist* the private tango between Anna and Guilia becomes a seductive spider's web that encircles the stiff Marcello. In *Luna*, Joe as a baby is trapped by a ribbon while his mother and father are dancing. Furthermore, Alida Valli (who plays Draifa in *The Spider's Stratagem*) plays in *Luna* the role of Giuseppe's (Joe's father) mother who gets trapped in her own knitting, recalling her spinning of Athos with a medical sarape in *Strategy*. Bertolucci, in one of his most famous and quoted interviews said:

> In nature it is usually the female that devours. Genetically, over the centuries, some males have understood her mechanisms, have understood the danger. Some spiders just approach the female, but stay within safe distance. Exciting themselves with her smell, they masturbate, collect their sperm in their mouth and wait to regain strength after orgasm. Because that is how they get devoured, when they are weak after ejaculation. Later, they inseminate the female with a minimal approach and thus she cannot attack them in the moment of their weakness. . . . What can develop (between a man and a woman) is only possessiveness . . . the destruction of the loved object.[29]

One cannot avoid comparing Bertolucci's reflection on this biological phenomenon with Simone de Beauvoir's. For de Beauvoir, this phenomenon "has crystallized the myth of the devouring femininity" and foreshadows "a feminine dream of castration." These biological facts, she emphasizes, create "a proclamation of the 'battle of the sexes' which sets individuals, as such, one against another."[30] Freud himself in his famous article "Femininity" gives the spiders as an example "that in some classes of animals the females are the stronger and more aggressive and the male is active only in the single act of sexual union."[31]

Metaphors of Sexual Repression/ Political Oppression

Bertolucci's consistent preoccupation with the motifs of sexual repression/political oppression, dance, incest, the Oedipal complex, sexual ambiguity, and anal metaphors contain the promise of liberated as well as liberating discourse. Hence, for example, dance sequences in his films have been interpreted as privileged moments of sexual and political liberation[32] and the incest motif as a metaphor for social transgression. Bertolucci himself acknowledged that his depiction of the incest in *Luna* "was supposed to serve as a kind of commentary on the decadence of modern society and the failure of the family as an institution to provide either solace or support." The reason Caterina and Joe "go so far in the movie," he said, "is a response to that destruction of values by society. They try to recreate a value even if it is painful. Their act is transgressive—subversive in a way. But through this traumatic experience they go toward a better life. I think there is a political gesture of hope at the end."[33]

Anality and sodomy are used by Bertolucci as metaphors for the exploitative, consumerist capitalist society. Yet, the repeated acts of violent sodomy and anal sex forced upon the female figures in his films (and also in Godard's, see chapter 5) make it questionable whether these acts can be taken as legitimate symbols of reification of social conditions under Capitalism. The anal motif so pervasive in Bertolucci's cinema is frequently used as a metaphor for the social relations under capitalism (see chapter 2). Perversions, on the other hand, are used ambivalently both as a promise of liberation and as a sign of decadence and degradation (as in *1900*). Yet the emancipating potential of the incest metaphor, to cite one example, is never fully realized. In *Before the Revolution*, as Aitken observes: "The replacement of Agostino by his aunt, Gina, the substitution of one taboo for another—a sort of homosexuality by a sort of incest—ultimately leads Fabrizio, in his quest for an unremarkable life, to ditch Gina and marry a respectable bourgeoisie."[34]

There is, then, some ambivalence in Bertolucci's treatment of incest and homosexuality. On the one hand they are presented (as in *Tango*) as manifesting a rebellion, and challenging bourgeois notions of propriety. In particular they attack the family as the nexus of civilized repression and political oppression imposed on the individual by the capitalist system. On the other hand, as in *The Conformist*, homosexuality and incest are presented as symptoms of bourgeois decadence regardless of actual political inclinations. Therefore both the Fascist Marcello and the anti-Fascist Anna are found guilty of decadence by Bertolucci.

In many of Bertolucci's movies, his heroes have been involved with women much older than themselves. In *Tango* this pattern is reversed. In *Partner*, however, Giacobbe is narcissistically in love with his double. The persistent search for the father in Bertolucci's cinema with its Oedipal overtones is in fact a search for the ultimate tutor. All the tutors (except for Anita, the teacher in *1900*) are males. Usually these tutor figures are unmarried or not presented in a family context. In *Before the Revolution*, at their final meeting, Fabrizio offers to take Agostino to visit his mentor, an older unmarried man, Professor Cesare (who on the film's self-reflexive level alludes to Cesare Zavattini). It is finally Gina and not Agostino whom Fabrizio takes to meet Professor Cesare. And it is here that Fabrizio and Gina read to each other from Oscar Wilde. "This Socratic relationship— older man teaching impressionable youth—runs in an ambigious refrain from *Before the Revolution* to *The Conformist* and gets intermingled with another strain—murder of the father by the son."[35] *The Conformist* like all of Bertolucci's movies is about the quest for the father, the absent patriarch. In *The Conformist* the Fascist state functions as a father-substitute. Quadri, as a potential spiritual father, is not good enough for Marcello. He is married to a lesbian and presumably derives pleasure from watching her engaged in homosexual acts with other women. The relationship between the Oedipal complex and the tutor motif reaches its climax in *The Last Emperor* (see chapter 4).

Ethno-Porno: From "Mama-China" to "Mama-Africa"

Bertolucci's quest in *The Last Emperor* and *The Sheltering Sky* for the non-Western Other involves as well a quest for another sexuality. Indeed, the two quests are one and the same in the sense that the allure of the Other is, presumably, grounded in his/her promise of different sexuality. In *The Last Emperor* (see chapter 4) racial otherness is homologous with sexual otherness. Yet, the film represents a fantasy of sexual otherness located within the boundaries of one race (the Chinese) and one class (the Imperial court). The most memorable erotic scene in the film is the suckling scene which foregrounds other sexuality by exploiting and exoticizing racial difference and geographical otherness. The location of Ar Mo in the center of the frame and the fondling and suckling of her breast by Pu Yi entrap the spectator not only because of the visual seductiveness and the voluptuous esthetics of the shot but, also because its composition frames a boundary of pleasure between spectacle and excess.

In the center of the frame are Ar Mo and the twelve-year-old Pu Yi. In the background the concubines are on boats sailing among exotic floating flowers and watching the scene with binoculars. On the right side of Pu Yi the camera reveals his younger brother Pu Chi eating his meal, a regular, normal nourishment. The spectator who looks at Ar Mo as an incestuous object of desire becomes complicit in Pu Yi's and Ar Mo's perversion, hence becoming as well a participant in the perverse pleasure of cinema itself. Moreover, the camera demands that the spectator participate in the concubines' voyeurism and in the mute but seeing presence of Pu Chi, who establishes the normative rules of child behavior by eating a regular meal.

The fetishization of Ar Mo as well as Pu Yi's regression to infantile orality become, to use Julia Kristeva's words, "metaphors of non-speech, of a 'semiotics' that linguistic communication does not account for."[36] This type of fetishization also occurs both in the *ménage à trois* scene between Pu Yi and his two wives, and in the scene between the woman pilot, Eastern Jewel, and Pu Yi's first wife. There fetishization is carried even further, culminating in the punishment of the deviant wife and her expulsion from history and the narrative alike.

In *The Sheltering Sky*, on the other hand, sexual and racial boundaries are transgressed in the form of inter-racial erotica. Whereas in *The Last Emperor*'s regime of desire the only imagized/eroticized bodies are the fantasized bodies of the Chinese Other, in *The Sheltering Sky* the protagonists' sexual encounters break racial and ethnic taboos. Nevertheless, Bertolucci's sexual politics do not transgress Western ethnocentrism. The American married couple Kit and Port Moresby are trying to resolve marital problems through a travel expedition through North Africa. Both of them have sexual encounters with natives. Port has an encounter with an Arab prostitute and Kit lives out a voluptuous affair with Belquassim, a

Tuareg tribal chief. The film's narrative focalization is the white couple; the natives (Arabs, Africans, and Tuaregs) are used as an ethnic backdrop aimed at magnifying and sanctifying white *angst*.

A deconstruction of the design of the major sexual encounters in *The Sheltering Sky* reveals that Bertolucci's sexual politics in this movie are heavily laced with traces of colonial discourse.[37] Port has a one-night stand with a Moroccan prostitute. Thus, her character is colonized twice: once as a subject of a colonized country under the French Protectorate and second as a prostitute whose body has been colonized by her pimp and clients. By contrast, Kit becomes the lover of a free subject. Tuareg nomadic culture resisted the Arab influence of the Islamic crusades and the attempts of the French colonization of the Magrheb. Furthermore, Belquassim is the chief of a Tuareg tribe; his status as a young Sahara desert prince counterbalances, to some extent, the inferiority implied by his racial difference.

Whereas the prime region of erotic interest for Port in the Moroccan prostitute's body is her full-breasted torso, Belquassim's sexual interest seems to concentrate on Kit's lower parts with an inclination towards foot fetishism (which is evident also in scenes in *The Conformist* and *The Last Emperor*, representing lesbianism). Port and the prostitute engage in phallic-mammal contact leading to Port's orgasm. The prostitute is the active partner in this encounter taking the responsibility for the seduction. She recites Arab love songs to Port with a soothing, musical voice. Like an infant who is reassured by a mother's voice, Port is shown with his head comfortably rested in the woman's full bosom. This pre-Oedipal, pre-genitally organized sexuality does not put any demands on Port's active virility, but expresses, rather, a regressive childish longing to refuse with the mother's body and thereby achieve an orgasm which means death.[38] In *The Sheltering Sky*, Port's desire to escape the fate of the American "lost generation" through fusion with Mother-Nature ("Mama-Africa") epitomized by the African continent (the origin of humanity according to current scientific thinking) indeed ends with his actual death.

It is worth noting in this context that the whole situation of prostitution is disguised in the film as a display of Oriental hospitality in which—according to the dictates of Arab tradition—tea is served to the guests. This disavowal of prostitution is perpetuated by the fact that no monetary payment is overtly transacted. The stealing of Port's wallet by the prostitute appears almost as a continuation of the disavowal of the act of selling which is taking place in this scene. However, as the prostitute cuddles Port to her bosom, Port takes back his wallet, thereby stealing in his turn, the sexual services he has been provided with. The spectator is put in an uneasy position in which identification oscillates between the exploited Western tourist and the exploited prostitute. When Port shows the wallet to the angry prostitute as he leaves the tent, his face expresses a greater satisfaction than it did during the sexual act itself, thus underlying the social vulnerability and exploitability of the humiliated Arab prostitute.

For a French audience familiar with the history of French colonialism in North Africa, the whole scene can be read as an allegory on French colonialism. Bertolucci, however, utilizes the pornographic potential of the cinema to comment on the exploitative nature of all colonial relations. Hence, Port's return home from a prostitute to the waiting Kit is not perceived as adultery. Rather, it points to the recourse of Port, as the traveler who explores the sexuality of the exotic other, to another sexual regime.

Bertolucci's poetics of sexual indeterminacy in *The Sheltering Sky* subliminally suggests an ethno-porno iconography. Kit's mimicry (her disguise as a Tuareg boy) allows her to enter Tuareg society. In the private chamber where she is kept confined, both sexual partners unwrap the traditional male Indigo turban. Kit by now has been transvested, her skin blackened. All this camouflage occurs so that Belquassin can enjoy her being sexually other (female) and racially different (white). The ritualistic, worshipping manner in which the African sexual partner tenderly undresses and reverently wipes the desert dust off Kit's body conjures forth an image of the American partner as a sex goddess rather than a sexual slave. Kit's cage/castle provides the couple, temporarily, with an intimate isolation free of the colonial outside world with its racial segregation. However, like in Bertolucci's *Tango*, the moment the door of this artificially constructed private space opens to the public space marked by racial separation, the couple's private Eden collapses. This recalls Albert Memmi's comment about the illusions of exogamy: there is no space free of socio-cultural contingencies.[39]It should also be stressed that, to put it provocatively, the fact that Belquassim does not look like the "Orangoutan husband of the Hottentot female"[40] but is stunningly beautiful and delicate, fetishistically assuages the transgression that traverses the text. Indeed, fetishism structures the whole scene that gives back to Kit her white skin and racial supremacy.

The potentially anxiety-inducing idea regarding contact between black manhood and white womanhood is soothed in the film by giving the Western partner an ego-reinforcing focus. Only the white male enjoys orgasm (as in the encounter between Port and the Moroccan woman) and the spectator is kept ignorant about the black male's subjectivity. Is he ravished by the delights of sexual difference, or by the discovery of Kit's white skin? Furthermore, Bertolucci's mise en scéne reproduces cultural codes of mastery and submission taken from popular erotica, thereby establishing white racial supremacy. This is most notable in the scene in the private chamber in which Kit is standing on the bed while Belquassim, sitting and kneeling, performs oral intercourse with her.

Both Kit's and Port's respective encounters with the exotic Other lead to sexual practices quite rare in mainstream cinema. Those practices allow the Western man to be nurtured without a display of virility, and permit the Western white woman to enjoy sexuality without phallic penetration. A feminist reading would gladly welcome this less phallocentric representation of human sexuality. However, the fact that, unwittingly or not, this reduction in phallocracy requires the recourse to an exotic Other as a flight from Western alienation is disturbing.

Bertolucci, just like Bowles four decades earlier, is a kind of "colonial traveler" in Said's sense of "displaced percipient."[41] Said describes colonial texts as "encapsulations" of the encounters between Europe and "primitivity" where a "vascillation" between the foreign and the familiar occurs. In *The Sheltering Sky* Port experiences precisely this kind of vascillation. He enjoys the delights of cultural differences as a freshly arrived American in Tangier but simultaneously disavows these differences by affixing universalist rules governing prostitution to his first North African experience (the encounter with the Moroccan woman). Homi Bhabha's analysis of colonial discourse may suggest a better insight into Bertolucci's fetishization of the Other along lines of race and sex. Bhabha reminds us that skin "unlike the sexual fetish, is not a secret, it is the most visible of fetishes which plays a public part in the racial drama which is enacted everyday in colonial societies."[42] In *The Sheltering Sky* the blackening of Kit's skin (her newly acquired sun-tan) metamorphoses the white skin of the Western female from a "visible fetish playing a public part in racial drama" into a secret fetish playing a part in private sexual drama. Not only does the scopic economy of the mise en scéne of the sexual drama enacted in the hidden room between Kit and Belquassim establish the idolization of white skin, but also the fetishistic textual regime of this scene leads to the sexualization of what Frantz Fanon refers to as the "epidermal schema."[43]

In the same thrust, Bhabha underlines the parallelism between sexual fetish and the fetish of colonial discourse (or of racial stereotypes). The first facilitates sexual relations ("It is the prop which makes the whole object desirable and lovable").[44] The second facilitates colonial or inter-racial relations. In *The Sheltering Sky* the scene between Port and the North African young woman demonstrates how the sexual fetish (signified by the Arab woman's dazzling erotic paraphenalia) facilitates colonial relations simulating a harem-like erotica. Similarly, the erotic scenes between Kit and Belquassim illustrate how the skin, the "key signifier of cultural and racial difference,"[45] facilitates and intensifies sexual relations. Bertolucci's exploitation of racial difference through the revitalization of tired libido (Port) or the investment of libidinal excess (Kit) seems to follow a prevalent tendency of our age of postmodern postcolonialism regarding the representation of sexual/racial relations.[46] It can be argued that this trend is triggered by the epidermal fetish which (due to its visibility) offers a tremendous voyeuristic potential to the scopophilic cinematic apparatus by injecting into the sexual fetish a new vitality.

Bhabha argues that colonial discourse is characterized by the holding of multiple contradictory beliefs. Bertolucci in *The Sheltering Sky* cultivates countless contradictory endemic beliefs about Africa and Africans/Arabs. Africa is both convivial and hostile, hospitable and rejecting, unpolluted and fly-infested. Africans are both ravishingly winsome and grotesquely repulsive. They have healthy, sculpted bodies or degenerate, demonized ones. They are capable of gratuitous, altruistic behavior or can reveal themselves as money-hungry and easily corruptible. In short, Arab/African culture within the economy of Bertolucci's quest for the Other is both utopia and dystopia.

Films, as products of the societies that consume them, give an expression to public consciousness and ideological orientations. As a product of the early 1990s, *The Sheltering Sky*'s latent phobia of inter-racial relations expresses Eurocentrist xenophobic fears of the Other. Questions of socio-cultural and national identity prevail in all their urgency in most countries at the outset of the 1990s. *The Sheltering Sky*, thus, relate to fears of First World metropolitan masses on both sides of the Atlantic, of being linguistically and culturally engulfed by unassimilable Others viewed as demographically, economically, and culturally threatening. The growing role of exile, expatriation, diaspora, and multiculturalism in the European and American urban landscape is libidinally invested in the textual and scopic organization of *The Sheltering Sky* in which postcolonialism is revealed both by its reproduction of racial hierarchies of the colonial order and by its nostalgic look at the "good old days of the Empire."

Conclusion

Despite Bertolucci's complex and sensitive engagement with the themes of male homosexuality and bisexuality, his female characters are represented and perceived exclusively within the boundaries of the sexual domain and are never depicted as able to transcend it (unlike, for example, Susan in *Tout va bien*). Women are excluded from the utopian vision portrayed in most of Bertolucci's films, and the *Last Emperor* even goes one step further and exiles them from the narrative.

The influence of Godard on the early Bertolucci is apparent, to a certain extent, in his representation of women as well. In fact, the seeds of all of Bertolucci's films are already planted in his first feature film *Before the Revolution*, which is a clearly post-Godardian film. The film contains many quotations that pay homage to Godard's New Wave films. Such for example is the beginning scene of the running Fabrizio which recalls Belmondo in the final scene of *Breathless*—a movie that affected the young, impressionable Bertolucci enormously.[47] There are also several allusions to Godard's *A Woman is a Woman*. The pick-up scene of Gina by a stranger in the street (the whole scene is voyeuristically observed by Fabrizio) is on the background of a billboard of *Una donna est una donna*, the Italian title of Godard's film. Later Fabrizio discusses the film with Cesare his spiritual father, the Communist tutor whose first name is the same as Cesare Zavattini's (who was also Bertolucci's father's friend). The billboard with the title of Godard's film is a sort of misogynist statement affirming that women are by definition treacherous creatures.

Bertolucci said in 1981, "When I made my first film in 1964, I considered myself more of a French director than an Italian director. I was influenced by the *Nouvelle Vague* and their experiments with cinema at the time."[48] *Before the Revolution* is an intertextual film and its plurality of shooting styles is based on a Godardian model. The film contains references not only to the New Wave Godard but also to a whole series of films from two decades of Italian neorealism.[49] The subject matter of *Before the Revolution* is an analysis of a segment of Italian society at a particular historical moment (Fabrizio accuses his apolitical aunt of living outside of history). Cesare, the Communist tutor, tells Fabrizio that "my education started at 45." *Before the Revolution*, thus, should be understood as referring to the way this chapter in Italian history has been embedded in the Italian cinema of the twenty years preceeding its making.

As much as Godard created Anna Karina, his first wife, as a new kind of woman to represent an era, so Bertolucci created Gina (played by the actress Adriana Asti, who was his first wife) to function as Fabrizio's other/mirror. Gina is the projection of Fabrizio/Bertolucci's neuroses (the nostalgia for the present, the fear of revolution, and the repudiation of politics) as well as a mirror of a whole generation of Italian intellectuals. The character of the aunt, Gina, an alienated modern woman (associated with Michelangelo Antonioni's woman but also with Roberto Rossellini's), recalls also the Godardian woman of the New Wave period. Her haircut is very French (the Care style), recalling Godard's Luis Brooks type of woman. Gina is a cinematic composition of constructions of female types in French and Italian cinema. Her meaning is created by allusions to cinematic female types and their relationship to trends in

Charlotte (Macha Méril) and Robert (Bernard Noël) in *The Married Woman*. Courtesy of The Museum of Modern Art, Film Stills Archive.

The fragmented bodies of Godard's New Wave period are revisited in *Passion*. Courtesy of The Museum of Modern Art, Film Stills Archive.

Godard's influence is most evident in Bertolucci's first auteurist film, *Before the Revolution*. Gina (Andriana Asti) and Fabrizio (Francesco Barilli) are framed in a typically fragmented Godardian composition. Gina, an alienated modern woman, recalls the Godardian woman of the New Wave period. Courtesy of The Museum of Modern Art, Film Stills Archive.

film and society (Italian neorealism, French New Wave, Antonioni's modernism) and not by psychological depth. Gina represents the idea of the new Italian woman. She is independent of her family in Milan, the most modern and industrial city of Italy.

Fabrizio epitomizes the contradiction between the power of the bourgeois past and the felt need for the revolution to be carried out by the Communist party. Fabrizio's conflicts with the other characters, each representing another segment of Italian society, turn the film into an analytic metamovie. The major conflict between Cesare (representing the political aspect) and Gina (representing the sexual apolitical aspect) is resolved only in Bertolucci's following films which synthesize Freud with Marx. *Before the Revolution* is a film "before the analysis" (the beginning of Bertolucci's analysis was in 1969) in which both the political and the sexual are betrayed by the young, immature protagonist. And, indeed, the film not only identifies with Fabrizio but also criticizes him on every level. Fabrizio is criticized by both Gina and Cesare. Gina criticizes Fabrizio for capitulating to bourgeois morality while Cesare criticizes him for being incapable of acting correctly on either the personal or political level. Gina in *Before the Revolution* (giving voice to the reactionary position from a leftist point of view) argues with Cesare that people cannot change. To support her argument she quotes Oscar Wilde's dictum, "You can't change even one person." In *The Last Emperor*, however, (which coincides with the end of Bertolucci's first analysis)[50] Bertolucci based his thesis on the belief that man can change. If we take Bertolucci as representing the authorial position of *Before the Revolution*, then we can take Fabrizio's capitulation as a signifier of Bertolucci's forthcoming career, his capitulation to bourgeois filmmaking. Although the film, through its shifting narrative and character focalization, privileges Gina's and Cesare's positions, Bertolucci's career has followed Fabrizio's path.

In *Partner*, to give another example of Godard's influence on the young Bertolucci, the scene of the soapgirl invokes the linking in *Two or Three Things* of female prostitution to consumer society. A more substantial theme in Bertolucci's cinema, which is not far from Godard's representation of women, is the association of the masculine as exterior and transcendental (evident also in Godard's *Masculin/Feminin*, *Numero Deux*, and others) in contrast to the association of the feminine with the interior and the immanent. Not even one woman in Bertolucci's cinema escapes this immanence or manages to exist beyond the realms of the senses. The two aspects of the Other as discussed by Erik Cohen (see chapter 4) are according to him "strikingly united in R.M. Rilke's Third Duino Elegy, in which the lover declares his love for the primaeval monster, his mother, in which he himself was 'dissolved' in a pre-natal state."[51] This view of the M/Other is not alien to Bertolucci's films and in particular *Tango* where the apartment assumes the role of the prenatal state similar to that of the Forbidden City in *The Last Emperor*.

The traditional association of femininity with the forces of nature and sensuality devoid of the grandeur of male existential *angst* or intellect (evident in particular in the fictional figures of Paul and Port) subverts Bertolucci's utopian attempts to foreground different sexuality. It is particularly disturbing that his two most recent films to date do not show any progress in this respect despite Bertolucci's more recent public pronouncements.[52] *The Last Emperor* symbolically annihilates women, while *The Sheltering Sky* punishes the white woman who was swept away into irrational sexual adventure. Sexual fantasies and political utopias in Bertolucci's cinema seem to be the exclusive privilege of men. What is left for women in his films, as in most of mainstream cinema, is to be gazed upon, to be erotically contemplated, and finally to be possessed and devoured as symbolic objects of desire.

Conclusion:
Past and Future Utopias

Perhaps the most significant phase of Bertolucci's career was the 1980s. The quest for the Other in this stage paralleled Bertolucci's moving to England as a sort of exile. Not surprisingly, Bertolucci's voluntary exile coincided with a larger trend affecting Italian society and cinema at that time of which Bertolucci, in our interview, complained bitterly. Between the late 1970s and the mid 1980s, as Stephen Gundle observes,

> the distinctive features of Italian society that marked it off, for good or ill, from other European nations, and which constituted the raw material of much of the domestic cinema, diminished greatly. In politics, economics, society and culture Italy now conforms broadly to the typical models of an affluent capitalist country. The collective dimension of social life had been undermined and replaced by a network of more individual and consumption-motivated orientations, while American themes and ideas find a ready audience with most of the more urbanized and modern sectors of the population. In these circumstances, it should hardly be cause for surprise that the cinema has ceded the primary role to television, as it did elsewhere in the industrial world up to thirty years previously.[1]

Bertolucci's fatigue with television-dominated Italy and the West (which he conveyed to me in our conversation in no uncertain terms) is expressed in *Emperor*, *The Sheltering Sky*, and *Little Buddha*. *The Sheltering Sky*, in particular, stresses the existential way of exile through its adaptation of the novel by the voluntary exile Paul Bowles. This is the way, not only of Bowles, but also of Port and Bertolucci himself. Exile is perceived as a privileged status through which the author detaches himself, in a Brechtian-style estrangement, from his immediate surroundings and assumes the condition of a spiritual exile in order to relate to reality from an unfamiliar perspective. It is quite interesting to note that Bertolucci's status as a semi-voluntary exile exists in tandem with his complete capitulation to Hollywood-style spectacle. The nine Oscars awarded to him by the Academy of Motion Pictures register his total assimilation into mainstream cinema and the ultimate recognition of his conformism by the film industry.

The irony of course is that Bertolucci, who began his film career as an admiring disciple of Godard, reached the climax of his career by repudiating his most important tutor. Godard, considered by many to be the most important living filmmaker, has remained completely marginal in terms of mainstream cinema. His Swiss exile, perceived in the 1970s as a temporary aberration, appears now to be permanent. In fact, today it may be possible to claim that the Paris period was the real exile and only today is Godard finally at home in his Swiss village of Rolle. Still, in terms of popularity and centrality there is no doubt that Godard's return to Switzerland represented his physical and symbolic choice of marginality and the periphery over the metropolitan centers. One cannot resist comparing Godard's voluntary exile with the voluntary exile of some of the German romantic writers for whom Godard bears a great admiration. Who else, as Frederic Jameson rightly asks, would reaffirm "by way of that unexpected permutation of his otherwise grotesque self-mockery (the invalid of *Carmen* [1982], the fool of *King Lear* [1987], the Prince Myshkin of *Soigne ta droite* [1987]) . . . the conception of the Romantic genius and creator in the strongest and most unreasonable expression it has found in our own time?"[2]

It is both telling and interesting that the end of the radical periods for both Godard and Bertolucci is the late 1970s. Godard made *Sauve qui peut (la vie)* and Bertolucci made *La Luna*. Both films can be seen as transitional in their anticipation of the impending " dialogue with the cosmos." One may claim that the shift in both directors' work signifies a larger cultural phenomenon typical of European intellectuals, the refugees of the radical 1960s and the confused 1970s. Bertolucci's newly born interest in the East and in Buddhism and Godard's fascination with Catholicism can be compared with the disappointment felt by intellectuals of the 1950s with Soviet Communism, "the God that failed," to use Stephen Spender's words. If, as Henri-Bernard Levi maintains, the belief in Soviet Stalinism spawned the first betrayal of the intellectuals, then the second betrayal was the one engendered by their subsequent conversion to Chinese Maoism. Bertolucci's romantic revolutionism and Godard's fanatic and dogmatic Maoism have currently been displaced by the quest for a new faith.

Godard's most recent film *Allemagne année 90 neuf zero* (*Germany Year 90 Nine Zero*) (1991) is a reflection on the relationship between story and history (in French the word *histoire* stands for both)[3] and expresses disappointment with both the West and the East (the former Eastern block). The film is a sort of a political thriller in which Godard explores the reunified Germany with skeptical eyes. Godard brings back Lenny Caution (Eddie Constantine) from *Alphaville* and turns him into the "last spy of the cold war." While apparently searching for a missing girl, Caution meets up with several characters, including Don Quixote, in the shattered landscape of former East Germany. In the film Caution asks repeatedly: "Where is the West?" The question becomes Godard's own expression of disappointment with the two political systems.[4]

It is of interest to conclude this comparative study by examining how Godard and Bertolucci relate to video, perhaps cinema's future technology. Godard has always been interested in new video technologies not so much for the sake of innovation but for what he considers video's potential to revolutionize conventional channels of production and dissemination. In fact, the success of the New Wave itself is partially indebted to the filmmakers' introduction of new technologies such as hand-held portable cameras which enabled the directors to shoot on location and to provide their films with more authentic atmospheres. In his video work with Miéville, Godard was trying to produce an alternative to standard, institutional television.[5]

Already in *Numero Deux* Godard experimented with video techniques such as overlaying images or inserting several images onto the same screen. Godard, Colin MacCabe observes, unlike many filmmakers, "has never regarded work in television as an inferior version of cinema."[6] In the past Godard has also been assisted by French and Mozambique television, which comissioned him to produce programs for them. Godard's embracing of new video technologies is part of his ongoing struggle as an iconoclast. During his New Wave and hyper-politicized periods Godard utilized new technologies so as to unmask "the treachery of images." Godard's exploration of the image in these periods is partially indebted to René Magritte's endlessly resourceful exploration of the theme of the image within an image. This exploration is perhaps best exemplified by the hand-painted poster of 1952 which recapitulates *The treachery of images,* the most famous of the word-pictures which Magritte

painted during his three years in Paris. In this word picture, the profile of a pipe is captioned in copperplate "Ceci n'est pas une pipe"
(This is not a pipe). Godard's famous dictum "Ce n'est pas une image juste, c'est juste une image" (This is not a just image, this is just
an image) is thus an echo of Magritte's preoccupation with the
treachery of images. In his cosmic period, however, the search for the
treachery of the image is replaced by the search for true, i.e., religious
and divine images of creation.[7] Surprisingly, this search seems to
bring Godard closer to Bertolucci, whose acute sense of nostalgia is
imbued with a Pasolini-like rejection of advanced capitalist society.
Bertolucci's recent quest for the other in ancient pre-industrialized
civilizations is not theoretically too distant from Godard's semi-
religious quest.[8]

Bertolucci's attitude toward video is diametrically opposed to
that of Godard. He has confessed in many interviews his fear of technology, claiming that he is not even able to take a simple picture
with an automatic still camera. The paradox, of course, is that despite Bertolucci's denial of complicity in technology, he is well
known as a visually oriented director, unlike the wordy, logos-
oriented Godard. Bertolucci's films bear the look of, to use Frederic
Jameson's words, "the technological 'perfection' of the new nostalgia glossy-film product."[9] It is also interesting to note that Godard's
embracing of the most advanced film-and-video laboratory, is, indeed, as Jameson explains, a continuation of his "aesthetic of imperfect cinema"[10] which renounces the "perfection" of capitalist
products by showing solidarity with the "poverty" and "imperfec-
tion" of the Third World. Like most avant-garde filmmakers, Godard's concern is to break away with the fetish character of the film
image. Indeed, as Jameson observes, "it is in one sense video itself
that inherits the virtues attributed to a formerly imperfect cinema:
triumphantly retaining its status as the latter's poor cousin, while
ambiguously connoting 'advanced technique' and 'trash' all at
once."[11]

Bertolucci's work, as well as his public pronouncements, express the contradictions of postmodernism. On one hand, his films,
in particular *Emperor* and *The Sheltering Sky*, are the ultimate images of commodified elegance and perfection produced by postmodern late capitalism. On the other hand, these very films, as well as
his earlier films, are immersed with nostalgia and yearning for non-
capitalist cultures. In light of this seeming contradiction, it is not
surprising that Bertolucci, like many other serious filmmakers, is an
opponent of television and video. In fact his attitude, like that of

many Italian filmmakers, is quite hostile to television. In our conversation Bertolucci discussed the "collective universality" of television (what Pasolini denounced as *cultura homoginieta*) saying that the model that television offers is "a model of culture that is completely degraded." It is almost, he added, "like it is the reality that is happening in order to be seen by television. It is almost like this television set was much more beyond the set, the whole country was a television set. . . . If I was a television maker I would be working all the time because I think Italy is behaving in order to be on television. It is not only something that happens in Italy. It is interesting. It is more or less everywhere." Three years before at the Mill Film Festival he said that the "20th century has chosen cinema as the language to represent itself. . . . Now television is the chosen language." For me, he said, "electronics is just exploited and not explored yet."[12]

Bertolucci's criticism of the global colonization of the imagination by television recalls Pasolini's attitude towards television as "the modern institution which he most loathed."[13] Pasolini's attitude, which influenced Bertolucci, derived from his Gramscian-inspired beliefs regarding the need to resurrect a "national-popular" culture and to investigate the role of the intellectual in this process. The kind of culture Pasolini longed for and Bertolucci laments the loss of is based on a plurality of popular cultures as opposed to neo-capitalist mass culture. In fact, Bertolucci's sentiments are shared by most Italian directors: Fellini, Visconti, Torrantore, and Scola, among others. The Italian economic miracle of the 1960s and the country's rapid industrialization was resented by many Italian directors who combined their distaste for the new Italy with a strong nostalgia "for the healthy and uncompromised values of a pre-industrial past."[14] This nostalgia reached its zenith in the 1980s with the rapid spread of the television culture and the decline of cinema as a form of popular entertainment. A group of Italian films were released in the late 1980s, all set in movie houses and all dealing with the spectatorial experience: Ettore Scola's *Splendor* (1988), Giuseppe Tornatore's *Cinema Paradiso* (1988), and Luciano Odorisio's *Via Paradiso* (1988). Scola's *Splendor* as well as Tornatore's *Cinema Paradiso* and *Tuto stanno bene* portray the degraded world created by television culture and compare it nostalgically to the paradise-lost world of cinema. In *Cinema Paradiso* the spectatorial experience is compared to a collective religious experience performed in a cathedral. Giuliana Bruno describes a tendency in Italian cinema towards the nostalgic mythologization "of cinema as a final bastion of collective life and the last symbol of a dying popular culture."[15] At the

1988 Mill Valley Film Festival Bertolucci discussed cinema in similar terms: "I still believe in the movie theatres as special spaces,
cathedrals for hypnosis for all of us to dream our collective dreams."

The Italian filmmakers' hostility to television is rooted in the
distinction existing in Italian culture between *Cultura di massa*
(mass culture) and *cultura popolare* (popular culture). Whereas the
former refers to manipulative consumer culture, the latter refers to
culture created by the people for the people. Until recently Italian
culture was grounded in the provincial rural life of small communi-
ties where the cinema house (as in *Cinema Paradiso*) was one of the
popular centers for social interaction. Since the 1976 Constitutional
Court ruling which abolished the state's monopoly on broadcasting,
television culture spread rapidly, leading to the loss of cinema's audience. Atomized television viewing replaced cinema's social viewing and led to a flood of cheap television game-shows and prolific
importing of American programs. It also suppressed other expressions of popular culture. The nostalgia of Bertolucci, Pasolini, and
other Italian directors for Italy's rural culture reflects the crisis provoked by the transition from cinema culture (associated with the
meaning assigned to popular culture in Italy) to television culture
(carrying the negative connotations assigned in Italy to mass culture).

Bertolucci uses organic (live) versus mechanic (dead) metaphors
(which recall Gramsci's distinction between organic and official ideology) to describe the difference between the old cinema and the cinema of the future as envisioned by Francis Ford Coppola (a cinema
beamed by satellite all over the world simultaneously).

> I have never felt inspired by this technological perspective and
> have persisted in conceptualising the cinema as something that
> is made in an artisanal, craftsmanlike environment, maintain-
> ing a constant relationship with living things and with people.
> The super technological cinema that is beginning to take shape
> would force me to accept the supremacy of all things dead. To
> move from the cinema I like to make to the one I might have
> to watch is like being catapulted from an agricultural civilisa-
> tion to an industrial one. Filmmakers will cease to be peasants
> to become factory workers. We would no longer work with na-
> ture but in endless assembly lines.[16]

This celebration of artisan culture as opposed to technological,
mass production society sounds strange coming from a filmmaker,
whose very involvement with the medium signifies complicity, indeed embracement, of the age of mechanical (if not electronic) re-

production. One cannot but raise, in this context, McLuhan's question: Is not the medium the message itself? There may be another way to resolve this contradiction by claiming that today only film, perhaps, can restore the aura typical of artisan society. Indeed the history of Italy's popular reception of cinema and its embracement during the 1930s, the 1950s, and the 1960s by the poor as "essential to life, as vital almost as food and clothing"[17] turned it into a truly popular culture.

Yet despite Bertolucci's "nostalgic popular utopianism," which points to the past as a visionary model for the future, the glossiness and technological commodification of the nostalgic images manufactured by his films locates his cinema within the dimension of the "postmodern geopolitical aesthetic." Cinema, Godard suggests in *Scenario du film Passion* and *Soft and Hard*, is a factory of images. But in these films, as in his other films from the cosmic period, images of production collide with images of creation and creativity, thus rendering visible contemporary Western cinema's oscillation between a utopia of artisan, organic society and the reality of technological, mechanical society.

Despite the danger inherent in any attempt to generalize I tend to view Godard's seemingly bizzare nouvelle religion and Bertolucci's search for uncontaminated civilizations as cultural and political symptoms. These symptoms reflect the accumulative reaction to the political 1960s and 1970s, the apolitical 1980s, and to the even more confusing 1990s with their celebratory rhetorics of a new world order, perhaps masking a new old world disorder. As much as Bertolucci's postmodern nostalgic gaze backward has replaced Godard's high modernist glance forward, so Godard's new religious gaze has replaced a futuristic political radicalism with a return to the theology of the biblical image. The potential of this theology for defining other graven images remains to be seen.

Notes

Notes to the Introduction

1. Robert Phillip Kolker, *Bernardo Bertolucci* (New York: Oxford University Press, 1985), 1.
2. In 1991 *Before the Revolution* was selected by the *Cahiers du Cinéma*'s critics as one of the forty best films ever made.
3. In Bloom's original text this reads as follows: "Poetic history . . . is held to be indistinguishable from poetic influence, since strong poets make that history by misreading one another, so as to clear imaginative space for themselves" Harold Bloom, *The Anxiety of Influence: A Theory of Poetry* (New York: Oxford University Press, 1973), 5.
4. Ibid.
5. Ibid, 7.
6. Bloom (see pp. 7–8) claims that "Poetic influence . . . is necessarily the study of the life-cycle of the poet as poet. When such study considers the context in which that life-cycle is enacted, it will be compelled to examine simultaneously the relations between poets as cases akin to what Freud called the family romance, and as chapters in the history of modern revisionism, 'modern' meaning here post-Enlightenment." (Nietzsche and Freud are, as Bloom says, the prime influences upon the theory of influence presented in his book).
7. Leonard Probst, "Maria Schneider of 'Last Tango': I'm More Beautiful than Marlon Brando," *The Village Voice* (February 8, 1973): 79.
8. For an interesting anecdote regarding Godard's reaction to *The Conformist* after its premiere in Paris see Donald Ranvaud and Enzo Ungari, *Bertolucci by Bertolucci* (London: Plexus, 1987), 237.
9. The idealization of the south and particularly Italy as a sun-drenched utopia was a common theme of the German romantic writers and especially Goethe who was in love with Italy. The *Romische Elegien* (1788) is a set of poems in classical meter celebrating both his amorous and cultural experiences in Rome. In the press conference at the 1991 Venice Film Festival (following the screening of his film *Allemagne Année 90 Neuf Zero* (*Germany Year 90 Nine Zero*), Godard attested to the influence of German literature and in particular German romanticism on his life and work. He mentioned that there has never been any book which moved him more than Goethe's *Whertur*.

10. The idea of replacing "difference" with "disjunction" was suggested by Dudley Andrew in his lecture on "Films or Francs? How to Measure the Industry Health," delivered in a panel on "History and Historiography of National Cinemas: The Example of France" at the 1989 Society for Cinema Studies Conference in Iowa City.

11. Jacques Aumont, "The Fall of the Gods: Jean-Luc Godard's *Le Mépris* (1963)" in *French Film: Texts and Contexts,* ed. Susan Hayward and Ginette Vincendeau (London and New York: Routledge, 1990), 227.

12. It should be noted that Godard's early movies are less emphasized in this book because they have already been extensively studied.

13. Bertolucci himself expressed envy at Godard's amazing productivity. He told Ranvaud and Ungari that "While I was shooting *Partner* I was terribly jealous of Godard who managed to shoot two, or even three, films a year and improved all the time while making them" (51).

14. *Partner,* Bertolucci's most Godardian film, was an anti-spectacle film. Bertolucci said: "The rejection of the ideas of spectacle and entertainment was a rallying point for a great many film-makers. *Partner* now stands out as a manifesto for those shared feelings." See Ranvaud and Ungari, 52.

15. T. Jefferson Kline, *Bertolucci's Dream Loom: A Psychoanalytic Study of Cinema* (Amherst: The University of Massachusetts Press, 1987).

16. Robert Burgoyne, *Bertolucci's 1900: A Narrative and Historical Analysis* (Detroit: Wayne State University Press, 1991). Burgoyne's excellent and exhaustive analysis freed me, to a certain extent, from the need to rediscuss Bertolucci's *1900.*

17. Angela Dalle Vacche, *The Body in the Mirror: Shapes of History in Italian Cinema* (Princeton: Princeton University Press, 1992).

Notes to Chapter 1

1. The "green utopia" of May 1968 was a springboard for the *Greens* and the growing world, and especially European, consciousness of issues of ecology.

2. See Dana Polan in " 'Above All Else to Make You See': Cinema and the Ideology of Spectacle," in Jonathan Arac, ed., *Postmodernism and Politics* (Minneapolis: University of Minnesota Press, 1986); and Bruce F. Kawin, *Mindscreen: Bergman, Godard, and First-Person Film* (Princeton, New Jersey: Princeton University Press, 1978), 159.

3. Colin MacCabe, *Godard: Images, Sounds, Politics* (Bloomington: Indiana University Press, 1980), 20.

4. The subject of May 1968 and film culture has been exhaustively examined in several lengthy and excellent studies. Among these are: Sylvia Harvey, *May '68 and Film Culture* (London: BFI, 1978); Maureen Turim, "The Aesthetic Becomes Political: A History of Film Criticism in *Cahiers du Cinéma,*" *The Velvet Light Trap,* 9 (Summer, 1973): 13–17; Thomas Elsaesser, "French Film Culture and Critical Theory: Cineth-

ique," Monogram, 2 (Summer, 1971): 31–37; and George Lellis, "A New Politicization," *Bertolt Brecht Cahiers du Cinéma and Contemporary Film Theory* (Ann Arbor: UMI Research Press, 1982). For a more specific but excellent study of the effect of the May 1968 events on three films, see Robin Bates, "Holes in the Sausage of History: May '68 as Absent Center in Three European Films," *Cinema Journal* 24, no. 3 (Spring, 1985): 24–42. For a more recent and reflective exploration of the relationship between the 1968 conflict and film culture see special issue on "May 68: 20 Years After," in *Spectator* 8, no. 2 (Spring 1988).

5. In Godard's *Tout va bien* (1972), Yves Montand plays Jacques, a commercial filmmaker who is, to a certain extent, the surrogate and alter-ego of Godard himself. In his long monologue the fictional Jacques defines himself as a former *Nouvelle Vague* director who in May 1968 became disgusted with his "films d'esthete."

6. Louis Althusser, *Lenin and Philosophy, and Other Essays,* trans. Ben Brewster (New York and London: Monthly Review Press, 1971). For a further discussion of this point see Jacques Aumont's review of Mac-Cabe's book *Godard: Images, Sounds, Politics* in *Camera Obscura* 8-9-10 (Fall, 1982): 212–213. This is a special issue on Jean-Luc Godard.

7. Michael Kelly, *Modern French Marxism* (Baltimore, Maryland: The Johns Hopkins University Press, 1982), 140.

8. Ibid., 142.

9. The notion of organic versus traditional intellectuals is the central argument of Gramsci's essay on intellectuals. See Antonio Gramsci, "The Intellectuals," *Selections from the Prison Notebooks,* ed. and trans. Quintin Hoare and Geoffrey Nowell Smith (New York: International Publishers, 1971), 5–23. Gramsci influenced Pasolini, Bertolucci's first mentor, and also, though to a lesser extent, Bertolucci himself.

10. "Bernardo Bertolucci Seminar," American Film Institute *Dialogue on Film,* vol. 3, no. 5, (April 1974), 26.

11. During the 1960s, Godard's average shooting time was less than a month; writing and directing lasted three months. Godard commissioned Aaton to make a 35mm camera that combined the advantages of the quantity of information contained in a 35mm film image with the ease of handling and unobtrusiveness of super 8 cameras. This was before the video age. Godard was ahead of his time in appropriating video technology for films such as *Numero Deux* (1975).

12. The name Patricia is very significant here. First it alludes to the heroine of *Breathless* who bears the same name. However, the second Patricia, unlike the first one, is politically correct. The name Patricia also recalls the name of the African leader Patrice Lumumba.

13. "Complaining that his movie (*One Plus One*), which costars the Rolling Stones and Black Power leader Frankie Y., was mangled by the addition of an extra Stones song, Godard stormed the stage of London's National Film Theatre, exhorted the audience to demand its money back and contribute it to the defense of Black Power leader Eldridge Cleaver, called

those who didn't a bunch of 'bourgeois fascists,' and punched Canadian producer Iain Quarrier in the jaw." *International Herald Tribune* (December 2, 1968).

14. See for example Marc Cerisuelo, *Jean-Luc Godard* (Paris: Quatres-vents, 1989).

15. Annette Michelson, "Introduction," *The Writings of Dziga Vertov* (Berkeley: University of California Press, 1984), xxvii.

16. The idea of simulation as the central mode of signification in postmodern culture is formulated in Jean Baudrillard, *Simulations*, trans. Paul Foss, Paul Patton, and Philip Beitchman (New York: Foreign Agents Series, Semiotexte(e), 1983).

17. See for example Peter Wollen, "Godard and Counter Cinema: *Vent d'Est*" in *Reading and Writings: Semiotic Counter-Strategies* (London: Verso Editions and NLB, 1982), 79.

18. Kristin Thompson, "Sawing through the Bough: *Tout va bien* as a Brechtian film," *Wide Angle*, 1, no. 3 (1979): 40.

19. Ibid., 44.

20. Ibid., 50.

21. The allusion to Toto is interesting because Toto's style combined elements from the classic silent comedies as well as the *commedia dell'arte* and Neapolitan theatrical traditions. Vittorio Caprioli's imitation of Toto's style thus duplicates the carnivalesque elements in *Tout va bien*. The manager recalls also other famous cinematic managers. He recalls Fredersen, the Master of Metropolis in Fritz Lang's *Metropolis* (1926), and the factory manager in Chaplin's *Modern Times* (1935). (*Modern Times* itself alludes consciously to *Metropolis*.) The manager, in a long interview (which actually is presented as a monologue addressed directly to the spectators), presents his ideas about the class struggle and the anachronism of Marxist theory. The Master of *Metropolis* at the end of Lang's film comes to accept the idea of class cooperation as opposed to the idea of class struggle (the unification of mind, heart, and hands). The manager in *Tout va bien* asserts the same message: "the collaboration of the classes in order to find permanent material progress." Yet his comic performance and his portrayal as a culmination of cinematic figures (mostly comic figures) show his speech in a grotesque light. Furthermore, the manager (unlike the *gauchistes* and the workers) quotes his speech. His discourse is not an authentic one; it is a parodic mosaic of clichés cited from Jean Saint-Geour's *Vive la societe de consommation*.

22. Mikail Bakhtin says that "we must not forget that urine . . . is a gay matter, which degrades and relieves at the same time, transforming fear into laughter." *Rabelais and His World* (Cambridge: M.I.T. Press, 1968), 335.

23. The idea of "le patron" is further developed by Bertolucci. The concepts of father and patriarchy *padre* (father) and *padrone* (boss) are closely linked to his politicization of Oedipus. (Paolo and Vittorio Taviani also treat these concepts in *Padre Padrone* [1977] and in *The Meadow*

[1979]). In Bertolucci's *Tragedy of a Ridiculous Man*, the padre is also the padrone of a cheese factory. The film refers to *Tout va bien* "as a mark of difference" (Kolker *Bernardo Bertolucci*, p. 175). Bertolucci even uses Vittorio Caprioli, the Italian actor who plays the boss in *Tout va bien*, to play the *maresciallo*, the police marshal, in this film. As in Godard's film, Caprioli gives a comic performance.

24. Bakhtin, *Rabelais and His World*, 19–20.
25. Stephen Heath,"Lessons from Brecht," *Screen*, 15, no. 2 (Summer, 1974): 103. I should also mention at that point that in the beginning of *Deux ou trois choses que je sais d'elle* (Two or Three Things I Know about Her) Marina Vlady says: "Oui, parler comme des citations de vérité. C'est le père Brecht qui disait ça. Que les acteurs doivent citer" (Yes, to speak like citations of truth. It is Father Brecht who said that. That actors should cite).
26. Steven Clyde Simmons, " 'Modernism' in Film: Essays on Jean-Luc Godard," (Ph.D. dissertation, Stanford University, 1982), 192.
27. Ibid., 193.
28. MacCabe, *Godard: Images, Sounds, Politics*, 34.
29. Ibid., 34.
30. Martin Walsh, "Godard and Me: Jean Pierre Gorin Talks," *The Brechtian Aspect of Radical Cinema* (London: BFI, 1981), 122.
31. A good example (although not the sole one) exists in *Vivre sa vie* (1962). The guest philosopher of this film is Brice Parrain, the author of *Recherches sur la nature et les fonctions du langage* (Paris, 1942) who explains to Nana his philosophical/linguistic postulations.
32. George Lellis, *Bertolt Brecht, Cahiers du Cinéma and Contemporary Film Theory* (Ann Arbor: UMI Research Press, 1982), 125–126.
33. Lellis, *Bertolt Brecht*, 126–127.
34. Jean-Louis Comolli, "Film/Politique (2): *L'aveau*: 15 propositions," *Cahiers du Cinéma*, no. 224 (octobre 1970): 48. Quoted from Lellis, *Bertolt Brecht*, 127.
35. Comolli, quoted from Lellis, *Bertolt Brecht*, 128.
36. As quoted in MacCabe, *Godard: Images, Sounds, Politics*, 43:

In the *Cahiers du Cinéma* interview about *Tout va bien*, Jean Pierre Gorin went to some lengths to emphasize how important it had been for them to have unknown and unemployed actors, mainly young, in the role of workers at the Salumi plant where Yves Montand and Jane Fonda are held for twenty-four hours during a factory occupation. It might seem that it would have been more logical to have had workers in these roles but, for Gorin, the distance between the workers and superstars like Fonda and Montand would have been too great for the group in front of the camera to be more than a selection of bodies in a situation unified and determined by the script. By employing actors in the economic breadline, relations of envy, jealousy and guilt were established between them and Fonda and Montand which provided some of the raw material of the film in a way that escaped any unification by the script and which at the same time, would reproduce some of the features of the relations between militant workers and radical intellectuals.

37. To illustrate this point it is telling to quote Jean Pierre Gorin who told Martin Walsh (pp. 120–121) in an interview that:

> It was a fun film to make because we were dealing with big stars . . . And the thing was that obviously in the film they were *not* the stars. The stars were the twenty extras who were paid twenty bucks to play the workers and who really enjoyed themselves a lot . . . At one point, I mean, neither Jane nor Yves knew what they were doing in that film. It was a heavy problem for them to be doing the whole factory sequence, because they're not the centre of attention. I mean, they're on the doorstep and that's forty minutes of this film.

38. Thompson, "Sawing through the Bough," 45.
39. Lellis, *Bertolt Brecht,* 137.
40. Ibid., 138.
41. Ibid., 139.
42. Groupe Lou Sin d'intervention ideologique, p. 15. Quoted from Lellis, *Bertolt Brecht,* 139.
43. Thomas M. Kavanagh, "Godard-Gorin's *Tout va bien" Diacritics,* 4, no. 1 (Spring, 1974): 46.
44. Judith Mayne, "The Ideologies of Metacinema," (Ph.D. dissertation, Buffalo: S.U.N.Y. at Buffalo, 1975), 153.
45. Ibid., 153.
46. Ibid., 153. For a more detailed analysis of "Love story/class struggle" see Mayne's dissertation, pp. 162–166. Another interesting analysis is presented by Kristin Thompson's essay: "Sawing through the Bough: *Tout va bien* as a Brechtian Film." Her analysis of the separation of narrative conventions focuses on the contradiction of romance and quasi-documentary in *Tout va bien* (see pp. 44–50).
47. The subject has been exhausted by critical literature. Therefore, I deal with it very briefly. For a detailed analysis of sound/image in *Tout va bien* see Judith Mayne, pp. 159–162. For an excellent analysis of the operation of contradiction on the level of sound/image see Kristin Thompson, pp. 43–44. See also Simmons, "Modernism in Film," pp. 187–189 and Alan Williams, "Godard's Use of Sound," *Camera Obscura,* 8–10 (Fall, 1982): 199–204.
48. Walsh, *The Brechtian Aspect of Radical Cinema,* 119.
49. Thompson, "Sawing through the Bough," 43.
50. Mayne, "The Ideologies of Metacinema," 184.
51. Quoted from John Willett, *The Theatre of Bertolt Brecht* (London: Methuen, 1977), 137.
52. Walsh, *The Brechtian Aspect of Radical Cinema,* 122.
53. James Roy MacBean offers an interesting analysis of this tracking shot in *Film and Revolution* (Bloomington: Indiana University Press, 1975), 178:

Moreover, symbolically the two-storied plant evokes the classical Marxist description of society being built on the economic foundations of the working class's labor while the ruling exploiting class occupies the upper level of the superstructure. Except that in *Tout va bien* the workers have rebelled against this state of affairs (as Marx said they would) and have occupied, at least for a time, the whole works.

54. Although Godard regarded himself during the late 1960s and early 1970s as Vertov's follower and disciple, dismissing the importance traditionally attributed to Eisenstein, his efforts to establish structural/materialist cinema reflect Eisenstein's quest for non-representational means. Godard's struggle to equalize the means of representation (colors, sound, image, camera movements, etc.) recalls Eisenstein's impression of the *Kabuki* theater which he saw in Moscow in 1927. In "The Unexpected" (in *Film Form*) Eisenstein wrote that what most strongly impressed him was a "monistic ensemble" on the *Kabuki* stage. Sound, movement, space, and voice are elements of equal significance in the *Kabuki* and as such make a single unit. Moreover, he adds, *Kabuki* theater makes it possible for the audience to "hear movement" and to "see sound;" visual and aural perceptions are reduced to a common denominator.

55. Colin MacCabe, "Betaville," *American Film* (September 1985): 61.

56. On the relationship between the school system and Michel Foucault's ideas see Constance Penley's analysis of the film in *The Future of an Illusion: Film, Feminism, and Psychoanalysis* (Minneapolis: University of Minnesota Press, 1989), 93–118.

Notes to Chapter 2

1. For an excellent study of the relationship between *1900* and history see Robert Burgoyne, *Bertolucci's 1900: A Narrative and Historical Analysis* (Detroit: Wayne State University Press, 1991). A recent debate concerning Bertolucci's *1900* focused on the question of whether the resolution of the film is utopian or not. See Robert Burgoyne, "Temporality as Historical Argument in Bertolucci's *1900*," *Cinema Journal* 28, no. 3 (Spring, 1989): 57–68 and Angela Dalle-Vacche and Robert Burgoyne, "Dialogue on *1900*," *Cinema Journal* 29, no. 3 (Spring, 1990): 69–78.

2. Bertolucci himself responded to the questions, Have you changed? Have you really changed? as follows: "As Lampedusa once said in *The Leopard*: 'everything must change so that everything can remain as it is' " in Donald Ranvaud and Enzo Ungari, *Bertolucci by Bertolucci* (London: Plexus, 1987), 282.

3. The late 1960s and the 1970s saw the emergence of what came to be known as the BB of the Italian cinema: Bernardo Bertolucci and Marco Bellocchio, whose ideological stances were close (although Bellochio was farther to the left). However, the thematics and style of Bertolucci's cinema resemble Visconti's more than Bellochio's.

4. I am indebted for this idea to William G. Simon. I audited his class on "Italian Cinema," offered by the Department of Cinema Studies at New York University, in Fall 1989.

5. Bernardo Bertolucci, interview with Marilyn Goldin, "Bertolucci on *The Conformist*," *Sight and Sound* 40 (1971): 66.

6. Douglas Kellner, *Herbert Marcuse and the Crisis of Marxism* (Hampshire and London: Macmillan Education Ltd, 1984), 154.

7. Bernardo Bertolucci, *Film Comment* (December, 1987): 35.

8. Peter Bondanella, *Italian Cinema: From Neorealism to the Present* (New York: Frederick and Ungar Publishing Co., 1983), 286.

9. Joel Magny, "Dimension Politique de L'oeuvre de Bernardo Bertolucci: De *Prima della Rivoluzione* à *Novecento*," *Etudes Cinématographiques*, nos. 122–126 (1979): 49–76.

10. Bertolucci has said: "In *The Spider's Stratagem* the relationship between father and son is modelled on an imaginary one between Berlinguer and Togliatti: the son who discovers the betrayal of his" heroic "father is Berlinguer who discovers Togliatti's Stalinism. Both betrayals were necessary historically." Donald Ranvaud and Enzo Ungari, *Bertolucci by Bertolucci* (London: Plexus, 1987), 63.

11. This conception of time is not far from Borges's own: "These parallelisms (and others) between the story of Caesar and the story of an Irish conspirator lead Ryan to suppose the existence of a secret form of time, a pattern of repeated lines. He thinks of the decimal history conceived by Condorcet, of the morphologies proposed by Hegel, Spengler and Vico, of Hesiod's men, who degenerate from gold to iron." Jorge Luis Borges, "Theme of the Traitor and the Hero," *Labyrinths* (New York: A New Directions Book, 1962), 73.

12. The notion of the social practice of commemoration is "where the past, a person or event becomes the object of intentional commemoration and is ascribed some historical significance." Quoted from "Introduction," in David Middleton and Derek Edwards, eds., *Collective Remembering* (London: Sage Publications, 1990), 8.

13. The motif of the painted eyes appears also in *Partner*. The soap salesgirl, epitomizing the Godardian equation of consumerism and prostitution, has painted eyes alluding to the second strip in Man Ray's "Frames from Emek Bakia" (1927). In this strip, Kiki (the famous model and "queen" of Montparnasse's artists) closes her eyes and another pair of eyes, painted on her lids, opens. This is exactly what the soap saleswoman in *Partner* does.

14. Anton Kaes, "History and Film: Public Memory in the Age of Electronic Dissemination," *History and Memory* 2, no. 1 (Fall, 1990): 121.

15. For Freud's use of the term "inverted" for female and male homosexuals, see Sigmund Freud, "Inversion," in *On Sexuality*, vol. 7 of The Pelican Freud Library (London, 1979), 46–52.

16. Bertolucci changed her name from Lina to Anna in order to allude to Anna Karina, Godard's first wife, who starred in most of Godard's early

films. Bertolucci at first wanted her to play the character in his movie in order to steal Godard's (i.e., his father's) wife.

Bertolucci himself has said in an interview with Marilyn Goldin, "*The Conformist* is a story about me and Godard. When I gave the professor Godard's phone number and address I did it as a joke, but afterwards I said to myself, well, maybe all that has some significance. . . . I'm Marcello and I make Fascist movies and I want to kill Godard who's a revolutionary who makes revolutionary movies and who was my teacher." "Bertolucci on *The Conformist*," *Sight and Sound* 40 (1971): 66.

17. Richard D. Chessick "The Search for the Authentic Self in Bergson and Proust," in Maurice Charney and Joseph Reppen, eds., *Psychoanalytic Approaches to Literature and Film* (Cranbury, New Jersey: Associated University Presses, 1987), 27. Luchino Visconti, the Italian director who is closest to Bertolucci in his sense of contradiction between progress and decadence, planned to make a film based on Proust's novel, but managed only to complete a script.

18. Ibid., 27. The "mystical ecstasy" discussed by Chessick is very similar to the secularization of the notion of epiphany by Joyce. Joyce's adaptation of the Christian concept to secular experience signifies a sense of sudden radiance and revelation while observing a commonplace object. Indeed, it is not far from the notion of involuntary memory triggered by mundane experiences such as the madeleine. The most famous example of epiphany in Joyce's work is the revelatory moment experienced by Stephen at the sight of a young girl on the beach in *A Portrait of the Artist as a Young Man*, chapter 4. Both writers' vocational discoveries are indebted to these moments of grace, manifested in Proust's novel through involuntary memory and in Joyce's through epiphany. Walter Benjamin uses the term rejuvenation to describe the same phenomenon: "Proust has brought off the tremendous feat of letting the whole world age by a lifetime in an instant. But this very concentration in which things that normally just fade and slumber consume themselves in a flash is called rejuvenation." Walter Benjamin, "The Image of Proust," in *Illuminations* ed. Hannah Arendt (New York: Schocken Books, 1989), 211.

19. According to Chessick ("The Search for the Authentic Self," 27–28), Proust insisted in an interview "that he made a distinction between involuntary and voluntary memory that Bergson did not make." Chessick argues, however, that Bergson clearly made such a distinction and that, like Proust, he stressed

the importance of true or pure memory, although they disagree about how one should relate to the images called up by memory. . . . The main difference between Bergson and Proust lies in Bergson's failure to distinguish the relationship between pure duration, the essential self, and the *elan vital* [life force]. Bergson lumped all this together as representing Reality, but Proust insisted that the appearance of pure memory even transcends real concrete duration and all the rest. This shows the difficulty with intuitive kinds of philosophy, in which the intuition of one person, when cognitively produced as in writing, collides with the intuition of another.

20. Joan Mellen, "Fascism in Contemporary Film," *Film Quarterly* XXIV, no. 4 (Summer, 1971): 5.

21. The relationship between involuntary memory and the Freudian notion of memory does not escape Chessick ("The Search for the Authentic Self," 33) who observes:

> Proust therefore presents what he calls 'a three dimensional psychology,' in which the spontaneous memories emerge outside of the dimension of time, in their original form. This remarkable idea coincides exactly with Freud's notion that memories in the unconscious are timeless; they are unaffected by the passage of time and they continue to exert the same pressures as they always did without mellowing. When they emerge in psychoanalysis, they emerge with the same force and vigor and vividness that even the passage of a whole lifetime fails to modify.

22. For the association between the Proustian involuntary memory and Joyce's epiphany see note 18 above. Chessick observes that: "There is a close relationship of this notion of pure duration to [William] James's famous concept of the stream of consciousness" (ibid., 23). However, it should be noted that it is not in the manner of Joyce's *Ulysses* which is a passive reproduction of the stream of consciousness.

23. Chessick observes that although Proust "considers at great length dreams as a possible mode for the rediscovery of memories, unlike Freud he rejects dreams and prefers the spontaneous emergence of complex memories in the awakened consciousness" (ibid., 34). Bertolucci's position in this respect is closer to Freud's.

24. Chessick, 32.

25. It is interesting to quote here from Proust himself: "Some wished the novel to be a sort of cinematographic parade. This conception was absurd. In reality, nothing is farther removed than this cinematographic view from what we have perceived." Marcel Proust,"The Past Recaptured," *Remembrance of Things Past*, trans. Frederick A. Blossom (New York: Random House, 1932), 1003–1004.

26. Mellen, "Fascism in Contemporary Film," 2–19.

27. Ranvaud and Ungari, *Bertolucci by Bertolucci*, 11.

28. Benjamin, "The Image of Proust," 202.

29. The notion of socially constructed oblivion is used by M. Douglas in *Evans-Pritchard* (London: Fontana, 1980). It demonstrates "the interest of psychologists in the socially oriented research agenda on remembering and forgetting," quoted in Middleton and Edwards, "Introduction," 6.

30. "Bernardo Bertolucci Seminar," American Film Institute *Dialogue on Film*, 3, no. 5 (April, 1974): 16.

31. Quoted in T. Jefferson Kline, *Bertolucci's Dream Loom: A Psychoanalytic Study of Cinema* (Amherst: The University of Massachusetts Press, 1987), 90. The original interview appears in Enzo Ungari, *Scena madri* (Milan: Ubulibri, 1982), 71.
32. Kaes, "History and Film," 121.
33. Benjamin, "The Image of Proust," 202.
34. Ibid.
35. Magny, "Dimension politique," 66.
36. This phrase was coined by Susan Sontag in "Fascinating Fascism," which appeared originally in *The New York Review of Books* (February 6, 1975). The article is reprinted, among other places, in *Movies and Methods I*, ed. Bill Nichols (Berkeley: University of California Press, 1976), 31–43.
37. Benjamin, "The Image of Proust," 214.
38. For a detailed analysis of this scene see Kolker, *Bernardo Bertolucci*, 96–100.
39. The subject is only briefly touched upon here because it has been exhausted by the critical literature on the film.
40. A further referent of the name is Godard who, after his father stopped sending him money because he was not studying in Paris, began stealing and writing articles for the monthly *La gazette du cinéma*, which he founded with Jacques Rivette and Eric Rohmer under the name Hans *Lucas* (the German equivalent of Jean-Luc). The professor and his wife Anna are thus a surrogate couple for Godard and Anna Karina (cf. note 16 above). The reference to the dream about the operation conducted by Quadri in Switzerland on the blind Marcello who can then see again, with the result that the professor's wife falls in love with him is not a coincidence either. It further enacts the Oedipal crime on the level of cinematic struggle by alluding to the revolutionary Godard who resigned to Switzerland in order to break with the capitalist circuits of production and distribution. Bertolucci, being financially backed by the capitalist enemy, Paramount, regards himself as the conformist rather then the pure rebel à la Godard.
41. I will not discuss this subject in great detail as it has been exhausted in the literature on the film.
42. In Moravia's novel Manganiello's name is Angelo. His name in the film (Manganiello) alludes to the *santo manganello*, the nickname for the club used by the Fascist *squadristi* to beat up dissidents. The Fascist *squadrismo* or armed terrorism of political opposition by strong-arm men with clubs (the *santo manganello*) was founded in 1920. They used the clubs and castor oil while workers occupied factories and peasants seized farm lands. Torture with castor oil is frequently recalled in the film. Marcello asks his father in the scene of his visit to the asylum about the punitive expeditions in which he had been involved, presumably as a member of the Fascist *squadrismo*: "Did you use clubs on

them, or just castor oil; did you torture them?" and finally "Did you actually kill?"

43. On the autobiographical level, Bertolucci's search for free space to differentiate himself from his father is well documented in many interviews. Because his father was a poet, Bertolucci decided to differentiate himself through the medium of film.

44. See for example Kolker, *Bernardo Bertolucci*, 217.

45. In Moravia's novel the motif of mask is predominant and the influence of Pirandello is evident. Quadri is associated with an imagery of mask and theater.

46. Goldin, "Bertolucci on *The Conformist*," 66. A similar hatred of the bourgeoisie is expressed by Pier Paolo Pasolini especially in his film *Teorema* (Theorem) (1968), which envisages the self-destruction of this class. Pasolini has bluntly declared, "The point of the film is roughly this: a member of the bourgeoisie, whatever he does, is always wrong." Oswald Stack, ed. *Pasolini on Pasolini* (Bloomington: Indiana University Press, 1970), 157.

47. To support my argument I should mention that the figure of Palmiro Togliatti had been used before by both Pasolini (Bertolucci's first mentor and cinematic father figure) and by the Taviani brothers, both of whom are close to Bertolucci in many respects (for example in their exploration of the padre/padrone theme). In *I souversivi* (1967) (*The Subversives*), the Tavianis study the personalities and behavior of four Communist party members before the funeral of Togliatti. One of the characters in the film is Giulia, the wife of a party official who gives in to her lesbian inclinations. In *Uccellaci e uccellini* (1966) (*Hawks and Sparrows*), Pasolini inserts newsreel footage of Togliatti's funeral.

48. The association between fascism and latent homosexuality is a recurrent and disturbing theme in post-war Italian cinema. The exception is Ettore Scola's *Una giornata speciale* (1977) (*A Special Day*) which presents a sympathetic homosexual, an anti-Fascist intellectual.

49. Goldin, "Bertolucci on *The Conformist*," 66.

50. Millicent Marcus reads the insertion of the allegory of Plato's cave in the *Conformist* as a "way of appropriating the moral teaching of Plato's myth," in *Italian Film in the Light of Neorealism*, (Princeton: Princeton University Press, 1986), 300.

51. Joan Mellen, "A Conversation with Bernardo Bertolucci," *Cinéaste* 5 (Summer, 1973), 24. This brings to mind Pierre Sorlin's thesis according to which the historical film always interprets the past from the perspective of the present. See Pierre Sorlin, *The Film in History: Restaging the Past* (Oxford, England: Basil Blackwell, 1980).

52. Quoted from Pauline Kael, "Introduction," *Last Tango in Paris*, by Bernardo Bertolucci (New York: Delacorte Press, 1973), 9–10.

53. *Tango* analyzes some of the problems that Bertolucci himself encountered in his private analysis.

54. I should point out here that I shall not try to prove the unprovable—that is, to trace which specific aspects of *Tango* derive from which lines in Marcuse's theoretical writings.
55. During the May 1968 events Paris was covered with the graffiti message "MMM," which stood for the names of the three inspiring prophets of this almost revolution: *Mao* Tse-tung, Herbert *Marcuse*, and *Malcolm* X.
56. Gideon Bachmann in interview with Bertolucci, "Every Sexual Relationship Is Condemned," *Film Quarterly*, 26 (1973): 6.
57. Ibid., 4.
58. Ibid.
59. Ibid.
60. Brando himself, according to the director, was hunting for all the secrets he had hidden in all his films. He loved and hated improvising his scenes. He loved it because it was new for him and hated it because it seemed a violation of his privacy. "The actor agreed, 'Never again will I make a film like this one,' he said. 'For the first time, I have felt a violation of my innermost self. It should be the last time.' " Quoted in David Downing, *Marlon Brando* (New York: Stein and Day, 1984), 160–162.
61. Bachmann, 4.
62. Ibid.
63. Brando/Paul's indulgence in anti-church rhetoric in *Tango* is also a statement on Brando's role in *On the Waterfront* (1954), in which he played a Christ-like figure. Furthermore, the 1954 film, which many labeled Fascist (Elia Kazan took a reactionary position vis-à-vis McCarthyism), portrayed the church as a progressive force. In *Tango*, the church and the symbolic Holy Family of Kazan's film (Edith as Mary, Terry/Brando as Jesus, and the priest as the father) are assailed in the scene where Paul sodomizes Jeanne and forces her to repeat his words against the repressive/oppressive family (the Holy Family as well as the bourgeois family institution). It should be noted, also, that the sodomy scene is visually represented as a crucifixion. Schneider is lying on the bare floor, her hands spread so that they form a shape of a cross.
64. Joan Mellen, "Sexual Politics and Bertolucci's *Last Tango in Paris*," in *Women and Their Sexuality in the New Film* (New York: Horizon Press, 1973), 132.
65. Herbert Marcuse, *Eros and Civilization: A Philosophical Inquiry into Freud* (Boston: Beacon Press, 1955), xxi.
66. Martin Jay, *The Dialectical Imagination*, 110.
67. Bertolucci told Gideon Bachmann (pp. 4–5) in "Every Sexual Relationship is Condemned," "that the sex in *Tango* is" simply a new kind of language that these two characters try to invent in order to communicate. They use the sexual language because the sexual language means liberation from the subconscious, means an opening up." The characters' use of animal sounds in re-naming themselves is a manifestation

of this attempt at liberation. It is also a refusal to enter the Lacanian symbolic whose signifier is language.

68. Marcuse, *Eros and Civilization*, 16. Jefferson Kline suggests parallels between the characters of *Tango* and those of the Orpheus myth. To him the film is "as much a perversion as a restatement of the myth" (*Bertolucci's Dream Loom*, p. 107). For Marcuse, Orpheus and Narcissus are the archetypal images of liberation and the symbols of the new reality principles he envisages in *Eros and Civilization*.
69. Kline, *Bertolucci's Dream Loom*, 35.
70. Ibid., 37.
71. Ibid., 106.
72. C. Fred Alford, "Nature and Narcissism: The Frankfurt School," *New German Critique* 36 (Fall, 1985): 179.
73. Marcuse, *Eros and Civilization*, 154–155.
74. Bertolucci, *Last Tango*, 146. The irony, of course, is that Jeanne is specifically not a worker in reality, but upper bourgeoisie. Her clothes are not blue overalls, but a fur coat and flower hat.
75. Marcuse, *Eros and Civilization*, 47.
76. Ibid., xii.
77. Ibid., 139.
78. Ibid., 141.
79. For an analysis of the theme of anality in Godard's film see Stuart Cunningham and Ross Harley, "The Logic of the Virgin Mother," *Screen*, 28, no. 1 (Winter, 1987): 67–69. The authors claim that *Prenom Carmen* pays tribute to *Tango* through its investigation of this theme.
80. Freud says, "We should rather be inclined to connect the simultaneous presence of these opposites [sadism and masochism] with the opposing masculinity and femininity which are combined in bisexuality—a contrast which often has to be replaced in psychoanalysis by that between activity and passivity." Sigmund Freud, "Three Essays on Sexuality," in *The Standard Edition of the Complete Psychological Works of Sigmund Freud*, trans. James Strachey (London: The Pelican Freud Library, 1979), Vol. 7:160.
81. Marcuse, *Eros and Civilization*, 49.
82. Ibid., 50.
83. Ibid., 59.
84. Bertolucci, *Last Tango*, 131–132.
85. Herbert Marcuse, *Studies in Critical Philosophy*, trans., Joris de Bres (Boston: Beacon Press, 1972), 141.
86. Marcuse, *Studies in Critical Philosophy*, 141.
87. For a detailed analysis of the sequence that epitomizes this conflict, see Kolker, *Bernardo Bertolucci* pp. 49–53.
88. Bachmann, 7.
89. Marcuse, *Eros and Civilization*, 19.
90. Ibid., 109.
91. Ibid., 198.

92. Ibid., 273.
93. It should be pointed out that the history of the tango is also a reflection of political and cultural history. The roots and development of the tango are associated with four different groups: (a) the Argentinian gauchos, (b) the Cuban African slaves, (c) the European immigrants in Argentina, and (d) the Italian anarchists, who used a tango melody as their banner. Initially the tango was rejected by the Argentinian aristocracy, which adhered to European manners and codes of behavior. Hence, the tango was pushed to the suburbs and brothels and became rooted in popular consciousness as expressing the feelings of the people. Only after it won sweeping success in Paris (where the tango was considered exotic and erotic) was it adopted by the Argentinian ruling class.
94. This is also what differentiates Godard's modernism from Bertolucci's postmodernism. Whereas modernism breaks with the past (it is "tradition against itself" to use Octavio Paz's definition), postmodernism revisits the past "but with irony, not innocently." "Umberto Eco," Postmodernism, Irony, the Enjoyable," *Postscript to the Name of the Rose* (New York: Harcourt, Brace, Janovich, Inc., 1984), 67.
95. For a discussion of these contradictions see Kolker's analysis of the film in *Bernardo Bertolucci*. For a narrative and historical analysis of the film see Robert Burgoyne, *Bertolucci's 1900*.

Notes to Chapter 3

1. The irony of course is that Godard was last at Cannes in May, 1968, when he and François Truffaut helped to shut down the festival which they called elitist and reactionary. Hence the last traces of Godard's radicalism vanish. For a further discussion of *Sauve qui peut (la vie)*, Godard's politics of its presentation to the public, and its reception by the American critical establishment and academic critics see Kristin Thompson, "Godard's Unknown Country: *Sauve qui peut (la vie)*," in *Breaking the Glass Armor: Neoformalist Film Analysis* (Princeton: Princeton University Press, 1988), 263–288.
2. This is according to Vincent Canby's report. See "Godard, at Cannes, Can Still Stir Up Film Furor," *The New York Times* (Saturday, May 24, 1980): 14. In an interview with Jonathan Cott (see "Godard: Born-Again Filmmaker," *Rolling Stone* [November 27, 1980]: 33) Godard said: "The other night [at the thirty-third Cannes Film Festival] I met someone who produced *Airplane!*, and he said, 'We're glad you're coming back.' It's funny, since I've never stopped making pictures. In the last ten years, I've made more hours of film than during the previous ten years." He also told Cott: "For ten years [the years in Grenoble] I was probably the only known filmmaker who made only failures from a commercial point of view."
3. See Richard Roud, "Bertolucci on *La Luna*," *Sight and Sound* 48, no. 4 (1979): 237.

4. Lawrence Cohen, "Jean-Luc Godard Enlivens New York: Auteur Theory Called Fraud," *Variety* (Wednesday, October 8, 1980): 32. Godard first moved to Grenoble and only then to Rolle, a small Swiss town between Geneva and Lausanne. As Colin MacCabe points out, "If Grenoble was not Paris, it was still too defined by its relation to Paris, by its not being Paris, and thus Godard and Miéville made another move: to Rolle." *Godard: Images, Sounds, Politics* (Bloomington: Indiana University Press, 1980), 24.

5. Cott, *Rolling Stone*, 33.

6. Ibid.

7. Quoted in Ric Gentry, "Bertolucci Directs *Tragedy of A Ridiculous Man*," *Millimeter* (December 1981): 56.

8. Ibid. *Tragedy* is not only a dialogue with *Tout va bien* but also with Godard's "revolutionary spaghetti" *Vent d'est* (1970). The film contains images accompanied by a voice-over narration saying "I kidnapped the son of the Citroen company."

9. Robert Phillip Kolker, *Bernardo Bertolucci* (New York: Oxford University Press, 1985), 192. Bertolucci said: "So-called reality was becoming more tenuous just as moral judgements were becoming more difficult to make. Certainly there is a relationship between the ambiguities of fact and the confusion over values" Gentry, 58–59. In another interview he said:

> The film is a repeated mugging that takes place in front of a mirror. Reality steals from the camera to take its revenge and for once be the vampire on the neck of the cinema. If my previous films played out the conflicts between documentary and fiction, prose and poetry, cinema and life, here we have the kidnap of the cinema and the novel, which are beaten by the world, by faces, landscapes, lights and the sounds of the real. This is felt throughout the whole system of representation and I refused to erect any barriers of defence. I let the harmony and equilibrium I had tried to achieve with my previous films, by controlling the relations between representation and reality, disappear. (Donald Ranvaud and Enzo Ungari, *Bertolucci by Bertolucci* [London: Plexus, 1987]: 216–217)

10. Jean Baudrillard, "Simulacra and Simulations," *Selected Writings* ed. Mark Poste, (Cambridge, UK: Polity Press, 1988), 174.

11. Ibid.

12. Ibid., 174–175. See also (pp. 175–176) Baudrillard's analysis of the declaration of Berlinger (the former leader of the Italian Communist party, the name of which was changed in October 1989 to PDS, *Partita Democratica della Sinistra* [The Democratic Party of the Left]): "We mustn't be frightened of seeing the communists seize power in Italy."

13. This is Kolker's as well as my interpretation. When I interviewed Bertolucci in London on July 27, 1991, he was rather surprised to hear my interpretation. According to him his last and most Godardian film is *Partner*.

14. Kolker, 175.
15. For a further discussion on the relationship between *Tragedy* and *Tout va bien* see Kolker, 174–176.
16. Gentry, 56.
17. As Kolker (p. 170) rightly observes, "*Tragedy of A Ridiculous Man* is a curious variation on *The Spider's Stratagem*." See his discussion of the relationship between the two films on pp. 170–172. On the relationship of *Tragedy of a Ridiculous Man* to *1900* see also Kolker's analysis. See also Ranvaud, 221. It should be pointed out, however, that whereas in *The Spider's Stratagem* the father stages the spectacle of treason/heroism, in *Tragedy* the son is, if not the manipulator of the terrorist spectacle, then at least one of the possible conspirators.
18. See for example the introduction in *Cahiers du Cinéma*, no. 437 (Novembre 1990), a special issue on: "Godard 30 ans depuis," and an interview with Roland Amstutz (pp. 82–87): "Les années 80: Voici venu le temps des années-cosmos. La nature prend-elle le dessus sur les hommes? Le ciel, l'eau, la terre . . . De *Passion* à *Nouvelle Vague*, fragments d'une histoire naturelle" (The 80s: Here the cosmic years have arrived. Does nature gain the upper hand over men? The sky, water, the earth . . . from *Passion* to *Nouvelle Vague*, fragments of a natural history). (p. 82).
19. See Marc Cerisuelo, "La trilogie du sublime," *Jean-Luc Godard* (Paris: Quatres-Vents, 1989), 207–232.
20. Cerisuelo, *Jean-Luc Godard* 209.
21. Isabelle's stuttering recalls the inarticulation of the working class so evident in *Tout va bien* (see chapter 1).
22. Peter Wollen, "*Passion* 1," *Framework* 21 (Summer, 1983): 4.
23. Gideon Bachmann, "In the Cinema It Is Never Monday," *Sight and Sound* (Spring, 1982): 119.
24. For a list of the tableaux invoked by Godard see Cerisuelo, *Jean-Luc Godard*, p. 244, note 2.
25. Ibid., 214.
26. Ibid., 207.
27. Godard said: (in Bachmann, "In the Cinema It Is Never Monday," *Sight and Sound*, 119): "One could say, as a subtitle, 'Passion, the world and its metaphor,' or, 'the social element and its metaphor.' And of course we don't know any more whether it's the metaphor which is 'real' or the reality which is only metaphorical." One cannot avoid seeing this disclaimer as a continuation of Godard's famous dictum "cinema is not the reflection of reality but the reality of reflection." This seems to echo Pasolini's belief in the metonymic reality of cinema.
28. Actually in *Scenario du film Passion* Godard says that the screen is a wall, thus alluding both to Brecht's fourth wall and to the illusionist nature of this wall which, like the sky, suggests the infinite without boundaries.

29. Rod Stoneman, "*Passion 2,*" *Framework* 21 (Summer 1983): 6. See Donald Ranvaud and A. Farassino, "An Interview with Jean-Luc Godard," for an explanation of why Godard made two video films.
30. Richard Kwietniowski, "Between Love and Labour—Godard's *Scenario of the Film Passion,*" *Screen* 24, no. 6 (November–December 1983): 53.
31. See on this matter Edward Ball, "Thinking Out Loud," *Afterimage* (October 1986): 22. "In *Scenario* we get a one-hour expose of the filmmaker or the job or, as they used to say, in the creative process. 'I didn't want to write the Scenario [for *Passion*], I wanted to see it,' the videomaker muses. Here, finally, is a moving picture treatise about the labor of conceiving a film."
32. Stoneman, "Passion 2," 6.
33. Bertolucci told me in our conversation on July 27, 1991, that he, as the president of the jury of the Venice Film Festival, influenced the other members of the jury to give the prize to Godard.
34. Quoted from Don Ranvaud, "An Interview with Jean-Luc Godard," *Framework* 21 (Summer 1983): 9.
35. They invoke the student militants of *La Chinoise*, the naive "anarchists" of *Bande à part*, the cannibals of *Weekend*, the *gauchistes* of *Tout va bien* (especially in the supermarket scene), and other "anarchist" groups that appear in Godard's films.
36. David Wills, "*Carmen*: Sound/Effect," *Cinema Journal* 25, no. 4 (Summer, 1986): 41.
37. Bertolucci received a two-month suspended jail sentence and lost his right to vote until 1981, a real punishment for a politically oriented filmmaker.
38. Robert Seidenberg, "Hail Godard," *Spin* (January 1986): 78.
39. Katherine Dieckmann, "Godard in His 'Fifth Period': An Interview," *Film Quarterly* 2, vol. XXXIX (Winter, 1985–1986): 2.
40. Ibid.
41. Seidenberg, "Hail Godard," 78.
42. Dieckmann, "Godard in His 'Fifth Period,' "2.
43. Ibid.
44. Baudrillard, "Simulacra and Simulations," 169–170.
45. Seidenberg, "Hail Godard," 78.
46. Perhaps Godard was influenced by the composer Olivier Messiaen who believes that the "collective improvisations" produced by birds are more advanced than Western music. To prepare his organ work "Book of the Holy Sacrament" he went to Israel to "hear the birds that Christ might have heard."
47. Dieckmann, "Godard in His 'Fifth Period,' " 4.
48. Seidenberg, "Hail Godard," 78.
49. The irony is that Godard ran out of the theater before seeing the end of *Tango*.
50. This thesis is suggested by Andre Dumas. See Andre Dumas, "Godard Protestant: A bout de foi," *Cahiers du Cinéma* 437:(Novembre 1990) 88–92.

51. Vincent Canby, "Nature's Splendor and Aphorisms in Godard's Latest," *New York Times* (September 29, 1990): 16.
52. Godard's original idea was, according to Roland Amstutz, to make the servants say the intelligent things and the rich say all the banal things. Thierry Jousse, "Entretien avec Roland Amstutz," *Cahiers du Cinema* 437 (Novembre 1990): 86.
53. It is ironic that Godard, who criticized Bertolucci for describing the world of rich decadence in *The Conformist*, is describing a similar world in *Nouvelle Vague*.
54. Amstutz, in *Cahiers du Cinema*, 437 (Novembre 1990): 86.
55. Robert Stam, "The Lake, The Trees," *Film Comment* (January-February, 1991): 65. Stam suggests seeing the film as upholding the radical politics promulgated in earlier Godards. My reading of the film, and of Godard's evolving career during the 1980s and the early 1990s suggests the opposite.
56. Stam, "The Lake, The Trees," 64.
57.   Dans un premier temps—l'ancien testament—
       un être humain
       (un homme)
       est sauvé de la chute
       par un autre être humain
       (une femme).

   Dans un deuxième temps—le nouveau testament—
   un être humain
   (une femme)
   (la même)
   est sauvé de être la chute
   par un être humain
   (un autre homme).

   Mais la femme découvre que l'autre homme est aussi le même que le premier,
   que le deuxième est (encore et toujours) le même que le premier.

   C'est donc une révélation.
   Et si l'homme a dit le mystère,
   la femme a révélé le secret.

   At first—the old testament—
   a human being
   (a man)
   is saved from the fall
   by another
   (a woman).

   Subsequently—the new testament—
   a human being
   (a woman)
   (the same)

is saved from the fall
by a human being
(another man).

But the woman discovers that the other man is also the
same as the first,
that the second is (again and always) the same as the
first.

It is therefore a revelation.
And if the man told the mystery,
the woman revealed the secret.

    The parenthetical phrase "(encore et toujours)" could be trans-
lated several ways, since *encore* means "again" and "still" and *toujours*
means "always" and "still." The words in French are therefore syn-
onyms yet may be subtly distinguished, whereas they must be translated into English as the same or as different words. The poet may wish
to evoke any of the following meanings:

    1) *encore* as "again" because this line is a repetition of the previ-
ous one,

    2) *encore et toujours* as "still" and "always" which resembles the
"now" and "forever" of the Lords' Prayer,

    3) *encore et toujours* as "still and still."

I have chosen a fourth possibility, *encore et toujours* as "again and always," because it captures the repetition of #1, the "forever" of #2, and
avoids the overlapping definition of #3, for by choosing not to repeat the
same word the poet prioritized the words' difference in appearance over
their similarity in meaning.

58. Stam, "The Lake, The Trees," 64.
59. Peter Bondanella, *Italian Cinema*, 281.
60. Dumas, "Godard Protestant," 90.

Notes to Chapter 4

1. See Johannes Fabian, *Time and the Other: How Anthropology Makes Its
Object* (New York: Columbia University Press, 1983) and Bernard Mc-
Grane, *Beyond Anthropology: Society and the Other* (New York: Columbia University Press, 1989). See also *Quarterly Review of Film and
Video* 13, Nos. 1–3 (1992). This is a special issue on "Discourse of the
Other: Postcoloniality, Positionality, and Subjectivity."
2. Ella Shohat, "Imaging Terra Incognita: The Disciplinary Gaze of Empire," *Public Culture* 3, no. 2 (Spring, 1991): 50.
3. Jane Desmond, "Ethnography, Orientalism and the Avant-Garde Film,"
Visual Anthropology 4 (1991): 155. Desmond makes this pronounce-
ment in a separate case.
4. Tommaso Chiaretti, "Allegro Con Pessimismo," *China is Near*, by Marco
Bellochio, trans. Judith Green (London: Calder and Boyars, 1970), 1.

5. Ibid.
6. Bertolucci said in response to a question about his impressions of China before 1968:

> I lived through the Cultural Revolution as if it was a grandiose mise-en-scène with an old director called Mao Tse-tong in charge of millions of young extras conceived and raised for the sole purpose of being there at that glorious moment. I was attracted above all by the aesthetics of the Cultural Revolution, like a form of street theatre: post-Living Theatre, pre-Pina Bausch. But I also felt somewhat uneasy; today I would describe that feeling in terms of the absence of the ghost of freedom. In other words, I was never a Sino-phile in the way that many of my friends were. (Donald Ranvaud and Enzo Ungari, *Bertolucci by Bertolucci* [London: Plexus, 1987], 237)

7. Zhang Longxi, "The Myth of the Other: China in the Eyes of the West," *Critical Inquiry* 15 (Autumn, 1988): 110.
8. Umberto Eco, "*De interpretazione*; or, The Difficulty of Being Marco Polo: On the Occasion of Antonioni's China Film" in *New Challenges for Documentary*, ed. Alan Rosenthal (Berkeley: The University of California Press, 1988), 532.
9. Ranvaud and Ungari, *Bertolucci by Bertolucci*, 238.
10. Longxi, "The Myth of the Other," 117.
11. Both Bertolucci and his cinematographer, Vittorio Storaro, have described Pu Yi's evolution as the "voyage of a man from darkness into light." Each stage in the protagonist's journey is visualized in the film by one type of color: "His years in the palace are in 'forbidden' colors, the warmest colors, because it was both a protective womb for him and a kind of prison," whereas his years outside the city are symbolized by new colors, new chromatics. The dialectics of color is echoed and mirrored in the concept of lighting whereby, as Storaro suggests, knowledge is compared with light. In the Forbidden City, Pu Yi is

> never exposed to direct sunlight, he is always in penumbra. At this point in his life, he is still shielded mentally from the outside world. Later, the more he learns from his tutor RJ [Peter O'Toole], the more we should feel the rays of the sun reaching him. Gradually, a fight develops between light and shade, just as you have a fight within you between conscious and unconscious . . . And the more he understands, the more the light and shadows come into balance. (Vittorio Storaro quoted in Tony Rayns, "Model Citizen: Bernardo Bertolucci on Location in China," *Film Comment* [December 1987]: 36)

12. Leonardo de la Fuente, "Le Dernier Empereur: Multiples Splendeurs," *Telerama*, 28 (4 Decembre, 1987): 41.
13. Bertolucci in the Mill Valley Film Festival (April 9 & 10, 1988) called the Forbidden City "The Forbidden Mama." It is worth quoting here Luce Irigaray on man's relation to the maternal womb:

> one finds imperatives dictated by the enactment of sadomasochistic fantasies, these in turn governed by man's relation to his mother: the

desire to force entry, to penetrate, to appropriate for himself the mystery of this womb where he has been conceived, the secret of his begetting, of his "origin." Desire/need, also to make blood flow again in order to revive a very old relationship-intrauterine, to be sure, but also prehistoric-to the maternal. (*This Sex Which Is Not One*, trans. Catherine Porter [Ithaca: Cornell University Press, 1985], 25)

14. Joelle de Gravelaine, Jean-Pierre Lavoignat, et Christophe d'Yvoire, "Bernardo Bertolucci: La confusion magnifique," *Studio magazine* 9 (Decembre, 1987): 61.
15. The notion of "emplotment" was coined by Hayden White in his article, "The Historical Text as a Literary Artifact," *Clio* 3 (1974): 273–303.
16. The imagery of theater and spectacle, as Robert Burgoyne correctly observes, pervades the film. I use the notion of the "stage" of history here to invoke both its Marxist meaning (history as a process that progresses through different stages) as well as its association with spectacle and theater. For a further discussion of this issue, see Robert Burgoyne, "The Last Emperor: The Stages of History," *Substance*, 59 (1989): 93–101.
17. The term *will-to-spectacle* is used by Dana Polan in his article " 'Above All Else to Make You See': Cinema and the Ideology of Spectacle" in *Postmodernism and Politics*, ed. Jonathan Arac (Minneapolis: University of Minnesota Press, 1986), 60. According to Polan, the "*will-to-spectacle*" asserts that the world only has substance—in some cases, only is meaningful—when it appears as image, when it is shown, when it exists as phenomenal appearance."
18. Burton Pike, in his book, *The Image of the City in Modern Literature* (Princeton: Princeton University Press, 1981), 127–128, points out that the cities in *Invisible Cities* by the contemporary Italian writer Italo Calvino all bear female names, and that they all seem to be the same city, perhaps Marco Polo's native *Venezia*. Marco Polo, we should bear in mind, revealed China to the West and furnished it with a stock of dreams, fantasies, and utopias of Otherness. The typing of cities as female, Pike observes, "recalls on one hand Mumford's depiction of early settlements as containers, symbolizing the female principle, and on the other hand Balzac's Paris and Angouleme, cities also under the sign and domination of woman. (Women in Balzac's cities are the divinities of place, the sacred goddesses whom his upward-striving hunter-heroes must both propitiate and conquer in order to possess *le monde*.)"

For further information on the structure and history of the Forbidden City and, in particular, on the use of screens as walls, see Roderick MacFarquhan and the editors of the *Newsweek* Book Division, "The Forbidden City in History," in *The Forbidden City* (New York: Newsweek, 1972), 48–90, 112–136.
19. Bertolucci, at the Mill Valley Film Festival, April 9 and 10, 1988 stated: "The exploration of the Forbidden City can never be said to be over; it is by definition a work in progress."

20. Sigmund Freud, "Femininity," in *New Introductory Lectures on Psychoanalysis*, ed. and trans. James Strachey. The Pelican Freud Library, vol. 2 (London: Penguin Books, 1979), 146. For a major feminist critique of this article's assumptions, see Luce Irigaray, "The Blind Spot of an Old Dream of Symmetry" in *Speculum of the Other Woman* (1974), trans. Gillian C. Gill (Ithaca: Cornell University Press, 1985). Interestingly, Laura Mulvey, uses this article's presuppositions in regard to women's sexuality. She uses them uncritically in order to support her arguments concerning the "masculinized" position of the female spectator. Laura Mulvey, "Afterthoughts on 'Visual Pleasure and Narrative Cinema,'" Inspired by *Duel in the Sun*," *Framework* 15/16/17 (Summer, 1981): 12–15.

21. On the processes of conceptualization by the film viewer (as opposed to the reader of fiction), see Robert Scholes, "Narration and Narrativity in Film" in *Film Theory and Criticism*, eds. Gerald Mast and Marshall Cohen (New York: Oxford University Press, 1985), 390–410.

22. Nancy Chodorow, *The Reproduction of Mothering: Psychoanalysis and the Sociology of Gender* (Berkeley: University of California Press, 1978).

23. Jessica Benjamin, "Master and Slave: The Fantasy of Erotic Domination" in *Powers of Desire: The Politics of Sexuality*, eds., Ann Snitow, Christine Stansell and Sharon Thompson (New York: Monthly Review Press, 1983), 293 and note 19.

24. Longxi, "The Myth of the Other," 114–115.

25. Quoted in Ranvaud, 245.

26. Ibid., 281.

27. Roland Barthes, "Myth Today," in *Mythologies*, ed. and trans. Annette Lavers (New York: Hill and Wang, 1980), 152.

28. Desmond Ryan, *The Philadelphia Inquirer*, (December 13, 1987): 1–G. Bertolucci repeated the same idea in many interviews.

29. Roland Barthes, "Striptease," in *Mythologies*, 84.

30. In Luce Irigaray *This Sex Which Is Not One*, 26:

> Woman takes pleasure more from touching than from looking, and her entry into a dominant scopic economy signifies, again, her consignment to passivity: she is to be the beautiful object of contemplation. While her body finds itself thus eroticized, and called to a double movement of exhibition and of chaste retreat in order to stimulate the drives of the "subject," her sexual organ represents *the horror of nothing to see*. A defect in this systematics of representation and desire. A "hole" in its scoptophilic lens. It is already evident in Greek statuary that this nothing-to-see has to be excluded, rejected, from such a scene of representation. Woman's genitals are simply absent, masked, sewn back up inside their "crack."

31. Teresa De-Lauretis, *Alice Doesn't: Feminism, Semiotics, Cinema* (Bloomington: Indiana University Press, 1981), 113, claims that *Oedipus* is "paradigmatic of all narratives."

32. The Confucian scholar class arose in the Han dynasty (206 BC–220 AD) when the political philosophy of Confucius (551–479 BC) was adopted by the state.

33. Taisuke Mitamura, *Chinese Eunuchs: The Structure of Intimate Politics* (Tokyo: Charles E. Tuttle Company, 1970). According to Mitamura, the eunuch system in China lasted for more than two thousand years and through twenty-five dynasties. Only in the republican revolution was the system banned, although thirteen years after the launching of the revolution eunuchs still existed.

34. Laura Mulvey, "Visual Pleasure and Narrative Cinema," *Screen* 16 (Autumn, 1975): 6–18. The citations in this article are from the reprint in Bill Nichols, ed., *Movies and Methods* (Berkeley: University of California Press, 1985), vol. 2, 303–314.

35. In Imperial China, as Mitamura explains, "the term *huan kuan* was used in two senses. It meant simply a castrated man in one sense, while in the other it meant one who served in the Imperial Palace" 21. Chinese autocracy cultivated the eunuch system in order to maintain its interests and the emperor's "mandate of heaven." Freud explains circumcision as "the symbolic substitute for the castration which the primal father once inflicted upon his sons in the plenitude of his absolute power, and whoever accepted that symbol was showing by it that he was prepared to submit to the father's will, even if it imposed the most painful sacrifice on him." Sigmund Freud, "Moses and Monotheism," *The Origins of Religion*, The Pelican Freud Library, vol. 13 (London: Penguin Books, 1979), 369–370.

36. Mitamura claims that "the relationship between a monarch and a eunuch was very much like that of a man and his shadow," *Chinese Eunuchs*, 50.

37. For discussions of the use of Plato's cave myth in *The Conformist* as a self-reflexive critique of cinema, see Robert Philip Kolker, *Bernardo Bertolucci* (New York: Oxford University Press, 1985), pp. 87 and 96; and Jefferson Kline, *Bertolucci's Dream Loom: A Psychoanalytic Study of Cinema* (Amherst: University of Massachusetts Press, 1987), 98–99.

38. Robin Wood, "Return of the Repressed," *Film Comment* 14, no. 4, (July–August, 1978): 26.

39. Although Pu Yi's homosexuality is never explicitly expressed in the movie, Bertolucci hints at it through Lone's face which he perceives as having androgynous quality.

40. In the scene where Pu Yi rebels against the lifestyle being imposed on him in the city and climbs on the roof of one of the palaces (the film leaves it open whether this is a suicide attempt or an accident due to his short-sightedness), he is saved by Johnston (who finds out that Pu Yi needs glasses) and by two eunuchs who stand out among the collective group of eunuchs and whose names are Big Foot and Hunchback. The two nicknames are significant: Big Foot alludes to Oedipus and to the binding of Oedipus's feet (a symbolic castration), while Hunchback refers to the deformed deficient man.

41. Johnston, the enlightened Scottish tutor, is a sort of eunuch himself, a life-long bachelor. The first conversation he has with Pu Yi is about the

custom of wearing a kilt. Could the topic be interpreted as being a subtly indirect allusion to a desexed skirt, or to an item of apparel that is of equivocal sexual character? The casting of Peter O'Toole in this role adds another dimension of sexual ambiguity to the character, when one recalls O'Toole's role in David Lean's *Lawrence of Arabia*. O'Toole's presence, on the one hand, indicates genre awareness (both *Emperor* and *Lawrence* belong to the epic tradition and deal with the exoticism of non-Western cultures), and on the other hand, alludes to Lawrence's alleged homosexuality and to its portrayal by O'Toole in the Lean production.

42. Relying on Stent's account, Mitamura (*Chinese Eunuchs*, 32–34) explains that the severed parts known as *pao*, or "treasure,"

> were processed by a specialist, put into a container . . . sealed, and then placed on a high shelf. This was called *kao sheng*, or "high position," and it is said to have been symbolical of the original owner attaining a high position. . . . There were two reasons for the careful preservation of the *pao*. First, the eunuchs had to show their *pao* upon being advanced in rank, and advancement would be impossible without it. . . . The second reason for preserving the *pao* was so that it could be buried with the eunuch after his death. . . . The eunuchs hoped to be restored to masculinity in the next world, for the Chinese had great fear of deformity. Also, it was believed that Jun Wang, the king of the underworld, would turn those without their *pao* into female asses.

43. Mitamura (Chinese Eunuchs, 25.) notes:

> the Chinese had an explanation for the existence of the court eunuchs. . . . there are four "eunuch" stars located in the astronomical map to the west of the Emperor's constellation. The idea of four eunuch stars, although thought by some to have been derived from the number of women intimately connected with the Emperor, indicated that the eunuchs already had roles as attendants to the Emperor in the heavenly world. The Chinese firmly believed that the heavenly order of things applied to all humans and was behind all happenings. Thus they were able to accept the eunuch system as a matter of destiny or divine order.

44. Indeed *Emperor* is linked to *The Conformist* through a complex intratextual network of allusions. In the film *The Conformist* the search for the father figure in the "healthy" and "normal" Fascist state is also motivated by cultural decadence epitomized by Clerici's old and decaying family mansion and by his opium addicted mother who keeps a young chauffeur, as a lover. A very similar kind of decadence (opium addiction, love affair with a chauffeur, and so on) is portrayed in *Emperor* which presents it as a cause for the emergence of Pu Yi's fascism.

45. Kolker, *Bernardo Bertolucci*, 225.

46. Bertolucci may have derived the inspiration for this image from a picture in MacFarquhar's book on the Forbidden City. In this picture only one woman appears. The three women allude to the three women singing in the recording studio in *The Conformist* and looking like an Italian version of the American Andrews Sisters.

47. On the relationship between the "gaze," castration and "knowing," see Luce Irigaray, *Speculum of the Other Woman*.

48. Kolker, *Bernardo Bertolucci*, 52.

49. Julia Kristeva, "Stabat Mater" in *The Kristeva Reader*, ed. Toril Moi (New York: Columbia University Press, 1986), 164.

50. One of the major scenes to be considered regarding the figure of Eastern Jewel is the erotic one between her and the emperor's first wife. The representation of this seduction scene is charged with images of decadent and perverted eroticism (opium smoking, blue light, foot fetishism, lesbianism, and so on). The eroticism of the scene, accentuated by its foot fetishism, alludes also to the scene in a film directed by Luis Buñuel (one of Bertolucci's heros), *L'Age d'Or*, where the protagonist sucks the toe of a statue in a mock gesture symbolizing the sublimation of Western civilization. In Chinese culture, the foot, as Bertolucci himself indicated in interviews, is the most erotic part of the female body. On the origins of foot fetishism according to Freud, see his "Unsuitable Substitutes for the Sexual Object: Fetishism" in *On Sexuality*. See in particular note 1, p. 68 in the Penguin edition.

51. Victor Turner, *The Ritual Process*, (Harmondsworth: Penguin), 1974.

52. For a discussion of this issue, see Lloyd Demause, "The History of Childhood: The Basis for Psychohistory" in *History of Childhood Quarterly*, 1, No. 1 (Summer, 1973): 1–4.

53. Bertolucci said: "You know, the Chinese have quite a lot of sympathy for Pu Yi, even though he was a very cruel person. He was imprisoned, forced to endure a sort of *psicanalisi forzata*. He had to change, and he did. I think the movie will be a success if it makes acceptable the notion of brainwashing. Mao said, if you can wash your hands, you can wash your brain. I am not talking about Korean War-style brainwashing with lamps, but about a change that is far more subtle. And that is the transformation faced by the last emperor. Write this down again and again— "*He changed, Lui e cambiato!*." Quoted by Allen Kurzweil, "Out to Lunch with Bernardo Bertolucci," *Vanity Fair* (December, 1986): 160.

54. Kolker, *Bernardo Bertolucci*, 194. For an interesting discussion on the place of utopia and women in *1900* see Angela Dalle-Vacche and Robert Burgoyne, "Dialogue on *1900*," *Cinema Journal*, 29, no. 3 (Spring 1990): 69–78.

55. Bertolucci quoted by Cheng Jing, "Emperor's Conflict of Reality," *China Daily* (October 16, 1988). Bertolucci's approach brings to mind the view offered by Hayden White—who is partially indebted here to Jacques Lacan—of "narration and narrativity as the instruments by which the conflicting claims of the imaginary and the real are mediated, arbitrated, or resolved in a discourse." Hayden White, "On the Value of Narrativity in the Representation of Reality" in W. J. T. Mitchell, ed., *On Narrative*, (Chicago: The University of Chicago Press, 1981), 4. For White, who studies the relationship between narrative and history, "narrativity, certainly in factual storytelling . . . is intimately related to,

if not a function of, the impulse to moralize reality." Hence, every story "is a kind of allegory" which "points to a moral, or endows events, whether real or imaginary, with a significance that they do not possess as a mere sequence." Ibid., 13–14. The narrative of *Emperor*, in a self-re-flexive manner surpasses the boundaries of realism and history, and be-comes a universal allegory for everybody. In Bertolucci's words, the coronation scene of the child-emperor becomes "the scene of the birth of omnipotence" and "a very profound echo, not just in me but in every-one. Everyone has been a baby, everyone has been the center of the uni-verse, the center of the family. And representing that, at that level, obviously provoked great anxiety." *Studio Magazine*, 62. In preferring the imaginary to the real, Bertolucci not only questions "the very dis-tinction between real and imaginary events, basic to modern discus-sions of both history and fiction" (White, "On the Value," 5), but also provides the "discourse of desire." In addition, Bertolucci consciously expresses the impulse "for moral meaning, a demand that sequences of real events be assessed as to their significance as elements of *moral drama*," (White, "On the Value," 21).

56. Longxi, "The Myth of the Other," 113.

57. Louis Althusser, *Lenin and Philosophy, and Other Essays*, trans. Ben Brewster (New York and London: Monthly Review Press, 1971), 133.

58. *The Sheltering Sky: A Film by Bernardo Bertolucci Based on the Novel by Paul Bowles*, edited and produced by Livio Negri and Fabien S. Ger-ard (London: Scribners, 1990), 11.

59. For a summary of sources on this debate see Erik Cohen, "Pilgrimage and Tourism: Convergence and Divergence," in *Sacred Journeys: The Anthropology of Pilgrimage*, ed. Alan Morinis (Westport, Connecticut and London: Greenwood Press, 1992), 47–61.

60. The term "thick description" was coined by the anthropologist Clifford Geertz. See "Chapter 1/Thick Description: Toward an Interpretive The-ory of Culture," *The Interpretation of Cultures* (New York: Basic Books, 1973), 3–30. Geertz views anthropology not as an "experimental science in search of law but an interperative one in search of meaning" (p. 5). For Geertz ethnography is thick description and anthropological writ-ings are themselves interpretations and thus fictions—"fictions, in the sense that they are 'something made,' 'something fashioned' "(p. 15).

61. Negri and Gerard, *The Sheltering Sky*, 35.

62. Ibid., 35.

63. John Urry, *The Tourist Gaze: Leisure and Travel in Contemporary So-cieties* (London, Newbury Park: Sage Publications, 1990), 3.

64. From Paul Bowles, *The Sheltering Sky* (New York: The Ecco Press, 1978 [1949]), 14:

Whereas the tourist generally hurries back home at the end of a few weeks or months, the traveler, belonging no more to one place than to the next, moves slowly, over periods of years, from one part of the earth to another . . . another important difference between tourist and traveller is that the former accepts his own civilization without question; not so the traveler, who compares it with the others, and rejects elements he finds not to his liking.

From Bernardo Bertolucci's *The Sheltering Sky*:

Kit: Tunner we are not tourists we are travellers!
Tunner: Oh! What's the difference?
Port: Tourist is someone who thinks about going home in the moment they arrive, Tunner.
Kit: Whereas a traveller might not come back at all.

A strong sense of nostalgia towards older forms of travel is expressed by Bowles: "If travelling today still meant taking ships, I would have gone on travelling. But taking the airplane for me isn't travelling. It's just going from one place to another in as little time as possible. When you go on a trip, you shouldn't know for how long. That's travelling." Quoted in "What Happened to Kit," an Interview by Fabio Troncarelli "in Negri and Gerard *The Sheltering Sky*, 40. A surprisingly similar nostalgia was expressed by Claude Levi-Strauss in an interview with Bernard Pivot which he gave to *Apostrophes* in 1986.

65. Martin Blythe, "The Romance of Maoriland: Ethnography and Tourism in New Zealand Film," *East-West Film Journal* 4, no. 2 (June, 1990): 90–91.

66. Cohen, "Pilgrimage and Tourism," 49.

67. The model of the world prevalent in traditional society can be conceived, according to Cohen, "as consisting of a sacred Center, an ordered, hallowed Cosmos, and a surrounding dangerous but alluring chaos." He argues that "within this socially constructed space, two prototypical, non-instrumental movements can be distinguished: *Pilgrimage*, a movement toward the Center, and *Travel*, a movement in the opposite direction, toward the Other, located beyond the boundaries of the Cosmos, in the surrounding Chaos." Cohen (Pilgrimage and Tourism," 50–51) observes that:

> While the Center is well-defined and frequently discussed in the literature, the Other is a much more ambigious and relatively rarely considered deep-structural theme. Ambiguity belongs to its very nature it stands for the strange and the attractive, the threatening and the alluring, in short—the fascinating primordial, unformed and unknown, lurking in the recesses of chaos surrounding the ordered, 'civilized' cosmos. In its malignant aspect it is monstrous . . . the embodiment of evil as cognitive and moral confusion; it is appalling and repelling. . . . In its benign aspect, the Other is alluring, promising the seeker the innocent happiness of losing himself in the primordial pre-creational (or pre-natal) unity of all things, often identified with an effortless, creaturely satisfaction of all desires, unhindered by the restriction of the socio-moral order.

68. Cohen, "Pilgrimage and Tourism," 52.

69. Ibid.

70. Ibid.

71. From Cohen, "Pilgrimage and Tourism," 55: In the experimental mode
    the tourist tries out various alternative life-styles in an effort to dis-
    cover the one which he would like to adopt for himself. . . . The fre-
    quently repeated claim that people travel in order "to find themselves"
    is the inward-looking facet of that mode. . . . In the "existential"
    mode, finally, the tourist commits himself to an alternative which be-
    comes for him a new, "elective" center. . . . His existential experience
    at that Center is homologous to that of the idealized pilgrim.

72. From Cohen, "Pilgrimage and Tourism," 55:

    While the experience of the "existential" tourist at the "elective" Cen-
    ter is homologous to that of the idealized pilgrim, his structural posi-
    tion is not: the pilgrim's Center is that of his own society and culture,
    whereas that of the 'existential' tourist is not; rather, the latter trans-
    forms a point in the periphery of that world into his 'elective' Center.
    Moreover, unlike MacCannell's attractions, that Center here is not
    'museumized' into modernity. . . . Rather, the 'existential' tourist opts
    out, spiritually, from modernity; his Center lies outside it . . . he re-
    turns home, if at all, only for instrumental purposes.

    In his interview ("What Happened to Kit?" in *The Sheltering Sky*, eds.
    Livio Negri and Fabien S. Gerard) with Fabio Troncarelli Bowles said: "I
    don't know whether I have been influenced by the fatalism of the Arabs
    and whether I have chosen to live amongst them because I see my fa-
    talism mirrored in their fatalism" (p. 40). In response to the following
    observation (p. 41): "In your book you describe disintegration, lack of
    balance, the precariousness of individuals who are constantly in crisis—
    a crisis which involves the whole of Western culture," Bowles said:
    "The collapse of culture which is already on the verge of breaking down
    is inevitable." To the question (p. 41) "In other words, does this mean
    that the Western value system no longer works?" he answered: "The so-
    called Western 'values,' what kind of values are they? I don't think, for
    instance, that the America of today is a country with values or 'culture':
    it is a huge monstrous 'non-culture,' a 'non-civilization'. . . . It's an
    apocalypse."

73. Pasolini's assumptions recall the discourse of travel literature with its
    romantic vision regarding the uncontaminated state of non-European
    cultures. As McGrane in *Beyond Anthropology* observes (p. 106), "With
    regard to the non-European Polynesians, the central visibles of Melville's
    horizon of concern are that (a) they are in the state of nature, and (b) con-
    tact with white European civilization corrupts them. These two rela-
    tively clear and distinct forms are common to much of mid-nineteenth
    century Europe's experience of the alien Other. "See also Ali Behdad,
    "Orientalist Tourism," *Peuples mediterraneens* 50, (janv-mars 1990):
    59–73. This is a special issue called "L'Orientalisme. Interrogations."

74. Giuliana Bruno, "Heresies: The Body of Pasolini's Semiotics," *Cinema
    Journal* 30, no. 3 (Spring, 1991): 39. Bruno's article is an attempt to re-
    think Pasolini's theory in light of postmodernist thought. In her view

Pasolini's ideas, which were strongly criticized at the time he expressed
them, can be seen as anticipating some aspects of postmodernism.

75. The other two films in the trilogy are: *The Decameron* (1971) and *The
Canterbury Tales* (1972). It should be pointed out, however, that in his
last essay, "Abiura dalla Trilogia della vita" (Disavowal of the "Trilogy
of Life"), which he published as a preface to the scripts of the three films,
he rejected the triology.

> In an era of sexual liberation, *all* forms of sexuality have been assimi-
> lated into a cultural system Pasolini despises: consumer capitalism;
> even Pasolini's three films celebrating the liberating potential of hu-
> man sexuality have been co-opted into the system of values he rejects.
> Now, Pasolini declares, it is clear that the lower-class characters he
> had always admired in other films and had seemed to discover in the
> Third World were always potentially petit-bourgeois figures, anticul-
> tural members of an ignorant lumpenproletariat whose only remain-
> ing function was that of consumer.

(Peter Bondanella, *Italian Cinema: From Neorealism to the Present*
(New York: Frederick Ungar Publishing Co., 1983), 293–294).

76. The disguise of Kit (Debra Winger) as a man recalls a similar disguise in
The Arabian Nights by Zumurrud (Inez Pellegrini), the clever slave girl.
77. Edward Said, *Orientalism* (New York: Random House, 1978), 167.
78. Said, *Orientalism*, 190. See also Ali Behdad, "The Discursive Formation
of Orientalism: The Threshold of (Pseudo) Scientificity," *Peuples
mediterraneens* 50: 163–169.
79. For a very interesting discussion of this issue and related topics see
James Roy MacBean, "Between Kitsch and Fascism: Notes on Fassbinder, Pasolini, (Homo)sexual Politics, the Exotic, the Erotic & Other
Consuming Passions," *Cineaste* XIII, no. 4 (1984): 12–19.
80. MacBean, "Between Kitsch and Fascism," 15.
81. Ibid., 15–16.
82. Millicent Dillon, "The Marriage Melody," in *The Sheltering Sky*, eds.
Livio Negri and Fabien S. Gerard, 47.
83. Paul Bowles, *The Sheltering Sky*, 272–273.
84. "The Physiology of Feelings," an Interview with Bertolucci by Renato
Leys, in *The Sheltering Sky*, eds. Livio Negri and Fabien S. Gerard, 60.
Debra Winger in a promotion film (*Behind the Scenes of The Sheltering
Sky*) on the making of *The Sheltering Sky* said:

> A lot of things in the end were changed because when we actually did
> reach Niger it was clear that these people that Paul had written about,
> he had used the names of the Tuaregs but it was a lot of fantasy there
> was not a lot of empirical study and so I felt that we had either to
> change the name of the people or we had to show them for the benev-
> olent race that they are—and they are amazingly beautiful—and I just
> couldn't, so it was one or the other and we went with what was more
> the reality of that place. Paul had never travelled that far south so this
> part of the book was not based on experience so I think we all under-
> stand that that's an acceptable change.

The paradox, of course, is that the Tuaregs were the victims of white violence. The European (mostly French) colonial penetration into the Sahara, the land of the Tuaregs (called in their language *balad el-atsh*—the land of thirst) was violent. From the middle of the nineteenth century forward the Tuaregs fought against modern armies with traditional swords. With African decolonization thirty years ago, the situation of the Tuaregs, who found themselves split among different countries, deteriorated. When Mali gained independence in 1960, the country's black-dominated goverment in Bamako imposed its rule over the nomads of the north, brutally crushing a Tuareg rebellion in 1963. In 1973, a severe famine wiped out most of the Tuareg livestock. Another severe drought followed in 1984–1985. As a result many Tuareges fled to other countries and remained as miserable refugees in Algeria and Mauritania. Some of the youth joined the Libyans and the Polisario (the rebel group fighting for independence in Western Sahara). In April 1986 Algeria transferred thousands of Tuareg nomads to Mali and Niger where they were persecuted and murdered. The former "knights of the desert" are today the victims of colonization and decolonization in a peripheral region of the globe. The stark contrast between their image in the film and the reality of their contemporary situation is therefore even more problematic. For another contemporary literary portrayal of the Sahara desert and the Tuaregs see Jean Marie Gustave Le Clezio *Desert* (Paris: Gallimard, 1980).

85. Jane Bowles had several affairs with women, one of them a Moroccan prostitute. In his interview with Renato Leys (*The Sheltering Sky,* eds. Livio Negri and Fabien S. Gerard, 57) Bertolucci said: "To me John appears like a centaur—these strong soccer-player thighs—whereas the upper part of his body seems softer, becoming at times almost effeminate. (In the same manner, Debra's incredible energy at times seems to have something almost boyish about it)."

86. Shohat observes that "the psychoanalytical postulation of id and superego parallels, to some extent, the primitive/civilized dichotomy permeating colonial discourse." "Imaging Terra Incognita," 66.

87. The Tuaregs were called by different names in Arabic texts. One of them is Al-Multhamin (the veiled people). Gendered metaphors such as "unveiling," Shohat observes, "had become recurrent in archeology and psychoanalysis (for example, "unveiling the past")" Shohat, 58.

88. Bertolucci, in Renato's "The Physiology of Feelings," *The Sheltering Sky,* eds. Livio Negri and Fabien S. Gerard, 58.

89. Said, *Orientalism,* 167.

90. Ibid., 188.

91. Ibid., 90.

92. Ibid., 190.

93. Bertolucci, in Renato's "The Physiology of Feelings," *The Sheltering Sky,* eds. Livio Negri and Fabien S. Gerard, 58.

94. David Thomson, "Gone Away," *Film Comment* 27, no. 3 (May-June, 1991): 20.

95. John Urry, *The Tourist Gaze*, 141. Marry Morris says that: "While there were such intrepid 'lady travelers' of the Victorian era as Isabella Bird, Freya Stark, and Mary Kingsley, they were considered eccentric, though the best of them were gifted, acclaimed writers (still underrated today)." She adds that: "Historically, the popular impression was that to journey meant to put oneself at risk not only physically but morally. The language of sexual initiation is oddly similar to that of travel. We speak of sexual 'exploits' or 'adventures.' Both body and globe are objects for exploration, and the great 'explorers,' whether Marco Polo or Don Juan, have been men." "Women and Travel," *Ms.* (May–June 1992): 68.

   See also Mary Louise Pratt, *Imperial Eyes: Travel Writing and Transculturation* (London: Routledge, 1992) and the book review by James Clifford in *TLS* (September 11, 1992): 3–4, as well as his article "Traveling Cultures," in Lawrence Grossberg et al. *Cultural Studies* (London: Routledge, 1992), 96–116.

96. Quoted from the promotion film "Behind the Scenes of *The Sheltering Sky.*"

97. Graham Dann and Erik Cohen, "Sociology and Tourism," *Annals of Tourism Research* 18 (1991), a special issue on "Tourism Social Science," 158.

98. For an interesting discussion of this issue see Donald Pizer, "The Sexual Geography of Expatriate Paris," *Twentieth Century Literature*, vol. 36, no. 2 (Summer 1990): 173–185. Bertolucci's *Last Tango in Paris* invokes and plays with the myth of expatriate Paris.

99. In Troncarelli's "What Happened to Kit" (*The Sheltering Sky*, eds. Livio Negri and Fabien S. Gerard), 44, Bowles himself denied his acclaimed status as a guru of the Beat Generation. "In the sixties, at the time of the hippies, many came to Tangier to visit Jane and me. But they came here to see us as an object of curiosity. . . . I took Allen Ginsberg to Marakesh; but this has not made me a poet of the Beat generation." According to his biographer, "Bowles does not regard himself as a guru. He simply has the impression of having arrived on the scene in time to be present at the end of a certain conception of nature and the world" (in Robert Briatte's, "The Territories of the Sky," *The Sheltering Sky*, eds. Livio Negri and Fabien S. Gerard, 36). Homi Bhabha constructs his article "Postcolonial Authority and Postmodern Guilt" (in *Cultural Studies*, pp. 56–68) around the analysis of Roland Barthes's attempt in a gay bar in Tangier "to enumerate the stereophony of languages within earshot." For Bhabha "Tangier simultaneously becomes the space for the writing of sexual difference" (p. 58).

100. Quoted from a Palace Pictures release, 1990, p. 11.

101. Said, *Orientalism*, 170.

102. Briatte, 35.

103. Quoted from A Palace Pictures Release, p. 32.

104. Said, *Orientalism*, 157.
105. From Bernard McGrane (*Beyond Anthropology*, 104): "For Marlow [the narrator of Conrad's darkly profound *Heart of Darkness* (1890)] journeying up the African Congo, as for the anthropologist, to look into this primitive area was to look back in time and to travel into this primitive space was the equivalent of traveling back in time. For nineteenth-century evolutionary anthropology going beyond Europe now took on the meaning of going back in time. Going beyond is going back."
106. Bowles, *The Sheltering Sky*, 313
107. William Aldrich, "Thirty Years in the Making," in *The Sheltering Sky*, eds. Livio Negri and Fabien S. Gerard, 86. Hence the fictional figures of Port and Kit, as well as their creator Paul Bowles, can be seen as rebels whose search for the id of civilization is a manifestation of revolt. This invokes what Graham Dann and Erik Cohen say, in Negri and Gerard's book, about existential tourism: "While the less profound, 'recreational' tourism is socially functional, serious 'existential' tourism is not—except perhaps in the oblique sense that it deflects away deeply alienated individuals who might otherwise engage in activities aimed at the destruction or revolutionary transformation of the existing order of their society of origin."
108. A Palace Pictures Release, 1990, 33. Bertolucci's *The Last Emperor* was also the first Western movie to venture behind the walls of China's Forbidden City. Bertolucci's new "obsession" with discovering new virginal spaces for the spectator's gaze recalls Werner Herzog's *Aguirre, The Wrath of God* (1972) and *Fitzcarraldo* (1980–1981). The exploitation of the Mosquito Indians by Herzog (to a large extent the protagonists' madness in these films reflects Herzog's own) is a well known and disturbing fact. The question of Bertolucci's exploitation of the Tuaregs is more complicated. He can be criticized for exploiting their exoticism and transforming them into the spectator's object of pleasure. However, there is no way to compare his treatment of the Tuaregs (on the level of production) and Herzog's treatment of the Mosquitos; the latter was clearly cruel and abusive. In 1984 Herzog, with French-German journalist Denis Reichle, made *Ballad of the Little Soldier* (*Ballade von kleinen Soldaten*), a forty-five-minute documentary about the Mosquito Indians and their rebellion against the Sandinistas. Interestingly Herzog made also *Fata Morgana* (1968–1970) a documentary on life in the Sahara desert.
109. A Palace Pictures Release, 1990, 34.
110. For a further discussion of ornamentalism in Bertolucci's cinema see Yosefa Loshitzky, "More than Style: Godard's Modernism versus Bertolucci's Postmodernism," *Criticism* XXXIV, no. 1 (Winter 1992): 119–142.
111. John Frow, "Tourism and the Semiotics of Nostalgia," *October* 57 (Summer, 1991): 144.

112. Marc Peploe, "Life as a Road Movie," in *The Sheltering Sky*, eds. Livio Negri and Fabien S. Gerard, 84.
113. The theme of lost identity appears in many road films such as Antonioni's *The Passenger* (written by Marc Peploe), Fonda's *Easy Rider*, and Wenders' *Paris/Texas*. The latter uses the landscape of the American desert as a backdrop and geographic metaphor for the protagonist who literally lost his identity.
114. A Palace Pictures Release, 1990, 17.
115. In 1946 John Huston directed Bowles's adaptation of Sartre's *Huis Clos* in New York. *No Exit*, the play, was a hit, later winning the Drama Critics' Award for Best Foreign Play of the year. Both Bertolucci's *Agonia* and *The Last Tango in Paris* take place in a closed room. Bertolucci himself reflected on the similarities between *Last Tango in Paris* and *The Sheltering Sky* from an existentialist point of view. He told me in an interview in London on July 27, 1991: "I was thinking, isn't the empty flat of *Last Tango* a kind of a desert and isn't the desert an empty flat?."
116. See, for example, McGrane in *Beyond Anthropology*.
117. Bertolucci, in Renato's "The Physiology of Feelings," *The Sheltering Sky*, eds. Livio Negri and Fabien S. Gerard, 59.
118. Georges-Louis Bourgeois, "The Road from Parma," *The Sheltering Sky*, eds. Livio Negri and Fabien S. Gerard, 66.

Notes to Chapter 5

1. See Colin MacCabe and Laura Mulvey, "Images of Woman, Images of Sexuality," in Colin MacCabe, *Godard: Images, Sounds, Politics*.
2. *Camera Obscura* 8–9–10 (Fall 1982) a special issue on Jean-Luc Godard. The three articles on *Sauve qui peut (la vie)* are reprinted in the MOMA Catalog *Godard: Son + Image*.
   See Laura Mulvey's essay "The Hole and the Zero: The Janus Face of the Feminine in Godard" in *Jean-Luc Godard: Son + Image*, ed. Raymond Bellour (New York: Harry N. Abrams, Inc, 1992). For a brief but interesting feminist critique of Godard's cinema until *Letter to Jane* see Molly Haskell, *From Reverence to Rape: The Treatment of Women in the Movies* (Chicago and London: The University of Chicago Press, 1987 [1973]), 299–302. For different critical perspectives on *Hail Mary*, see Maryel Locke and Charles Warren, eds., *Jean-Luc Godard's Hail Mary: Women and the Sacred in Film* (Carbondale: Southern Illinois University Press, 1993).
3. For an interesting discussion of Godard as a frustrating public speaker see David Rodowick, "Godard and Silence," *Camera Obscura* 8–9–10, 187–190.
4. Martin Walsh, "Godard and Me: Gorin Talks," *The Brechtian Aspect of Radical Cinema* (London: British Film Institute, 1981), 123.

5. Quoted in Walter S. Ross, "Splicing Together Jean-Luc Godard," *Esquire* (July 1969): 75.

6. Ross, "Splicing Together," 75.

7. William G. Simon, "The Influence of the Director: Jean-Luc Godard and Anna Karina," in *Great Film Actresses* (Catalogue for retrospective at the Art Institute of Chicago, 1979).

8. Ibid.

9. Leaud's image of a child-male is used in *Tango* to satirize Godard. Molly Haskell notes that Jean-Pierre Leaud, though functioning as the alter-ego of both Godard and Truffaut, is indelibly associated with Truffaut. Leaud, she says, is "the fumbling, eternally innocent male, straightfor-ward and guileless, whose inexperience is no match for the instinctive wisdom and wiles of a woman." Molly Haskell, *From Reverence to Rape*, 302.

10. Janet Bergstrom, "Violence and Enunciation," *Camera Obscura*, 21.

11. Bertolucci attempted, in a way, to use the same female type in *Before the Revolution*, which is a typical post-Godardian film.

12. Quoted in Walter S. Ross, "Splicing Together," 42.

13. The story as Moravia describes it "sets out to relate how, while I con-tinued to love her and not to judge her, Emilia, on the other hand, dis-covered, or thought she discovered, certain defects in me, and judged me and in consequence ceased to love me." Alberto Moravia, trans. Angus Davidson, *A Ghost at Noon* (New York: A Signet Book, 1956 [1955]), 5.

14. Walter Korte, "Godard's Adaptation of Moravia's *Contempt*," *Litera-ture/Film Quarterly* II, no. 3 (Summer, 1974): 284.

15. Korte, 285.

16. Sylvie Pierre, "Fritz movie," *Cahiers du Cinéma* no. 437: 32.

17. Jacques Aumont, "The Fall of the Gods: Jean-Luc Godard's *Le Mépris* (1963)" in *French Film: Texts and Contexts*, ed. Susan Hayward and Ginette Vincendeau (London and New York: Routledge, 1990), 217. See note 3 p. 228. Aumont, quoting Leonard Martin, says that Godard used to send telegrams addressed to "Mussolini Ponti" and "King Kong Levine."

18. See for example Jacques Aumont, p. 219.

19. I borrow the term from Eisabeth Lyon, "Unspeakable Images, Unspeak-able Bodies," *Camera Obscura* 24 (September, 1990): 169–193.

20. Jean-Luc Godard, "Introduction a une veritable histoire du cinéma," *Camera Obscura* 8–9–10, 76.

21. Simon, "The Influence of the Director," 6.

22. Joel Haycock, "The Sign of the Sociologist: Show and Anti-Show in Godard's *Masculin Feminin*," *Cinema Journal* 29, no. 4 (Summer, 1990): 51.

23. Haycock, "The Sign of the Sociologist," 60.

24. Haycock, 62–63. For a discussion of this parody see also Robert Stam, *Subversive Pleasures: Bakhtin, Cultural Criticism, and Film* (Baltimore and London: The Johns Hopkins University Press, 1989), 178–179.

25. Tania Modleski, "Lethal Bodies," in *Feminism Without Women: Culture and Feminism in a "Postfeminist" Age* (New York and London: Routledge, 1991), 135.

26. These comments appeared originally in *Le Nouvelle Observateur* in 1966, Paris, and Agence Laure Forestier. Original French text edited by Sylvain Regard. Translated by *Sight and Sound*.

27. Roger Greenspun, *"Weekend"* in Royal S. Brown ed. *Focus on Godard* (Englwood Cliffs, New Jersey: Prentice Hall, Inc., 1972), 76.

28. On Jane Fonda, Godard said in 1980 at the thirty-third annual Cannes International Film Festival: "She looks much healthier, much happier, much more beautiful in her latest films. She's much more beautiful than they are. At last, someone who benefited from Vietnam." Quoted in Vincent Canby, "Godard, at Cannes, Can Still Stir Up Film Furor," *The New York Times* (Saturday, May 24, 1980): 14.

29. Jim Hoberman, "He-e-ere's Jean-ee: TV a la Godard," *Village Voice* (April 28, 1986): 46.

30. I am borrowing the term "metapornography" from Robert Stam. See Stam, *Subversive Pleasures*, 178.

31. Julia Lessage, *Jean-Luc Godard: A Guide to References and Resources* (Boston: G.K. Hall & Co., 1979), 122.

32. Godard said: "I wouldn't be able to film a nude woman today. And still less, a nude man." ("Introduction a une veritable histoire du cinéma," *Camera Obscura* 8–9–10, 80) Yet, only a year after he said this he showed a nude woman in *Passion* (1981).

33. "Introduction," *Camera Obscura* 8–9–10, 6.

34. Elisabeth Lyon, "La passion, c'est pas ca," *Camera Obscura* 8–9–10, 7. For a further discussion of the significance of Duras within the overall conceptual and stylistic economy of the film see the rest of this article.

35. Constance Penley, "Pornography, Eroticism," *Camera Obscura* 8–9–10, 13.

36. Penley, "Pornography, Eroticism," 15.

37. Ibid., 16.

38. Ibid., 17.

39. Bergstrom, "Violence and Enunciation," 39.

40. Quoted in Phil Anderson, "Godard: X-rays of the Child," *Twin Cities Reader* (February 25, 1981). Godard also said: "I'm judging myself as a man, too, in the film. This is how the world is, not how I'd like it to be. The world we live in, at least in Europe—and Europe is only a colony of America—is not a very happy one. To me, the world is pessimistic. And to me, the two girls in the picture are not pessimistic at all." Quoted in Joanna Connors, "Women Zap Godard, *Every Man*," *Minneapolis Star* (Monday, February 23, 1981): 1c.

41. This recalls her role in Michael Cimino's *Heaven's Gate*. For a discussion between Godard and Pauline Kael on the film see "The Economics of Film Criticism: A Debate Jean-Luc Godard and Pauline Kael," *Camera Obscura* 8-9-10, 167–171.

42. Vincent Canby, "Godard at Cannes, Can Still Stir Up Film Furor," 14.
43. Jonathan Cott, "Godard: Born-Again Filmmaker," *Rolling Stone* (November 27, 1980): 33.
44. Bergstrom, "Violence and Enunciation," 28.
45. Quoted in Phil Anderson, "Godard: X-rays of the Child."
46. Marc Cerisuelo, *Jean-Luc Godard* (Paris: Quatres-vent, 1989), 214.
47. David Wills, "*Carmen*: Sound/Effect," *Cinema Journal* 25, no. 4 (Summer 1986): 35.
48. Ibid.
49. Stuart Cunningham and Ross Harley, "The Logic of the Virgin Mother: A Discussion of *Hail Mary*," *Screen* 28, no. 1 (Winter, 1987): 65.
50. For a discussion of the myth of the goddess and its relationship to the moon see Anne Baring and Jules Cashford, *The Myth of the Goddess: Evolution of an Image* (London: Viking, 1991).
51. Katherine Dieckmann, "Godard in His 'Fifth Period': An Interview," *Film Quarterly*, no. 2, vol. XXXIX (Winter 1985–1986): 4.
52. Dieckmann, "Godard in his 'Fifth Period,' " 3.
53. Ibid.
54. Ibid.
55. Cunningham and Harley, "The Logic of the Virgin Mother," 63.
56. Cerisuelo, 234–235.
57. Bertolucci told me in an interview on July 27, 1991, in London that when Godard was asked in the 1984 Cannes Film Festival to identify his major desire he said "to be cured of my fatigue."
58. Cerisuelo, *Jean-Luc Godard* 235.
59. Myron S. Meisel, "An Interview Composed by Jean-Luc Godard," *Reader* (January 23, 1981): 11.
60. John Fiske, *Reading the Popular* (Boston: Unwin Hyman, 1989).
61. Urry, *The Tourist Gaze*, 152.
62. Mary Ann Doane, "The Economy of Desire: The Commodity Form in/of the Cinema," *Quarterly Review of Film and Video* 11, no. 1 (1989): 23. This is a special issue on Female Representation and Consumer Culture.
63. Doane, "The Economy of Desire," 28.
64. See for example Alice Gagnard, "A Sociocultural Close-Up: Body Image in Advertising," and Linda Lazier-Smith, "A New 'Genderation' of Images to Women," in *Women in Mass Communication: Challenging Gender Values*, ed. by Pamela J. Creedon (Newburry Park and London: Sage, 1989), 247–262.
65. For a different account of narcissism as a "fundamental ('primary') and *identificatory* relation of the ego to the other, that grounds both sexual difference and social identification" see Elisabeth Lyon, "Unspeakable Images, Unspeakable Bodies," 169–193.
66. Brian Darling, "Jean-Luc Godard: Politics and Humanism," Notes for discussion at BFI Education Department Seminar, April 17, 1969.
67. Constance Penley, "Pornography, Eroticism," in *The Future of an Illusion: Film, Feminism, and Psychoanalysis* (Minneapolis: University of Minnesota Press, 1989), 16.

68. Jane Fonda specialized in the role of a courageous investigative journalist in Hollywood movies such as *The Electric Horseman* (1980) and *The China Syndrome* (1979). As Bordwell et al. note, *Tout va bien* resembles the story of *The China Syndrome* in several ways. See David Bordwell, Janet Staiger, and Kristin Thompson, *The Classical Hollywood Cinema: Film Style and Mode of Production to 1960* (London: Routledge, 1988), 372.

69. For an interesting analysis of the theme of anality in Godard's film see Stuart Cunningham and Ross Harley, "The Logic of the Virgin Mother."

70. Frederic Strauss, "La scene primitive," *Cahiers du Cinéma* 437 (Novembre 1990): 94.

71. The issue of pornography is one of the major topics in contemporary discourse on film. I advise the interested reader to refer to Tania Modleski's "Lethal Bodies" (in *Feminism Without Women*) for an extremely valuable discussion of the controversy surrounding pornography and in particular that concerned with lesbian sadomasochism.

72. According to Robert Stam, the " 'metapornography' practiced by Jean-Luc Godard has precisely this quality of exposing cinematic eroticism, especially, as a discursive and linguistic construct. From his films in the late fifties through the films coauthored with Anne-Marie Miéville in the seventies and eighties, Godard has conducted what Bakhtin would call a 'submerged polemic' with pornography, a kind of metatextual dialogue with porn as a preexisting body of texts. Time and again Godard returns to the scene of pornography, to the sexual fascination of its images and the frustration implicit in its lure." Stam, 178.

73. Strauss, "La scene primitive," 95.

74. It is interesting to note that Bertolucci portrays Dominique Sanda, the French actress, as a Botticceli type of woman in one of the scenes in *1900*.

75. Robert Stam, "The Lake, The Trees," *Film Comment* (January-February, 1991): 64.

76. This is of course a polemic point. If indeed Godard wanted to invest his heroine flesh with spirituality then, to revert to Molly Haskell's question, "why is it that the most memorable scenes are of a girl dressing and undressing, undressing and dressing, boyish from the waist down, but seductively large-breasted, her face always hidden by cascading sheaves of brown hair?" Molly Haskell, "Immaculate Deception," *Vogue* (October, 1985).

Notes to Chapter 6

1. Joelle de Gravelaine, Jean-Pierre Lavoignat, and Christophe d'Yvoire, "Bernardo Bertolucci: La Confusion Magnifique," *Studio magazine* 9 (Decembre, 1987): 60. This recalls Susan Sontag's observation: "What is more beautiful in virile men is something feminine; what is more beautiful in feminine women is something masculine." Susan Sontag, "Notes

on 'Camp'," in *Against Interpretation* (New York: Dell, Laurel Edition, 1969), 279. The celebration of androgyny is one of the principles of the credo of camp. As a matter of fact many of the features of camp (the aestheticist attitude, the preference of artifice to nature, the love of exaggeration, and the cult of the androgyny) show an amazing resemblance to nineteenth century decadence. Freud discusses the androgynous structure in mythology in his study of Leonardo Da Vinci. See Sigmund Freud, "Leonardo Da Vinci and a Memory of His Childhood (1910)," in *Art and Literature*. The Pelican Freud Library, vol. 14 (London: Penguin Books, 1979), 185–186.

See also Sandra M. Gilbert and Susan Gubar, "Cross-Dressing: Transvestism as Metaphor," in *No Man's Land: The Place of The Woman Within the Twentieth Century*, Vol. 2: Sexexchanges (New Haven and London: Yale University Press, 1989), 324–376 and Chris Straayer, "Redressing the 'Natural': The Contemporary Transvestite Film," *Wide Angle* 14, No. 1 (January, 1992): 36–55.

Angela Dalle Vacche's emphasizes in her discussion of Bertolucci's *Spider's Stratagem* what she calls "gender confusion and role contamination." Angela Dalle Vacche, *The Body in the Mirror: Shapes of History in Italian Cinema* (Princeton, New Jersey: Princeton University Press, 1992), 241.

2. Will Aitken, "Bertolucci's Gay Images: Leaving the Dance," *Jump Cut* 16 (November 1977): 24.

3. Bertolucci confessed to me in an interview in London, July 27, 1991 that Fassbinder is one of the filmmakers he loves and to whom he feels close.

4. Bertolucci said: "In *Last Tango in Paris*, Brando, the father, is confronted by a bisexual and bifocal character represented by Maria Schneider and Jean-Pierre Leaud. In *Tragedy* . . . we have the same thing, but in addition, there is a mother who is very active from the beginning while in *Last Tango* she's dead from the start. Leaud, instead of making love to Maria, films her, just as Adelfo, who before being a worker is a priest, has a platonic, intellectual relationship with Laura." Donald Ranvaud and Enzo Ungari, *Bertolucci by Bertolucci* (London: Plexus, 1987), 222.

5. Barbara Creed, "From Here to Modernity: Feminism and Postmodernism," *Screen* 28, no. 2 (Spring, 1987): 66.

Chris Straayer distinguishes a new sexual type, the she-man, within the context of postmodern performance. The she-man, according to her, "is glaringly bi-sexed rather than obscurely androgynous or merely bisexual. Rather than undergoing a downward gender mobility, he has enlarged himself with feminine gender *and* female sexuality." Chris Straayer, "The She-Man: Postmodern Bi-Sexed Performance in Film and Video," *Screen* 31, no. 3 (Autumn, 1990): 263.

6. For a feminist critique of Bertolucci's sexual politics see Robert Kolker, *Bernardo Bertolucci* (New York: Oxford University Press, 1985), 225–240. For a critique of *Tango*, see Joan Mellen, "Sexual Politics and

Bertolucci's *Last Tango in Paris*," in *Women and Their Sexuality in the New Film* (New York: Horizon Press, 1973), 128–146.

7. Jerry Tallmer, "The Feminists 'Will Kiss Me'," "The Week in Entertainment," *New York Post* (Saturday, February 3, 1973): 15.

8. Aitken, "Bertolucci's Gay Images," 26. Aitken adds that the last scene in which Jeanne is dressing Paul in her father's military cap and gunning him down is "curiously, touchingly reminiscent of the final scene of Godard's *Breathless*," Ibid.

9. Straayer, "The She-Man," 262.

10. Straayer, 263.

11. *Newsweek*, February 12, 1973, 56.

12. In our interview Bertolucci said: "after I finished working [on *The Sheltering Sky*] I thought that there were strong links between *The Sheltering Sky* and *Last Tango*. I thought that the two movies were closer than it seems . . . both films are about the difficulty of the couple . . . they both are the most, I think, existentialist of my movies. Both Marlon and John . . . have an aura of danger, they are both dangerous men. Also I thought that they carry with them a strong sense of death. . . . Both films are full of death and in both films the man dies and the woman survives."

13. Bertolucci, *Last Tango in Paris* (New York: Delacorte Press, 1973), 136.

14. Bertolucci, *Last Tango*, 135.

15. The portrayal of the Colonel as an archetypal Fascist links *Tango* to *The Conformist*, which attempts (like the original text of Moravia's novel) to explain the formation of a Fascist personality.

16. Julian C. Rice, "Bertolucci's *Last Tango in Paris*," *The Journal of Popular Film*, 3 (1974): 171. For an interesting and nostalgic discussion of the "generational effect" of Brando on the adolescents of the 1950s (Bertolucci's generation) see Richard Schickel," Accomplices: Brando and the Fifties, and Why Both Still Matter," *Film Comment* 27, no. 4 (July-August, 1991): 30–36.

17. Rice, "Bertolucci's *Last Tango in Paris*," 169.

18. Bertolucci, *Last Tango*, 180.

19. Pauline Kael, "Introduction," *Last Tango in Paris*, 18.

20. The shot of Paul's death is an allusion not only to *Viva Zapata*. The background (the roofs of Paris) recall visually and thematically the shot of Kelly sitting on the roof in *An American in Paris*. It also echoes the imagery of the roofs of New York in *On the Waterfront*.

21. Ann Guarino, "It's Impact He Wants," *New York News* (October 6, 1979).

22. Vittorio Storaro, "Writing with Light," in *The Sheltering Sky: A Film by Bernardo Bertolucci Based on the Novel by Paul Bowles*, edited and produced by Livio Negri, and Fabien S. Gerard (London: Scribners, 1990), 88. The mythological association of femininity with the moon is joined with the association of masculinity with the sun. In his discussion of the case history of Schreber, Freud mentions that he was able "to ex-

plain the sun as a sublimated 'father symbol' " by recognizing the connection between the patient's peculiar relation to the sun and the "wealth of its bearing upon *mythology.*" Sigmund Freud, "Postscript" (1912 [1911]) to "Psychoanalytic Notes on an Autobiographical Account of a Case of Paranoia (Dementia Paranoides) (Schreber) (1911 [1910])," in *Case Histories II: 'Rat Man', Schreber, 'Wolf Man', Female Homosexuality,* ed. and trans. James Strachey, The Pelican Library, vol. 9 (London: Penguin Books, 1979), 221.

23. Mellen, "Fascism in Contemporary Film," 4.
24. Lynda K. Bundtzen, "Bertolucci's Erotic Politics and the Auteur Theory: From *Last Tango in Paris* to *The Last Emperor.*" *Western Humanities Review* 44, no. 2 (Summer, 1990): 202.
25. An opposite view on the character of Anna is conveyed by Aitken. According to him: "Anna, at first a butch-lesbian caricature [actually she imitates the pose of Marlene Dietrich] striding about, hands thrust firmly in trouser pockets—quickly becomes the epicenter of repressed erotic desires in the film. Anna alone, of all the characters in the perhaps over-simplified Reichean schema of the film, is a free sexual agent, radiating a determined sensuality that at once frightens and fascinates Marcello." p. 25.
26. Kolker, *Bernardo Bertolucci,* 233.
27. Kline, *Bertolucci's Dream Loom: A Psychoanalytic Study of Cinèma* (Amherst: The University of Massachusetts Press, 1987), 66.
28. Kline, 74.
29. Cited in Gideon Bachmann, "Every Sexual Relationship Is Condemned: An Interview with Bernardo Bertolucci," *Film Quarterly* 26 (Spring, 1973): 3–4.
30. Simon de Beauvoir, *The Second Sex,* trans. and ed. H. M. Parshley (Harmondsworth: Penguin Books, 1974 [1949]), 50.
31. Sigmund Freud, "Femininity," in *New Introductory Lectures on Psychoanalysis,* ed. and trans. James Strachey. The Pelican Freud Library, vol. 2 (London: Penguin Books, 1979), 148.
32. See Marsha Kinder and Beverle Houston, "Bertolucci and the Dance of Danger," *Sight and Sound* 42 (1973): 186–191.
33. Michiko Kakutani, "Bertolucci: He's Not Afraid to Be Shocking," *The New York Times* (Thursday, October 4, 1979): C17.
34. Aitken, "Bertolucci's Gay Images," 24.
35. Aitken, 25.
36. Julia Kristeva, "Stabat Mater," *The Kristeva Reader,* ed. Toril Moi (New York: Columbia University Press, 1986), 175.
37. My analysis of inter-racial relations in *The Sheltering Sky* is indebted to Jocylin Tinestit.
38. In many interviews that Bertolucci has given on *Tango* he has emphasized the fact that in French the expression "le pétit mort" means orgasm. He also added that the feeling of death is characteristic of sexual relations in our alienated age. The intertextual relationships between

Tango and *The Sheltering Sky* only reinforce this Eros/Thanatos-invested association.

39. See Albert Memi, *L'Homme Domine* (Paris: Gallimard, 1968).

40. Sander Gilman, *Stereotypes of Sexuality, Race and Madness* (Ithaca and London: Cornell University Press, 1985), 85.

41. Edward Said, "Orientalism Reconsidered," in *Literature, Politics and Theory: Papers from the Essex Conference 1976–84*, eds. Francis Barker, Peter Hulme, Margaret Iversun, and Diana Loxley (London: Methuen, 1986), 224.

42. Homi Bhabha, "The Other Question: Difference, Discrimination and the Discourse of Colonialism," in *Literature, Politics and Theory*, 166–167.

43. See Frantz Fanon, *Black Skin, White Masks*, trans. Charles Lam Markmann (London: Pluto Press, 1986).

44. Bhabha, "The Other Question," 166.

45. Bhabha, 165.

46. From the mid 1980s up to the present date one can detect the emergence of films (among others *Heat and Dust, The Gods Must Be Crazy, A Passage to India, Out of Africa*) that portray imperialism with nostalgia. See Renato Rosaldo, "Imperialist Nostalgia," in *Culture and Truth: The Remaking of Social Analysis* (Boston: Beacon Press, 1989), 68–87. The 1990s, however, witness a new wave of French films (*L'Amant, Indochine,* and *La Guerre Sans Nom*) on the French colonial experience in Indochina and Algiers. Much like *The Sheltering Sky*, these films look on the French colonial era with nostalgia. The plots involve doomed love affairs used to allegorize, nostalgically, the colonial experience.

47. On the impression of *Breathless* on the young Bertolucci, see Ranvaud and Ungari, *Bertolucci By Bertolucci*, 30. In Franco Citti, as Ranvaud and Ungari note (p. 32), Bertolucci recognized "not only the sacred double of Jean-Paul Belmondo *A Bout de Souffle* but also his profane counter-part."

48. Ric Gentry, "Bertolucci Directs *Tragedy of a Ridiculous Man, Millimeter* (December, 1981): 58.

49. Some of my ideas on *Before the Revolution* are influenced by William Simon's discussion of the film in his class on "Italian Cinema," offered by the Department of Cinema Studies at New York University, in Fall, 1989.

50. In an interview that I conducted with Bertolucci on August 7, 1991, in London he told me that he began his analysis in 1969. This analysis, he said, "ended one or two times officially, but then started again." He added, laughingly, that he remembers "there is an essay of Freud called 'Analysis or Interminable Analysis'." He said, "I think that "I'm the first case of interminable analysis."

51. Quoted in Erik Cohen, "Pilgrimage and Tourism," regarding Rainer Maria Rilke's *The Duino Elegies* (New York: Harper and Row, 1972): 45.

52. At the Mill Valley Film Festival in April 9 and 10, 1988, on the subject of "Cinematic, Psychoanalytic, and Historical Viewpoints," Bertolucci said: "I think that feminism is the most important thing happening in the last 15 years." I would like to thank Bruce Sklarew for giving me access to the video recording of the discussion with Bertolucci.

Notes to the Conclusion

1. Stephen Gundle, "From Neo-Realism to *Luci Rosse*: Cinema, Politics, Society, 1945–85," in Zygmunt G. Baranski and Robert Lumley, eds. *Culture and Conflict in Postwar Italy: Essays on Mass and Popular Culture* (New York: St. Martin's Press, 1990), 222.

2. Frederic Jameson, "High-Tech Collectives in Late Godard," in *The Geopolitical Aesthetic: Cinema and Space in the World System* (Bloomington and Indianapolis: Indiana University Press, 1992), 162–163.

3. In a press conference at the 1991 Venice Film Festival Godard said jokingly that when he was a child he used to invent stories and his parents told him not to make up stories. When he became a filmmaker everybody told him that he must make stories (Godard, obviously, has never followed this advice and his total work is a struggle against the "story"). He also said that the English title of the film does not convey the pun created by the French title. Neuf in French also means new. In the French title Godard obviously alludes both to Roberto Rossellini's *Germania anno zero* (*Germany Year zero*) (1947) and to *Deutschland im Herbst* (*Germany in Autumn*), a collective film undertaken by some of the German New Wave filmmakers in the aftermath of the politically stormy autumn of 1977 when the activity of the terrorist groups in Germany was at its peak.

   I would like to thank Uri and Irma Kline for lending me the material from the press conference which was (together with the film) broadcast on French Television by Antenne 2 as part of its series on Solitude (Godard explained that in his film he wanted to show the solitude of a nation).

4. In the Venice press conference Godard criticized both the democratic system of the West and the failure of the Russian revolutions (the Bolshevik as well as the *perestroika*) to bring true liberation. He quoted Musil's definition of democracy in *The Man Without Qualities* ("We did not succeed in freeing ourselves and we call it democracy") claiming that this is the best definition of democracy he could find. He emphasized that the Russians, at least, have tried to liberate themselves twice, while we (the West) accepted our inability to free ourselves and implemented democracy in a "second-best" exchange.

5. For a discussion of Godard's relationship to technology and television see MacCabe, chapters 5 and 6 in *Godard: Images, Sounds, Politics*. See also the MOMA catalog *Godard: Son + Image*.

6. Colin MacCabe, *Godard: Images, Sounds, Politics,* (Bloomington: Indiana University Press, 1980) 138.

7. In his press conference at the 1991 Venice Film Festival Godard discussed in some detail the religious meaning of the notion of the image. Quoting St. John who said that on the cross there is no image, Godard claimed that the image comes from the resurrection (which is indeed the theme of his *Nouvelle Vague*). This means that on the cross there is no image, only picture.

8. Godard's experiments with video culminate, according to Raymond Bellour, in *Puissance de la parole* (*The Power of Words*) (1988) a videotape produced by Telecom (the French telephone company). Bellour claims that the images and the words of the film "speak among themselves and take shape among themselves in ways that have never been seen or heard . . . in a fiction film." Raymond Bellour, "The Power of Words, The Power of Images," *Camera Obscura* 24 (September, 1990): 9.

9. Frederic Jameson, *Signatures of the Visible* (New York and London: Routledge, 1990), 219.

10. Jameson, *Signatures of the Visible,* 219.

11. Ibid.

12. My interview with Bertolucci was conducted on August 7, 1991 at his home in London.

13. Zygmunt G. Baranski, "Pier Paolo Pasolini: Culture, Croce, Gramsci," in *Culture and Conflict in Postwar Italy,* 139.

14. Gundle, "From Neo-Realism to *Luci Rosse*," 216.

15. Giuliana Bruno, "Review: Giampiero Brunetta, *Buio in sala: cent'anni di passioni dello spettatore cinematografico.* Venezia: Marsilio, 1989," *Screen* vol. 32, no. 2 (Summer, 1991): 229.

16. Ranvaud and Ungari, *Bertolucci by Bertolucci,* (London: Plexus, 1987) 65.

17. Gundle, "From Neo-Realism to *Luci Rosse*," 201.

Bibliography

Adorno, Theodor W. "Cultural Criticism and Society," in *Critical Sociology*, ed. Paul Connerton. New York: Penguin Books, 1976, pp. 258–276.

Adorno, Theodor W., Else Frenkel-Brunswik, Daniel J. Levinson and R. Nevitt Stanford. *The Authoritarian Personality*. New York: Harper, 1950.

Aitken, Will. "Bertolucci's Gay Images: Leaving the Dance," *Jump Cut* 16 (November 1977), pp. 23–26.

Alford, C. Fred. "Nature and Narcissism: The Frankfurt School," *New German Critique* 36 (Fall, 1985), pp. 174–192.

Althusser, Louis. *For Marx*, trans. Ben Brewster. New York: Pantheon Books, 1969.

———. *Lenin and Philosophy, and Other Essays*, trans. Ben Brewster. New York and London: Monthly Review Press, 1971.

Altman, Rick, ed. *Genre: The Musical*. London: Routledge and Kegan Paul, 1981.

Anderson, Phil. "Godard: X-rays of the Child," *Twin Cities Reader* (February 25, 1981).

Andrew, Dudley. *The Major Film Theories*. Oxford: Oxford University Press, 1976.

———. *Concepts in Film Theory*. Oxford: Oxford University Press, 1984.

Annals of Tourism Research 18 (1991). A special issue on "Tourism Social Sciences."

Artaud, Antonin. *The Theatre and Its Double*, trans. Mary Caroline Richards. New York: Grove Press, 1958.

Aumont, Jacques. "The Fall of the Gods: Jean-Luc Godard's *Le Mepris* (1963)," in *French Film: Texts and Contexts*, ed. Susan Hayward and Ginette Vincendeau. London and New York: Routledge, 1990, pp. 217–229.

Bachmann, Gideon. "Every Sexual Relationship Is Condemned: An Interview with Bernardo Bertolucci apropos *Last Tango in Paris*," *Film Quarterly* 26 (1973), pp. 2–9.

———. "In the Cinema It Is Never Monday," *Sight and Sound* (Spring, 1982), pp. 118–120.

Bakhtin, Mikail. *Rabelais and His World*. Cambridge: M.I.T. Press, 1968.

Ball, Edward. "Thinking Out Loud," *Afterimage* (October 1986).

Baranski, Zygmunt and Robert Lumley, eds. *Culture and Conflict in Postwar*

Italy: Essays on Mass and Popular Culture. New York: St. Martin's Press, 1990.

Baring, Anne and Jules Cashford. *The Myth of the Goddess: Evolution of an Image*. London: Viking, 1991.

Barthes, Roland. *Image/Music/Text*, trans. Stephen Heath. New York: Hill and Wang, 1977.

———. *Mythologies*, ed. and trans. Annette Lavers. New York: Hill and Wang, 1980.

Bates, Robin. "Holes in the Sausage of History: May '68 as Absent Center in Three European Films," *Cinema Journal* 24, No. 3 (Spring, 1985), pp. 24–42.

Baudrillard, Jean. "Simulacra and Simulations," in *Selected Writings*, ed. Mark Poster. Cambridge, UK: Polity Press, 1988, pp. 166–184.

———. *Simulations*, trans. Paul Foss, Paul Patton and Philip Betichman. New York: Agentz Series, Semiotexte(e), 1983.

Baudry, Jean-Louis. "The Apparatus: Metapsychological Approaches to the Impression of Reality in the Cinema," in *Film Theory and Criticism*, eds. Gerald Mast, Marshall Cohen and Leo Brandy. New York and Oxford: Oxford University Press, 1992, pp. 690–707.

Behdad, Ali. "Orientalist Tourism," *Peuples mediterraneens* 50 (January-March 1990), pp. 59–73.

———. "The Discursive Formation of Orientalism: The Threshold of (Pseudo) Scientificity," *Peuples mediterraneens* 50 (January-March 1990), pp. 163–169.

Bellour, Raymond. "The Power of Words, the Power of Images," *Camera Obscura* 24 (September, 1990), pp. 7–9.

———, ed. *Jean-Luc Godard: Son* + Image: 1974–1991. New York: The Museum of Modern Art, 1992.

Benjamin, Jessica. "Master and Slave: The Fantasy of Erotic Domination," in *Powers of Desire: The Politics of Sexuality*, eds., Ann Snitow, Christine Stansell and Sharon Thompson. New York: Monthly Review Press, 1983, pp. 280–299.

Benjamin, Walter. "The Image of Proust," in *Illuminations*, ed. Hannah Arendt. New York: Schocken Books, 1989, pp. 203–217.

Bertolucci, Bernardo. "Versus Godard," *Cahiers du Cinema* 186 (Jan. 1957), pp. 29–30.

———. "Bernardo Bertolucci Seminar." *American Film Institute Dialogue on Film* 3, no. 5 (April 1974), pp. 14–28.

———. *Last Tango in Paris*. New York: Delacorte Press, 1973.

Bhabha, Homi. "The Other Question: Difference, Discrimination and the Discourse of Colonialism," in *Literature, Politics and Theory* eds. Francis Barker, Peter Hulme, Margaret Iversen and Diana Loxley. London: Methuen, 1986, pp. 148–172.

———. "Postcolonial Authority and Postmodern Guilt," in *Cultural Studies*, eds. Lawrence Grossberg, Carry Nelson, and Paula Treichler. London: Routledge, 1992, pp. 56–68.

Bloom, Harold. *The Anxiety of Influence: A Theory of Poetry.* New York: Oxford University Press, 1973.

Blythe, Martin. "The Romance of Maoriland: Ethnography and Tourism in New Zealand Films," *East-West Film Journal* 4, no. 2 (June, 1990), pp. 90–110.

Bondanella, Peter. *Italian Cinema: From Neorealism to the Present.* New York: Frederick Ungar Publishing Co., 1983. New expanded edition: New York: A Frederick Ungar Book, 1990.

Bordwell, David. "Dziga Vertov: An Introduction," *Film Comment* 8, No. 1 (Spring 1972), pp. 38–42.

Bordwell, David, Janet Staiger and Kristin Thompson. *The Classical Hollywood Cinema: Film Style and Mode of Production to 1960.* New York: Columbia University Press, 1985.

——. *Narration in the Fiction Film.* Madison: University of Wisconsin Press, 1985.

Borges, Jorge Luis. "Theme of the Traitor and the Hero," *Labyrinths.* New York: A New Directions Book, 1962.

Bowles, Paul. *The Sheltering Sky.* New York: The Ecco Press, 1978 (1949).

Brecht, Bertolt. *Brecht on Theatre,* ed. and trans. John Willett. New York: Hill and Wang, 1964.

——. "Against Georg Lukacs," in *Aesthetics and Politics,* ed. E. Bloch et al. London: NLB, 1977, pp. 68–85.

——. "Sur le Cinéma," trans. Julia Lesage. *Cineaste* V, No. 2 (Spring, 1972), pp. 34–37.

Brooks, Peter. *The Melodramatic Imagination.* New York: Columbia University Press, 1985.

Bruno, Giuliana. "Heresies: The Body of Pasolini's Semiotics," *Cinema Journal* 30, no. 3 (Spring, 1991), pp. 29–42.

——. "Review: Giampiero Brunetta, *Buio in sala: cent'anni di passioni dello spettatore cinematografico,*" *Screen* 32, no. 2 (Summer, 1991), pp. 228–233.

Buache, Freddy. "La Dame du Lac," *L'Avant Scene Cinéma* 396–397 (November/December 1990), pp. 3–7.

Bundtzen, Lynda. "Bertolucci's Erotic Politics and the Auteur Theory: From *Last Tango in Paris* to *The Last Emperor,*" *Western Humanities Review* 44, no. 2 (Summer, 1990), pp. 198–215.

Burgoyne, Robert. "The Last Emperor: The Stages of History," *Substance* 59 (1989), pp. 93–101.

——. "Temporality as Historical Argument in Bertolucci's *1900,*" *Cinema Journal* 28, no. 3 (Spring, 1989), pp. 57–68.

——. *Bertolucci's 1900: A Narrative and Historical Analysis.* Detroit: Wayne State University Press, 1991.

Cahiers du Cinéma 437. "Special Godard-Trente Ans depuis," Paris (Novembre 1990).

Calinescu, Matei. *Five Faces of Modernity.* Durham, North Carolina: Duke University Press, 1987.

Camera Obscura 8–9–10 (Fall 1982). A special issue on Jean-Luc Godard.

Canby, Vincent. "Godard, at Cannes, Can Still Stir Up Film Furor," *The New York Times* (Saturday, May 24, 1980), p. 14.

———. "Nature's Splendor and Aphorisms in Godard's Latest," *New York Times* (September 29, 1990), p. 16.

Cerisuelo, Marc. *Jean-Luc Godard*. Paris: Quatres-vents, 1989.

Chessick, Richard D. "The Search for the Authentic Self in Bergson and Proust," in *Psychoalytic Approaches to Literature and Film* ed. Maurice Charney and Joseph Reppen (Cranbury, New Jersey: Associated University Presses, 1987).

Chiaretti, Tommaso. "Allegro Con Pessimismo," in *China is Near* by Marco Bellochio, trans. Judith Green. London: Calder and Boyars, 1970, pp. 1–12.

Chodorow, Nancy. *The Reproduction of Mothering: Psychoanalysis and the Sociology of Gender*. Berkeley: University of California Press, 1978.

Clifford, James. "Traveling Cultures," in *Cultural Studies* eds. Lawrence Grossberg, Carry Nelson, and Paula Treichler. London: Routledge, 1992, pp. 96–116.

———. A review of Mary Louis Pratt's *Imperial Eyes: Travel Writing and Transculturation, TLS* (September 11, 1992), pp. 3–4.

Cohen, Erik. "Pilgrimage and Tourism: Convergence and Divergence," in Alan Morinis, ed., *Sacred Journeys: The Anthropology of Pilgrimage*. Westport, Conn. and London: Greenwood Press, 1992, pp. 47–61.

Cohen, Lawrence. "Jean-Luc Godard Enlivens New York: Auteur Theory Called Fraud," *Variety* (October 8, 1980), p. 32.

Connors, Joanna. "Women Zap Godard, *Every Man*," *Minneapolis Star* (February 23, 1981), p. 1c.

Cott, Jonathan. "Godard: Born-Again Filmmaker," *Rolling Stone* (November 27, 1980), p. 33.

Creed, Barbara. "From Here to Modernity: Feminism and Postmodernism," *Screen* 28, no. 2 (Spring 1987), pp. 47–67.

Creedon, Pamela J. *Women in Mass Communication: Challenging Gender Values*. Newburry Park and London: Sage, 1989.

Culler, Jonathan. *Structuralist Poetics: Structuralism, Linguistics, and the Study of Literature*. Ithaca: Cornell University Press, 1975.

Cunningham, Stuart and Ross Harley. "The Logic of the Virgin Mother: A Discussion of *Hail Mary*," *Screen* 28, no. 1 (Winter, 1987), pp. 62–76.

Dalle Vacche, Angela. *The Body in the Mirror: Shapes of History in Italian Cinema*. Princeton: Princeton University Press, 1992.

Dalle Vacche, Angela and Robert Burgoyne. "Dialogue on *1900*," *Cinema Journal* 29, no. 3 (Spring, 1990), pp. 69–78.

Dann, Graham and Erik Cohen. "Sociology and Tourism," *Annals of Tourism Research* 18, no. 1 (1991), pp. 155–169.

Darling, Brian. "Jean-Luc Godard: Politics and Humanism." Notes for discussions at BFI Education Department Seminar, April 17, 1969.

de Beauvoir, Simone. *The Second Sex*. trans. and ed. H. M. Parshley. Harmondsworth: Penguin Books, 1974 (1949).

De Gravelaine, Joelle, Jean-Pierre Lavoignat and Christophe d'Yvoire. "Bernardo Bertolucci: La confusion magnifique," *Studio magazine* 9 (Decembre 1987), pp. 58–64.

De la Fuente, Leonardo. "Le Dernier Emperor: Multiples Splendeurs," *Telerama* 28 (4 December, 1987), pp. 40–41.

De-Lauretis, Teresa. *Alice Doesn't: Feminism, Semiotics, Cinema.* Bloomington: Indiana University Press, 1981.

Demause, Lloyd. "The History of Childhood: The Basis for Psychohistory," in *History of Childhood Quarterly* 1, no. 1 (Summer, 1973), pp. 1–4.

Descombes, Vincent. *Modern French Philosophy*, trans. L. Scott-Fox and J. M. Harding. Cambridge: Cambridge University Press, 1980.

Desmond, Jane. "Ethnography, Orientalism and the Avant-Garde Film," *Visual Anthropology* 4 (1991), pp. 147–160.

Dieckmann, Katherine. "Godard in his 'Fifth Period': An Interview," *Film Quarterly* 2, vol. XXXIX (Winter, 1985–86), pp. 2–6.

Doane, Mary Ann. "The Economy of Desire: The Commodity Form in/of the Cinema," *Quarterly Review of Film and Video* 11, no. 1 (1989), pp. 23–33.

Downing, David. *Marlon Brando.* New York: Stein and Day, 1984.

Dumas, Andre. "Godard Protestant: A bout de foi," *Cahiers du Cinéma* 437 (Novembre 1990), pp. 88–92.

Eco, Umberto. "Postmodernism, Irony, the Enjoyable," in *Postscript to the Name of the Rose.* New York: Harcourt Brace Janovich, Inc., 1984.

———. "*De interpretazione;* or, The Difficulty of Being Marco Polo: On the Occasion of Antonioni's China Film," in *New Challenges for Documentary*, ed. Alan Rosenthal. Berkeley: The University of California Press, 1988.

Eisenstein, Sergei. "The Unexpected," in *Film Form: Essays in Film Theory* ed. and trans. Jay Leyda. New York: Harcourt Brace and World, Inc., 1949, pp. 18–27.

Elsaesser, Thomas. "Reflection and Reality," *Monogram* 2 (Summer, 1971), pp. 2–9.

———. "French Film Culture and Critical Theory: *Cinéthique*," *Monogram* 2 (Summer, 1971), pp. 31–37.

———. "Tales of Sound and Fury: Observations on the Family Melodrama," *Monogram* 4 (1973).

Esslin, Martin. *Brecht: A Choice of Evils.* London: Eyre and Spottiswoode, 1959.

———. *The Theatre of the Absurd.* New York: Doubleday, 1961.

———. "Modernist Drama: Wedekind to Brecht," in *Modernism*, ed. Malcolm Bradbury and James MacFarlane. London: Penguin Books, 1976, pp. 527–60.

Fabian, Johannes. *Time and the Other: How Anthropology Makes Its Object.* New York: Columbia University Press, 1983.

Fanon, Frantz. *Black Skin, White Masks*, trans. Charles Lam Markmann. London: Pluto Press, 1986.

Feuer, Jane. "The Self-Reflective Musical and the Myth of Entertainment," *Quarterly Review of Film Studies* 2, No. 7 (August 1977), pp. 313–326.

———. *The Hollywood Musical*. Bloomington: Indiana University Press, 1982.

———. "Melodrama, Serial Form and Television Today," *Screen* 25, Vol. 1 (January-February 1984), pp. 4–16.

Fiske, John. *Reading the Popular*. Boston: Unwin Hyman, 1989.

Fletcher, John and James MacFarlane. "Modernist Drama: Origins and Patterns." in *Modernism*, ed. Malcolm Bradbury and James MacFarlane. London: Penguin Books, 1976, pp. 499–513.

Foster, Hal, ed. *The Anti-Aesthetic: Essays on Postmodern Culture*. Port Townsend: Bay Press, 1983.

Frederickson, Don. "Modes of Reflexive Film," *Quarterly Review of Film Studies* 4, No. 3 (1979), pp. 299–320.

Freud, Sigmund. "Femininity," in *New Introductory Lectures on Psychoanalysis* vol. 2 , pp. 145–169; "On Sexuality," vol. 7; "Postscript" (1912 [1911]) to "Psychoanalytic Notes on an Autobiographical Account of a Case of Paranoia (Dementia Paranoides) (Schreber) (1911 [1910])," in *Case Histories II: 'Rat Man', Schreber, 'Wolf Man', Female Homosexuality*, pp. 220–223; "Moses and Monotheism," in *The Origins of Religion* vol. 13 pp. 237–386; "Leonardo Da Vinci and a Memory of His Childhood (1910)," in *Art and Literature* vol. 14, pp. 145–231, in *The Standard Edition of the Complete Psychological Works of Sigmund Freud*, trans. and ed. James Strachey. London: The Pelican Freud Library, 1979.

Frow, John. "Tourism and the Semiotics of Nostalgia," *October* 57 (Summer, 1991), pp. 123–151.

Gablik, Suzi. "The Human Condition," in *Magritte*. New York: New York Graphic Society, 1976, pp. 75–101.

Geertz, Clifford. *The Interpretation of Cultures*. New York: Basic Books, 1973.

Gentry, Ric. "Bertolucci Directs *Tragedy of A Ridiculous Man*," *Millimeter* (December, 1981), p. 56.

Gerould, Daniel, ed. *Melodrama*. New York: New York Literary Forum, 1980.

Gilbert, Sandra and Susan Gubar. "Cross-Dressing: Transvestism as Metaphor," in *No Man's Land: The Place of The Woman Within the Twentieth Century*, vol. 2: Sexexchanges. New Haven and London: Yale University Press, 1989, pp. 324–376.

Gilman, Sander. *Stereotypes of Sexuality, Race and Madness*. Ithaca and London: Cornell University Press, 1985.

Godard, Jean-Luc. *Godard on Godard*, ed. and trans. Tom Milne. New York: Viking Press, 1972.

Goldin, Marilyn. "Bertolucci on the *Conformist*: Interview," *Sight and Sound* 40 (1971), pp. 64–66.

Gombrich, E. H. *Art and Illusion: A Study in the Psychology of Pictorial Representation*. London: Phaidon, 1960.

Gramsci, Antonio. *Selections from the Prison Notebooks*, ed. and trans. Quintin Hoare and Geoffrey Nowell- Smith. New York: International Publishers, 1971.

———. *Selections from Cultural Writings*, ed. David Forgacs and Geoffrey Nowell-Smith. Trans. William Boehower. Cambridge, Mass.: Harvard University Press, 1985.

Greene, Naomi. "Artaud and Film: A Reconsideration," *Cinema Journal* 23, No. 4 (Summer 1984), pp. 28–40.

Greenspun, Roger. "*Weekend*," in Royal S. Brown, ed., *Focus on Godard*. Englewood Cliffs, New Jersey: Prentice Hall, Inc., 1972.

Guarino, Ann. "It's Impact He Wants," *New York News* (October 6, 1979).

Gundle, Stephen. "From Neo-Realism to *Luci Rosse*: Cinema Politics, Society, 1945–85," in *Culture and Conflict in Postwar Italy: Essays on Mass and Popular Culture*, eds. Zygmunt G. Baranski and Robert Lumley. New York: St. Martin's Press, 1990.

Hak Kyung Cha, Theresa, ed. *Apparatus: Cinematographic Apparatus, Selected Writings*. New York: Tanam Press, 1980.

Harvey, Sylvia. *May '68 and Film Culture*. London: British Film Institute, 1978.

Haskell, Molly. *From Reverence to Rape: The Treatment of Women in the Movies*. Chicago and London: The University of Chicago Press, 1987 (1973).

———. "Immaculate Deception," *Vogue* (October, 1985).

Haycock, Joel. "The Sign of the Sociologist: Show and Anti-Show in Godard's *Masculin Feminin*," *Cinema Journal* 29, no. 4 (Summer, 1990), pp. 51–74.

Heath, Stephen. "Lessons from Brecht," *Screen* 15, no. 2 (Summer, 1974), pp. 103–128.

Hoberman, Jim. "He-e-ere's Jean-ee: TV a la Godard," *Village Voice* (April 28, 1986), pp. 45–46.

Horkheimer, Max and Theodor W. Adorno. *Dialectics of Enlightenment*. New York: Herder and Herder, 1972.

Hutcheon, Linda. *Narcissistic Narrative: The Metafictional Paradox*. Waterloo: Wilfrid Laurier University Press, 1980.

Irigaray, Luce. *This Sex Which Is Not One*, trans. Catherine Porter. Ithaca: Cornell University Press, 1985.

———. "The Blind Spot of an Old Dream of Symmetry," in *Speculum of the Other Woman*, trans. Gillian C. Gill. Ithaca: Cornell University Press, (1974), 1985.

Jakobson, Roman. "On Realism in Art," in *Readings in Russian Poetics: Formalist and Structuralist Views*, ed. and trans. Ladislav Matejka and Krystyna Pomorska. Ann Arbor: University of Michigan, 1978.

Jameson, Frederic. *Signatures of the Visible*. New York and London: Routledge, 1990.

————. *The Geopolitcal Aesthetic: Cinema and Space in the World System.* Bloomington and Indianapolis: Indiana University Press, 1992.

Jansen, Sue, Curry. "Power and Knowledge: Toward a New Critical Synthesis," *Journal of Communication* 33, No. 3 (Summer, 1983), pp. 342–354.

Jay, Martin. *The Dialectical Imagination: A History of the Frankfurt School and the Institute of Social Research 1923–1950.* Boston: Little Brown, 1973.

Jing, Cheng. "Emperor's Conflict of Reality," *China Daily* (October 16, 1988).

Kaes, Anton. "History and Film: Public Memory in the Age of Electronic Dissemination," *History and Memory* 2, no. 1 (Fall, 1990), pp. 111–129.

Kakutani, Michiko. "Bertolucci: He's Not Afraid to Be Shocking," *The New York Times* (October 4, 1979), p. C17.

Katz, Barry. *Herbert Marcuse and the Art of Liberation.* London: Verso, 1982.

Kavanagh, Thomas. "Godard-Gorin's *Tout va bien,"* *Diacritics* 4, No. 1 (Spring, 1974), pp. 42–48.

————. "Godard's Revolution: The Politics of Meta-Cinema," *Diacritics* 3, No. 2 (Summer, 1973), pp. 49–56.

Kawin, Bruce F. *The Mind of the Novel: Reflexive Fiction and the Ineffable.* Princeton: Princeton University Press, 1982.

————. *Mindscreen: Bergman, Godard, and First-Person Film.* Princeton: Princeton University Press, 1978.

Kellner, Douglas. *Herbert Marcuse and the Crisis of Marxism.* Hampshire and London: Macmillan Education Ltd., 1984.

Kelly, Michael. *Modern French Marxism.* Baltimore: The John Hopkins University Press, 1982.

Kinder, Marsha and Beverle Houston. "Bertolucci and the Dance of Danger," *Sight and Sound* 42 (1973), pp. 186–191.

Kline, T. Jefferson. *Bertolucci's Dream Loom: A Psychoanalytic Study of Cinema.* Amherst: The University of Massachusetts Press, 1987.

Kolker, Robert Philip. *Bernardo Bertolucci.* New York: Oxford University Press, 1985.

Korte, Walter. "Godard's Adaptation of Moravia's *Contempt,"* *Literature/Film Quarterly* II, no. 3 (Summer, 1974), pp. 284–289.

Kreidl, John. *Jean-Luc Godard.* Boston: Twayne Publishers, 1980.

Kristeva, Julia. "Stabat Mater," in *The Kristeva Reader,* ed. Toril Moi. New York: Columbia University Press, 1986.

Kurzweil, Allen. "Out to Lunch with Bernardo Bertolucci," *Vanity Fair* (December 1986), p. 160.

Kwietniowski, Richard. "Between Love and Labour—Godard's *Scenario of the Film Passion,"* *Screen* 24, no. 6 (November-December 1983), pp. 52–69.

Lacan, Jacques. *The Language of the Self,* trans. Anthony Wilden. Baltimore: Johns Hopkins University Press, 1968.

Le Clezio, Jean Marie Gustav. *Desert.* Paris: Gallimard, 1980.

Lellis, George. *Bertolt Brecht, Cahiers du Cinema and Contemporary Film Theory.* Ann Arbor: UMI Research Press, 1982.

Lesage, Julia. "The Films of Jean-Luc Godard and Their Use of Brechtian Dramatic Theory." Ph.D. dissertation. Bloomington: Indiana University, 1976.

———. *Jean-Luc Godard: A Guide to References and Resources.* Boston: G.K. Hall, 1979.

Levin, Harry. "On the Dissemination of Realism," in *Grounds for Comparison.* Cambridge: Harvard University Press, 1972, pp. 242–261.

Locke, Maryel and Charles Warren, eds. *Jean-Luc Godard's Hail Mary: Women and the Sacred in Film.* Carbondale: Southern Illinois University Press, 1993.

Longxi, Zhang. "The Myth of the Other: China in the Eyes of the West," *Critical Inquiry* 15 (Autumn, 1988), pp. 108–131.

Loshitzky, Yosefa. " 'Memory of My Own Memory': Processes of Private and Collective Remembering in Bertolucci's *The Spider's Stratagem* and *The Conformist,*" *History and Memory* 3 No. 2 (Fall/Winter, 1991), pp. 87–114.

———. "More than Style: Godard's Modernism versus Bertolucci's Postmodernism," *Criticism* XXXIV No. 1 (Winter, 1992), pp. 119–142.

———. "The Tourist/Traveler Gaze: Bertolucci and Bowles' *The Sheltering Sky,*" *East-West Film Journal* 7 No. 2 (July, 1993), pp. 110–132.

———. and Raya Meyouhas. " 'Ecstasy of Difference': Bertolucci's *The Last Emperor,*" *Cinema Journal* 31 No. 2 (Winter, 1992), pp. 26–44.

Lovell, Terry. *Pictures of Reality: Aesthetics, Politics and Pleasure.* London: BFI, 1983.

Lukacs, George. "Critical Realism and Socialist Realism," in *Realism in Our Time.* New York: Harper Torchbooks, 1971, pp. 93–135.

Lyon, Elisabeth. "Unspeakable Images, Unspeakable Bodies," *Camera Obscura* 24 (September 1990), pp. 169–193.

MacBean, James Roy. *Film and Revolution.* Bloomington: Indiana University Press, 1975.

———. "Between Kitsch and Fascism: Notes on Fassbinder, Pasolini, (Homo)sexual Politics, the Exotic, the Erotic & Other Consuming Passions," *Cineaste* XIII, no. 4 (1984), pp. 12–19.

MacCabe, Colin. "Realism and the Cinema," *Screen* 15, No. 2, 1974.

———. *Godard: Images, Sounds, Politics.* Bloomington: Indiana University Press, 1980.

———. "Betaville," *American Film* (September 1985), pp. 61–63.

MacFarquhan, Roderick. "The Forbidden City in History," in *The Forbidden City.* New York: Newsweek, 1972.

Macherey, Pierre. "The Problem of Reflection." *Sub-Stance* 15 (1976), pp. 6–20.

Magny, Joel. "Dimension Politique de L'oueuvre de Bernardo Bertolucci: De *Prima della Rivoluzione* A *Novecento*," *Etudes Cinématographiques* 122–126 (1979), pp. 49–76.

Marcus, Millicent. *Italian Film in the Light of Neorealism*. Princeton: Princeton University Press, 1986.

Marcuse, Herbert. *The Aesthetic Dimension: Toward a Critique of Marxist Aesthetics*. Boston: Beacon Press, 1978.

———. "Art as a Revolutionary Weapon." Los Angeles: Pacifica Tape Library, 1970.

———. *Eros and Civilization: A Philosophical Inquiry into Freud*. Boston: Beacon Press, 1955.

———. *An Essay on Liberation*. Boston: Beacon Press, 1969.

———. *Five Lectures: Psychoanalysis, Politics and Utopia*. Trans. Jeremy J. Shapiro and Shirley M. Weber. Boston: Beacon Press, 1970.

———. *One-Dimensional Man: Studies in the Ideology of Advanced Industrial Societies*. Boston: Beacon Press, 1964.

———. "Reason and Revolution Today." Los Angeles: Pacifica Tape Library, 1970.

———. *Studies in Critical Philosophy*. Boston: Beacon Press, 1972.

Mast, Gerald and Marshall Cohen. *Film Theory and Criticism*. New York: Oxford University Press, 1985.

Maynard, Solomon, ed. *Marxism and Art*. New York: Alfred A. Knopf, 1973.

Mayne, Judith. "The Ideologies of Metacinema," Ph.D. dissertation. Buffalo: S.U.N.Y. at Buffalo, 1975.

McGrane, Bernard. *Beyond Anthropology: Society and the Other*. New York: Columbia University Press, 1989.

Meisel, Myron S. "An Interview Composed by Jean-Luc Godard," *Los Angeles Reader* (January 23, 1981), pp. 9–11.

Mellen, Joan. "Sexual Politics and Bertolucci's *Last Tango in Paris*," in her *Women and Their Sexuality in the New Film*. New York: Horizon Press, 1973, pp. 128–146.

———. "A Conversation with Bernardo Bertolucci," *Cineaste* 5 (Summer, 1973), pp. 21–24.

———. "Fascism in Contemporary Film," *Film Quarterly* XXIV, no. 4 (Summer, 1971), pp. 2–19.

Memi, Albert. *L'Homme Domine*. Paris: Gallimard, 1968.

Metz, Christian. *The Imaginary Signifier: Psychoanalysis and the Cinema*. Trans. Ben Brewster, et al. Bloomington: Indiana University Press, 1982.

Michelson, Annette. "Introduction," in *The Writings of Dziga Vertov*. Berkeley: University of California Press, 1984.

Middleton, David and Derek Edwards eds. *Collective Remembering*. London: Sage, 1990.

Millicent, Marcus. *Italian Film in the light of Neorealism*. Princeton: Princeton University Press, 1986.

Mitamura, Taisuke. *Chinese Eunuchs: The Structure of Intimate Politics*. Tokyo: Charles E. Tuttle Company, 1970.

Modleski, Tania. *Feminism Without Women: Culture and Feminism in a "Postfeminist" Age.* New York and London: Routledge, 1991.

Moeller, Hans-Bernhard. "Brecht and 'Epic' Film Medium: The Cineaste Playwright, Film Theoretician and His Influence," *Wide Angle* 3, No. 4 (1980), pp. 4–11.

Moravia, Alberto. *A Ghost at Noon,* trans. Angus Davidson. New York: A Signet Book, 1956 (1955).

Morris, Marry. "Women and Travel," *MS.* (May-June 1992), pp. 68–71.

Mulvey, Laura. "Visual Pleasure and Narrative Cinema," *Screen* 16 (Autumn, 1975), pp. 6–18.

——. "Notes on Sirk and Melodrama," *Movie* 25 (Winter 1977–78), pp. 53–56.

——. "Afterthoughts on 'Visual Pleasure and Narrative Cinema' Inspired by *Duel in the Sun,*" *Framework* 15/16/17 (Summer 1981), pp. 12–15.

——. "The Hole and the Zero: The Janus Face of the Feminine in Godard," in *Jean-Luc Godard" Son & Image, 1974–1991,* eds. Raymond Bellour and Mary Lea Bandy. New York: The Museum of Modern Art, 1992, 75–88.

Negri, Livio and Fabien S. Gerard eds., *The Sheltering Sky: A Film by Bernardo Bertolucci Based on the Novel by Paul Bowles.* London: Scribners, 1990.

Nichols, Bill. *Ideology and the Image: Social Representation in the Cinema and Other Media.* Bloomington: Indiana University Press, 1981.

——, ed. *Movies and Methods,* Vol. 1. Berkeley: University of California Press, 1976.

——. *Movies and Methods,* Vol. 2. Berkeley: University of California Press, 1985.

Ortega Y Gasset, J. *The Dehumanization of Art and Other Essays on Art, Culture and Literature.* Princeton: Princeton University Press, 1972.

Palace Pictures publicity release for *The Sheltering Sky.* London: 1990.

Penley, Constance. *The Future of an Illusion: Film, Feminism, and Psychoanalysis.* Minneapolis: University of Minnesota Press, 1989.

Pierre, Sylvie. "Fritz Movie," *Cahiers du Cinema* 437 (Novembre 1990).

Pike, Burton. *The Image of the City in Modern Literature.* Princeton: Princeton University Press, 1981.

Pizer, Donald. "The Sexual Geography of Expatriate Paris," *Twentieth Century Literature* 36, no. 2 (Summer, 1990), pp. 173–185.

Poirier, Richard. *The Performing Self: Compositions and Decompositions in the Languages of Contemporary Life.* New York: Oxford University Press, 1971.

Polan, Dana Bart: "Brecht and the Politics of Self-Reflexive Film," *Jump Cut* 17 (April 1978), pp. 29–32.

——. "Image-Making and Image-Breaking: Studies in the Political Language of Film and the Avant-Garde." Ph.D. dissertation. Stanford University, 1981.

——. *The Political Language of Film and the Avant-Garde.* Ann Arbor: UMI Research Press, 1985.

————. " 'Above All Else to Make You See': Cinema and the Ideology of Spectacle," in Jonathan Arac, ed. *Postmodernism and Politics*.Minneapolis: University of Minnesota Press, 1986, pp. 55–69.

Pratt, Mary Louis. *Imperial Eyes: Travel Writing and Transculturation*. London: Routledge, 1992.

Probst, Leonard. "Maria Schneider of 'Last Tango': I'm More Beautiful than Marlon Brando," *The Village Voice* (February 8, 1973):79.

Proust, Marcel. *Remembrance of Things Past*, trans. Frederick A. Blossom. New York: Random House, 1932.

Quarterly Review of Film and Video 13, nos. 1–3. "Discourse of the Other: Postcoloniality, Positionality, and Subjectivity," (1992).

Ranvaud, Donald and A. Farassino. "An Interview with Jean-Luc Godard," *Framework* 21 (Summer 1983), pp. 8–9.

Ranvaud, Donald and Enzo Ungari. *Bertolucci by Bertolucci*. London: Plexus, 1987.

Rayns, Tony. "Model Citizen: Bernardo Bertolucci on Location in China," *Film Comment* (December 1987), pp. 31–36.

Rice, Julian C. "Bertolucci's *Last Tango in Paris*," *The Journal of Popular Film* 3 (1974), pp. 157–173.

Rosaldo, Renato. "Imperialist Nostalgia," in *Culture and Truth: The Remaking of Social Analysis*. Boston: Beacon Press, 1989, pp. 68–87.

Ross, Walter S. "Splicing Together Jean-Luc Godard," *Esquire* (July 1969), pp. 72–75.

Roud, Richard. *Jean-Luc Godard*. London: Thames and Hudson, 1967.

————. "Bertolucci on *La Luna*," *Sight and Sound* 48 No. 4 (1979).

Said, Edward. *Orientalism*. New York: Random House, 1978.

————. "Orientalism Reconsidered," in *Literature, Politics and Theory* eds. Francis Barker, Peter Hulme, Margaret Iversun and Diana Loxley. London: Methuen, 1986.

Schickel, Richard. "Accomplices: Brando and the Fifties, and why Both Still Matter," *Film Comment* 27 no. 4 (July- August, 1991), pp. 30–36.

Schneede, Uwe M. *Rene Magritte: Life and Work*. New York: Barron's Educational Series, Inc., 1982.

Scholes, Robert. "Narration and Narrativity in Film," *Film Theory and Criticism*, eds. Gerald Mast and Marshall Cohen. New York: Oxford University Press, 1985, pp. 390–410.

Screen Reader 1: Cinema/Ideology/Politics. London: The Society for Education in Film and Television, 1977.

Screen 15, No. 2 (Summer 1974). Special Number: "Brecht and Revolutionary Cinema."

Screen 16, No. 4 (Winter 1975/76). A Special Issue: "Brecht and the Cinema/Film and Politics."

Seidenberg, Robert. "Hail Godard," *Spin* (January, 1986), p. 78.

Sherwood, Richard. "Introduction to Documents from *Lef*," *Screen* 12, No. 4 (Winter 1971), pp. 25–32.

Shohat, Ella. "Imaging Terra Incognita: The Disciplinary Gaze of Empire," *Public Culture* 3, no. 2 (Spring 1991), pp. 41–70.

Siegle, Robert. "Chapter One" in *The Politics of Reflexivity: Narrative and the Constitutive Poetics of Culture*. Baltimore: The Johns Hopkins University Press, 1986.

Simmons, Steven Clyde. " 'Modernism' in Film: Essays on Jean-Luc Godard." Ph.D. dissertation. Stanford University, 1982.

Simon, William G. "The Influence of the Director: Jean-Luc Godard and Anna Karina," in *Great Film Actresses* (Catalogue for retrospective at the Art Institute of Chicago, 1979), pp. 4–6.

Siska, William C. "Metacinema: A Modern Necessity," *Literature/Film Quarterly* 7 (1979), pp. 285–90.

Sontag, Susan. *Styles of Radical Will*. New York: Farrar, Strauss and Giroux, 1969.

———. *Against Interpretation*. New York: Dell, Laurel, 1969.

———. "Fascinating Fascism," in *Movies and Methods* I, ed. Bill Nichols. Berkeley: University of California Press, 1976, pp. 31–43.

Sorlin, Pierre. *The Film in History: Restaging the Past*. Oxford: Basil Blackwell, 1980.

Spectator 8, no. 2 (Spring 1988). A special issue on "May 68: 20 Years After."

Stack, Oswald, ed. *Pasolini on Pasolini*. Bloomington: Indiana University Press, 1970.

Stam, Robert. *Reflexivity in Film and Literature: From Don Quixote to Jean-Luc Godard*. Ann Arbor: UMI Research Press, 1985. (A revised edition. New York: Columbia University Press, 1992.)

———. *Subversive Pleasures: Bakhtin, Cultural Criticism, and Film*. Baltimore and London: The John Hopkins University Press, 1989.

———. "The Lake, The Trees," *Film Comment* (January-February 1991), pp. 63–66.

Stoneman, Rod. "*Passion 2*," *Framework* 21 (Summer 1983), pp. 5–6.

Straayer, Chris. "The She-Man: Postmodern Bi-Sexed Performance in Film and Video," *Screen* 31, no. 3 (Autumn, 1990), pp. 262–280.

———. "Redressing the 'Natural': The Contemporary Transvestite Film," *Wide Angle* 14, no. 1 (January, 1992), pp. 36–55.

Strauss, Frederic. "La scene primitive," *Cahiers du Cinéma* 437 (Novembre, 1990).

Tallmer, Jerry. "The Feminists 'Will Kiss Me'," *New York Post* (February 3, 1973), p. 15.

Thompson, Kristin. "Sawing through the Bough: *Tout va bien* as a Brechtian Film," *Wide Angle* 3, no. 1 (1979), pp. 38–51.

———. "Godard's Unknown Country: *Sauve qui peut (la vie)*," in *Breaking the Glass Armor: Neoformalist Film Analysis*. Princeton: Princeton University Press, 1988, pp. 263–288.

Thomson, David. "Gone Away," *Film Comment* 27, no. 3 (May-June 1991), pp. 18–23.

Turim, Maureen. "The Aesthetic Becomes Political: A History of Film Criticism in *Cahiers du Cinéma*," *The Velvet Light Trap* 9 (Summer, 1973), pp. 13–17.

Turner, Victor. *The Ritual Process*. Harmondsworth: Penguin, 1974.

Ungari, Enzo. *Scena Madri*. Milan: Ubulibri, 1982.

Urry, John. *The Tourist Gaze: Lesiure and Travel in Contemporary Societies*. London, Newbury Park: Sage, 1990.

Vertov, Dziga. "The Vertov Papers," trans. Marco Carynnyk. *Film Comment* 8, No. 1 (Spring 1972), pp. 38–42.

Walker, Michael. "Melodrama and the American Cinema," *Movie* 29/30 (Summer 1982), pp. 1–38.

Walsh, Martin. *The Brechtian Aspect of Radical Cinema*. London: British Film Institute, 1981.

White, Hayden. "The Historical Text as a Literary Artifact," *Clio* 3 (1974), pp. 273–303.

———. "On the Value of Narrativity in the Representation of Reality," in W. J. T. Mitchell, ed. *On Narrative*. Chicago: The University of Chicago Press, 1981, pp. 1–25.

Wide Angle 1, No. 3 (1977). "On the Film of Jean-Luc Godard."

Willeman, Paul. "Distanciation and Douglas Sirk," *Screen* 12, No. 2 (Summer 1971), pp. 63–67.

Willet, John. *The Theatre of Bertolt Brecht*. London: Methuen and Co., 1977.

Williams, Christopher, ed. *Realism and the Cinema*. London: Routledge and Kegan Paul, 1980.

Williams, Raymond. "A Lecture on Realism," *Screen* 18, No. 1 (Spring, 1977), pp. 61–74.

Wills, David. "*Carmen*: Sound/Effect," *Cinema Journal* 25, no. 4 (Summer, 1986), pp. 33–43.

Wollen, Peter. "Godard and Counter Cinema: *Vent d'Est*," in his *Reading and Writings: Semiotic Counter-Strategies*. London: Verso Editions and NLB, 1982.

———. "*Passion 1*," *Framework* 21 (Summer 1983), p. 4.

Wood, Robin. "The Return of the Repressed," *Film Comment* 14, no. 4, (July- August, 1978), pp. 25–32.

Young, Robert. *White Mythologies: Writing History and the West*. London and New York: Routledge, 1990.

Filmography

Jean-Luc Godard

Opération Béton (1954). Production company: Actua-Films. Producer, director and screenwriter: Jean-Luc Godard. Cinematographer: Adrien Porchet. Editor: Jean-Luc Godard.

Une femme coquette (1955). Production company: Jean-Luc Godard. Producer and director: Jean-Luc Godard. Cinematographer and editor: Hans Lucas (pseudonym for Jean-Luc Godard). Cast: Marie Lysandre, Roland Tolma, Jean-Luc Godard.

Tous les garçons s'appelent Patrick (Charlotte et Véronique) (*All Boys Are Called Patrick*) (1957). Production company: Les Films de la Pléïade. Producer: Pierre Braunberger. Director: Jean-Luc Godard. Screenwriter: Eric Rohmer. Cinematographer: Michel Latouche. Editor: Cécile Decugis. Cast: Jean-Claude Brialy, Anne Colette, Nicole Berger.

Une Histoire d'eau (1958). Production company: Les Films de las Pléïade. Producer: Pierre Braunberger. Directors: Jean-Luc Godard and François Truffaut. Screenwriter: François Truffaut. Cinematographer: Michel Latouche. Editor: Jean-Luc Godard. Cast: Jean-Claude Brialy, Caroline Dim, Jean-Luc Godard (narrator).

Charlotte et son jules (1959). Production company: Les Films de la Pléïade. Producer: Pierre Braunberger. Director and screenwriter: Jean-Luc Godard. Cinematographer: Michel Latouche. Editor: Cécile Decugis. Cast: Jean-Paul Belmondo, Anne Colette, Gerard Blain.

A bout de souffle (*Breathless*) (1960). Production company: Société Nouvelle de Cinéma. Producer: Georges de Beauregard. Director: Jean-Luc Godard. Screenwriter: Jean-Luc Godard; based on an idea by François Truffaut. Cinematographer: Roul Coutard. Editors: Cécile Decugis, Lila Herman. Cast: Jean Seberg, Jean-Paul Belmondo, Henri-Jacques Huet, Daniel Boulanger.

Le Petit Soldat (1960). Production company: Société Nouvelle de Cinéma. Producer: Georges de Beauregard. Director and screenwriter: Jean-Luc Godard. Cinematographer: Roul Coutard. Editors: Agnès Guillemot, Nadine

Marquand, Lila Herman. Cast: Michel Subor, Anna Karina, Henri-Jacques Huet, Paul Beauvais.

Une Femme est une femme (A Woman is a Woman) (1961). Production company: Rome-Paris Films/Unidex, Euro International. Producers: Georges de Beauregard, Carlo Ponti. Director: Jean-Luc Godard. Screenwriter: Jean-Luc Godard; based on an idea by Geneviève Cluny. Cinematographer: Raoul Coutard. Editors: Agnès Guillemont, Lila Herman. Cast: Anna Karina, Jean-Paul Belmondo, Jean-Claude Brialy, Marie Dubois.

La Paresse (sketch in *The Seven Capital Sins*) (1961). Production company: Les Films Gibe/Franco-London Films/Titanus. Director and screenwriter: Jean-Luc Godard. Cinematographer: Henri Decae. Editor: Jacques Gaillard. Cast: Eddie Constantine, Nicole Mirel.

Vivre sa vie (My Life to Live) (1962). Production company: Les Films de la Pléiade. Producer: Pierre Braunberger. Director and screenwriter: Jean-Luc Godard. Cinematographer: Raoul Coutard. Editor: Agnès Guillemot, Lila Lakshmanan. Cast: Anna Karina, Sady Rebbot, Andre S. Labarthe, Peter Kassovitz.

Le Nouveau Monde (sketch in *Rogopag*) (1962). Production company: Société Lyre/Arco Film. Director: Jean-Luc Godard. Cinematographer: Jean Rabier. Editor: Agnès Guillemot, Lila Lakshmanam. Cast: Alexandra Stewart, Jean-Marc Bory, Jean-André Fieschi, Michel Delahaye.

Les Carabiniers (1963). Production company: Rome-Paris Films/Les Films Marceau/Laetitia Films. Producers: Georges de Beauregard, Carlo Ponti. Director: Jean-Luc Godard. Screenwriters: Jean-Luc Godard, Roberto Rosellini, Jean Gruault. Cinematographer: Roul Coutard. Editor: Agnès Guillemot, Lila Lakshmanan. Cast: Marino Mase, Albert Juross, Geneviève Galéa, Catherine Ribeiro.

Le Grand Escroc (sketch in *Les Plus Belles Escroqueries du monde*) (1963). Production company: Ulysse Productions/Primex Films/Lux/C.C.F Vides Cinematografica/Toho/Caesar Film Productie. Producer: Pierre Roustang. Director: Jean-Luc Godard. Cinematographer: Roul Coutard. Editor: Agnès Guillemot, Lila Lakshmanan. Cast: Jean Seberg, Charles Denner, Laszlo Szabo.

Le Mépris (Contempt) (1963). Production company: Rome-Paris Films/ Les Films Concordia/Compagnia Cinematografica Champion. Producers: Georges de Beauregard, Carlo Ponti, Joseph E. Levine. Director: Jean-Luc Godard. Cinematographer: Raoul Coutard. Editor: Agnès Guillemot, Lila Lakshmanan. Cast: Brigitte Bardot, Jack Palance, Fritz Lang, Michel Piccoli.

Bande à part (*Band of Outsiders*) (1964). Production company: Anouchka Films/Orsay Films. Director: Jean-Luc Godard. Cinematographer: Raoul Coutard. Editors: Agnès Guillemot, Françoise Collin. Cast: Anna Karina, Claude Brasseur, Sami Frey, Louisa Colpeyn.

Une Femme mariée (*A Married Woman*) (1964). Production company: Anouchka Films/Orsay Films. Director: Jean-Luc Godard. Cinematographer: Raoul Coutard. Editors: Agnès Guillemot, Françoise Collin. Cast: Macha Méril, Bernard Noel, Philippe Leroy, Roger Leenhardt.

Alphaville, une étrange aventure de Lemmy Caution (1965). Production company: Chaumiane Production/Filmstudio. Producer: André Michelin. Director and screenwriter: Jean-Luc Godard. Cinematographer: Raoul Coutard. Editor: Agnès Guillemot. Cast: Eddie Constantine, Anna Karina, Akim Tamiroff, Howard Vernon.

Montparnasse-Levallois (sketch in *Paris vu par*) (*Six in Paris*) (1965). Production company: Les Films du Losange. Producer: Barbet Schroeder. Director and screenwriter: Jean-Luc Godard. Cinematographer: Albert Maysles. Editor: Jacqueline Raynal. Cast: Joanna Shimkus, Philippe Hiquily, Serge Davri.

Pierrot le fou (1965). Production company: Rome-Paris Films/Dino de Laurentiis Cinematografica. Producer: Georges de Beauregard. Director: Jean-Luc Godard. Cinematographer: Raoul Coutard. Editor: Françoise Collin. Cast: Jean-Paul Belmondo, Anna Karina, Dirk Sanders, Raymond Devos.

Masculin Féminin (1966). Production company: Anouchka Films/Argos Films/Svensk Filmindustri/Sandrews. Director and screenwriter: Jean-Luc Godard. Editor: Agnès Guillemot. Cast: Jean-Pierre Léaud, Chantal Goya, Marlène Jobert, Michel Debort.

Made in U.S.A (1966). Production company: Rome-Paris Films/Anouchka Films/SEPIC. Producer: Georges de Beauregard. Director and screenwriter: Jean-Luc Godard. Cinematographer: Raoul Coutard. Editor: Agnès Guillemot. Cast: Anna Karina, Laszlo Szabo, Jean-Pierre Léaud, Yves Afonso.

Deux ou Trois Choses que je sais d'elle (*Two or Three Things I Know about Her*) (1966). Production company: Anouchka Films/Argos Films/Les Films du Carrosse/Parc Film. Director and screenwriter: Jean-Luc Godard. Cinematographer: Roul Coutard. Editors: Françoise Collin, Chantal Delattre. Cast: Marina Vlady, Anny Duperey, Roger Montsoret, Roul Lévy.

Anticipation ou l'amour en l'an 2000 (sketch in *Le Plus Vieux Métier du monde*) (1967). Production company: Francoriz/Les Films Gibé/Rialto Films/Rizzoli Films. Director and screenwriter: Jean-Luc Godard. Cinematographer: Pierre Lhomme. Editor: Agnès Guillemot. Cast: Jacques Charrier, Anna Karina, Marilu Tolo, Jean-Pierre Léaud.

Caméra-Oeil (sequence in *Loin du Viêtnam*) (1967). Production company: S.L.O.N. Director and screenwriter: Jean-Luc Godard. Cinematographer: Alain Levent. With commentary by Jean-Luc Godard.

La Chinioise (1967). Production company: Anouchka Films/Les Productions de la Guéville/Athos Films/Parc Films/Simar Films. Director: Jean-Luc Godard. Cinematographer: Raoul Coutard. Editors: Agnès Guillemot, Delphine Desfons. Cast: Anne Wiazemsky, Jeanne-Pierre Léaud, Michel Semeniako, Lex de Bruijn.

L'Aller et retour andate e ritorno des enfants prodigues dei figli prodighi (sketch in *Amore e rabbia/vangelo 70*) (1967). Production company: Anouchka Films/Castoro Film. Director: Jean-Luc Godard. Editor: Agnès Guillemot. Cast: Nino Castelnuovo, Catherine Jourdan, Christine Guého, Paolo Pozzesi.

Weekend (1967). Production company: Films Copernic/Ascot Cineraid/Comacico/Lira Films. Director: Jean-Luc Godard. Cinematographer: Raoul Coutard. Editor: Agnès Guillemot. Cast: Mireille Darc, Jean Yanne, Jean-Pierre Kalfon, Jean-Pierre Léaud.

Le Gai Savoir (1968). Production company: Anouchka Films/Bavaria Atelier/O.R.T.F./Suddeutschen Rundfunk. Director: Jean-Luc Godard. Cast: Jean-Pierre Léaud, Juliet Berto.

Ciné-Tracts (1968). (Series of 2–4 minute shorts). Produced, directed and edited by Jean-Luc Godard and others.

Un film comme les autres (*A Movie like Any Other*) (1968). Production company: Anouchka Films. Director, screenwriter, cinematographer and editor: Jean-Luc Godard and Groupe Dziga Vertov.

One Plus One (*Sympathy for the Devil*) (1968). Production company: Cupid Productions, Inc. Director: Jean-Luc Godard. Cinematographer: Anthony Richmond. Editors: Ken Rowles, Agnès Guillemot. Cast: Anne Wiazemsky, Ian Quarrier, Danny Daniels, The Rolling Stones.

One American Movie (One A.M.) Abandoned during production in 1968. The footage shot and footage from a film being made about the original film, were released as *One P.M.* (1971). Production company: Leacock-Pennebaker. Directors and screenwriters: Jean-Luc Godard and D.A. Pennebaker. Editor: D.A. Pennebaker. Cast: Richard Leacock, Jean-Luc Godard, Anne Wiazemsky, Eldridge Cleaver.

British Sounds (See You at Mao) (1969). Production company: Kestrel Productions (for London Weekend Television). Director: Jean-Luc Godard and Jean-Henri Roger. Cinematographer: Charles Stewart. Editor: Elizabeth Koziman.

Pravda (1969). Production company: Centre Européen Cinéma Radio Télévision. Producer: Claude Nedjar. Directors, cinematographers, editors: Groupe Dziga Vertov (Jean-Luc Godard, Jean-Henri Roger, Paul Burron).

Vent d'est (Wind from the East) (1969). Production company: Poli Film/Anouchka Films/Kuntz Film. Directors: Groupe Dziga Vertov (Jean-Luc Godard, Jean-Pierre Gorin, Gérard Martin). Screenwriters: Jean-Luc Godard, Daniel Cohn-Bandit, Sergio Bazzini. Cinematographer: Mario Vulpiani. Editors: Jean-Luc Godard, Jean-Pierre Gorin. Cast: Gian Maria Volonté, Anne Wiazemsky, Paolo Pozzesi, Christiana Tullio Altan.

Luttes en Italie (Lotte in Italia) (1969). Production company: Cosmseion for RAI. Directors and screenwriters: Groupe Dziga Vertov (Jean-Luc Godard, Jean-Pierre Gorin). Cast: Christiana Tullio Altan, Anne Wiazemsky, Jérôme Hinstin, Paolo Pozzesi.

Vladimir et Rosa (Vladimir and Rosa) (1971). Production company: Grove Press Evergreen Films/Telepool. Directors, screenwriters, and cinematographers: Groupe Dziga Vertov (Jean-Luc Godard, Jean-Pierre Gorin). Cast: Anne Wiazemsky, Jean-Pierre Gorin, Juliet Breto, Ernest Menzer.

Tout va bien (1972). Production company: Anouchka films/Vicco Films/Empire Film. Directors, and screenwriters: Jean-Luc Godard and Jean-Pierre Gorin. Cinematographer: Armand Marco. Editor: Kenour Peltier. Cast: Yves Montand, Jane Fonda, Vittorio Caprioli, Jean Pignol.

Letter to Jane (1972). Production company: Jean-Luc Godard and Jean-Pierre Gorin. Directors and screenwriters: Jean-Luc Godard and Jean-Pierre Gorin.

Ici et allieurs (1974). Production company: Sonimage/I.N.A. Directors and screenwriters: Jean-Luc Godard and Anne-Marie Miéville. Cinematographer: William Lubtchansky. From footage shot in 1970 by Groupe Dziga Vertov as *Jusqu'à la victoire.*

Numéro deux (1975). Production company: Sonimage/Bela Prod./S.N.C. Directors: Jean-Luc Godard, Anne-Marie Miéville. Cinematographer: William Lubtchansky. Video: Gérard Teissedre. Cast: Sandrine Battistella, Pierre Oudry, Alexandre Rignault, Rachel Stefanopoli.

Comment ça va (1976). Production company: Sonimage/I.N.A./Bela Prod./S.N.C. Directors and screenwriters: Jean-Luc Godard and Anne-Marie

Miéville. Cinematographer: William Lubtchansky. Cast: Anne-Marie Miéville, M. Marot.

Six fois deux/Sur et sous la communication (1976). Production company: Sonimage/I.N.A. Directors, screenwriters and editors: Jean-Luc Godard, Anne-Marie Miéville. Cinematographer: William Lubtchansky, Gérard Teissedre.

France/tour/détour/deux enfants (1977–78). Production company: I.N.A. for Antenne 2/Sonimage (Grenoble). Directors and screenwriters: Jean-Luc Godard and Anne-Marie Miéville. Cinematographers: Pierre Binggeli, William Lubtchansky, Dominique Chapuis, Philippe Rony. Cast: Camille Virolleaud, Arnaud Martin, Betty Berr, Albert Dray.

Scénario de Sauve qui peut (la vie) (1979). Production company: JLG Films. Director: Jean-Luc Godard.

Sauve qui peut (la vie) (Every Man for Himself) (1979). Production company: Sara Films/MK2/SagaProduction/Sonimage/C.N.C./Z.D.F./S.S.R./ O.R.F. Director: Jean-Luc Godard. Screenwriters: Anne-Marie Miéville, Jean-Claude Carière. Cinematographers: William Lubtchansky, Renato Berta, Jean-Bernard Menoud. Editors: Jean-Luc Godard, Anne-Marie Miéville. Cast: Isabelle Huppert, Jacques Dutronc, Nathalie Baye, Cecile Tanner, Roland Amstutz.

Lettre à Freddy Buache (1981). Production company: Film et Vidéo Productions. Director and screenwriter: Jean-Luc Godard. Cinematographer: Jean-Bernard Menoud. Editor: Jean-Luc Godard.

Changer d'image (sequence for the broadcast *Le Changement a plus d'un titre*) (1982). Director: Jean-Luc Godard.

Passion (1982). Production company: Sara Films/Sonimage/Films A2/Film et Vidéo Production SA/S.S.R. Director, screenwriter and editor: Jean-Luc Godard. Cinematographer: Raoul Coutard. Cast: Isabelle Huppert, Hanna Schygulla, Michel Piccoli, Jerzy Radziwilowicz, Laszlo Szabo.

Scénario du film Passion (1982). Production company: JLG Films/Studio Trans-Vidéo/Télévision Suisse Romande. Director: Jean-Luc Godard in collaboration with Jean-Bernard Menoud, Anne-Marie Miéville, Pierre Binggeli.

Prénom Carmen (First Name Carmen) (1983). Production company: Sara Films/Jean-Luc Godard Films. Director: Jean-Luc Godard. Screenwriter: Anne-Marie Miéville. Cinematographer: Raoul Coutard, Jean Garcenot. Editors: Suzanne Lang-Villar, Jean-Luc Godard. Cast: Maruschka Detmers, Jacques Bonnaffé, Myriem Roussel, Christophe Odent.

Petites Notes à propos du film Je vous salue Marie (1983). Production company: Jean-Luc Godard Films. Director: Jean-Luc Godard. Cast: Jean-Luc Godard, Myriem Roussel, Thierry Rode, Anne-Marie Miéville.

Je vous salue Marie (Hail Mary) (1985). Production company: Pégase Films/S.S.R./JLG Films/Sara Films/Channel 4. Director and screenwriter: Jean-Luc Godard. Cinematographers: Jean-Bernard Menoud, Jacques Firmann. Editor: Anne-Marie Miéville. Cast: Myriem Roussel, Thierry Rode, Philippe Lacoste, Anne Gauthier, Manon Andersen.

Détective (1985). Production company: Sara Films/JLG Films. Director: Jean-Luc Godard. Screenwriters: Alain Sarde, Philippe Setbon, Anne-Marie Miéville. Cinematographer: Bruno Nuytten. Editor: Marilyne Dubreuil. Cast: Nathalie Baye, Claude Brasseur, Stéphane Ferrara, Johnny Hallyday, Jean-Pierre Léaud, Laurent Terzieff.

Grandeur et décadence d'un petit commerce de cinéma (1986). Production company: TF1, "Série Noire"/Hamster Prod./JLG Films. Director and screenwriter: Jean-Luc Godard. Cinematographer: Caroline Champetier, Serge Le François. Cast: Jean-Pierre Léaud, Jean-Pierre Mocky, Marie Valera.

Soft and Hard (A Soft Conversation between Two Friends on a Hard Subject) (1986). Production company: JLG Films/Channel 4. Directors: Jean-Luc Godard, Anne-Marie Miéville. With: Jean-Luc Godard and Anne-Marie Miéville.

J.L.G. Meets W.A./Meetin' WA (1986). Production company: Jean-Luc Godard. Director: Jean-Luc Godard. With: Woody Allen, Jean-Luc Godard.

Armide (sequence for *Aria*) (1987). Production company: Lightyear Entertainment/Virgin Vision. Producer: Don Boyd. Director and editor: Jean-Luc Godard. Cinematographer: Caroline Champetier. Cast: Marion Peterson, Valérie Allain, Jacques Neuville, Luke Corre.

King Lear (1987). Production company: Cannon Films (Golan-Globus). Director, screenwriter and editor: Jean-Luc Godard. Cinematographer: Sophie Maintigneux. Editor: Jean-Luc Godard. Cast: Burgess Meredith, Peter Sellars, Molly Ringwald, Woody Allen, Léos Carax.

Soigne ta droite (Keep up Your Right) (1987). Production company: Gaumont/JLG Films/Xanadu Films. Director, screenwriter and editor: Jean-Luc Godard. Cinematographer: Caroline Champetier de Ribes. Cast: Jean-Luc Godard, Jacques Villeret, Philippe Rouleau, François Périer, Jane Birkin.

On s'est tous défilé (1988). Production company: JLG films.

Puissance de la parole (1988). Production company: Gaumont/JLG Films/France Télécom. Director: Jean-Luc Godard. Cinematographer: Caroline Champetier, Pierre-Alain Besse. Cast: Jean Bouise, Laurence Cote, Lydia Andrei, Michel Iribarren.

Le Dernier Mot/Les Francais entendus par (for the broadcast series *Les Français vus par*) (1988). Producers: Anne-Marie Miéville, Hervé Duhamel, Marie-Christine Barrière/Erato Films/Scopresse/Le Figaro/JLG Films. Director: Jean-Luc Godard. Cinematographer: Pierre Bingelli. Cast: André Marcon, Hans Zichter, Catherine Aymerie, Pierre Amoyal.

Histoire(s) du cinéma (1989–). Production company: Gaumont/JLG Films/La Sept/FR 3/Centre National de la Cinématographie/Radio Télévision Suisse Romande/Véga Films. Director, screenwriter and editor: Jean-Luc Godard.

Le Rapport Darty (1989). Directors: Jean-Luc Godard, Anne-Marie Miéville.

Nouvelle Vague (1990). Production company: Sara Films/Périphéria/Canal +/Vega Films/Télévision Suisse Romande/Films A2/C.N.C./Sofia Investimage/Sofia Créations. Director, screenwriter and editor: Jean-Luc Godard. Cinematographer: William Lubtchansky. Cast: Alain Delon, Domiziana Giordano, Roland Amstutz, Laurence Cote.

L'Enfance de l'art (sequence for the film *Comment vont les enfants/How Are the Kids*) (1990). Production company: JLG Films/UNICEF. Directors and screenwriters: Jean-Luc Godard, Anne-Marie Miéville.

Allemagne année 90 neuf zéro (*Germany Year 90 Nine Zero*) (1991). Production company: Antenne 2/Brainstorm Production. Director and screenwriter: Jean-Luc Godard. Cinematographers: Christophe Pollock, Andréas Erben, Stépan Benda. Cast: Eddie Constantine, Hanns Zischler, Claudia Michelsen, André Labarthe, Nathalie Kadem.

Hélas pour moi (1993). Production company: Les Films Alain Sarde, Véga Films, Périphéria. Direcor: Jean-Luc Godard. Cinematographer: Caroline Champetier. Cast: Gérard Départieu, Laurence Masliah, Bernard Verley, Jean-Louis Loca, François Germond, Jean-Pierre Miquel, Anny Romand, Roland Blanche.

Bernardo Bertolucci

La commare secca (*The Grim Reaper*) (1962). Production company: Cinematografica Cervi. Director: Bernardo Bertolucci. Screenwriters: Bernardo Bertolucci, Sergio Citti, from an idea by Pier Paolo Pasolini. Cinematographer: Gianni Narzisi. Editor: Nino Baragli. Cast: Francesco Ruiu, Giancarlo

De Rosa, Vincenzo Ciccora, Alvaro D'Ercole, Romano Labate, Lorenzo Benedetti, Emy Rocci, Erina Troiani, Allen Midgette, Marisa Solinas.

Prima della rivoluzione (Before the Revolution) (1964). Production company: Iride Cinematografica. Director: Bernardo Bertolucci. Screenwriters: Bernardo Bertolucci, Gianni Amico. Cinematographer: Aldo Scavarda. Editor: Roberto Perpignani. Cast: Adriana Asti, Francesco Barilli, Allen Midgette, Morando Morandini, Cristina Pariset, Gianni Amico, Domenico Alpi, Cecrope Barilli, Emilia Borghi, Iole Lunardi.

La via del petrolio (The Oil Trail) (1965–66). Production company: Giorgio Patara through Rai television and L'Eni (organizzazione generale Giovanni Bertolucci). Director and screenwriter: Bernardo Bertolucci. Cinematographers: Ugo Piccone, Louis Saldanha, Giorgio Pelloni, Maurizio Salvadori. Editor: Roberto Perpignani.

Il canale (The Canal) (1966) (not released). Production company: Giorgio Patara. Director: Bernardo Bertolucci. Cinematographers: Maurizio Salvadori, Ugo Piccone. Editor: Roberto Perpignani.

Agonia (Agony) (1967). Production company: Castoro Film. Director and screenwriter: Bernardo Bertolucci. Cinematographer: Ugo Piccone. Editor: Roberto Perpignani. Cast: Julian Beck, Members of the Living Theatre Group, Giulio Cesare Castello, Milena Vukotic, Adriano Apra, Romano Costa.

Partner (1968). Director: Bernardo Bertolucci. Screenwriters: Gianni Amico, Bernardo Bertolucci. Cinematographer: Ugo Piccone. Editor: Roberto Perpignani. Cast: Pierre Clementi, Stefania Sandrelli, Tina Aumont, Sergio Tofano, Giulio Cesare Castello, Romano Costa, Antonio Maestri, Mario Venturini, John Ohettplace, Ninetto Davoli.

Strategia del ragno (The Spider's Stratagem) (1970). Production company: Giovanni Bertolucci through Rai television and the Red Film. Director: Bernardo Bertolucci. Screenwriters: Marilu Parolini, Eduardo De Gregorio, Bernardo Bertolucci. Cinematographers: Vittorio Storaro, Franco Di Giacomo. Editor: Roberto Perpignani. Cast: Giulio Brogi, Alida Valli, Pippo Campanini, Franco Giovannelli, Tino Scotti.

Il conformista (The Conformist) (1970). Production company: Maurizio Lodi-Fe through Maris Film Maran Film (Munich). Director and screenwriter: Bernardo Bertolucci. Cinematographer: Vittorio Storaro. Editor: Franco Arcalli. Cast: Jean-Louis Trintignant, Stefania Sandrelli, Dominique Sanda, Enzo Tarascio, Pierre Clementi, Gastone Moschin, José Quaglio, Milly, Giuseppe Addobbati, Yvonne Sanson, Fosco Giachetti, Benedetto Benedetti.

La saluta è malata, or *I poveri muoioni prima* (1971). Director: Bernardo Bertolucci.

Ultimo tango a Parigi (Last Tango in Paris) (1972). Production company: PEA through Alberto Grimaldi (Rome), Artistes Associés (Paris). Director: Bernardo Bertolucci. Screenwriters: Bernardo Bertolucci, Franco Arcalli. Cinematographer: Vittorio Storaro. Editor: Franco Arcalli. Cast: Marlon Brando, Maria Schneider, Jean-Pierre Léaud, Massimo Girotti, Maria Michi, Giovanna Galletti.

Novecento (1900) (1976). Production company: PEA through Alberto Grimaldi (Rome). Director: Bernardo Bertolucci. Screenwriters: Bernardo Bertolucci, Franco Arcalli, Giuseppe Bertolucci. Cinematographer: Vittorio Storaro. Cast: Burt Lancaster, Sterling Hayden, Robert De Niro, Gérard Dépardieu, Donald Sutherland, Laura Betti, Stefania Sandrelli, Dominique Sanda.

La Luna (1979). Production company: Fiction Cinematografica of Giovanni Bertolucci. Director: Bernardo Bertolucci. Screenwriters: Giuseppe and Bernardo Bertolucci, Clare Peploe. Cinematographer: Vittorio Storaro. Editor: Gabriella Cristiani. Cast: Jill Clayburgh, Matthew Barry, Fred Gwynne, Elisabetta Campeti, Veronica Lazar, Peter Eyre, Julian Adamoli.

La tragedia di un uomo ridicolo (The Tragedy of a Ridiculous Man) (1981). Production company: Fiction Cinematografica of Giovanni Bertolucci. Director and screenwriter: Bernardo Bertolucci. Cinematographer: Carlo di Palma. Editor: Gabriella Cristiani. Cast: Ugo Tognazzi, Anouk Aimée, Laura Morante, Victor Cavallo, Olimpia Carlisi, Vittorio Caprioli, Riccardo Tognazzi.

The Last Emperor (1987). Production company: The Recorded Picture Company. Director: Bernardo Bertolucci. Screenwriters: Mark Peploe, Bernardo Bertolucci. Cinematographer: Vittorio Storaro. Editor: Gabriella Cristiani. Cast: John Lone, Joan Chen, Peter O'Toole, Ying Ruocheng, Victor Wong, Dennis Dun, Wu-Tao, Richard Wu.

The Sheltering Sky (1990). Production company: The Recorded Picture Company. Director: Bernardo Bertolucci. Screenwriters: Mark Peploe, Bernardo Bertolucci. Cinematographer: Vittorio Storaro. Editor: Gabriella Cristiani. Cast: Debra Winger, John Malkovich, Campbell Scott, Jill Bennett, Timothy Spall, Eric Vu-An, Amina Annabi.

Little Buddha (1993). Production company: The Recorded Picture Company (Jeremy Thomas) and Ciby 2000. Director and screenwriter: Bernardo Bertolucci. Cinematographer: Vittorio Storaro. Editor: Pietro Scalia. Cast: Keanu Reeves, Ying Ruocheng, Chris Isaak, Alex Wiesendanger, Bridget Fonda.

Index

Jarry, Alfred, 35
"Jean-Luc" (Godard and Miéville), 52
Jefferson Airplane, 29
Je vous salue Marie. See *Hail Mary*
John Paul II, Pope, 94
Johnston, Sir Reginald, 101
Joyce, James: *A Portrait of the Artist
as a Young Man,* 215 n.18
Jusqu'à la victoire (Until Victory)
(Dziga Vertov Group, 1970), 32,
34, 49

Kael, Pauline: on *Last Tango in
Paris,* 68
Kaes, Anton, 58, 62
Karina, Anna, 136, 142; in *Vivre sa vie
(My Life to Live),* 169
Karmitz, Marin, 53; *Coup pour coup
(Blow for Blow),* 44
Kaufman, Denis. *See* Vertov, Dziga
Kavanagh, Thomas, 45
Kawin, Bruce, 23
Kazan, Eli, 219 n.63
Kellner, Douglas, 55
Kelly, Michael, 25
Kinoki, 29
Kline, T. Jefferson, 220 n.68;
*Bertolucci's Dream Loom: A
Psychoanalytic Study of Cinema,*
18, 19
Kolker, Robert: *Bernardo Bertolucci,*
18, 19; on Bertolucci's images of
women, 112; on Bertolucci's
stature, 13; on Bertolucci's struggle
with Godard, 14; on *La Luna,* 113;
padre/padrone theme, 65–66; on
symbolic orders in *1900,* 116; on
Tragedy of a Ridiculous Man,
86–87, 223 n.17
Korte, Walter, 138
Kristeva, Julia, 114, 190

Lacan, Jacques, 80; imaginary vs.
symbolic, 102, 103, 106
La Cause du Peuple, 37
La Chinoise (Godard, 1967), 23,
100–101
La Luna (Bertolucci, 1979), 22,
81, 82–83, 183–84; incest as
metaphor, 188; moon as
symbol of feminine, 184;

spider woman myth, 187; as
transitional film, 201
Lang, Fritz: *Metropolis,* 210 n.21
Langlois, Henri, 24
Language: Godard on, 39; in *Le Gai
Savoir,* 27–28; and sexuality in *Last
Tango in Paris,* 144, 185; and
sexuality in *Masculin Féminin,*
144; in *The Sheltering Sky,* 185
*La salute e malata o I poveri muoiono
prima (Health is Sick, or The Poor
Die First)* (Bertolucci, 1971), 56
The Last Emperor (Bertolucci, 1987),
19, 89; Chinese Cultural
Revolution in, 116, 118; color and
light, 103, 227 n.11; and *The
Conformist,* 231 n.44; dialectics,
102–3, 111, 116; doubling motif
(Dopplegänger), 109–10, 117; as
epic film, 115; eunuchs, 108–12;
expulsion scene, 110–11; fetishism,
190, 232 n.50; Forbidden City,
103–8, 228 n.18; freedom from
Godard, 16; homosexuality motif,
110, 230 n.39; images of women,
102–8, 112–18; issue of analysis,
115–16; Oedipal theme, 102–3;
quest for the Other, 21; sexual
indeterminacy, 110–12, 114–15,
231 n.41; as spectacle, 228 n.16;
symbolic orders, 116; as universal
allegory, 232 n.55; utopian vision,
101, 102; *will-to-spectacle,* 104, 107
La strategia del ragno. See *The
Spider's Strategem*
Last Tango in Paris (Bertolucci, 1972),
20, 56; anality, 74; apartment in,
72–73, 77–78, 79, 103, 133; critique
of capitalist/consumer society, 72;
critique of religion, 76, 219 n.63;
doubling motif *(Dopplegänger),* 73,
79, 183; family in, 75–76; feminist
critique of, 22, 178–79; influence of
Artaud, 69; influence of Hollywood
melodrama, 69; influence of
Marcuse, 68–71, 72–80;
international success, 76; Jeanne
character, 180–81; and Lacanian
imaginary, 103; language and
sexuality, 144, 185; as liberation
from Godard, 15; marriage in, 185;

Books in the Contemporary Film and Television Series